JN247317

ゆまに書房

書誌書目シリーズ(110)

フランク・ホーレー旧蔵

# 「宝玲文庫」資料集成

第2巻

［編著・解題］横山　學

# 凡　例

一、本書は、「宝玲文庫」に関するフランク・ホーレー旧蔵資料を影印復刻したものであります。原資料の大半は編著者が保持しています。

二、第一回配本（全四巻）には、日本政府から蔵書が「敵国財産」に指定・没収されることを予期したホーレーが、昭和十六年（一九四一）に急いで作成した蔵書目録と、戦後になってＧＨＱから返還された際に書類に添付されていた目録、慶應義塾図書館の返還目録、さらに、返還本の確認作業に用いたホーレー自身のノート類を収録しました。

三、各資料の「書入れ」「記号」「削除」「加筆」等は、大部分がホーレー自身の手によるもので、整理の段階で加えられています。「資料23」の本文（手書）は、ホーレーの筆跡です。

四、復刻にあたっては「原資料に対して無修正」を原則として、書き込み等もそのままとしました。但し、実際のインク・鉛筆色が赤・青・黒などとなっていますが、製版の都合で判別が難しいかもしれません。ノート類の無記述頁は割愛しました。

五、欧文（横書き）の資料はページ順に従い、右開きとして製本しました。

六、原資料の寸法は様々ですが、Ａ５判に収めるために縮尺率を調整しました。

七、底本の記録状態や経年劣化等により、読み難い箇所がありますが、御了解をお願い致します。

八、各資料には便宜的に番号を付しました。（　）内は「原資料の形態と表紙の記述・資料の冒頭の記述」です。

九、各資料の解題・解説は、第五巻に掲載します。

十、第一回配本（全四巻）の内容は以下の通りです。

第一巻　資料01（ノート・辞源）
資料02（ノート・標注令義解）
資料03（ノート・金剛謹之助）
資料04（ノート・十一月五日）
資料05（ノート・欧文　帰国後）
資料06（貼付ノート・宗因）
資料07（貼付ノート・六部成語）
資料08（貼付ノート・雲遊帖）

第二巻　資料09（貼付ノート・Acker,W.）
資料10（貼付ノート・Ashbee: Library Catalogue）
資料11（貼付ノート・Transaction of the Asiatic Society of Japan）
資料12（目録・List of 364 missing or imperfect books）

第三巻　資料13（書類添付・File No.05264 Enclosure No.4 [Separate book No.1]）
資料14（慶應義塾用箋・十六世紀地図）
資料15（手書目録・アイヌ語を通じて観たるアイヌの族性他）
資料16（タイプ目録・アイヌ語を通じて観たるアイヌの族性他）

第四巻　資料17（目録・嵯峨志　嵯峨自治会）
資料18（目録・愛書趣味）
資料19（書類添付・File No.05264 Enclosure No.5 [Separate book No.2]）
資料20（慶應義塾用箋・Japan and China）
資料21（タイプ目録・A LIST OF BOOKS TO BE RETURNED BY KEIO UNIVERSITY）
資料22（タイプ目録・Merryweather, F.S.Biliomania）
資料23（HW自筆手書目録・Poppe,N.N.）

以上

# 第二巻　目　次

# 資料09（貼付ノート・Acker,W.）

資料 09（貼付ノート・Acker,W.）

資料 09（貼付ノート・Acker,W.）

資料09（貼付ノート・Acker,W.）

1309. At Acker, W., The Fundamentals of Japanese Archery, 東洋弓道(?)… , 1 vol. Ichitsu, Kyoto, 1937

1061. Nv (D) Ackermann, E., Der Vater Kehrt Zurück : ZiZi Kaeru by Kikutzi Kwan, Schobundo, Tokyo, 1935

174. Hy Adams, F. O., The History of Japan, 2 vols., Henry S. King & Co., London, 1875

981. Lg Ahn, F., First German Course, Allman & Son, London

515. Lg Aim and Method of the Romaji Kai, Romaji-Kai, Tokyo, 1885

1107. By Akimoto, S., Lord Ii Naosuke And New Japan, (Translated from Ii Tairo To Kaiko 井伊大老と開港) by Nakamura, K.), Published by Nakamura, K., Tokyo, 1909

1096. Tr Akiyama, A., A Complete Guide To Nara, Published by the Author, Zushi, 1937

85. Na Alcock, Sir R., The Capital of the Tycoon, 2 vols., Longman, Green, Longman, Roberts & Green, London, 1863

101. Mr Allen, B. M., The Rt. Hon. Sir Ernest Satow - A Memoir, Kegan Paul, Trench, Trubner & Co., London, 1933

958. So Allen, G.C., Modern Japan And Its Problems, George Allen & Unwin, London, 1928

420. Li (F) Allusions Littéraires: Corentin Pétillon, Mission Catholique, Changhai, 1909, 2 vols.

273. Gy Alvarez, J. M., Formosa, 2 vols, Luis Gili, Barcelona, 1930

485. Na Andersson, J. G., Children of the Yellow Earth, Kegan Paul, Trench, Trubner & Co., London, 1934

1220. Ct, Pa Anderson, W., Descriptive And Historical Catalogue Of A Collection Of Japanese And Chinese Paintings In The British Museum, Longmans & Co., London, 1886

1388. At Anderson, W., The Portfolio, No. 17 (Japanese Wood Engravings), Seeley &Co., London, 1895

776. Ct Andrews, F.H., Descriptive Catalogue Of Antiquities, Manager of Publications, Delhi, 1935

1091. So Anesaki, M., The Religions And Social Problems Of The Orient The Macmillan Co., New York, 1923

620. Rn Anesaki, M., History Of Japanese Religion, Kegan Paul, Trench, Trubner & Co., London, 1930

42. At Anesaki, M., Art, Life and Nature in Japan, Marshall Jones Co., Boston, 1933

683. Rn Anesaki, M., A Concordance To The History Of Kirishitan Missions, Office of the Academy, Tokyo, 1930

1245. Rn Anesaki, M., Religious Life Of The Japanese People, K.B.S., Tokyo, 1938

912. Rp Annual Report of The American Council of The Institute of Pacific Relations Incorporated, 1940-1941

1226. Rp Annual Report On Reforms And Progress In Chosen, Government-General Of Chosen, Keijô, 1912

1117. Ms Arber, E., Areopagitica, by John Milton, Constable & Co., London, 1925

1390. Es Armstorng, R.C., Light From The East, University Of Toronto, 1914

1065. Es Arnold, E., The Light Of Asia Or The Great Renunciation, Kegan Paul, Trench, Trubner & Co., London, 1932

1437. Rs (P) Arquivos de Macaw, 19 parts,

277. Hy Asakawa, K., The Documents of Iriki, Yale University Press, New Haven, 1929

717. Cu Asakawa, K., The Early Institutional Life Of Japan, The Waseda-daigaku-shuppan-bu, Tokyo, 1903 (2 copies)

1215. Rn Asakawa, K., The Life Of A Monastic Shō In Medieval Japan, Government Printing Office, Washington, 1919

1231. Hy Asakawa, K., Some Of The Contribution Of Feudal Japan To The New Japan, (Reprinted from The Journal of Race Development, Vol. 3, No. 1, July, 1912)

293. Gy Asia Major, Schindler, B. and Weller, F. etc., Verlag der Asia Major, 1924-1932, 10 vols.

885. Rs (P) Asia De Barros, 8 vols., Lisboa, 1778

886. Rs (P) Asia De Couto, 14 vols., Lisboa, 1778-1788

887. Rs (P) Asia De Barros : Vida E Indice, Lisboa, 1778

888. Rs (P) Asia De Couto : Indice Geral, Lisboa, 1788

873. Rn Aston, W.G., Shinto : The Ancient Religion Of Japan, Constable & Co., London, 1921

516. Rn Aston, W.G., Shinto: The Way Of The Gods, Longmans, Green, & Co., London, 1905

8

資料 09（貼付ノート・Acker,W.）

535. Gr Aston, W. G., Grammar of the Japanese Written Language, Trubner & Co., London, 1877 -

536. Gr Aston, W. G., Japanese Grammar, Office of the "Phoenix", London, 1872

1019. Hy (F) Aston, W.G., Hideyoshi's Invation Of Korea, Ryubun-Kwan, Tokyo, 1907

544. Li Aston, W. G., Japanese Literature, William Heinemann, London, 1899

588. Hy Aston, W. G., Nihongi, Kegan Paul, Trench, Trubner & Co., London, 1924

983. Lg Aston, W., A Grammar Of The Japanese Written Language, Luzac & Co., London, 1904

984. Gr Aston, W.G., A Grammar Of The Japanese Spoken Language, Kelly & Walsh, Yokohama, 1888

1348. Li (F) Aston, W.G., Histoires Des Littératures : Littérature Japonaise, Librairie Armand Calin, Paris, 1902

1468. Sc Atkinson, R.W., Memoirs Of The Science Departments, Tôkyô Daigaku, No.6, The Chemistry Of Saké-Brewing, Tôkyô Daigaku, Tôkyô, 1881

779. Ms Culin, S., Korean Games, University Of Pennsylvania, Philadelphia, 1895

151. " Aux Portes de la Chine les Missionnaires du Seizième Siècle, Hautes Études, Tientsin, 1933

1269. Cu Ayrton, M.C., Child-Life In Japan, Griffith, Farran, Okeden & Welsh, London,

69. Hy F. O. Adams - The history of Japan (1853-1872), 2 vols.

44. Lg(F) Actes du premier congrès international de linguistes à la Haye du 10-15 avril 1928, Lyden, 1930.

171. Et Te R. C. Armstrong - Light from the East, studies in Japanese Confucianism, University of Toronto, 1914.

75. Li(F) W. G. Aston - Littérature japonaise.

52. Jr Pl Atlantic monthly, No. 5 (1932), No. 3 (1934), No. 4 (1935), 3 vols.

170. At Sp W. Anderson - Japanese wood engravings.

37. Dc(R) A. Alexandrow - Russian-English dictionary.

119. Fa AEsop's fable with illustrations, Hokuseido.

Annuaire de la Société des Études Japonaises 1881-2

Annual Report on Administration of Chosen 1932-1933, Compiled by Gov-General of Chosen, Keijo, 1933.

✓ Annales du Musée Guimet, Tome Dixième, Paris, 1887

✓ Arberry, A. J.; The Library of the India Office; The Secretary of State for India at the India Office, London; 1938

✓ Arquivo Historico da Marinha, Vol 1. No1., 1933

✓ Aston, W. G.; Writing, Printing & the Alphabet in Korea (From the "Journal of the Royal Asiatic Society, July 1895)

✓ Annual Bibliography of Indian Archaeology for the Year 1926; 1 vol. 1928.

✓ Fifty-fourth Annual Report of the Minister of State for Education for 1926~1927, 1932

✓ Fifty-sixth Annual Report of the Minister of State for Education for 1928~1929, 1934

✓ Alekseev, Kitaiskaya Ieroglificheskaya Ieaimennost 1932

10

資料 09（貼付ノート・Acker,W.）

819. Cu Bacon, A.M., Japanese Girls & Women,
Houghton, Mifflin & Co., Boston, 1902

697. Tr (P) Baião, A., Asia De Joam De Barros, vol. I.,
Imprensa Da Universidade, Coimbra, 1932

699. Gy Baião, A., Carta Anua Da Vice- Provincia Do Japão,
Imprensa de Universidade, Coimbra, 1933

946. Gy Baker, J.N.L., A History Of Geographical Discovery And Exploration,
George G. Harrap & Co., London, 1931

520. Gr Balet, C., Grammaire Japonaise de la Langue Parlée, 2 copies,
Sansaisha, Tokyo, 1908 and 32nd Year of Meiji

1054. Cu Bälz, E., Über Die Todesverachtung der Japaner,
J.Engelhorns Nachf Stuttgart,

478. By Bälz, T., Erwin Bälz (Das Leben eines dutschen Arztes im erwachenden Japan, J. Engelhorns Nachf. Stuttgark, 1931

354. Ps Balfour, A. J., A Defence of Philosophic Doubt, Hodder and Stoughton, London

446. Si Ball, J. D., Things Chinese, Kelly & Walsh, Shanghai, 1925

1171. Po . Baring, M., Selected Poems,
William Heinemann, London, 1930

355. La St Barnes, H. E., The Story of Punishment, The Stratford Co.,
Boston, Mass., 1930

679. Jy (I) Bartoli, P.D., Dell' Istoria Della Campagna Di Gesù Il Giappone, 5 vols.,
Per Giacinto Marietti, Torino, 1825

945. Ta Basedow, H., The Australian Aboriginal,
F.W. Preece & Sons, Adelaide, 1925

803. Ta Batchelor, J., The Pit- Dwellers Of Hokkaido And Ainu Place- Names Considered,
Sapporo, 1925

800. Ta Batchelor, J., Ainu Fireside Stories,
Kyo Bun Kwan, Tokyo, 1924

801. Dc Batchelor, J., An Ainu- English- Japanese Dictionary,
Kyo Bun Kwan, Tokyo, 1926

705. B Baty, T., The Private International Law Of Japan,
"Pyrsos" Ltd., Athens, 1939

815. Cu (D) Baumann, F., Japanese Madel,
Gross- Lichterfelde- Ost, Berlin,

~~605. Si/Ta Baddeley, J. F., Russia - Mongolia -China, 2 vols,
Macmillan & Co., London, 1919~~

214. Bo Bailey, L. H., How Plants Get Their Names, The Macmillan Co.,
New York, 1933

383. Ca Jy Barghoorn, A., Kokumin Nenju Gyoji, Deutschen Gesellschaft für Natur-und Völkerkund Ostasiens, Tokyo, 1926

547. Li Na Beaujard, A., Sei Shonagon' Son Temps et Son Oeuvre, Librairie Orientale et Américane G. P. Maisonneuve, Paris, 1934

1075. Ad Beard, C.A., The Administration And Politics Of Tokyo, The Macmillan Co., New York, 1923

653. Pc Beck, A., The Ghost Plays Of Japan, The Japan Society, New York, 1933

990. Lg Becker, Japanese Self Taught, Kelly & Walsh, Yokohama

714. La Becker, J.E., The Criminal-Code Of Japan, Kelly & Walsh, Yokohama, 1907

337. Tr Beechey, F. W., Narrative of a Voyage to the Pacific, Carey & Lea, Philadelphia, by authority of the Lords Commissioners of the Admiralty, 1832

1121. Rs Benfow, J., Manuscript & Proof, Oxford University Press, New York, 1937

1003. Lg Benneville, J.S., More Japonico, Published by The Auther, Yokohama, 1908

916. Mr Berlin Academy Memoirs : Chiefly On Central Asia, 1908-1926, (German bulletins bound in a volume), Verlag Der Königl Akademie Der Wissenschaften, Berlin,

1183. St Bennett, A., How to Live 24 Hours a Day, The Hokuseido Press, Tokyo, 1931

126. Es Bernard, R. P. H., La Decouverte de Nestoriens Mongols aux Ordos et l'Histoire Ancienne du Christianisme en Extreme-Orient, Hautes Études, Tientsin, 1935

127. " Bernard, R. P. H., Sagesse Chinoise et Philosophie Chretienne, Hautes Études, Tientsin, 1935

128. " Bernard, R. P. H., L'Apport Scientifique du Père Matthieu Ricci à la Chine, Hautes Études, Tientsin, 1935

129. " Bernard, R. P. H., Aux Origines du Cimetière de Chala, Hautes Études, Tientsin, 1934

124. Es Bernard, R. P. H., Le Père Matthieu Ricci et la Société Chinoise de son Temps 1552-1610, 2 vols., Hautes Études, Tientsin, 1937

125 Es Bernard, R. P. H., Les Iles Philippines du Grand Archipel de la Chine, Hautes Études, Tientsin, 1936

301. Bb The Best Hundred Japanese Books, The Isseido Bookstore, Tokyo, 1930

111. Dp Berchet, G. D., Le Antiche Ambasciate Giapponesi in Italia, Venezia, 1877

資料09（貼付ノート・Acker,W.）

583. Li Beul, O., Tsurezureguśa (Aufzeichnungen aus Mussestunden), Japanisch-Deutschen Kultur-Institut, Tokyo, 15th Year of Showa 1940

1284. Li (D) Bezzenberger, A., etc., Die Osteuropäischen Literaturen, Druck Und Verlag Von B.G. Teubner, Berlin, 1908

1286. Lg Bhandarkar, R.G., First Book Of Sanskrit, Gopal Narayan & Co., Bumbay, 1930

701. Bb Bibliographischen Alt- Japan- Katalog 1542- 185?, Deutsches Forschungsinstitut, Kyoto, 1940

1469. Rn Bibliotheca Buddhica, 7 parts.

257. By Bibliographie von Japan, 3 vols., Hans Praesent, Oskar Nachod, etc., Verlag Karl W. Hiersemann, Leipzig, 1937

258. By Bibliography of Japan, 4 vols, Fr. von Wenckstern, Oskar Nachod, etc., Verlag Karl W. Hiersemann, Leipzig, etc., 1928

710a Bibliographischer Alt-Japan-Katalog 1542–1853 Deutsches Forschungsinstitut, Kyoto, 1948

242. Bb Bibliographie Abrégée des Livres Relatifs au Japon en Français, Italien, Espagnol, et Portugais, K.B.S., Tokyo, 1936

320. Bb K.B.S. Bibliographical Register of Important Works written in Japanese on Japan and the Far East, 2 vols., K.B.S., Tokyo, 1937-1938

673. Pri Binyon, L., Catalogue Of Japanese And Chinese Woodcuts In British Museum London, 1916

1227. At Binyon, L., etc., Japanese Art, The Encyclopaedia Britannica Co., London, 1933

357. Cu Biot, F. E., Le Tcheou-Li ou Rites des Tcheou, 3 vols., L'Imprimerie Nationale, Paris, 1851; Reprinted at Wen Tien Ko, Peking, Mingoku 29th Yr.

1237. Lg Boas, F., Handbook Of American Indian Language, Government Printing Office, Washington, 1922

881. Es Boas, F., Instituttet For Sammenlignende Kuturforskning, H. Aschehong & Co., Oslo, 1927

1282. Lg Boas, F., Handbook Of American Indian Languages, Government Printing Office, Washington, 1911

429. By Bodde, D., China's First Unifier (A Study of the Ch'in Dynasty as soon in the Life of Li Ssŭ), E. J. Brill, Leiden, 1938

456. Cu Le Bogan, M. L. C., Manchu Customs and Superstitions, China Booksellers Ltd., Tientsin, 1928

610. In Bögel, F.N., etc., Equivalents of The Principal Japanese and Foreign Measures and Weights in 4 Tables., Tokyo, 1894

611. Dm (F) Bonazet, A., Le Théatre Au Japon, Ernest Leroux, Editeur, Paris, 1901

318. Hy Böhner, H., Jinnô-Shôtô-Ki, 2 vols., Japanisch-Deutsches Kultur-Institut, Tokyo, 1935

291. Bu Böhner, H., Legenden aus der Frühzeit des Japanischen Buddhismus (Nippon Koku Gembo Zenaku Ryo-i-Ki), 2 vols., Deutsche Gesellschaft Für Natur-und Völkerkunde Ostasiens, Tokyo, 1934-1935

1441. Rn Boletin Eclesiástico Da Diocese De Macaw, Nos.394-452

933. Lg Bolling, G.M., edited, Language Journal Of The Linguistic Society Of America, vols. 1, 2, 3, 4, 5, 6, 7, 8. Waverly Press, Baltimore, 1925-1929

1221. Lg Bolling, G.M., Language Dissertations, Nos. 7-11, 5 vols., Linguistic Society Of America, Philadelphia, 1932

1222. Lg Bolling, G.M., Language Monographies, Nos. 8-12, 5 vols., Waverly Press, Baltimore, U.S.A., 1931-1932

1223. Lg Bolling, G.M., Language, Vol. 7, 8, 3 vols. 8 parts Waverly Press, Baltimore, U.S.A., 1931-1932

1211. Pt Bonar, H.A., On Maritime Enterprise In Japan, (Read February 9th, 1887)

1271. Po (F) Bonneau, G., Rythmes Japonaise, 4 vols., (4, 5, 6, 7) Librairie Orientaliste Paul Geuthner, Paris, 1933-1934

1272. Po (F) Bonneau, G., L'Expression Poetique Dans Le Folk-Lore Japonais, 3 vols., Librairie Paul Geuthner, Paris, 1933

249. Ct Books from Japan (Catalogue of Important Publications), Tokyo Shuppan Kyokai, Tokyo, 1937

770. Bb Book Reviews, (Reprint from Vol. 1 Fasc. 1, 1935 )

1103. Dc Bourgois, G., Dictionary And Glossary For The Practical Study Of The Japanese Ideographs, Kelly & Walsh, Yokohama, 1916

505. Pt The Boundary Question between China and Tibet (A valuable record of the Tripartite Conference between China, Britain and Tibet held in India 1913-1914), Peking, 1940

298. Ms (D) Bourke, J. G., Der Unrat, Ethnologischer Verlag, Leipzig, 1913

66. At Bowes, J. L., Notes on Shippo, Printed for Private Circulation, Liverpool, 1895

593. Sp At Bowes, J. L., Japanese Marks and Seals, (印章), Henry Sotheran & Co., London, 1882

14

資料 09（貼付ノート・Acker,W.）

28. At Bowie, H. P., On the Laws of Japanese Painting, Paul Elder & Co., San Francisco, 1911

155. Es Boxer, C. R., Jan Compagnie in Japan 1600-1817, Martinus Nijhoff, The Hague, 1936

153. Dp Boxer, C. R., A Portuguese Embassy to Japan 1644-47, Kegan Paul, Trench, Truber & Co., London, 1928

150. Dp Boxer, Capt. C. R., The Embassy of Capt. Gomçalo de Siqueira de Souza to Japan in 1644-47, Macau, 1938

151. Hy Boxer, Major C. R., Breve Relação du Vida e Feitos de Lopo e Inacio Sarmento de Carualho, Macau, 1940

998. Es Boxer, C.R., Ruy Freyre De Andranda Commentaries, George Routledge & Sons, London, 1929

84. Na Block, J. R., Young Japan (Yokohama and Yedo: A Narrative of the Settlement of the City from the Signing of the Treaties in 1858 to th close of the Yr. 1879), 2 vols., Baker, Pratt & Co., New York, 1883

970. Dp Blakeslee, G.H., Japan And Japanese-American Relations, G.E. Stechert & Co., New York, 1921

312. Bb Blackwell, B., The World of Books, J. M. Dent & Sons, London, 1932

144. Blake, R., The Needle-Watcher, Wm. Heinemann Ltd., London, 1934

539. Cal Blakney, R. B., A Course in the Analysis of Chinese Characters, The Commercial Press, Shanghai, 1926 (1927)

943. Ta Bland, J.O.P., China : The Pity Of It, William Heinemanne, London, 1932

852. Sc (D) Bloch, I., Sexualpsychologische Bibliothek, Erste Serie, Louis Marcus Verlagsbu-chhandlung, Berlin,

~~1382. Li Brandt, J.J., Introduction To Literary Chinese, Henri Vetch, Peking, 1936~~

502. Lg Brandt, J. J., Wenli Particles (虛字指南), The North China Union Language School, Peiping, 1929

503. Li Si Brandt, J. J., Introduction to Literary Chinese (漢文進階), Henri Vetch, Peiping, 1936

685. Ct (F) Brandt, J., Catalogue Des Principaux Ouvrages Sortis Des Presses Des Lazarites, Société Française De Librairie Et D'Edition, Pekin, 193[illegible]

72. At Brankston, A. D., Early Ming Wares of Ching Techen, Henri Vetch, Peking, 1938

207. Bo Bretschneider, E., Botanicon Sinicum (Notes on Chinese Botany from Native and Western Sources), 3 vols., Trubner & Company, London, 1882, and Kelly & Walsh, Shanghai, 1892 & 1895

1235. Ay, Po Brereton, F., An Anthology Of War Poems, W.Collins Sons & Co., London, 1930

15 Bongbun, a, Kokumin Nenpu Ryoji, Tokyo, 1926

382. Nv Brewitt-Taylor, C. H., San Kuo (or Romance of the Three Kingdoms), 2 vols., Kelly & Walsh, Shanghai, 1925

1356. Es /37 ~~Briffault, R., The Mothers : A Study Of The Origin Of Sentiments And Institutions, 3 vols., George Allen & Unwin, London, 1927~~

954. Lg Bright, J.W., An Anglo-Saxon Reader And Grammer, George Allen & Unwin Ltd., London, 1917

549. Ar Britton, R. S., Yin Bone Rubbings, Chalfant Publication Fund, New York, 1937

550. Ar Britton, R. S., Yin Bone Photographs, Chalfant Publication Fund, New York, 1935

439. Jr Britton, R. S., The Chinese Periodical Press, Kelly & Walsh, Shanghai, 1933

1234. Po Brophy, J., etc., Soldiers' Songs And Slang, Eric Partridge, London, 1931

10. At Brown, L. N., Block Printing and Book Illustration in Japan, George Routledge & Sons, London, etc., 1924

1333. Jr Brown, W.N., Supplement To The Journal Of The American Oriental Society, ~~3 vols.~~, (6 copies), 3 parts (1, 2, 4). The American Oriental Society, Maryland, 1925-1939

523. Lg Brown, S. R., Colloquial Japanese, Presbyterian Mission Press, Shanghai, 1863

367. Si Pt Brunnert, H. S. and others, Present Day Political Organization of China, translated from the Russian by Beltchenko, A., Kelly & Walsh, Shanghai, 1912

1144. Cl (F) Bruyere, Les Caractères Ou Les Moeurs De Ce Siècle, Froideuoux, Paris,

811. Nv Bryk, F., Neger- Eros, A. Marcus & E. Weber's Verlag, Berlin, 1928

859. Cl Bryan, J.I., The Civilization Of Japan, Thornton Butterworth, London, 1929

860. Li Bryan, J.I., The Literature Of Japan, Thornton Butterworth, London, 1929

759. Po (D) Buch, V., Aus Der Gedichten Tu Fu's, (Reprint from Vol. 1, Fasc. 1, Oct., 1935)

601. In Buck, J. L., Land Utilization in China, 2 vols., The Commercial Press Ltd., Shanghai, 1937

371. In Si Buck, J. L., Land Utilization in China, Commercial Press, Shanghai, 1933

1202. Rn Bulletin of the Catholic University of Peking, ~~9, 1928-1934~~ 9 parts. ~~Vol. 5, 6, 8,~~

10. Bn /0/ Bulletin de la Societe Academique Indo-Chinoise, Au Siege de la Societe, Paris, 1883 6 vols 12 VI ~ 1890

16

資料 09（貼付ノート・Acker,W.）

1?. At Bulletin of Eastern Art, 2 phgs., Society of Friends of Eastern Art, Tokyo– Jan–Dec 1940; 1941 + Jan–March 1942.

327. Bn 54 Bulletin de L'école Francaise d'Extrême-Orient, 42 vols., Hanoi, 1901-1930

325. Bn 46 Bulletin de la Maison Franco-Japonaise, 23 vols., Mitsukoshi Book Dept., Tokyo, 1927-1939

326. At (Book Bindings: Historical and Decorative, Maggs Brothers, (London, 1927

1430. Bn (F) Bulletin de la Société Franco-Japonaise de Paris XXVI-XXII, Juin-Septembre (1 part) 1912, Palais du Louvre-Pavillon de Marsan, Paris

137 878. Bn Bulletin of The School of Oriental Studies, London Institution, 38 parts. The School of Oriental Studies, London Institution, London, 1917-1940

879. Mi Burkitt, M.C., Prehistory, The University Press, Cambridge, 1925

1219. Ms Burton, R., The Kasidah Of Hâji Abdû El-Yezdi, Philip Allen & Co., London, 1925

858. Ps Bury, J.B., A History Of Freedom Of Thought, Thornton Butterworth, London, 1928

73. Ce Bushell, S. W., Description of Chinese Pottery and Porcelain, The Clarendon Press, Oxford, 1910

~~265. Cu 134 Buxton, L. H. D., The Peoples of Asia, Kegan Paul, Trench, Trubner & Co., London, 1925~~

197. Lg F. Brinkley - New guide to English self-taught, Sanseido, To-Kyo, 1909 (明42).

154. Nv(D) Vicki Baum - Helene Willfüer.

1321. Hy Becker, J.E., Notes On The Mongol Invasion Of Japan, "Japan Gazette" Press, Yokohama

46. Bn Pl(F) Bulletin de la Maison Franco-Japonaise, Mitsukoshi Book dpt, Tokyo, No. 4 - 1938.

124?. Tr(F) François Bernier - Voyages à Grand Mogol, Tome I (1709), Tome II (1710), Amsterdam, Total 2 vols.

147. Ey(I) Gino Bottiglioni - Atlante linguistico etnografico italiano della Corsica, Pisa, 1932.

55. Bb Li G. Bonneau - Bibliographie de la littérature japonaise contemporaine, Maison Franco-Japonaise, 1938.

47. Li Po(F) G. Bonneau - Rythmes Japonais, Paul Geuthner, Paris, 1933-34.

~~143. Gy Hy John F. Baddeley - Russia, Mongolia & China, Macmillan & co., 1919, 2 vols.~~

48. Jy Cl(F) Henri Bernard - Les premiers rapports de la culture européenne avec la civilisation japonaise.

✓ 134. Hy Cl Buxton - The people of Asia, Kegan Paul, London, 1932.

✓ 121. Li Brandt - Introduction to literary Chinese, Henri Vetch, Peking, 1936.

(✓) 7. Dc F. Brinkley - An unabridged Japanese-English dictionary.

✓ 137. Es Robert Briffault - The mothers, a study of the origin of sentiments and institutions, George Allen & Unwin, London, 1927, 3 vols.

(✓) 54. Bn Pl Bulletin de l'ecole française d'extrême-orient, Tome I (1901) - Tome IX (1909), Hanoi, Total 9 vols.

21 (✓) Baedeker, K., the United States with an excursion into Mexico., Karl Baedeker, publisher, Leipzig, 1904

(✓) X Bernard, H., Aux Portes de la Chine les Missionaires du Seizieme Siecle 1514-1588, 1933

23 (✓) Boutflower, C. H. Bishop, The Individual versus Society in Japan, (Reprinted from the Transactions of the Japan Society of London, Vol. XXXVI )

12 (✓) Bulletin de la Société de Geographie Paris, 1868

(✓) Bland, J. O., Verse & Worse, Shanghai, 1902

(✓) Bott, Alan: Eastern Flights, Penguin Book, 1920 126 pal

(✓) Bible in the Korean Language

(✓) Browne, E. G., A Year Amongst the Persians (Impressions as to the Life, Character & Thought of the People of Persia), Cambridge Univ. Press, 1927.

(✓) Bulletin de la Kokusai Bunka Shinkokai, Vol 1-No 4, Kokusai Bunka Shinkokai, Tokyo, 1936

18

48. At Caiger, G., Dolls on Display (Japan in Miniature), The Hokuseido Press, Tokyo, 1933

~~Calder, G., A Gaelic Grammar, Alex. MacLaren Sons, Glasgow~~

951. Gr Calder, G., A Gaelic Grammar, Alex. MacLaren & Sons, Glasgow, 1923

710. Rn (P) Camara Manovel, J.P.A., Missões Das Jesuitas No Oriente, Impresa Nacional, Lisbon, 1894

911. Sc (F) Carnoy, A., La Science Du Mot, Editions Universitas Louvain, 1927

1236. Ms Caron, P., Benkyôka No Tomo, Imprimerie Nazareth, Hongkong, 1892

82. Tr Caron, F. and Schouten, J., A True Description of the Mighty Kingdoms of Japan and Siam, The Argonaut Press, London, 1935

303. Pri Carter, T. F., The Invention of Printing in China, Columbia University Press, New York, 1931

1267. Ct Catalogue Of The K.B.S. Library, K.B.S., Tokyo, 1938

248. Ct Catalogue of the Asiatic Library of Dr. G. E. Morrison, 2 vols., The Oriental Library, Tokyo, 1924

319. Ct Bb Catalogue of the Möllendorff Collection, Peiping, 1932

316. Bb Catalogue of the Library of S. Ichikawa, privately printed, Tokyo, 1924

(F) 317. Do Chavannes, E., Documents sur Turcs Occidentaux, Buntenkaku, Mingoku 29th Yr.

321. Ct Bb Catalogue of Periodicals written in European Languages and Published in Japan, K.B.S., Tokyo, 1936

322. Ct Catalogue of Books written in European Languages and Published in Japan, K.B.S., Tokyo, 1936

~~94. Ct Catalogus Librorum et Manuscriptorum Japonicorum a Ph. Fr. de Siebold Collectorum, 1845~~

1293. Ct Catalogue Of Marine, Freshwater And Land Shells Of Japan, Imperial Geological Survey Of Japan, Tokyo, 1931

58. Pa Catalogue of Paintings recovered from Tun-Huang by Sir Aurel Stein, Waley, A., The British Museum of the Government of India, London, 1931

1045. Ms Cautata, Kaidō-Tosei, Nippon Bunka Chuo Renmei, Tokyo, 1941

Chalfant, F. H. The Hopkins Collection of Inscribed Oracle Bone, New York 1939

A Catalogue of the Principal Works of Art at Chequers

19

1252. Sc Chikashige, M., Oriental Alchemy, Rokakuho Uchida, Tokyo, 1936

729. Hy (F) Chaille-Long-Bey, La Corée, Ernest Leroux, Editeur, Paris, 1894

669. Rn (F) Chaillet, J.B., La Resurrection Catholique Du Japon, Chaillet, 1919

275. Cal Chalfant, F. H., Early Chinese Writing, Buntenkaku, Pekin, Mingoku 29th Yr.

276. Ea Couling, S., The Encyclopaedia Sinica, Kelly & Walsh, Shanghai, 1917

548. Ar Chalfant, F. H. and others, The Hopkins Collection of Inscribed Oracle Bone, Chalfant Publication Fund, New York, 1939

551. Ar Chalfant, F. H., Seven Collections of Inscribed Oracle Bone, Chalfant Publication Fund, New York, 1938

552. Cal Chiang Yee, Chinese Calligraphy, Methuen & Co. Ltd., London, 1938

531. Lg Chamberlain, B. H., Romanized Japanese Reader, 3 vols., Kelly & Walsh, Yokohama, 19th Yr. of Meiji (3 parts in one Vol.)

571. Cal Chamberlain, B. H., The Study of Japanese Writing (Moji-no-Shirube), 2 copies, Crosby Lockwood & Son, London, 1905

993. Lg Chamberlain, B.H., Colloquial Japanese, 4th edition, Crosby Lockwood & Son, London, 1907

844. Tr Chamberlain, B.H., A Handbook For Travellers In Japan, John Murray, London, 1894

818. Ed Chamberlain, B.H., Educational Literature For Japanese Women, Trubner & Co., London, 1898

563. Hy Chamberlain, B. H., Translation of "Kojiki", J. L. Thompson & Co. (Retail) Ltd., Kobe, 1932

533. Lg Chamberlain, B. H., The Japanese Language, Kelly & Walsh, Yokohama, 19th Yr. of Meiji

467. Jy Chamberlain, B. H., Things Japanese, reprinted from the 1905, revised 5th edition, J. L. Thompson & Co., Kobe, 1927

468. Jy Chamberlain, B. H., Things Japanese, 6th revised edition, Kegan Paul, Trench, Trubner & Co., London, 1939

469. Jy Chamberlain, B. H., Things Japanese, arranged for College use, Daito Shobo, Tokyo, 1933

967. So Chapman, H.O., The Chinese Revolution 1926-'27, Constable & Co., London, 1928

Chavannes, E.: Documents sur Les Tou-Kiue (Turcs) Occidentaux

20

資料 09（貼付ノート・Acker,W.）

(F) 339. Na Champagne de L'alcmene en Extreme-Orient, Société Anonyme de L'Imprimerie Ch. Thèze, Rochefort, 1907 (F)

703. Rn (F) Charlevoix, R. P., Histoire Du Christianisme Au Japon, 2 vols., Chez Vanlinthout Et Vandenzande, Louvain, 1829

(F) 9. Sp Chavannes, E., Six Monuments de la Sculpture Chinoise, G. Van Oest & Cie, Bruxelles, etc., 1914

358. Chavannes, E., Les Memoires Historiques de Se-Ma Ts'ien, 6 vols., Ernest Leroux, Paris, 1895-1905

1. Si (F) Chavannes, E., Documents Chinos Decouverts Par Aurel Stein, Imprimerie De L'Univ rsite, Oxford, 1913

142. Bu Chavannes, E., Contes et Légendes du Buddhisme Chinois, Bossard, Paris, 1921

1155. St Chesterton, G.K., All Things Considered, Methuen & Co., London, 1928

722. D (F) Chevalier, H., Annales Du Musée Guiment, Ernest Leroux, Editeur, Paris, 1897

400. Tr Chiang Yee, The Silent Traveller in War Time

254. Sc Chikashige Masumi, Oriental Alchemy (The Civilization of Japan and China in Early Times as soon from the Chemical Point of View), Rokakuho Uchida, Tokyo, 1936

10 . Hy Cholmondeley, L. B., History of the Bonin Islands, Constable & Co., London, 1915

1357. By Cho-Yuan Tan(譚卓垣), The Development Of Chinese Libraries Under The Ch'ing Dynasty, 1644-1911, 清代図書館発展史, The Commercial Presw, Shanghai, 1935

846. Pt Chung, H., The Case of Korea, Fleming H. Revell Co., London, 1921

1304. Jr The Chrysanthemum : A Monthly Magazine, Vol.1-3, Kelly & Co., Yokohama, 1881- 1883

105. Hy Clark, T. B., Oriental England (A Study of Oriental Influence in the 18th Century England as reflected in the Drama), Kelly & Walsh, Shanghai, 1939

509. Ms Clark, E. B., Stray Leaves, Kenkyusha, Tokyo, 1936

754. Pn Clark, C.A., Religions of Old Korea, Fleming H. Revell Co., New York,

997. Lg Clark, W.J., International Language, J.M.Deut & Sons, London, 1912

1185. St Cleland, J., Memories Of Fanny Hill, London, 1749

1041. La Clement, E.W., Constitutional Imperialism In Japan, The Academy Of Political Science, Columbia University, New York, 1916

159. Bu Coates, Rev. H. H., etc., Honen, The Buddhist Saint, Kodokaku, Tokyo, 1930

90. Hy Cohen, G., Some Early Russo-Chinese Relations, "The National Review" Office, Shanghai, 1914

23. The Collection of Old Bronzes of Baron Sumitomo (泉屋清賞). Kichizaemon Sumitomo, Kyoto, 1934

1138. St Collis, M., Siamese White, Penguin Books, 1941

78. Bu A Comparative Analytical Catalogue of the Kanjur Division of the Tibetan Tripitaka (西蔵大蔵経甘殊爾勘同目録), Otani Daigaku Library,, Kyoto, 1930-32.

110. Jr The Complete Journal of Townsend Harris, Doubleday Doran & Co. for the Japan Society, New York, 1930

~~1350. Gy 129 中華坤輿詳誌, Comprehensive Geography Of The Chinese Empire And Dependencies : T'Usewei Press, Shanghai, 1908~~

. Ga Conder, J., Landscape Gardening in Japan, 1 vol. & Supplement, Kelly & Walsh Ltd., Yokohama, etc., 1893

764. At Conder, J., The Flowers Of Japan And The Art Of Floral Arrangement, 1 vol. 1 chitsu, Hakubun-sha, Tokyo, 1892

734. At Conder, J., The Theory of Japanese Flower Arrangements Thompson & Co., Kobe, 1935

692. Cal (D) Conrady, A., Die Chinesischen Handschriften-und Sonstigen Kleinfunde Sven Hedins in Lou-Lan, Generalstabens Litografiska Anstalt, Stockholm, 1920

61. At Conrady, A., Das Alteste Dokument zur Chinesischen Kunstgeschichte Tien-Wen, Verlag Asia Major, Leipzig, 1931

753. So The Conspiracy Case In Chosen, "Seoul Press", 1912

1225, Jr Contemporary Japan, Vol.1 No. 1-4, The Foreign Affairs Association Of Japan, Tokyo, 1932-1933

1438. Do Contemporary Japan, 26 parts, The Foreign Affairs Association Of Japan, Tokyo,

1446. Jr Cocil, H.G., ed., The Oriental Magazine, 1st No.5, Orientalia, New York, 1927-1928

979. Lg Cook, L.A., Macmillan's Shorter Latin Course, Macmillan & Co., London, 1937

804. Bb Coole, A.B., A Bibliography On Far Eastern Numismatics And An Union Index Of The Currency, Charms, And Amulets Of The Far East, California College In China, Peking, 1940

6?6. At Coomaraswamy, A.K., The Transformation Of Nature In Art, Harvard University Press, Cambridge, 1935

Couto, M. J.: O Plano Colonial de Affonso de Albuquerque; Lisboa, 1929

22

資料 09（貼付ノート・Acker,W.）

1471 Henri Cordier, Bibliotheca Sinica, Dictionnaire Bibliographique des ouvrages relatifs a l'empire Chinois vol. IV 文殿閣、北京、民國二十七年

438. Cordier, H., Ser Marco Polo (Notes and Addenda to Sir Henry Yule's edition, containing the Results of Recent Research and Discovery ), John Murray, London, 1920

331. Bb Cordier, H., Bibliotheca Sinica, 5 vols., Buntenkaku, Peiping, 27th Year of Mingoku

694. Bb Cordier, H., Bibliotheca Japonica, Imprimerie Nationale, Paris, 1912

257-A Hy 123 Gy Cordier, H., Mélanges d'Histoire et de Géographie Orientales. 4 vols., Jean Maisonneuve & Fils, Paris, 1914-1923

499. Lg Cordier, G., Langue Chinoise Ecrite: Grammaire et Exercices, Tan-Dan, Hanoi

108. Rp Cosenza, M. E., The Establishment of the College of the City of New York as the Free Academy in 1847 - Townsend Harris, Founder, The Associate Alumni of the College of the City of New York, N.Y., 1925

283. Si The Couling - Chalfant Collection of Inscribed Oracle Bone (庫方二氏藏甲骨卜辭), edited by Britton, R. S., The Commercial Press, Shanghai, 1935

1084. Dp The Counter-Case Presented, By The Imperial Japanese Government To The Tribunal Of Arbitration

1462. Si (F) Courant, M., De L'Utilité Des Études Chinoises, Librairie Chevalier-Marescq, Paris, 1899

473. Sy Courant, M., En Chine, Félix Alcan, Paris, 1901

569. Do 141 Couvreur, F. S., Dictionnaire Classique de la Langue Chinoise, Ho Kien Fou Imprimerie de la Mission Catholique, 1911

1418. Hy (F) Couvreur, S., Tch'ouen Ts'ion Et Tso Tchouan, 春秋左傳, 3 vols., Imprimerie de la Mission Catholique, Ho Kien Fon, 河間府 1914

1419. Te 175 (F) Couvreur, S., Li Ki 禮記, 2 vols., Imprimerie de la Mission Catholique, Ho Kien Fou 河間府, 1913

1420. Po (F) Couvreur, S., Chen King 詩經, Imprimerie de la Mission Catholique, Sien Hsien 獻縣, 1934

1421. Te 174 (F) Couvreur, S., Les Quatre Livres, 四書, Imprimerie de la Mission Catholique, Sien Hsien 獻縣, 1930

1422. Te (F) Couvreur, S., Cérémonial 儀禮, Imprimerie de la Mission Catholique, Sien Hsien 獻縣, 1928

1423. Te 177 (F) Couvreur, S., Chou King 書經, Imprimerie de la Mission Catholique, Sien Hsien 獻縣, 1935

Chiba: Research into the nature & scope of accent in the light of Experimental Phonetics.

23

17. At Ac Cram, R.A., Impressions of Japanese Architecture and the Allied Arts, Marshall Jones Co., Boston, Mass., 1930

27. Pa Crane, L., China in Sign and Symbol, Kelly & Walsh Ltd., Shanghai, 1926

821. Cu Cranmer- Byng, etc., Women And Wisdom Of Japan, John Murray, London, 1914

663. Pc Cranmer-Byng, L., etc., Nōgaku, Japanese Nō Plays, John Murray, London, 1932

408. Rs Creel, H. G., The Birth of China (A Study of the Formative Period of Chinese Civilization), Reynal & Hitchcock, N.Y.

384. Cl Si Creel, H. G., Studies in Early Chinese Culture, Waverly Press, Baltimore, 1938

495. Li Creel, H. G., Literary Chinese by the Inductive Method, University of Chicago Press

1067. Ms Crooke, W., Hobson-Jobson, John Murry, London, 1903

1068. Dr Constant, S.V., English-Chinese Military Terms, China Booksellers, Peking, 1927

1165. Ml Crookshank, F.G., Individual Diagnosis, Kegan Paul, Trench, Trubner & Co., London, 1930

1051. Cl Cultural Nippon Vol. I no. 1 — Vol. IX no. 1 1 bound vol. + 28 parts

599. At Cutler, T. W., A Grammar of Japanese Ornament and Design, B.T. Batsford, London, 1880

600. Hy Chani, A. B., Historia Mongolorum et Tatarorum, Casani, 1825

~~589. Rn Cybikow, G. C., Buddhist Palomnik U Svyatyn' Tibeta, 1919~~

947. Hy Czaplicka, The Turks Of Central Asia in History and at the Present Day, Clarendon Press, Oxford, 1918

948. Gy Czaplicka, M.A., Aboriginal Siberia : A Study In Social Anthropology, Clarendon Press, Oxford, 1914

195. Jr Samuel Couling - The New China review, ~~No. 1, 1919; No. 4 &~~ No. 5, 1920, Kelly & Walsh, Shanghai, 4 vols. complete

196. Dc(F) G. Cesselin - Dictionaire Japonais-Francais, Maruzen Co Ltd., Tokyo, 1939.

199. Tr Charington (A.J.H.) - Le livre de Marco Polo, Albert Nachbaur, Pékin, 1924, '26, '28, 3 vols.

50. Hy Current history, No. 2 (1932), No. 6 (1932), 2 vols.

1315. Jr China Review, 73 vols., China Mail Office, Honkong, 1875-1901

資料09（貼付ノート・Acker,W.）

175. Et Te(F) F. S. Couvreur - Li Ki (禮記), Mission Catholique, Ho Kien Fou, 1913, 2 vols.

176. Et Te(F) -,,- - Cérémonial (儀禮), Sien Hsien, 1928.

177. Et Te(F) -,,- - Chou King (書經), Sien Hsien, 1935, 2 vols.

174. Et Te(F) F. S. Couvreur - Les Quatre Livres (四書), Mission Catholique, Sien Hsien, 1934.

92. Hy Si Gl Cho-Yüan-Tan (譚卓垣) - The development of Chinese libraries under the Ching dynasty, 1644-1911 (清代圖書館發達史), The Commercial Press, Shanghai, 1935.

123. Hy Gy(F) H. Cordier - Mélange d'histoire et de geographie orientales, Jean Maisonneuve, Paris, 1914-23, 4 vols.

96. Bu Rn(R) G. C. Cybikov - Buddist Palomnik u svyatyn' Tibeta,1919.

89. Cal Chamberlain - The study of Japanese writing, Crosby Loskwood, London, 1905.

141. Dc(F) F. S. Couvreur - Dictionnaire classique de la langue Chinoise, Mission Catholique, Ho Kien Fou, 1911.

204. Tr(F) Antoine Charignon et Melle Medard - A Propos des voyage aventureux de Ferdinand Mendez Pinto, in chitsu (秩), Imperimerie de la Politique de Pekin, 1934.

The Collected Poems of G. K Chesterton, 1927.

Catalogue of Reproductions of Oriental Painting, Ohtsuka Kogeisha

Creel, H. G, Sinism, a study of the Evolution of the Chinese World-view. the Open Court Publishing Co., Chicago, 1929

10 Cary. F., Only Forty Years Ago, Thompson & Co, Kobe, 1933

19. Dc(D) Cassel's German dictionary (German-English & English-German).

182. Pt Th. F. Carter - The invention of printing in China and its spread westward, Columbia University Press, N. Y., 1931.

106. Tr G. Caiger - From Japan to Japan.

25

92. Hy Dahlmann, J., Japans Beziehungen zum Westen (1542-1614), Ferder & Co., Berlin, etc., 1923

999. By Dakin, E.F., Mrs. Eddy, The Biography of a Virginal Mind, Blue Ribbon Books, New York, 1930

767. Fn (F) Dallet, C., Histoire De L'Eglise De Corée, 2 vols., Librairie Victor Palme, Edituer, Paris, 1874

81. Tr Damper, W., Voyages and Discoveries, The Argonaut Press, London, 1931

591. Rn Darmesteter, J., Le Zend-Avesta (Annales du Musée Guimet), 3 vols., Ernest Leroux, Paris, 1892-93

122. Hy Danvers, F. C., The Portuguese in India (Being a history of the rise and decline of their Eastern Empire), Vol. II only, W. H. Allen & Co., London, 1894

205. Sc Davis, T. L. and Chao Yün-Ts'ung, Essay on the Understanding of the Truth (Chinese Alchemy), The American Academy of Arts and Sciences, 1939

64. Bu Davids, Mrs. R., A Manual of Buddhism, The Macmillan Co., New York, 1932

49. Bu Davids, Mrs. R., Sakya or Buddhist Origins, Kegan Paul, Trench, Trubner & Co., London, 1931

186. Rp Davison, C., The Japanese Earthquake of 1923, Thomas Murby & Co., London, 1931

521. Gr De Forest, J. H., Japanese Verbs of Saying, Speaking, Telling, etc., Methodist Publishing House, Tokyo, 1900

55. Le (F) De Milloué, L. and Kawamoura, S., Coffre A Trésor, Ernest Leroux, Paris, 1896

341. Gy Denuce, J., Les Iles Lequios (Bulletin de la Société Royale Belge de Géographie), Société Royale Belges de Géographie, Bruxelles, 1907

408. Le De Benneville, J. S., Saito Musashi-Bo Benkei, 2 vols., published by the author, Yokohama, 1910

192. Ml De Zwaan, J.P.K., Die Heilkunde der Chinesen und Japaner, De Erven Loosjès, Haarlem, 1917

397. Na De Benneville, J. S., Bakemono Yashiki (Retold from the Japanese Originals), published by the Author, Yokohama, 1921

278. Ed (F) De Harlez, C., La Siao Hio ou Morale de la Jeunesse, Ernest Leroux, Paris, 1889

396. Na De Benneville, J. S., Oguri Hangwan, published by the Author, Yokohama, 1915

208. Zo De Rosny, L., Education des vers a Soie au Japon (養蚕訳説), Department de L'Agriculture, Paris, 1868

26

資料 09（貼付ノート・Acker,W.）

37. Bu De Visser, M. W., Ancient Buddhism in Japan, 2 vols., Libraire Orientaliste Paul Geuthner, Paris, 1928-1935

425. Ip Gy Dennys, N. B., Treaty Ports of China and Japan, Trubner & Co., London, 1867

670. D'Elia, P.M., The Catholic Mission In China, The Commercial Press, Shanghai, 1934

892. Rp Despatch from Sir R. Alcock Respecting, The Murder of Major Baldwin And Lieutenant Bird, Kamakura, 1865 (Kamakura In Japan)

1296. So Dewar, D., Difficulties Of The Evolution Theory, Edward Arnold & Co., London, 1931

1149. By Dickinson, T.H., Robert Green, T. Fisher Unwin, London,

512. Na Dickins, F. V., The Old Bamboo-Hewer's Story, or The Tale of Taketori, San Kaku Sha, Tokyo, 9th Yr. of Showa

545. Lg Dickins, F. V., Japanese Texts, 2 vols., The Clarendon Press, Oxford, 1906

510. Na Dickins, F. V., Ho-Jo-Ki by Kamo no Chomei (Notes from "A Ten-Feet Square Hut"), Gowans & Gray Ltd., London, 1921 (2 copies: 1 copy published by San Kaku Sha, Tokyo, 8th Yr. of Showa)

403. Li Diaries of Court Ladies of Old Japan, translated by Annie Shepley Omori and Kochi Doi, Kenkyusha, Tokyo, 1935

1066. Ta Dickins, F.V., Chiushingura Or The Loyal League, Gowan & Gray, London, 1930

966. Ps Dimnet, E., The Art Of Thinking, The Musson Book Co., Toronto, 1930

972. So Dingwall, E.J., The Girdle Of Chastity (A Medico-Historical Study), George Routled & Sons, London, 1931

1206. Ta Dickins, F.V., tr., The Old Bamboo-Hewer's Story : The Tale Of Taketori, 竹取物語, Sankaku-sha, Tokyo, 1934

713. Rn (F) Doctrina Christan Na Lingoa De Japão, Toyo Bunko Ronso, Tokyo, 1928

960. So Dodge, R., etc., The Craving For Superiority, Yale University Press, New Heaven, 1931

390. Tr Doflein, F., Ostasienfahrt, B.G.Teubner, Leipzig, 1906

440. Rp Rn Dossier de la Commission Synodale, Commissio Synodalis in Sinis, Peiping, 1938

978. Lg (F) Dombrowski, Methode Pratique De Russe, Librairie Garnier Frères, Paris, 1920

125. Tr(P) Da Asia de Diogo de Couto, Decada Duodecima, Parte Primeira, Parte Segunda, Parte Ultima, Lisboa, 1788, 3 vols. (2 vols only)

677. Cl Doi, K., Journal Of The Sendai International Cultural Society, Sendai International Cultural Society, 1940

1412. Hy (D) Dohi, K., Beitrage zur Geschichte der Syphilis, Verlag von Nankodo, Tokyo, 1923

562. Cal Driscoll, L. and Toda, K., Chinese Calligraphy, The University of Chicago Press, Chicago, 1935

387. Hy Si Dubs, H. H. and others, The History of the Former Han Dynasty: Pan Ku, Waverly Press, Baltimore, 1938

1108. Ms Duddington, N.A., December The Fourtheenth, by Merezhkovsky, (Translated from Russian), Jonathan Cape, London

149. Hy Dudgeon, J., Historical Sketch of the Ecclesiastical, Political and Commercial Relations of Russia with China (中俄政教訳略), Wen Tien Ko, Peking, 1940

1345. Mr (F) Dulauries, E., Mémoires De La Societe Académique, Indo-Chinoise De France, Siège De La Société, Paris, 1879

1346. Bn (F) Dulaurier, E., Bulletin De La Société Académique Indo-Chinoise Challamel Aine, Paris, 1890

~~1143. By Dumas, A., The Countess Dubarry, Collins' Clear-type Press, London.~~

949. Dc Dwelly, E., The Illustrated Gaelic Dictionary, The Compiler, Fleet Hants, Scottland, 1930

16. Dc Davidson-Houston - Modern military dictionary - Chinese and English.

1302 Diary of Richard Cocks vol. II, Murakami, N. Sankosha, Tokyo 1899

22 De Benneville, Saito Musashi-bo Benkei, 西塔武蔵坊弁慶, 1910 2 vols.

32. Lg Dc A. De Smedt & c. - Le dialecte Monguor, dictionnaire Monguor-Français, L'université Catholique, Peiping, 1933.

79. Hy Ad J. E. de Becker - Feudal Kamakura from A.D. 1186-1333.

169. Hy Av(F) Léon de Rosny - Le livre canonique (書紀) de l'antique japonaise, Paris, 1887, 2 vols.

165. Nv Alexandre Dumas - The Countess Dubarry, Collins Clear-Type Press, London.

151. Sc Nh Dewar - Difficulties of the evolution theory, Edward Arnold, London, 1931.

28

資料 09（貼付ノート・Acker,W.）

117. Es Floyd Dell - Love in the machine age (Psychological), George Routledge, London, 1929.

25. Gr(F) Deny - Grammaire de la langue Turque.

36. Dc Sarat Chandra Das - Tibetan-English dictionary.

Das, Sarat Chandra; Introduction to the Grammar of the Tibetan Language with the Texts of Situ Sum-rtag, Dag-je Salwai Melong & Situi Shal-Lung; Darjeeling, 1915

Dahlgren, E. W; Les débuts de la Cartographie du Japon; Upsal 1911.

Dai-Nippon, 1935

~~Dictionary of Chinese-Japanese Words,~~

29

Ellis, H., Studies in the Psychology of Sex, Vol VI. 1925

" " , Vol III, 1926

30

資料 09（貼付ノート・Acker,W.）

68. Sp East Indian Sculpture (From the 12th Century to the 18th Century), The Toledo Museum of Art, Toledo, Ohio.

382. Li Eby, C. S., The Tsure- Dzure-Gusa (Meditations of a Recluse), San Kaku Sha, Tokyo, 9th Year of Showa 1934

727. At Eckardt, A., History Of Korean Art, Edward Goldston, London, 1929

748. Lg (D) Eckardt, P.A., Schlussel Zur Koreanischen Konversations=Grammatik, Julius Groos, Heidelberg, 1923

749. Lg (D) Eckardt, P.A., Koreanischen Konversations- Grammatik, Julivs Groos, Heidelberg, 1923

479. By Eckstein, G., Noguchi, Harper & Bros., New York

63. St Edgerton, F., The Panchatantra Reconstructed, 2 vols., American Oriental Society, New Haven, Conn., 1924

1153. Ms Edinger, G., Pons Asinorum, Kegan Paul, Trench, Trubner & Co., London, 1929

141. Bu Edkins, Rev. J., Chinese Buddhism, Kegan Paul, Trench, Trubner & Co., London, 1893

791. Ed Education In Japan, The Foreign Affairs Association of Japan, Tokyo, 1938

940. Ta Edward Dowden, edited, The Tragedy Of Romeo And Juliet, Methuen & Co., London

347. Lg (F) Edwards, E.R., Etude Phonetique De La Langue Japonaise, Imprimerie B.G. Teubner, Leipzig, 1903

637. Dm, Pc Edwards, O., Japanese Plays And Playfellows, William Heinemann, London, 19ol

530. Lg Ehmann, P., Die Sprichwörter und Bildlichen Ausdrücke der Japanischen Sprache, Deutsche Gesellschaft fur Natur-und Völkerkunde Ostasiens, Tokyo, 1927

164. Bu Dc Eitel, E. J., Handbook of Chinese Buddhism (中国佛教梵漢字典), Sanshusha, Tokyo, 1904.

1278. Ps Ellis, H., Studies In The Psychology Of Sex, (vol. 4 ), F.A. Davis Co., Philadelphia, 1925

1218. Ps Ellis, H., Studies In The Psychology Of Sex, F.A. Davis Co., Philadelphia, 1926

918. Lg Ellis, A.J., Early English Pronunciation, 5 vols., Asher & Co., London, 1869-1889

98. Bu Eliot, Sir C., Japanese Buddhism, Edward Arnold & Co., London, 1935

97. Rn Eliot, Sir C., Hinduism and Buddhism, 3 vols., Edward Arnold & Co., London, 1921

1106. Lg Elisseeff, S., Elementary Japanese for University Students, 2 vols., Harvard Yenching Institute, Cambridge, U.S.A., 1941

(F) 30. Pa Elisséev, S., La Peinture Contemporaine au Japon (現代日本絵画小史), E. de Boccard, Paris, 1923

784. Es, Rp Elisseeff, S., etc., Harvard Journal Of Asiatic Studies, 13 vols., Yenching Institute, Harvard, 1936 - 1939, 4 vols complete.

848. Zo Elton, C., Animal Ecology & Evolution, The Clarendon Press, Oxford, 1930

1034. Dc English-Japanese- Dictionary Of Graphic Arts Terms, Nippon Insatsu-gakkai, Tokyo, 1938

238. Me English-Chinese Hospital Dialogue (Outline of Chinese Medical History and Bernard E. Read), The French Bookstore, Peking, 1930

1119. Na English Short Stories Of Today, Published for the English Association by the Oxford University Press, London, 1939

1327. La English Transaction of The Korean Laws etc., 1909

596. Mr Enthronement of the One Hundred Twenty-fourth Emperor of Japan, The Japan Advertiser, Tokyo, 1928

959. Lg Entwistle, W.J., The Year's Work In Modern Language Studies, Volume 1., Oxford University Press, London, 1931

807. Ta Ernest Crawley, The Mystic Rose, 2 vols., Methuen & Co., London, 1927

1011. Ca Erskine, W.H., Japanese Festival and Calender Lore, Kyo Bun Kwan, Tokyo, 1933

1010. Cu Erskine, W.H., Japanese Customs, Their Origin and Value, Kyo Bun Kwan, Tokyo, 1925

1306. Rs (F) Etudes Asiatiques, 2 Tomes, Ses Membres Et Ses Collaborateurs, Librairie Nationale D'art Et D'Histoire, 1925

34. Ar Excavation of a West Han Dynasty Site, Conducted by the Freer Gallery of Art, Washington, D.C., and the Shansi Provincial Library of Tai Yuan, Shansi, Kelly & Walsh Ltd., Shanghai, 1932

525. Lg Exercises in the Yokohama Dialect, compiled from original and reliable sources, Yokohama, 1874

986. Lg (D) Ey, L., Schlüssel zur Portugieseschen Konversations-Grammatik, two copies Julius Groos, Heidelberg, 1926

2 vols with key. O.K.

32

資料 09（貼付ノート・Acker,W.）

288.Cl Ekvall, R. B., Culture Relations on the Kansu-Tibetan Border, The University of Chicago Press, Chicago, 1939

41. Cu Ema, T., A Historical Sketch of Japanese Customs and Costumes, K. B. S., Tokyo, 11th Yr. of Showa

409. Fl Embree, J. F., Suye Mura: A Japanese Village, The University of Chicago Press, Chicago

155. La (F) Escarra, J., Le Droit Chinois, L Librairie Du Recueil Sirey, Paris, 1936

311. Bb Esdaile, A., A Students' Manual of Bibliography, George Allen & Unwin, London, 1931

603. Zo Ezaki, T., Zur Einführung in Ph. Fr. von Siebolds (Fauna Japonicaの解説), Shokubutsu Bunken Kankokai, Tokyo, 1935

198. Cu The Kisho Shuppan Sha (英書出版社) - Marriage customs in Japan, with descriptions of the Imperial Wedding, Tokyo, 1904 (明37).

156. Nv May Edginton - Life isn't so bad, London.

資料 09（貼付ノート・Acker,W.）

386. Jy Faber, H., Alt-Japan, Skizzen und Geschichten, Leipzig

463. Pt Fahs, C. B., Political Groups in the Japanese House of Peers; Reprinted from the American Political Science Review, Vol. XXXIV, No. 5, October 1940

876. Tr Fane, P., Kyoto, Rumford Printing Press, Hong Kong, 1931

31. Pa Fenollosa, E. F., Epochs of Chinese and Japanese Art, 2 vols., William Heineman, London, 1912 (G)

556. Cal Fenollosa, E., The Chinese Written Character, Stanley Nott, London, 1936 (F)

302. Bb Ferguson, J. C., Index to the China Review, Kelly & Walsh, Shanghai, 1918

306. Bb Ferguson, J., Some Aspects of Bibliography, George P. Johnston, Edinburgh, 1900

1127. St Ferguson, J., Death Of Mr. Dodsley, The Albatrose Crime Club, Liepzig, 1937

16. At Ferguson, J. C., Survey of Chinese Art, The Commercial Press Ltd., Shanghai, 1940

1374. Pa Ferguson, J.C., Ku K'ai-Chih's Scroll In The British Museum, (From The Journal Of The North China Branch Of The R.A.S., Vol. 49, 1918)

1375. At Ferguson, J.C., Early Chinese Bronzes, (From The Journal Of The North China Branch Of The R.A.S., Vol. 47, 1916)

1376. Pa Ferguson, J.C., Painters Among Catholic Messionaries And Their Helpers In Peking, (From The Journal Of The North China Branch Of The R.A.S., Vol. 45, 1934)

1377. At Ferguson, J.C., Inscriptions On Bronzes, (From The Journal Of The North China Branch Of The R.A.S., Vol. 66, 1935)

1378. Na Ferguson, J.C., The Six Horses Of T'ang T'ai Tsung, (From The Journal Of The North China Branch Of The R.A.S., Vol.67, 1936)

1379. Es Ferguson, J.C., Loyang As The National Capital, (From The Journal Of The North China Branch Of The R.A.S., Vol. 64, 1933)

1360. Na Ferguson, J.C., Fir-Flower Tablets, (From The Journal Of The North China Branch Of The R.A.S., Vol. 53, 1922)

1361. Hy Ferguson, J.C., General Survey Of Standard Chinese Histories, (From The Journal Of The North China Branch Of The R.A.S., Vol. 57, 1926)

1318. Mp Ferguson, J.C., Atlas Of China, Reprint from T'ien Hsia Monthly, October, 1936

35

1362. Pt Ferguson, J.C., Political Parties Of The Northern Sung Dynasty, (From The Journal Of The North China Branch Of The R.A.S., Vol. 58, 1927)

1363. By Ferguson, J.C., Recent Books By A Chinese Scholar, (From The Journal Of The North China Branch Of The R.A.S., Vol. 50, 1919)

1364. Ms Ferguson, J.C., Writing Appliances, North-China Daily New & Herald, Shanghai, 1933 (From The China Journal, Vol. 19 No. 3, September)

1365. At Ferguson, J.C., Three Unusual Bronze Vessels, (Reprinted from The China Journal, Vol. 21, No.1, July, 1934)

1366. Pa Ferguson, J.C., Chinese Landscapists,

1367. At Ferguson, J.C., Bronze Vessels, (Reprinted from The China Journal, Vol.11, No.6, December, 1929)

1368. By Liang Ch'i-Ch'ao, 梁啓超, (Reprinted from The China Journal, Vol. 12, No.4, April, 1 1930)

1369. Na Ferguson, J.C., Hyacienth, (Reprinted from The China Journal, Vol. 12, No. 6, June, 1930)

1370. Na Ferguson, J.C., Bretschneider, (Reprinted fromThe China Journal, Vol.13, No.5, November, 1930)

1371. Pa Ferguson, J.C., Stories In Chinese Paintings, 2 vols., (From The Journal Of The North China Branch Of The R.A.S., Vol. 61, 1930-1932)

982. Lg (D) Fick, R., Praktische Grammatik der Sanskrit-Sprache für den Selbstunterricht, A Hartleben's Verlag, Wien,

329. Fi An Financial and Economic Annual of Japan, 19 vols., Dept. of Finance, 1901-1930

1454. Rn (F) Finot, L., Rāstrapālapariprccha, Sutra Du Mahayana, Commissionnaire de L'Academie Imperial des Sciences, St.-Petersbourg, 1901

1056. La The First Japanese Constitution, (A Lecture by Sir George Samour), Asiatic Society Of Japan, Tokyo, 1938

135. Dp The First Japanese Embassy to the United States of America 1860, Translated by Miyoshi, S., The America-Japan Society, Tokyo, 1920

777. Es (D) Forke, A., Abhandlungen aus dem Gebiet der Auslandskunde, Band 46, Friederichsen, De Gruyter & Co., Hamburg, 1934

~~1009. Jr Fortune, vol. XIV, No. III September, 1936~~

36

資料 09（貼付ノート・Acker,W.）

1040. Dc Fowler, H.W., A Dictionary Of Modern English Usage, The Clarendon Press, Oxford,

~~264. Cu Fox, C. E., The Threshold of the Pacific, Kegan Paul, Trench, Trubner & Co., London, 1924~~

226. Bo Franchet, A. et Savatier, L., Enumeratio Plantarum Japonicarum, 2 vols., 1875 & 1879; Reprinted by the Shokubutsu Bunken Kankokai, Tokyo, 1940

51. Gr Franfurter, O., Elements of Siamese Grammar, Karl W. Hiersemann, Leipzig, 1900

300. Bb Fraser, E. D. H. and Lockhart, J. H. S., Index to the Tso Chuan, O.U.P., London, 1930

220. Bo Ga Freeman-Mitford, A. B., The Bamboo Garden, Macmillan & Co., London, 1896

936. Dp The French Yellow Book : Diplomatic Documents 1938-1939, Hutchinson & Co., London

130. " Le Frère Bento de Goes (Chez les Musulmans de la Haute Asie 1603-1607), Hautes Etudes, Tientsin, 1934

702. Hy Frois, P. L., Segunda Parte Da Historia De Japan, Edição da Sociedade Luso- Japonesa, Toquio, 1938

698. Hy (D) Frois, P. L., Die Geschichte Japans (1549- '78), Verlag Der Asia Major, Leipzig, 1926

342. Bb Fuchs, W., Beiträge zur Mandjurischen Bibliographie und Literatur, Deutsche Gesellschaft Für Natur und Völkerkunde Ostasiens, Tokyo, 1936

188. Me Fujikawa, Y. and others, Japanese Medicine, Paul B. Hoeber Inc., New York, 1934

261. By At On Watanabe-Kazan as a Painter, by Fujimori, S. and translated by Hawley, F., Nippon Bunka Chuo Renmei, Tokyo, 1939

826. Cu Fujimoto, T., The Nightside Of Japan, T. Werner Laurie, London, 1927

827. Cu Fujimoto, T., The Geisha Girl, T. Werner Laurie, London, 1927

269. Tr Gy Fujinami, K., Hot Springs in Japan, Maruzen Co., Tokyo, 1936

1047. Ta Fukada, I., Criss-Cross Of The Japanese Mind, The Sanseido Co., Tokyo, 1938

65. Fukui, K., Human Elements in Ceramic Art, K.B.S., Tokyo, 1934 (2 copies OK.)

432. Lg Fu Liu, Les Mouvements de la Langue National en Chine, Press de l'Université Nationale de Pékin, 1925

365. Ps Fung Yu-Lan, A History of Chinese Philosophy (中国哲学史：馮友蘭), translated by Bodde, D., Henri Vetch, Peiping, 1937

909. Lg (D) Funke, O., Iunere Sprachform, Sudetendentscher Verlag Franz Kraus, Reichenberg, 1924

Ferrand, Gabriel; Les Poids, Mesures et Monnaies des Mers du Sud aux XVI et XVII Siecles; Paris, 1921

Fahs, Charles Burton; The Japanese House of Peers

~~1549. Mi (D) Florenz, K., Japanische Mythologie : Nihongi, Hobunsha, Tokyo, 1901~~

292. Dc (D) Florenz, K., Wörterbuch Zur Altjapanischen Liedersammlung Kokinshu, Kommissionsverlag L'Freedrichsen & Co., Hamburg, 1925

542. Li Florenz, Dr. K., Geschichte der Japanischen Litteratur, C. F. Amelangs Verlag, Leipzig, 1906

1072. So Flowers, M., The Japanese Conquest Of American Opinion, George H. Doran Co., New York, 1916

~~1354. Na Floyd-Dell., Love In The Machine Age, George Routiedge & Sons, London, 1930~~

Fifty-Fourth Annual Report of the Minister of State for Education for 1926–1927, Department of Education, 1932, 1934 (1928–1929) 2 vols.

Franke O; Staatssozialistische Versuche im Alten und Mittelalterlichen China; Berlin 1931

Ferguson, John C; Recent Scholarship in China (Reprinted from the China Journal Vol X, #6 Dec 1929

Ferguson; Chinese Chronology (-Do-)

Ferguson; Books on Journeys to Western Regions (Reprinted from Vol XI, No. 2, Aug 1929

Ferguson; The Confucian Renaissance in the Sung Dynasty; Shanghai, 1902

38

資料 09（貼付ノート・Acker,W.）

(✓) Ferguson John C; 12 Articles reprinted from T'ien Hsia Monthly.

Frois, L., La Première Ambassade Du Japon En Europe., I., 1 vol., 1942

✓ Ferguson J. C; Porcelains of Successive Dynasties (From the Journal of the North China Branch of the Royal Asiatic Society, Vol. 63, 1932)

Ferguson: The Twin pagodas of Zayton

89

✓ 111. Mi Hy(D) Karl Florenz - Japanische Mythologie (Nihongi, "Zeitalter der Götter")( 日本紀 ), Hobunsha, Tokyo, 1901.

✓ 148. Jy Cu Fortune vol XIV, No. 3 - The Japanese Empire, 1936.

✓ 166. Hy Cl Fox - The threshold of the Pacific, Kegan Paul, London, 1932.

194. Jr Fortune- special number for Japan, Sept., 1936.

189. Mp Alexis Everett Frye - New geography book, Ginn & Co, 1920.

152. Nv R. A. Freeman - The puzzle lock, N.Y., 1926.

✓ Ferguson, J. C., Porcelains of Successive Dynasties,

" Wang An-shih (王安石)

40

資料09（貼付ノート・Acker,W.）

430. Ds Gale, E. M., Discourses on Salt and Iron (鹽鐵論), Late E. J. Brill Ltd., Leyden, 1931

752. Tr Gale, J.S., Korean Sketches, William Briggs, Toronto, 1898

762. Gr Gale, J.S., Korean Gra matical Forms, 辭課指南, Methodist Publishing House, Seoul, 1903

496. Si Ci Gale, E. M., Basics of the Chinese Civilization, Kelly and Walsh, Shanghai, 1934

725. Dc Gale, J.S., The Unabridged Korean-English Dictionary, The Christian Literature Society of Korea, Seoul, 1931

1114. Ms Galsworthy, J., The Forsyte Saga, William Henemann, London, 1922

458. Hy Le Gardner, C. S., Chinese Traditional History, Harvard University Press, Cambridge, 1938

465. Jy De Garis, F., We Japanese, Fujiya Hotel Ltd., Hakone, 1934

975. Lg Gaselee, S., The Oxford Book Of Medieval Latin Verse, The Clarendon Press, Oxford, 1928

595. Li Mi Gatenby, E. V., The Cloud-Men of Yamato (Being an Outline of Mysticism in Japanese Literature), John Murray, London, 1929

1460. Rn (F) Gauthiot, R., Le Sūtra Du Religieux Ongles-Lougs, Librairie Honore Champion, Paris, 1912

1461. Lg (F) Gauthiot, R., Essai Sur Le Vocalisme Du Sogdien, Librairie Paul Geuthner, Paris, ~~1899~~

~~1355. Es Gauthiot, R., Essai de Grammaire Sogdienne, 2 vols., Librairie Paul Geuthner, Paris, 1914-1923~~

~~1414. Bb (F) Gavel, H., Grammaire Basque, Tome 1, Imperimerie du "Courrier" Bayonne, 1929~~

934. Sc (F) Geerts, A.J.C., Les Produits De La Nature Japonaise Et Chinoise, 2 vols., C. Levy, Imprimeur-Editeur, Yokohama, 1878-1883

1193. Jr General Index To The Transactions Of The Asiatic Society Of Japan, Vols. 1-23, Kelly & Walsh, Yokohama

1203. Ct, Bb General Index of Subjects Contained in The Twenty Volumes of The Chinese Repository, Vol. 20, Shanghai, 1940

1083. Gy Geographical Review, July 1937, The American Geographical Society Of New York, New York,

1064. By (F) Georges Lecomte, La Vie Hiroique de Saint François Xavier, Editions Baudiniere, Paris,

938. Rn Geschichte Des Christentums In Japan ,1, Haas, P.H., Tokyo, 1902

89. Hy Gezelius, B., Japan: Västerländsk Framställning Till Omkring ar 700, A. B. Östyöta, Linkoping, 1910

586. Bb Giles, H. A., A Chinese Biographical Dictionary (古今姓氏族譜), Kelly & Walsh, Shanghai, 1898; reprinted in China, 1939

570. Dc Giles, H. A., Chinese English Dictionary, Kelly & Walsh, Shanghai, 1912

372. H A Giles, H. A., Adversaria Sinica, Kelly & Walsh, Shanghai, 1914 & 1915, 2 vols. コレハ押入

373. Rp Grigorieff, W. W., Travaux de la Troisième Session du Congrès International des Orientalistes, St. Petersbourg, 1876

296. Bb Giles, L., Index to the Chinese Encyclopaedia, The British Museum, London, 1911 (欽定古今図書集成)

493. Ta Si Giles, H. A., Strange Stories from a Chinese Studio, Kelly & Walsh, Shanghai, 1936

482. By Giles, H. A., Chuang Tzu (Mystic, Moralist, and Social Reformer), Kelly & Walsh, Shanghai, 1926

1130. St Gibbons, S., Nightingale Wood, Penguin Books, London, 1940

1428. Dc (F) Gibert, L., Dictionnaire Historique et Geographique de la Mandchourie, de la Société des Mission-Etrangeres, Hongkong, 1934

760. Cu Gifford, D.L., Every-Day Life in Korea, Fleming H. Revell Co., Chicago, 1898

567. Cu Fl Gillis, I. V. and Pai Ping-Ch'i, Japanese Personal Names, Hwa Hsing Press, Peking, 1940

568. Cu Fl (F) Gillis, I. V. and Pai Ping-Ch'i, Japanese Surnames, Hwa Hsing Press, Peking, 1939

56. At Goette, J., Jade Lore, Kelly & Walsh, Shanghai, 1936

708. Rn A Golden Jubilee 1865-1915 : General View of Catholicism In Japan, L. G. of the Foreign Mission of Paris, Nagasaki, 1914

864. Pt (F) Goncourt, E., Hokousai, Bibliotheque - Charpentier, Paris, 1896

1116. Mr Gore, J., King George V. A Personal Memoir, John Murray, London, 1941

956. Po Gow, J., Horace Odes And Epodes (2. Horati Flacci Carmina), The University Press, Cambridge, 1932

1339. An (D) Gragger, R., Ungaresche Jahbucher, Band 6, Walter De Gruyter & Co., Berlin, 1926

42

740. Gr (F) Grammaire Coréenne Et Exercise Gradués, Les Missionnaires De Coree, Yokohama, 1881

1260. Po (F) Granet, M., Fêtes Et Chansons Anciennes De La Chine, Librairie Ernest, Paris, 1929

917. Le (F) Granet, M., Danses Et Ligender De La Chine Ancienne, Librairie Felix Alcan, Paris, 1926

388. M Gray, L. H. and others, The Mythology of All Races, 13 vols., Marshall Jones Co., Boston, 1917

906. Lg Gray, H., Foundation of Language, The Macmillan Co., New York, 1939

218. The Greek Herbal of Dioscorides, translated by Goodyer, J. A.D.1655; University Press, Oxford, 1934

112. Hy Griffin, E., Clippers and Consuls (American Consular and Commercial Relations with Eastern Asia 1845-1860), Edwards Bros. Inc., Ann Arbor, Mich., 1938

761. Ta Griffis, W.E., Korean Fairy Tales, George G. Harrap & Co., London,

107. By Griffis, W. E., Townsend Harris, Houghton Mifflin & Co., New York, 1895

756. Cu Griffis, W.E., Corea, The Hermit Nation, W.H. Allen & Co., London, 1882

405. By Griffis, W. E., Honda the Samurai (A story of Modern Japan), Congregational Sunday School and Publishing Society, Boston

1001. Dc Gring, A.B., Eclectic Chinese-Japanese-English Dictionary, Kelly & Co., Yokohama, 1884

963. Lg Grose, F., Grose's Glossary, A Provincial Glossary, S.Hooper, London, 1787

903. Dc Grose, F., A Classical Dictionary Of The Vulgur Tongue, Issued for Private Subscribers by The Scholartis Press, London, 1931

1122. Rm Groot, J.J., The Religions System Of China, 6 vols.,

169. Bu Hy Grousset, R., In the Footsteps of the Buddhia, George Routledge & Sons Ltd., London, 1932

891. Lg (D) Grube, W., Goldisch-Deutsches Wörterverzeichniss mit vergleichender Berücksichtgung der übrigen tungusischen Dialekte, St. Petersburg, 1900

723. Lg (D) Grube, W., Die Sprache und Schrift Der Jucen, Kommissions - Verlag Von O. Harrassowitz, Leipzig, 1896

1255. Jy Gubbins, J.H., The Making Of Modern Japan, Seeley, Service & Co., London, 1922

1270. Dc Gubbins, J.H., A Dictionary Of Chinese-Japanese Wards, Maruya & Co., Tokyo, 1908

? (V) 119. Jy X Gubbins, J. H., The Progress of Japan 1853-1871, The Clarendon Press, Oxford, 1911

? (V) 270. Gy X Gubler, A., Die Kurilen, Aschmann & Scheller, Zürich, 1932

1105. Jy (V) A Guide To Japanese Studies, Kokusai Bunka Shinkokai, Tokyo, 1937

(O) 143. Rs (V) van Gulik, R. H., Monumenta Serica (Journal of Oriental Studies of the Catholic University of Peking), Henri Vetch, Peking,

280. (V) Hy Van Gulik, R. H., Monumenta Serica, Henri Vetch, Peking

67. (V) Van Gulik, R. H., Mi Fu on Ink Stones, Henri Vetch, Peking, 1938

798. At (V) Gulik, R.H., The Lore Of The Chinese Lute, 琴道,
Sophia University, Tokyo, 1940

829. At (V) Gulik, R.H., Hsi K'ang And His Poetical Essay On The Lute, Sophia University, Tokyo, 1941

45. At (V) Van Gulik, R. H., The Mounted Scroll in China and Japan, Reprinted from T'ien Hsia Monthly, Aug-Sept. 1941

1085. Tr (V) Gutzlaff, C., Journal Of Three Voyages Along The Coast Of China In 1831, 1832 & 1833, Thomas Ward & Co., London

(V) 872. Ta (F) Gyp, Celui qu'on aime, Flammarion,

(V) 57. Dc(F) Jules Guirand - Dictionnaire Anglais-Français, 1926.

521. Rb (D) X (V) Gundert, W., Japanische Religionsgeschichte, Taiheiyosha, Tokyo, 1935

(V) Giles, H. A., An Introduction to the History of Chinese pictorial Art, Kelly & Walsh, Shanghai, 1918

(V) Grossman F. N., Japanese Without a Teacher, Dawase & Son, Kobe, 1927

? (V) Gardner, C. S., A Union List of Selected Western Books on China In American Library, American Council of Learned Societies, Washington, 1938

44

152. Fl Cu(F) M. Marcel Granet - Fêtes et chansons anciennes de la Chine, Librairie Ernest, Paris, 1929.

40. Es Gr(F) Robert Gaunthiot - Essai de grammaire Sogdienne, Paul Geuthner, Paris, 1914-1923, 2 vols.

64. Gr(F) H. Gavel - Grammaire Basque, Tome I, Imprimérie du "Courrier", Bayonne, 1929.

13. Dc Gubbins - A dictionary, Chinese-Japanese words, Maruya & Co., Tokyo, 1908.

158. Nv Remy de Gourmont - Histoires magiques, Paris, 1924.

164. Nv John Galsworthy - A modern comedy, London, 1939.

108. Jy Tr Grenon - Verdant Simple's views of Japan, 1890.

Green, Robert: The Mermaid Series; Fisher Unwin Ltd, Lon.

Gaikoku Jinmei Chimei Hyo (Proper Names with Standard Chinese Equivalents.

Granet: La Civilisation Chinoise, 1929

Gardner; Chinese Studies in America, 1935 (A Survey of Resources & Facilities)

Grand Exhibition of Ancient Chinese & Corean Works of Art, Yamanaka & Co, Osaka.

Giles, Herbert A; The Hundred Best Characters, Kelly & Walsh Ltd, Shanghai, 1925.

Giles, Herbert A: The Second Hundred Best Characters; Kelly & Walsh Ltd, Shanghai, 1922.

Giles, Lionel; The Sayings of Lao-Tzu; John Murray, London; 1917

Government Publications; HM Stationery Office; 3 vols; Consolidated list for 1937; January & February 1938.

X Gunther: Greek Herbal of Dioscorides, 1934

X Guerreiro: Relacão, 2 vols.

218 LB021

85

452. Pi Haag-Pedersen, J., The Postage Stamps of Manchoukuo with Varieties, published by the author, Mukden, 1940

Case 3. 196. Nh Hachisuka, M.U., The Birds of Japan and the British Isles, Cambridge University Press, Cambridge, 1925

969. So Haire, N., Sexual Reform Congress, Kegan Paul, Trench, Trubner & Co., London, 1930

335. Tr Hall, B., Voyage to West Coast of Corea and the Great Loochoo Island, John Murray, London, 1818

91. Hy Hallberg, I., L'extreme Orient, Wald Zachrissons, Göteborg, 1906

345. Tr Halloran, A. L., Eight Months' Journal to Japan, Loochoo, etc., Longman, Brown, Green, Longmans & Roberts, London, 1856

1439. Dp (F) Halot, M., Conférence Sur L'Ile Formosa, Imprimerie E Cagniard, Rouen, 1910

1154. Te Hamerton, P.G., Human Intercourse, Macmillan & Co., London, 1928

871. Cu Hamerton, P.G., The Intellectual Life, The Hokuseido Press, Tokyo, 1925

1137. St Hampden, J., Great English Short Stories, Vol. ? Penguin Books, London, 1940

1313. Es Hanazono, K., Journalism In Japan And Its Early Pioneers, Osaka Shuppan-sha, Osaka, 1926

1216. Es Hanazono, K., The Development of Japanese Journalism, Osaka Mainichi, Osaka, 1924

211. Bo Pm Hanbury, D., Science Papers (Chiefly Pharmacological and Botanical), Macmillan & Co., London, 1876

618. Rn Handbook of The Old Shrines And Temples And Their Treasures In Japan, Bureau Of Religions Department Of Education, Tokyo, 1920

71. At Handbook of the Department of Oriental Art, The Art Institute of Chicago, Chicago, 1933

645. Pt Happer, J.S. Japanese Sketches And Japanese Prints, Kairyudo, Tokyo, 19?4

356. St Hara, K., An Introduction to the Story of Japan, G. P. Putnam's Sons, New York, 1920

262. Ct Harada, J., English Catalogue of Treasures in the Imperial Repository Shosoin, The Imperial Household Museum, Tokyo, 1932

5. At Harada, J., A Glimpse of Japanese Ideals, Kokusai Bunka Shinkokai, Tokyo, 1937

6. Ga Harada, J., The Gardens of Japan, The Studio Ltd., London, 1928

46

資料 09（貼付ノート・Acker,W.）

983B Harkness, A. A Latin Grammar for Schools & Colleges, American Book Company, New York

1053. Tr Harrington, J.P., Tobacco Among The Karuk Indians Of California, United States Government Printing Office, Washington, 1932

1445. Rn Havret, H., T'Ien-Tchon, 天主, Imprimerie De La Mission Catholique, Chang-Hai, 1909

870. Pt Hastings, C.H., Printed Cards L.C. : How To Order And Use Them, Government Ptinting Office, Washington, 1925

~~228. Bo~~ 181 ~~Hawkes, E., Pioneers of Plant Study, The Sheldon Press, London, 1928~~

307. Bb Hayakawa, S., Symbolae ex Libris, Herbarium Hayakawa, Tokyo, 1929

193. Ct Hayakawa, S. Symbolae ex Libris Hayakawa (植芳書屋図書目録), Herbarium Hayakawa, Tokyo, 1929

181. Bo E. Hawkes - Pioneers of plant study, The Sheldon Press, London, 1928.

58. Gr Hoffmann - Japanese grammar, A. W. Sythoff, Leiden, 1868.

149. La A. P. Herbert - Misleading cases in the common law, Methuen, London, 1931.

142. Ml(D) Fr. Hübotter - Die Chinesische Medizin (中華醫學), Bruno Scuindler, Leipzig, 1929.

110. Rn Cl Holton - The national faith of Japan, Kegan Paul, London, 1938.

116. Nv Sidney Horles - Hunters of death.

120. Es Th. H. Huxley - Selected essays (of).

155. Nv Aldous Huxley - Crome Yellow, London, 1929.

~~178. Pap Dard Hunter - A Paper-Making pilgrimage to Japan, Korea & China, Pynson Printers, N.Y., 1936.~~

~~179. Pap " - Paper-making tyrough 18th centuries, W.E. Rudge, N. Y., 1930.~~

51. Jr Pl Harper's monthly magazine, No 1022 (1935), No. 1023 (1935), No. 1030 (1936), 2 vols. 3 vols. No 1030

640. Pa Hirano, C., Kiyonaga,

48

資料09（貼付ノート・Acker,W.）

1257. Jy Hearn, L., Kokoro : Hints And Echoes Of Japanese Inner Life, Houghton Mifflin Co., Boston, 1893

133. Na Heco, J., The Narrative of a Japanese (What he has seen and the People he has met in the course of the last 40 years), 2 vols., Maruzen, Tokyo, 28th Yr. of Meiji

266. Tr Hedin, S., Jehol, City of Emperors, Kegan Paul, Trench, Trubner & Co., London, 1932

1182. Lg Henderson, B.L.K., Chats About Our Mother Tongue, Macdonald And Evans, London, 1927

1071. Ta Henderson, B., Wonder Tales Of Older Japan, Feederick A.Stokes Co., New York,

641. Jy Henderson, H.G., Etc., The Surviving Works Of Sharaku, The Society For Japanese Studies, New York, 1939

580. Po Henderson, H. G., The Bamboo Broom (An Introduction to Japanese Haiku), J. L. Thompson (Retail) & Co., Kobe, 8th Year of Showa

623. Rn Hepner, C.W., The Kurozumi Sect Of Shintō, The Meiji Japan Society, Tokyo, 1935

835. Po Herbert, A.P., A Book Of Ballads, Ernest Benn , London, 1931

1159. St Herbert, A.P., The Secret Battle, Methuen & Co., London, 1930

1160. St Herbert, A.P., Wisdom For The Wise, Methuen & Co., London, 1930

~~1157. La~~ 149 ~~Herbert, A.P., Misleading Cases In The Common Law, Methuen & Co., London, 1931~~

1186. Ms Hergesheimer, J., Tampico, Bernhard Tauchnitz, Leipzig, 1926

369. Jy History of the Empire of Japan, translated for the Imperial Japanese Commission of the World's Columbian Exposition, Chicago, 1893, by order of the Department of Education, Dai Nippon Tosho K.K., Tokyo

421. Si Hy Histoire des trois Royaumes Han, Wei et Tchao, by Tschepe, A., Mission Catholique, Changhai, 1910

180. Rs Hirth, F. and Rockhill, W. W., Chau Ju-Kua (諸蕃志 - His works on the Chinese and Arab trades in the 12th and 13th centuries, entitled Chu-Fan-Chi), The Imperial Academy of Sciences, St. Petersburg, 1912.

209. Bo Higgins, V., The Naming of Plants, Edward Arnold & Co., London, 1937

460. Te E Hiroike, S., Moralogy, The Institute of Moralogy, Chiba, 1937

457. Hy Hirth, F., The Ancient History of China (To the end of the Chou Dynasty), Columbia University Press, New York, 1923

501. Li Si Hirth, F., Notes on the Chinese Documentary Style, Kelly & Walsh, Shanghai, 1909

615. Rn Hibino, Y., Nippon Shin o Ron, The University Press, Cambridge, 1928

1125. Pa Hirano, C., Kiyonaga, AsStudy Of His Life And Works, 8 coloured prints & 138 plates in 1 chitsu, The Harvard University Press, Cambridge, 1939

1254. Jy Hildreth, R., Japan As It Was And Is, The Sanshusha, Tokyo, 1905

1250. Hy (F) Histoire De La Chine,

1434. Hy House, E.H., Japanese Expedition To Formosa, Tokyo, 1875

706. Cu, La Hozumi, N., Ancestor- Worship And Japanese Law, The Maruzen Co., Tokyo, 1912

Case 11. 346. Ms Hobhouse, L. T., Morals in Evolution, Chapman & Hall, London, 1925

(F) 223. Bo Hoffmann, J. et Schultes, H., Noms Indigènes d'un Choix de Plantes du Japon et de la Chine, E. J. Brill, Leyde, 1864;

304. Bb Holden, J. A., The Bookman's Glossary, R. R. Bowker Co., N.Y., 1931

497. By Holth, S., Micius (A Brief Outline of his Life and Ideas), The Commercial Press, Shanghai, 1935

~~559. Gr 58 Hoffmann, J. J., Japanese Grammar, A. W. Sythoff for H.M.'s Minister for Colonial Affairs, Leiden, 1868~~

~~614. Rn 110 Holtom, D.C., The National Faith Of Japan, Kegan Paul, Trench, Trabner & Co., London, 1938~~

631. Jy Holtom, D.C., The Japanese Enthronement Ceremonies, The Kyo Bun Kwan, Tokyo, 1928

747. Lg Hodge, J.W., The Stranger's Handbook Of The Corean Language, The Seoul Press-Hodge & Co., Seoul, 1902

1310. Bb Honjo, E., A Bibliography of Japanese Economic History written by some European Languages, Kyoto, 1933

1424. Hy Howorth, H.H., History of the Mongols, vols. 1, 2, 3, 5, 文殿閣書荘, Péking 民国27年

16. Ad (F) Hoang, P.P., Mélanges Sur L'Administration, Imprimerie De La Mission Catholique, Chan-Hai, 1902

902. Ps (D) Hochstetter, Studien zur Metaphysik und Erkenntnislehre Wilhelms von Ockham, Walter de Gruyter & Co., Berlin, 1927

1031. Cl Hodons, L., Careers For Students Of Chinese Language And Civilivation, The University Of Chicago Press, Chicago, 1933

50

資料 09（貼付ノート・Acker,W.）

1086. Po Housman, A.C., Last Poems,
Great Richards, London, 1922

1240. Ar Hopkins, L.C., The Honan Relics : A new investigator and some results,
From the Journal of The Royal Asiatic Society, Jan., 1921

1276. Hy Holmes, R., Caesar De Bello Gallico,
The Clarendon Press, Oxford, 1914

1297. Dc Hoffmann, J.J., Japanese- English Dictionary, ~~3 vols.~~,
The Dutch Government, Leyden, 1881-1892 found in a volume

1277. Bo (D) Hochschulen, Lehrbuch Der Botanik,
Verlag Von Gustav Fischer, Jena, 1921

1307. Fi The House Of Mitsui,
Mitsui Gomei Kaisha, Tokyo, 1933

910. Cl (F) Huart, C., La Perse Antique et La Civilisation Iranienne
La Renaissance du Livre, Paris, 1925

~~1409. Me~~ 142 ~~Hübotter, Fr., Die Chinesisch Medizin,~~
~~Verlag der "Asia Major" Dr. Bruno Scuindler, Leipzig, 1929~~

1256. Es Hudson, W.H., The Land's End,
J.M. Dent & Sons, London, 1926

123. Dp Hudson, G. F., Europe and China (A Survey of their Relations from the Earliest Times to 1800), Edward Arnold & Co., London, 1931

825. Cu Huggins, H.C., etc., Love And Society In Japan,
Tokyo, 1932

808. Ta Huggins, H., etc., Intimate Tales of Old Japan,
Nichibei- Insatsu- Sha, Yokohama, 1929

1059. Li Hughes, G., Three Women Poets Of Modern Japan,
University Of Washingyon Book Store, Seattle, 1930

728. Hy Hulbert, H.B., The Passing Of Korea,
William Heinemann, London, 1906

431. By Hummel, A. W., The Autobiography of a Chinese Historian
(顧頡剛古史辨自序), Late E. J. Brill Ltd., Leyden, 1931

481. Si Hunter, W. C., The "Fan Kwae" at Canton before Treaty Days
1825-1844, Oriental Affairs, Shanghai,

~~287. Pap~~ 179 ~~Hunter, D., A Papermaking Pilgrimage to Japan, Korea and~~ China,
~~Pynson Printers, N.Y., 1936~~

~~290. Pap~~ 179 ~~Hunter, D., Papermaking through Eighteen Centuries, William~~
~~Edwin Rudge, New York, 1930~~

1400. Po Huntley, F.L., The Study Of English Poetry,
Kaitakusha, Tokyo, 1932

51

483. Ps Hu Shih (Suh Hu), The Development of the Logical Method in Ancient China, The Oriental Book Co., Shanghai, 1921

484. Ps Hu Shih (Suh Hu), The Development of the Logical Method in Ancient China, The Oriental Book Co., Shanghai, 1928

1131. St Huxley, J., We Europeans, Penguin Books, London, 1939

529. Jy Huzii, O., Japanese Proverbs, Board of Tourist Industry, Japanese Government Railways, 1940

222. Ed Huzimoto, H. and others, Science Education in Japan, The 7th Word Conference of the World Federation of Education Association, 1937

381. Dc Ichikawa, S., The Kenkyusha Dictionary of English Philology, Kenkyusha, Tokyo, 1940

1042. Ta Ichikawa, H., Japanese Lady In Europe, Extracts from Press Reviews, Kenkyusha, Tokyo, 1937

Rp Ichikawa, S., The Ichikawa Mineral Laboratory Summary Reports, 2 vols., Ichikawa Mineral Laboratory, Fukui-ken, 1934 & 1935

1017. Ta Ichikawa, H., Japanese Lady In America, Kenkyusha & Co., Tokyo, 1938

1018. Ta Ichikawa, H., Japanese Lady In Europe, Kenkyusha & Co., Tokyo, 1937

707. Cu, La (D) Ikeda, R., Die Hauserbfolge In Japan, Mayer & Muller, Berlin, 1903

8. At Illustrated Catalogue of Chinese Government Exhibits for the International Exhibition of Chinese Art in London, edited by the Chinese Organizing Committee, 4 vols., The Commercial Press, Shanghai, 1936-1937

416. Pt (F) Imbert, H., Collection de la Politique de Pekin, 4 vols. in 1 chitsu, Pekin, 1921-1922

514. Gr Imbrie, Wm., Wa and Ga, Kyo Bun Kwan, Tokyo, 1914

991. Lg Imbrie, W., English-Japanese Etymology, 1st edition, T.Ishikawa & Son, Tokyo, 1884

992. Lg Imbrie, W., English-Japanese Etymology, second edition, Z.P. Maruya & Co., Tokyo, 1889

795. Ed The Imperial Rescript On Education, Translated Into Chinese, English, French & German, The Department of Education, Tokyo, 1907

630. Jy The Imperial Ordinance Relating To The Ascension To The Throne,

359. Dp The Imperial Japanese Mission to the United States, Carnegie Endowment for International Peace, Washington, D. C., 1918

518. Lg Inagaki, M., Langnage Text of Nippon, 2 vols., Kyobunkwan, Tokyo, 1938 and 1939

52

資料 09（貼付ノート・Acker,W.）

1331. Jr Index Journal Of The American Oriental Society, 20 vols., American Oriental Society, Connecticut, 1924

817. Cu Inouye, J., Sketches Of Tokyo Life, Kuruta Naka, Yokohama, 1895

822. Cu Inouye, J., Home Life In Tokyo, 1 vol. 1 chitsu, Tokyo, 1910

527. Lg Interim Report on Vocabulary Selection for the Teaching of English as a Foreign Language, P. S. King & Son Ltd., London, 1936

561. Li Introduction to Contemporary Japanese Literature, K.B.S., Tokyo, 1939

574. Po Isobe, Y., The Poetical Journey in Old Japan (Oku-no-Hoso-Michi - Basho), San Kaku Sha, Tokyo, 8th Yr. of Showa 1933

511. Na Itakura, J., The Ho-Jo-Ki (Private Papers of Kamo-no-Chomei of the Ten Foot Square Hut), Maruzen, Tokyo, 1935

575. Po Ito, S., Songs of a Cowherd, translated by Sakanishi, S., Marshall Jones Co., Boston, 1936

797. La Ito, H., Prince, Commontaries On The Constitution Of The Empire Of Japan, Chu-O Daigaku, Tokyo, 1931

654. Rn Iwai, T., The Outline Of Tenrikyo, Tenrikyo Doyu-sha, Yamato, 1932

900. Jr Izvestiya Vostoenago Instituta, 6 vols., Russia, 1900-1901

41. Lg Ed The Institute for Research in English Teaching - A commemorative volume - 10th annual conference of English teachers -1933.

Hoaler, S., Huntress of Death, 1933

Roger, G., Hitler, 1932

53

314. Bb Jackson, H., The Fear of Books, The Soncino Press, London, 1932

315. Bb Jackson, H., The Anatomy of Bibliomania, The Soncino Press, London, 1932

1078. Nv. Jackson, J.H., Water Margin, 2 vols., The Commercial Press, Shanghai, 1937

305. Pri Jacobi, C. T., Some Notes on Books and Printing, Chiswick Press, London, 1892

1128. St Jacobs, W.W., Night Watches, Penguin Books, London, 1940

930. Lg James, A.L., Broadcast English, The British Broadcasting Corporation, London, 1935

506. Fl Jameson, R. D., Three Lectures on Chinese Folklore, North China Union Language School, Peiping, 1932

1002. Dc Jones, J.I., etc., 6000 Chinese Characters With Japanese-pronounciation And Japanese And English Renderings, Kyo Bun Kwan, Tokyo, 1915

667. Rn (D) Jann, P.A., Die Katholischen Mission in Indien, China und Japan, Druck und Verlag von Ferdinand Schoningh, Paderborn, 1915

1433. Jy (F) Japan Et Extrême-Orient, No. 1-12, ~~(except No. 3)~~, Edmond Bernard, Editeur, Paris

148. Hy Japan het Verkeer met Europesche Natiën, J. A. Beijerinck, Amsterdam, 1847

875. Sta 60 The Japan Year Book, 4 vols., ( 1919-20, 1920-21, 1921-22, 1924-25) The Japan Year Book Co., Tokyo, 1919-1925

79. Bu Japanese Alphabetical Catalogue of Nanjio's Catalogue of the Buddhist Tripitaka ( 大蔵経南條目録補正索引 ), Nanjio-Hakushi Kinen Kankokwai, Tokyo, 1930

69. At Japanese Art (Screen paintings, fan paintings, and lacquer covering a period of over 600 years), The Toledo Museum of Art, Toledo, Ohio.

74. At The Japanese Arts thru Lantern Slides, 5 vols., K.B.S., Tokyo, 1937-1940

1082. Ta A Japanese Boy, (By Himself), E.B.Sheldon & Co., New ~~York~~ Heaven, 1889

215. Cu Japanese Cooking and Etiquette by the Graduating Class of Keisen Girls' School, K.B.K., Tokyo, 1940

~~793. Ed 76 Japanese Education, Monbusho (Department of Education), Tokyo, 1877~~

1380. Dp The Japanese Government's Statement of Observations on Lytton Report, The Japan Advertiser, Tokyo, 1932

54

資料 09（貼付ノート・Acker,W.）

1244. Pa Japanese Painting, Lantern Slide Catalogue, K.B.S., Tokyo, 1938

824. Cu Japanese Women, McClurg & Co., Chicago, 1893

572. Cal Jensen, Dr. P. H., Geschichte der Schrift, Orient-Buchhandlung Heinz Lafaire, Hannover, 1925

868. Zo (F) Jeune, P., La Societe Des Insectes, Les Editions Des Portiques, Paris

253. Sc Johnson, S. A Study of Chinese Alchemy, The Commercial Press, Shanghai, 1928

~~7. At 64 Joly, H.L., Legend in Japanese Art, John Lane The Bodley Head, London, 1908~~

1210. Jr (F) Journal Asiatique, Tome 229, La Société Asiatique, Librairie Orientaliste Paul Geuthner, Paris, 1937

1436. Jr (F) Journal Asiatique, ~~4 parts~~, Editions ~~Ernest Leroux~~, Paris, ~~1922~~

1324. Jr 49 Journal Of The China Branch Of The Royal Asiatic Society, vols.23, 30, Kelly & Walsh, Shanghai, 1895-1888

1196. Jr 49 Journal Of The Noth China Branch R.A.S., 55 vols., Kelly & Walsh, Shanghai,

1197. Jr Journal Of The Notth China Branch R.A.S., Vol. 69, 1938, New Series, Nos.1, 14, 19,25, 1864-1893

1198. Jr Journal Of The China Branch Of The Royal Asiatic Society, Vol. No.1, 3, 8, 11, 17, 20, 21, 22(2 copies), 23(2 copies), 24, 30, 42(2 copies), 71, 18 parts, 1864-1940, Kelly & Walsh, Shanghai,

1386. Jr 114 The Journal Of The Royal Asiatic Society Of Great Britain And Ireland, (2 copies) Published By The Society, London, 1921

1392. Jr The Journal Of The Royal Asiatic Society Of Great Britain And Ireland, Published By The Society, London, 1932

1353. Jr Journal Of The Royal Asiatic Society, 1929, Published By The Society, London, 1929

1201. Jr Journal Of The Shanghai, No. 1 June , 1858 Reprinted by Noronha & Sons, Shanghai, 1887

239. Bo Juel, H. O., Plantae Thunbergianae, Akademiska Bokhandeln, Uppsala, etc., 1918

163. Ds Julien, S., Méthode pour déchiffrer les Noms Sanscrits, A L'imprimerie Impériale, Paris, 1861

1302. Jy John, H.C., The Wild Coast Of Nipon, David Douglas, Edinburgh, 1880

919. Lg (F) Julieu, S., Syntaxe Nouvelle De La Langue Chinoise, 2 vols., bound together, Librairie De Maisonneuve, Paris, 1869-1870

1319. Jr Journal Of The Peking Oriental Society, 12 vols., Pei-T'ang Press, Peking, 1885-1895

76. Ed Japanese Department of Education - Japanese education, Philadelphia International Exhibition (1876).

84. At Le H. L. Joly - Legend in Japanese art, John Lane, London, 1908.

49. Jr Pl Journal of North China Branch of R. A. S. - 1860, 1868 (2 vols); 1874-5 (2 vols); 1878-9 (2 vols); 1881-3 (3 vols); 1889-1910 (16 vols); 1912-38 (28 vols including index), Total 53 vols.

60. Dr The Japan Year Book Office - The Japan year book, (1926).

192. Bo(D) Japanische Bergkirschen, ihre Wildformen und Kulturrassen, Imperial University of Tokyo, 1916. (With illustrations).

203. Rp Rs The Japanese Sericultural Association - The sericultural industry in Japan, Tokyo, 1910.

53. Jr Pl Journal of American Oriental Society (J. A. O. S.) from 45 (4 vols), 1925 to 58 (1-4), 1938 & 59 (1), 1939, Total 57 vols. O.K

30. Ps Gr Jespersen - Philosophy of grammar.

62. Lg O. Jespersen - Language, its nature, development and origin. 2 copies

11. Gr Jespersen - Modern English grammar.

26. Gr Jächke - Tibetan grammar.

Jaw Yuanrenn: Gwoyeu Romatzyh Chaing Yong Tzyh Beau, 1930,

56

資料09（貼付ノート・Acker,W.）

433. Hy Jy Kaempfer, E., The History of Japan, together with a Description of the Kingdom of Siam, 3 vols., M. D. James MacLehose & Sons, Glasgow, 1906

1110. Lg Kanazawa, S., The Common Origin Of The Japanese And Korean Languages, Sanseido, Tokyo, 1910

2 copies

750. Lg Kanazawa, S., The Common Origin Of The Japanese And Korean Language, Sanseido, Tokyo, 1910

1463. Gy (D) Kanazawa, S., Untersuchungen über Die Japanischen Und Koreanischen Ortsnamen In Alten Zeiten, General Gouvernement, Chōsen, 1912

1295. Dc Karlgren, B., Analytic Dictionary of Chinese and Sino-Japanese,

489. Lg Karlgren, B., Sound and Symbol in Chinese, O. U. P., London

622. Rn Katō, G., A Study Of Shintō, The Meiji Japan Society, Tokyō, 1939

585. Na Kato, G. and Hoshino, H., Kogoshui, or Gleanings from Ancient Stories (A History of Japan), Zaidan Hojin Meiji Seitoku Kinen Gakkai, Tokyo, 1925 and 1926 (2 copies)

350. Mr Kato, G., The Meiji Japan Society 25th Anniversary Commèmoration Volume, Zaidan Hojin Meiji Seitoku Kinen Gakkai, Tokyo, 1937

634. Rn Kato, G., Le Shinto, Librairie Orientaliste Paul Geuthner, Paris, 1931

664. Pc Kawatake, S., Development Of The Japanese Theatre Art, Kokusai Bunka Shinkokai, Tokyo, 1935

974. Fa Kaye, F.B., Mandeville : The Fable of the Bees, 2 vols., The Clarendon Press, Oxford, 19284

~~410. Gy Kenelly, M., L. Richard's Comprehensive Geography of the Chinese Empire and Dependencies, S. J. T'usewei Press, Shanghai, 1908~~

475. In Kennedy, M. D., The Changing Fabric of Japan, Constable & Co., London, 1930

790. Ed Kienleyside, H., History of Japanese Education & Present Educational System, The Hokuseido Press, 1937

787. Ed Kikuchi, D., Japanese Education, John Murray, London, 1909

609. Dm Pc Kincaid, Zoë, Kabuki: The Popular Stage Of Japan, Macmillan & Co., London, 1925

1081. At Kincaid, Z., Tokyo Vignettes, The Sanseido Co., Tokyo, 1933

587. Hy Kinoshita, I., Koziki (Aelteste Japanische Reichsgeschichte), Japanisch-Deutschen Kulturinstitut zu Tokyo und Japaninstitut zu Berlin, 1940

~~1140. Mo ~~ 157 ~~Kirchwey, F., Our Changing Morality, Albert and Charles Boni, New York, 1930~~

635. Jy Kirkwood, K.P., Renaissance In Japan, Meiji Press, Tokyo, 1938

1145. Po Kipling, R., Barrack-Room Ballads And Other Verses, Methuen & Co., London, 1929

1170. St Kipling, R., The Years Between, Methuen & Co., London, 1919

806. At Kishibe, S., The Origin Of The P'I P'A With Particular Reference To The Five- Stringed P'i P'a Preserved In The Shosoin, A Modified version of the article 琵琶の淵源, which appeared in the 考古学雑誌 Vol. 22(1936) Nos., 10 and 12 (Reprinted from the Transaction of the Asiatic Society of Japan, Second Series Vol. 19), 1940

Case 17. 719. Te (D) Kitamura, S., Grundriss der Ju-Lehre, Maruzen Co., Tokyo, 1935

(F)
14. An Klaproth, M. J., Nippon-O-Dai-Itsi-Ran ou Annales des Empereurs du Japon, The Oriental Translation Fund of Gt. Britain and Ireland, Paris, 1834

721. Do (F) Klaproth, J., San Kokf Tsou Ran To Sets, John Murry, Paris, 1832

2 copy

730. Do (F) Klaproth, J., San Kokf Tsou Ran To Sets, John Murry, Paris, 1832

731. At Koehn, A., Japanese Tray Landscapes, Lotus Court Publications, Peking, 1937

(F)
344. Lg Klaproth, J., Chrestomathie Mandchou, ou Recueil de Textes Mandchou, par autorisation de Mgr le Garde des Sceaux a L'Imprimerie Royale, 1828

In one bundle (Klette, Dr. E. and Knapp, Dr. H., Archiv Fur Buchbinderei, (Wilhelm Knapp, Halle, 1934
(
(Archiv-Fur Buchbinderei Zeitschrift Fur Einbandkunst, 1935

Case 10 (F)
1087. By Klien, H., The English Duden, Bibliographisches Institut Ag. , Leipzig, 1937

1023. By Kobayashi, N., The Sketch Book Of The Lady Sei Shōnagon, John Murry, London,

1024. Cu Kawanami, K.K., Japan And The Japanese, The Keiseisha, Tokyo, 1905

737. At Koehn, A., The Way of Japanese Flower Arrangement, Kyo Bun Kwan, Tokyo, 1937

626. Ms Kodokwanki, The Meiji Japan Society, Tokyo, 1937

206. Me Ko Hung on the Gold Medicine and on the Yellow and the White, translated from the Chinese by Lu-Ch'iang Wu, The American Academy of Arts and Sciences, 1935

58

1262. Rp Kokusai Bunka Shinkokai (Prospectus and Scheme), K.B.S., Tokyo

1263. Bb K.B.S. Bibliographical Register Of Important Works Written In Japanese On Japan And Far East, K.B.S., Tokyo, 1937

1264. Li Kikuchi, K., History And Trends Of Modern Japanese Literature, K.B.S., Tokyo, 1936

1265. Rp Kokusai Bunka Shinkokai (Prospectus And Scheme), K.B.S., Tokyo, 1939

1266. K.B.S. Quarterly, 4 Bands, K.B.S., Tokyo, 1935-1936

236. Ml Kollard, J. A., Early Medical Practice in Macao, Inspecção Dos Serviços Economicos, Macao, 1935

~~1397. Fl 90 Koop, A.L., Japanese Names And How To Read Them 銘字便覧, The Eastern Press, London, 1923~~

1329. Rs The Korean Repository, 5 vols, The Trilingual Press, Seoul, Korea, 1894-1898

1005. Lg (D) Korner, W., Methode Toussaint-Langenscheide (der Russischen Sprache), 41 copies under a cover, Langenscheidtsche Verlag, Berlin

1410. Gr de Körös, A.C., A Grammar Of The Tibetan Language, 文殿閣書莊, Peking, 1834

~~1391. Hy 172 Korostovelz, I.J., Von Ginggis Khan Zur Sowjetrepublik, (D) Walter De Gruyter & Co., Berlin, 1926~~

1026. Nv (D) Kosaka, Y., Der Kappa : Akutagawa Ryunosuke, Shobundo, Tokyo, 1934

~~1406. Dc 33 (F) Kowalewski, J.E., Dictionnaire Mongol-Russe-Français, 3 vols French Book Store, Peiping, 1933~~

(D) 299. Jy Krauss, F. S., Der Japaner, Ethnologischer Verlag, Leipzig, 1911

136. Cl Krieger, C. C., The Infiltration of European Civilization in Japan during the 18th Century, E. J. Brill, Leiden, 1940

116. Kuiper, Dr. J. F., Japan en de Buitenwereld in de Achttiende Eeuw, Martinus Nijhoff, 'S-Gravenhage, 1921

565. Li Kunitomo, T., Japanese Literature Since 1868, The Hokuseido Press, Tokyo, 1938

~~566. Cu 90 Fl Koop, A. J. and Inada, H., Japanese Names and How to Read Them, Bernard Queritch Ltd., London, 1923~~

908. Dc (D) Kunze, R., Praktisches Zeichenlexikon (Chinesisch-Deutsch-Japanisch), Nagoya, 1938

450. Pt Kuo-Cheng Wu, Ancient Chinese Political Theories, The Commercial Press, Shanghai, 1933

59

60. Es Kuo Hsi, An Essay on Landscape Painting, Translated by Shio Sakanishi, John Murray, London, 1935

1. Ce Kuo Pao-Ch'ang and Ferguson, J.C. etc., Noted Porcelains of Successive Dynasties ( 校注項氏歷代名瓷圖譜 ), Chih Chai Publishing Co., Peiping, 1931

649. Pt (D) Kurth, J., Harunobu, R. Piper & Co., Munchen, 1923

662. Pc Kwannami, Sotoda Komachi, The Japan-British Society, Tokyo, 1940

1274. Lg Kwong Ki Chiu, The Fisat Conmersation- Book, Wah Cheung, Shanghai, 1885

1275. Lg Kwong Ki Chiu, The Second Conversation- Book, Wah Cheung, Shanghai, 1885

1453. Fi Kyoto University Economic Reviw, Nos. 8 — 13 ~~8, 9, 11, 13~~, Kyoto Imperial University Department Of Economics, Kyoto, 1934

33. Dc(F) Kowalewski - Dictionnaire Mongol-Russe-Français, French Book Store, Peiping, 1933, 3 vols.

73. Hy Pt A. May Knapp - Feudal & modern Japan, Duckworth, London, 1898, 2 vols.

129. Gy Ml. Kenelly - Richard's comprehensive geography of the Chinese Empire ( 中國坤輿詳誌 ), T'Usewel Press, Shanghai, 1908.

82. Nv Kenzo Kai - Sakura no Kaori (war novel), Kenkyusha, 1933.

~~1142. Jy 73 Knapp, A.M., Feudal And Modern Japan, 2 vols., Duckworth & Co., London, 1898~~

167. Lt Kazuo Koizumi - Letters from B. H. Chamberlain to Lafcadio Hearn, Hokuseido, Tokyo, 1936, 1937, 2 vols.

172. Hy(D) I. J. Korostovetz - Von Ginggis Khan zur Sowjetrepublik, Geschichte der Mongolei, Leipzig, 1926.

157. Es Mo Freda Kirchwey - Our changing morality, a symposium, Albert & Charles Boni, N. Y., 1930.

90. Jy Koop & Inada - Japanese names & how to read them ( 銘字便覧 ), Bernard Quaritch, London, 1923.

88. Rp Mr Kyoto prefecture - Summary of the grand ceremonies of the Imperial Enthronement (Shôwa 3 y.)

186. Mp Kokusai Bunka Shinkokai - Map of Japan and Adjacent regions, Tokyo, 1937.

144. Ar Bb Kern Institute - Annual bibliography of Indian archaeology, Leiden, 1928.

207. Jr Красный Библиотекарь
Krasnij Bibliotekar (Red Library), issued Sept., Oct., Nov., Dec. 1931. 4 vols.

11 Kelling, R., Das Chinesische Wohnhaus, Tokyo, 1935

60

資料09（貼付ノート・Acker,W.）

957. Dm Mabbe, J., Translated from the Spanish, Celestina of The Tragi-Comedy Of Calisto And Melibea, George Routledge & Sons Ltd., London,

1341. Gr (H) Maatschappy, Grammatica Of Nederduitsche Spraakkunst, 和蘭文典（前編） 1822

1342. Gr (H) Maatschappy, Syntaxis of Woordvoeging, 和蘭文典，後編成句論, 1810 2 copies

1022. Lg Macauley, C., An Introductory Course In Japanese, Kelly & Walsh, Yokohama, 1906

~~604. Cl Madsen, V. etc., Anatomie Mandchoue, Copenhague, Bibliotheque Royale, 1928~~ B. C 24

285. Sc La Main (Les Sciences Occultes en Chine), Morant, G. S. de, Librairie Orientaliste, Paris

32. Pa Maler-und Sammler-Stempel aus der Ming und Ch'ing zeit gesammelt und bearbeitel von Victoria contag und Wang Chi-Ch'üan (明清画家印鑑), The Commercial Press Ltd., Shanghai, 1940

602. Po The Manyoshu, published for the Nippon Gakujutsu Shinkokai by the Iwanami Shoten, Tokyo, 1940

1020. Ta Marcus, M.C., The Pine-Tree, The Iris Publishing Co., London

932. Rn (F) Maruas, F., La Religion De Jésus Ressuscitée Au Japon, 2 vols., Delhomme Et Brignet, Éditeurs, Paris, 1896

263. Pa March, B., Some Technical Terms of Chinese Painting, Waverly Press Inc., Baltimore, 1935

1232, Ms Marett, R.R., An Outline Of Modern Knowledge, Victor Gallancz, London, 1931 左

1326. Jr ~~Margolis, M.M., etc., eds.~~, Journal Of The American Oriental Society, ~~162 vols., Vols. 32, 37 ...~~ 99 parts Yale University Press, U.S.A., ~~1912~~ 1917-1940

426. Li Margouliès, G., Évolution de la Prose Artistique Chinoise, Encyclopadie' Verlag, München, 1929

428. Li Si Margouliès, G., Le Kou-Wen Chinois, Paul Geuthner, Paris, 1926

1109. Gr Marsden, W., Torii, M., A Grammar Of The Malayan Language, Kaigai Jijo Fukyukai, Tokyo, 1930

617. Rn (F) Martin, J.M., Le Shintoisme, Imprimerie de Nazareth, Hongkong, 1924

Case 3. 176. Cl Martin, W. A. P., The Lore of Cathay (or The Intellect of China), Oliphant, Anderson & Ferrier, Edinburgh, 1901 B.C

1403. Cal Br Mason, W.A., A History Of The Art Of Writing, The Macmillan & Co., New York, 1928

61

1444. Li Mason, I., Notes On Chinese Mohammedan Literature, 文殿閣書莊, Peiping, 民国 27年

619. Rn Mi Mason, J.W.I., The Spirit Of Shinto Mythology, Fuzanbo Co., Tokyo, 1939

140. Ps Masson-Oursel, P., Esquisse d'une Histoire de la Philosophie Indienne, Paul Geuthner, Paris, 1923

1470. Me Materia Medica, one package,

187. Me Materia Medica (藥物學輯要), The Chinese Medical Association, Shanghai, 1933

1073. Po Matsuhara, I., Min-yo : Fork-Songs Of Japan, Shin-Sei Do, Tokyo, 1927

952. Lg Mathews, M.M., A Survey Of English Dictionaries, Oxford University Press, London, 1933

1052. Pc (F) Matsudaira, M., Résumé du "No" Théâtre, (one package) Published by the Author, Tokyo,

289. Na Matsudaira, M., Les Fêtes Saisonnières au Japon (Province de Mikawa), G. P. Maisonneuve, Paris, 1936

378. Rp Matsukata, Count M., Report on the Adoption of the Gold Standard in Japan, The Government Press, Tokyo, 1899

~~540. Lg Matsumiya, Y., Exercises in Japanese Conversation, 2 vols., The School of Japanese Language & Culture, Tokyo, 1937-1938~~

541. Gr Matsumiya, Y., A Grammar of Spoken Japanese, The School of Japanese Language & Culture, Tokyo, 1937

537. Lg Matsumoto, N., Austro-Asiatica (Le Japonais et les Langues Austroasiatiques), Paul Geuthner, Paris, 1928

1213. Sc Matsuo, I., The Japanese Journal of Gastraenterology, Vol. 6 No. 2, Gastraenterology Association of Japan, 1934

874. Rn Matsutani, M., The Ideals Of The Shinran Followers, Tokyo, 1920

1004. Lg Mayers, W.F., The Chinese Reader's Manual, The Presbyterian Mission Press, Shanghai, 1924

781. Lg McCune, G.M., etc., Romanization Of The Korean Language, (Reprint from The Transactions Of The Korea Branch Of The Royal Asiatic Society, Seoul, Korea)

994. Lg McGovern, W.M., Colloquial Japanese, Kegan Paul, Trench Trubner & Co., London, 1920

759. So McKenzie, F.A., Korea's Fight for Freedom, Simpkin, Marshall & Co., London, 1920

1340. Gr McIlroy, J.G., ed., Chamberlain's Japanese Grammar, 3 copies Kegan Paul, London, 1924

62

1115. Bb McKerrow, R.B., An Introduction To Bibliography, The Clarendon Press, Oxford, 1928

504. Pt Si Meadows, T. T., Desultory Notes on the Government and People of China, Wm. H. Allen & Co., London, 1847

1334. Tr (F) Medard, M., A Propos des Voyages Aventureux de Fernand Mendey Pinto, 1 vol. in 1 chitsu, Imprimerie de la Polique de Pekin, Pekin, 1934

118. Tr (F) Médard, M. M., A Propos des Voyages Aventureux de Fernand Mendez Pinto, 2 copies, Pekin, 1935

921. Lg (F) Meillet, A., Introduction A L'Étude Comparative Des Langues Indo-Europiennes, Librairie Hachette, Paris, 1924

922. Gr (F) Meillet, A., Traite De Grammaire Comparée Des Langues Classiques, Librairie Ancienne Honore Champion, Paris, 1927

1249. Lg (D) Meisinger, O., Vergleichende Wortkunde, C.H. Beck'seke Verlagsbuch Handlung, München, 1932

1290. Gr (D) Meissner, K., Lehrbuch Der Grammatik Der Japanischen Schriftsprache, Dentsche Gesellschaft Für Natur-U. Völkerkunde Ostasiens, Tokyo, 1927

380. Na Meissner, K., Der Krieg der alten Dachse, Kyobunkwan, Tokyo, 1932

470. Hy Meissner, K., Die "Heilige" Sutra und audere japanische Geschichten, Kyobunkwan, Tokyo, 1937

157. Meissner, K., Deutsche in Japan 1639-1930, Berlin, 1940

391. Ir Mélanges Japonais, 8 vols., Libraririe Sansaisha, Tokyo, 1904-1910

443. Hs Si Mélanges sur la Chronologie Chinoise, Havret et Chambeau, Imprimerie de la Mission Catholique, Chang-Hai, 1920

1161. St Mellon, J.W., Intermediate Inorganic Chemistry, Longmans, Green & Co., London, 1930

1466. Gy (F) Mémoires de L'Academie Imperial des Sciences de St. Pétersbourge VIII Serie, Index De La Section Géographique De La Grande Encyclopédie Chinoise T'ou-chou-tsi-tchéng, C de Waeber, St. Pétersbourg, 1907

1308. Mr Memoire Of The Research Department Of The Toyo Bunko, Nos. 1-10, The Toyo Bunko, Tokyo, 1926-1938

971. Rn Mencken, H.L., Treatise On The Gods, Alfred A. Knopf, New York, 1930

197. Bo Merrill, E. D. and Walker, E. H., A Bibliography of Eastern Asiatic Botany, The Arnold Arboretum of Harvard University, Mass., 1938

(1) Mombusho: An Outline History of Japanese Education; Tokyo, 1877.

(1) Monumenta Nipponica; Sophia University, 1939, Vol. II, Semi-Annual, No. 2.

(1) " Vol. V, Semi-Annual No. 1, 1942

1 Memoires de la Société Académique Indo-Chinoise de France. Tome I. 1879

64

資料 09（貼付ノート・Acker,W.）

# 資料10（貼付ノート・Ashbee: Library Catalogue）

資料 10（貼付ノート・Ashbee: Library Catalogue）

資料 10（貼付ノート・Ashbee: Library Catalogue）

Ashbee: Library Catalogue (3 voll.)
✓ Ashbee: Bibliography of the Barbary States – Tunisia
✓ Aretino: 1 Ragionamenti
✓ Anderson: Memo. on Chinese Currency
✓ Anderson: Japanese Wood-Engravings
✓ Anderson: Japanese Wood Engravings (8vo.)
✓ Apollinaire: Selected Poems Choix des Poesies
✓ Apollinaire: L'Oeuvre des conteurs allemands
✓ Auboyer: Influences au kondo du Horyuji et les Reminiscences Etrangeres
✓ Asakawa: Early Institutional Life of Japan
✓ Allen: A History of Georgian People – From the Beginning to the Russian Conquest in the 19th Century
✓ Allen: Japan and the Expedition thereto of the U.S., 1853
✓ Alpini: Medicina aegyptorum
✓ Andrews: Bibliopegy in the U.S. & kindred Subjects
✓ Appointment in Baker Street
✓ Albertinus: Historische relation ... im konigreich Iapon ...
Alcune lettere delle cose del Giappone (Milan edition)
✓ Acostae Historia Rerum in Oriente Gestarum (Paris '72)
✓ Al gioco cinese chiamato il rompicapo 1818
✓ Alcock's Specimens of Japanese Papers (2 voll.)

Same as Spuren –

✓ Artemis – Swiss Books in German Languages 1945–46

The Audience Question in China

Damaged 2

3

Aceur: La versification nationale Turque

Adam: Grammaire Mandchou
Antonii Panormitae Hermaphroditus ed. Forberg:
Aungervy le Society. Voyages of Vertomannus
Aubert: La petite pantoufle
Allen: Korean Tales
Arber: Herbals
Alcock: Art and Art Industry in Japan
Ananga-Ranga or the Hindu Art of Love
Aston: Grammar of Spoken Japanese, 4th ed.
Atkinson: Travels in the Amoor
Ament: Begriffe der Kindersprache
Andreae: Bibliotheca sinologica
Articles in Formosan, 1896
Adami: Ungarische Sprachkunst
Atkinson: Oriental and Western Siberia
Ars Asiatica, Vol. III, I (separately placed)
Arnold: Books of the Ancients
Arnold: Islamic Book
Arberry: British Orientalists
Akademik S.F.Oldenburg, 1934
Amyot: Dictionnaire Mantchou Tartare
Anesaki: Buddhist Art
Ambassades ~~vers l'Empereur~~ du Japon, 2 voll., 12 mo
Adamson: Camoëns, 2 voll.
Alexeev: Kitaiskaya Poema
Adam: Gr. de la langue tongouse
~~Amerusaban Kinkusha~~
A Model Japanese Villa
~~Ars Asiatica, I.~~
Adler: Dialectic
American Anthropologist vol. 34, #4.
Art Chretien Chinois
Apollinaire: L'oeuvre du Marquis de Sade
Albuquergue, 4 voll.
Aziatskiya Rossiya, 3 voll., 4 to., Atlas, folio
Ament: Deutung der ersten Kinderworte
Altaiskii Almanax
Arch. franc historici conspectus chronologicus
Alekseev: Japanese Gold and Silver Coins (Russian) 1913
Alfaric: Vie chretienne due Bouddha
Alaska Historical Museum Kashevaroff
Andreev: Yazgulemskii Yazyk
Authors and Printer's Dict.: Collins:
Anadyrskii Krai, 1893.
Art Militaire des Chinois (Uncoloured) Amiot & Deguignes:
Archivo Franciscanum Historici 1908–1927

Damaged 1

Astodan, & Recorded Instances of Children having been nourished by Wolves & Birds of Prey
Anstey: Index to Indian Antiquary (Part I)
" : Do. (Part II & III)
~~[illegible]~~

資料 10（貼付ノート・Ashbee: Library Catalogue）

B

Baker Street Inventory
Baker Street and Beyond
Baker Street Four-Wheeler
A Baker Street Song Book
Bang: Vom kokturkischen zum Osmanischen, 1917
Butler: Hudibras
Bickerstaffe: Araki the Daimio
Binyon: Spirit of Man in Asian Art
Beyer: Shell Ornament Sets (in the Middle American ...)
Beazley: Carpini and Rubruquis
Budge: the Monks of Kublai Khan, Emperors of China.
Boym: Flora sinensis (incomplete facsimile)
Biot: Villes de la Chine
Bethnal Green Museum: Catalogue of a collection of Oriental Porcelain & pottery 2nd edition
Bouvet: Portrait historique de l'empereur de la Chine (Paris edition)
Belloc: Avril
Beal: the Origin of the Spiritual Activity Developed in Buddhism - 1889
Bazin: Academie Imperiale de Peking
Ball: Is Buddhism a preparation for or a hindrance to Christianity in China?
Ball: Cultivation and Manufacture of Tea in China
Boym: Briefve Relation
Britton: Fifty Shang Inscriptions, 1940
Bisson: American Policy in the Far East
Blades: William Caxton (1st edit., 2 voll.)
Boode: Notes for collectors of Chinese Antiques
Bontius: De medicina Indorum (Leiden edition)
Bromsgrove School: A.E. Housman
Beal: Two Chinese Buddhist Inscriptions found at Buddha Gaya
Borton: Japan since 1931 - Its Political & Social Developments
Brinton: On the Words "Anahuac" and "Nahuatl"
Brand: Travels to China (Amsterdam edition, French)
Bushell: Oriental Ceramic Art, text volume, 8vo.
Bouger: the History of Silk
Bibliography of Brosset Bibliographie Analytique des ouvrages de M. F. Brosset
Bushnell: The World's Earliest Libraries
Bizonfy: Hungarian Dictionary
Brooke: the Collected Poems of Rupert Brooke
Bronte: Wuthering Heights
Bates: Intertraffic
Blades Exhibition Caxton Exhibition in Commemoration of the Centenary of Wm. Blades
Bushell: Notes on the Old Mongolian Capital of Shangtu
Bishop: Hist. Geography of Early Japan
Burgerstein: Untersuchung der von den Chinesen vor der Erfindung des Papiers benutzten Holztafelchen als Beschreibstoff
Berendt: Analytical Alphabet for the Mexican & Central American Languages
Bergen: the Sages of Shantung
Browne: Religio Medici, MacMillan edit. Greenhill
Bayer: Museum Sinicum
Bradley: Trans-Pacific Relations of Latin America
Baudelaire: La Beaute, Corydon Press

Damaged 1
Badly 1

5

Baudelaire: Les Fleurs du Mal
Boxer: Portuguese embassy to Japan (1644-1647)
Bowditch: Mayan Nomenclature
Belmar: Zapoteca-serrana y Zapoteca del Valle
Bolton: Language used to Domestic Animals
Bretschneider: Botanicon sinicum, 3 voll.
Beazley: Dawn of modern geography, 3 voll.
Beal: Suhkililihkiu
Boispreaux: La vie de Pierre Aretin
Batabiyashimbun (6 voll.)
Brosset: Études sur les monuments géorgiens photographiés par M. Iermakof, et sur leurs inscriptions. (Mélanges Asiat.
Bibliothèque Libre - Procès des Raretés (18
another copy

Brosset: Arakel de Tauriz, Registre Chronologique
Brosset: Rapport sur l'ouvrage intitule Numizmaticeskie fakty
Bibliotheca Lindesiana - Cat. of Chinese Books
Bedevian: Polyglottic Dict. of Plant Names
Bang: Monographien zur türkischen Sprachgeschichte, 1918

Browne's, Sir T., Works, Bohn, 3 voll.
Brown, I.: Books of Words
Bipphy: Britain Needs Books

6

Bang & Marquart: Ostturkische Dialektstudien
Becker: Feudal Kamakura from AD1186 to 1333
Brief Summary of Do Ka Zang 1895
Brockelmann: Mittelturkischer Wortschatz
Blochet Histoire des Mongols (texte)
Blades: Enemies of Books, 2nd ed.
Burton: Catallus the Carmina of
Brown: Pilgrims Progress (Cambridge English Classics)
Beal: Travels of Buddhist Pilgrims
Bibliographie des oeuvres de H. Cordrer
Beveridge: Babur Nama in Engl., 2 voll.
~~Bayer: De Horis Sinicis~~ (See "de")
Boxer: Affair of the Madre de Deus
Bibliotheca Curiosa ~~Monacensis~~ et Erotica Stern-Szana: Bibli—
Binyon: Flight of the Dragon
Bhuyan: Early British Relations with Assam
Binyon: Chinese Art and Buddhism
Blochet: Babar Nama
Bretschneider: Chinese Silkworm Trees
Bunakov: Oracle Bones from Honan
Blochet: Introd. a l'histoire des Mongols
Bartold: Istoriya izuceniya Vostoka v Europe
Bartold: Turkestan down to the Mongol Invasion
Bonaparte: Documents de l'epoque Mongole
Budenz: Az ugor nyelvek osszehasonlito alaktana 1884-1894
Bonneau: Curiosa - 1887
Bohtingk: Spracheder Jakuten
Balfour: Chuang Tsze (The Divine Classic of Nan-Hua)
Birdwood: Report of Old Records of the India Office
Baranov: Kitaiskii noyi gord
Burford's Canton
Bullock: Etajima, the Dartmouth of Japan
Brooks: Account of Weights
Beveridge: Babar Nama, Turkitext
Beal: Romantic History of Buddha
Benyowsky's Travels, 2 voll., 4to.
Brodrick: Little China
Burton's Camoens, 6 voll. the gem of the Orient Earth
Ball: Macao: the Holy City, the gem & other essays
Browne's Religio Medici (tall 4to.)
Bailey: Lucretius on the Nature of Things
Bowring: Flowery Scroll
Blake: Grammar of Tagalog Language
Biot: Etoiles Filantes
Ball: The Pith of the Classics (the Chinese Classics in Everyday Life)
Brit. Museum: Japanese Books, 2 voll., 4to.
Balfour: Waifs and Strays from Far East
Ballagi: Hungarian Dict.
Buck: Sun Yat Sen
Baber Nama 1857 Ili zapiski Sultana Babera
Busbequi Episbolae
Ballagi: Nemet-Magyar Szotara

Damaged 2

7

Bang: Manichaeische Hymnen
Bibliotheca Asiatica #452 - 1924
#455 - 1924
Bauer: Woman
Brookes: Intern. Rivalry in Pacific Islands 1800-1875
Braithwaite: Life of Sogoro, the farmer Patriot of Sakura.
Bouillard: Attitudes des Buddhas
Bloch: German Interests + Policies in Far East
Bellows German Dict.
Blochet: Babar Nama
Bacon: Advancement of Learning
Bickerstaffe: Araki the daimio
Berjeau: Calcoen; Dutch Narrative of the 2nd voyage of Vasco da Gama to Calicut
Bretschneider: Mediaeval Geography & History of Central + Western Asia
Bingham: Founding of T'ang Dynasty
Balfour: Leaves from my Chinese Scrapbook
Benneville: Yotsuya Kaidan
Beveridge: Notes on MSS of Babar's Memoirs
Bang: Turkischen Namen einiger Grosskatzen
Bulletin de la Maison franco-jap. I
Ballagi: Pocket Hungarian Dict.
Bang: Kokturkische Inschrift über die
Braga: Camoens, 2 voll., ms.
Bogoras: Koryak Texts (Vol V)
Bruce: Humanness of Chu hsi - 1925
Bacof: Ecriture cursive tibetaine
Bang: Türkische Bruchstücke
Beveridge: Babar Nama (Pamphlet) Critical Notice by Blochet
Bramsen: Coins of Japan
Bibliographie clerico-galante
Bloch: Leben unserer Zeit
Batchelor: Ainu Fireside Stories
Bang: Turcica - 1917
Boas Anniversary Volume
Brit. Museum Japanese and Chinese Paintings
Bouvat: (Pamphlet) Notice Bio-Bibliographique sur Athir ed-Din Mohammad ibn Yousouf Abou Hayyan Al-Gharnati
Bute: Ancient Language of T
Bishop of Victoria: Lewchew
Beveridge: Further Notes on the Babar-nama MSS

Comerford's Private Journal 1868
Coxe: Russian Discoveries, 2nd. ed.
Catalogue of Philatelic Library of Earl of Crawford
Camoens' Passion of Christ Prestage;
Chavannes: Les religieux eminents
Christopher: Palaeography and Archives
Courteille: Memoires de Baber, 2 voll. in 1.
Covell: Under the Seal of Sesshu
Catalogue Turkestan Public Library (R)
Clifton: Fortune Telling by Japanese Swords
Codex Cumanicus
Cornish: Borderlands of Language in Europe
Cahen: Livre de comptes de la Caravane Russe a Pekin - 1911
Cat #673: Books Printed Between 1476 + 1944 on a Variety of Subjects. (Francis Edwards)

8

資料 10（貼付ノート・Ashbee: Library Catalogue）

Cole: Index to Bibliographical Papers

Canadian Arctic Exp. Report, 15 B

Chamberlain: Ainu Language and Folklore

Chino-Sinhalese Relations, 2 voll.

Carpenter: Emerson and Asia

Clark: Indian Sign Language

~~Complete Sherlock Holmes~~

Claremont Oriental Studies, ~~Part~~ 5 april 1943

Covarrubias: Atlas

C

Charlevoix: Histoire du Japon (4to, 2 voll.)

Classics: (Chinese M. of Information Pamphlet #7)

Collocott: Tongan astronomy & Calendar - 1922

Cordier: Bibliotheca Japonica

Cordier: Bibliotheca Sinica (5 voll.) Damaged!

Cordier: Conflit entre la France & la Chine

Coushnir: Chinese coins without currency

Catalogue of Swiss Books (2 voll.) (See Cat. & Book Lists)

Catalogue Chinese Maritime Customs, Collection, Philadelphia 1876

Catalogue of the Caxton Exhibition 1877

Catalogue des Russica (2 voll.)

Catalogue of Chinese Books in the Asiatic Department, St. Petersburg

Cowley: Bibliographical Description and Cataloguing

Christian: Modern Burma

Chwolson: Syrisch-nestorianische Grabinschriften, aus Semirjetsche all series

Chase: The Tyranny of Words

Constable's Miscellany (Voll. 1-3)

Camoens: Lusiadas, 1776 (Hall's Image)

Cressey: China's Geographic Foundations

Carrington: Beauty - a Legend of Georgia

Criterion Miscellany No. 5: Pornography & Obscenity Lawrence:

Chang: Chinese Ingot of the Twelfth Century (Numismatic Note & Monograph #103)

Couplet: Confucius sinarum philosophus sive Scientia Sinensis

Castren: Burjatische sprachlehre

Carus: The Canon of Reason and Virtue

Corson: Introduction to the Works of John Milton

Cunningham: History of the Szechuen Riots

Crasset: History of Japanese Christianity, German edition

Concise Oxford Dictionary

Copinger: The Elzevier Press

Chesterton: Collected Poems The Collected Poems of G. K. Chesterton

Curtis: A History of Ireland

Chinese Medical Journal, March 1933

Cox: The Poems of Sappho

The Chinese and Japanese Repositories (Voll.1-3, in 2 Voll.) Summers:

Craigie: ~~Japan and~~ Behind the Japanese Mask

Cowley's Poems, Nonsuch Press 1926

Chen: Taxation in China in Tsing Dynasty

Carroll: Alice in Wonderland

Chambers: Papers for the People, Vol. 12

R.W.Chambers: 1874-1942

9

✓Collis: Courts of the Shan Princes
✓Collis: New Sources for the life of Empress Dowager Tz'u Hsi

✓Cunningham, Kilborn, Maxwell, Morse, Mullett & Dickinson: The Nosu Tribes of West Szechwan

× ✓Cat. of the Tracey Woodward Collection of Japan

✓Currall: Three Tales by Pushkin

✓Chinese, Corean & Japanese Potteries

✓Computation Tables + Intervals + Multiples

✓Cat 434: Important & Rare Books on the Fine Arts (Quaritch Ltd)
✓Coyerand: La Vie du Bien Heureux Père François Xavier
Cat #18 d'un Beau Melange d'ouvrages anciens & modernes sur l'extrême-orient et l'océanie (librairie orientale et americaine)
✓Calthrop: Book of War
✓Chardin's, Sir T.: Travels in Persia (Argonaut)
~~Couto: Da Asia, 24 voll.~~
✓Campbell: Arabian Medicine, 2 voll.
~~Cocks: Diary, 2 voll.~~
✓Cogan: The Voyages & Adventures of Ferdinand Mendez Pinto, the Portuguese (Transl. of Fernd. Mendez Pinto)

✓catalog #106: The Oriental & Travel Supplement
✓catalogs, Nos 246 & 247, Grafton & Co
✓catalog of Rare & Valuable Books, #438 (Bernard Quaritch, Ltd)
✓Carus: T'ai-Shang Kan-Ying P'ien
✓Courant: La presse periodique japonaise (Journal Asiatique)
✓Compar. Tables of Christian and Muham. Dates
✓Chavannes: T'ai chan
✓Conder: Notes on Japanese Architecture
✓Conferences Musee Guimet 1903-04
✓Closter-documente
✓Chinese Hist., 4 voll., 12 mo Hau Kiou Choaan or The Pleasing History
✓Camoes: Liricas (School Texts)
✓Couling: Luminous Religion
Catalogue de la Litterature mondiale, 2 voll., 4to.
✓Comptes rendus des expéditions pour l'exploration du Nord de la Mongolie, 1925.
Caucasus polyglottus, I.
✓Collinson: Soul of Grammar & the Philosophy of Gr. with Special Reference to the question
✓Chavannes: Les livres chinois avant l'invention du papier (Journal Asiatique)
✓Coxwell: Siberian & Other Folk Tales
✓Chavannes: La Sculpture
✓Cat. #245 (Grafton & Co)
✓Collins: Attempt at a Catalogue of the Library of the Late Prince Louis-Lucien Bonaparte

10

資料 10（貼付ノート・Ashbee: Library Catalogue）

Catalog #674; Books of All Ages (Francis Edwards Ltd)
Catalog IV; A Selection of Rare & Notable Books on Many Subjects (Rosenthal Ltd)
Catalog: Lagerkatalog #720
Catalog: Supplement #7 Jan. 1940: A Short List of Second-Hand Books.
Cordier: Narrative of Recent Events in Tongking 1875
Cordier: La France en Chine, Vol. I only
Courteille: Dictionnaire Turk-Oriental
Castren: Ostjakischen Sprachlehre
Conrady: Indochinesische Causativ-denominativ-bildung, 1896
Catalogue of Mollendorff Manchu Library
Castagne: Congres de turkologie de Bakou
Campbell: List of Birds Collected in Corea
Cardim: Notes on Port.-English Anglo-Port. Grammars to 1830
Campbell: A Recent Journey in N. Korea
Catalogue of Lockhart ~~Library~~ (general)
Churchill: Beach-la-Mar
Catalogue of Chinese Works in Bodleian Library
Contributions ~~on~~ Folklore, Kwatiungue 3 voll.
Clement: Article on the Poppy, 1908
Chamberlain: Japanese Poetry.
Charpentier: W. of Rubruk & Roger Bacon
Courant: L'Asie Centrale
Cahen: Histoire des relations de la Russie avec la Chine
Chrestomatia arcaica (Textos literarios)
Chamberlain: Romanized Japanese Reader
Couvreur: Dictionnaire classique, ~~folio~~ de la Langue Chinoise
~~Catolikku Daijiten, I.~~
Chukaminkoku Shinchizu
Chalfant: Early Chinese Writing — Damaged 1
Cordier: Quelques données nouvelles
Catalogue titles and index entries — Badly 2
Castren: Tungusische Sprachlehre
Cordier: Merveilles de l'Asie
Camus: Voyages de Thevenot
Campbell: Journey in N. Korea 1899
Collis: Land of the Great Image
Catalogue of Drujon
~~Chamberlain: Japanese Written Grammar~~
Ceylon and the Hollanders 1658-1796 – Pieris:
Certenaire de l'Ecole des Langues orientales vivantes 1795-1895
Chater Collection ~~Catalogue, 4to~~. Orange:
Clark: Formosa
Carlo: Paleografia Espanola, 2 voll.
Curtius: Jap. Spraakkunst - 1857
Costumes of China
Chamberlain: Moji no Shirube
Civil Code of Japan, 2 voll. Gubbins:
Castagne: Congres de turkologie de Bakou (1926) (see back of page)
~~Catholic Native Episcopacy in China~~
Culin: Chinese in America: A Study in the Social Life of the Chinese in the Eastern U.S.
Chavannes: L'Expression des voeux
Cat. Rostor Museum
Clark: Abbey of St. Gall
Campos: History of the Portuguese in Bengal
Catalog: Rare & Unusual Books on a Variety of Subjects (Rosenthal Ltd)
Catalog: Ephemerides Orientalistes Nos 108 & 111; 2 vols.
Catalog: Orientalia #66-1930
Chappe: Voyage en Sibérie, 2 vols.

11

✓ Contents of and Indices to Useful Plants of Japan Described & Illustrated or Yuyo Shokubutsu Zusetsu Mokuroku Oyobi Sakuin

✓ Cat. of the Library of the Late A. G. Ellis, M.A (Bibliotheca Orientalis XLIII) Luzac & Co

✓ Cat #439 of Rare & Valuable Books relating to the Occult Sciences (Quaritch Ltd)

✓ Cats. 732 & 736 - Voyages & Travels (Maggs Bros).

✓ Cats 669 (1943) & 670 (1944) - Edwards Ltd

✓ Cat. 245: Bibliography: Unusual Books: Railways (Grafton & Co)

✓ Cats of Sotheby & Co (7 volumes) none

12

- 6 -

D'Elia: Catholic Native Episcopacy in China 1300-1926
Diosy: Yamato-damashi-i
Dictionary of English Book Collectors
Danvers: Portuguese in India, 2 voll.
da Orta: Simples and Drugs of India
Dickins: Chushingura of the Loyal League
Dickins: Old Bamboo Hewer's Story
de Korne: The Fellowship of Goodness (a Chinese Secret Religious Society)
Douglas: South Wind
Dingwall: Kakiemon Designs
Douglas: Fortunate Union
Davidson: The Island of Formosa-Past and Present
Dorfler: Ahron ben Elia über die Manichaer
Dandin: Sigillographie sino-annamite
Dalgado: Glossario luso-asiatico, 2 voll.
Davis: Fortunate Union, 2 voll.
Donner: Zur Phonetik des samojedischen, 1920
du Halde: History of China, 2 voll. folio
Dagestan, 1847
Davis: Chinese Miscellanies
J. de la Societe finno-origienne, 37.
Dühren: Le Marquis de Sade et son Temps
De Horis Sinicis: Bayer
Deeters: Kharthwelische Verbum
Dickins: Japanese Odes, or Hyakunin Isshiu
Douglas: Birds and Beasts of GR Anthology
Dandolo: Art of Rearing Silkworms 1825
Dautremer: Nikko passe et present, 1894
Duhren: Neue Forschungen über den Marquis de Sade und seine Zeit
Dennys: Folklore of China
Douglas: Paneros
Dahlgren: Debuts de la cartographie du Japon
Dickins: Old Bamboo-Hewer's Story, 1888
Drevnayya Rossiiskaya Bibliotheka, 20 voll.
de Corbeil: Lettres sur l'histoire philos. des langues, 1820
de Landes: Glossaire erotique de la Langue Francaise
Diccionario do Povo, No 4.
Duhren: Der Marquis de Sade und seine Zeit
da Costa: Uma Carta nautica portuguesa
d'Arcy: Hao-Khieou-tchouan, ou La Femme Accomplie
Duhren: Der Marquis de Sade u. seine Zeit
Dulaure: Des cultes qui ont precede l'idolatrie
Duhren: R. de la Bretonne
Diwan Lughat, 3 voll.
Davis: Han Koong Tsew, 1829
Donisthorpe: Loveliest of Friends
d'Auteroche: Voyage en Siberie, 3 voll.
Descriptio Regii Japoniae (Armsterdam)
Derbend-Nameh Kazem-Beg
Davis: San-yu-low or the Three Dedicated Rooms
Dandin: Sigillographie Sino-Annamite
Davis: Chinese Romance & Tragedy, 2 vols.
de Couto: Da Asia, 24 vols.
Donner: Bei den Samojeden in Sibirien

13

✓ Diary of a Journey Overland thru the Maritime Province of China from Manchao on the South Coast of Hainan to Canton

✓ Douglas: Cat. of Japanese Printed Books & MSS in the British Museum, 1898

✓ Ditto: 1899-1903 none

14

D

✓Dorn: Erster Beitrag zur geschichte der georgier, ... 1843
✓Dellon: Nouvelle relation d'un Voyage aux Indes orientales
✓Dellon: Inquisition de Goa (3 voll.)
✓Dumezil: Introduction a la grammaire des langues caucasiennes du Nord
✓ " Recherches comparatives sur Le verbe caucasien
Deshayes: La Ceremonie du the au Japon
✓Dunn: Grammar of the Portuguese Language
✓Davidson: Hebrew Grammar
✓Delepierre: Philobiblon de Londres
✓Duff: Early Printed Books
✓Dubray: F. Rops, Seheur
✓Day: Songs of D'urfey
✓Doyle: The True Conan Doyle (John Murray)
✓Doyle: The True Conan Doyle
Documents preserved in the National Museum of Peiping
✓Dawes: 6 Essays on The Ancients, their Music & Instruments 1893
✓Dennett: Americans in Eastern Asia
✓Donne: A Sermon of Valediction
✓Dyn 1-6 (1 vol.)
Diary of a Journey overland through the Maritime Provinces of China, from Manchao to Canton
✓Dulaurier: Les Mongols d'apres les Historiens Armeniens

4.

✓De Ricci: A Census of Caxtons
✓De Ricci: Editions originales de Ronsard
✓Del Castillo: Discovery and Conquest of Mexico 1517-1521
✓De Guignes: Voyages a Peking (3 voll. text, 1 vol. atlas) atlas
✓De Quincy: Selected Writings
✓d' Avezac: Note sur une Mappemonde turke
✓Dickins: Megalithes du Japon
✓Dickins: Guide to Sericulture
✓The De La Cruz-Badiano Aztec Herbal of 1552
✓De Christiana Expeditione apud Sinas AB Societate Iesu Suscepta.
✓Doyle: The Complete Sherlock Holmes
✓De Rebus Japonicis Indicis et Peruanis - 1605
✓Dalette: Niederlandischen Konversations-Grammatik 1923

Damaged 2

15

E

✓Edwards:Lives of founders of British Museum
✓Ellis: Sonnets & Folk Songs
✓Ellis: Kanga Creek
✓Elton: The Great Book Collectors
✓Epistolae indicae, epistolae Japanicae (2 voll. in one Louvain edition)
✓Epistolae indicae, Louvain'66 1566
✓Epitome of History of Pellew Islands
✓Erdberg: Chinese Influence on European Garden Structures
✓Ey: Portuguese Grammar (2 voll.)
2 another copy of 1570)

✓Exercises in Yokohama Dialect, 1879 Bishop of Homoco;
✓Erdmann: Muhammed's Geburt u. Abrahah's Untergang
✓Epic of Bogdo-khan Janggar, Kalmuck text.
✓Elferink: Het oordeel
✓Ecke: Twin Pagodas of Zayton
✓Emelyanov: Grammatika votyackogo yazyka
✓Etnograficeskii Sbornik, Vol. I.
✓Eastern Art, 4 parts (plus 2 voll.) (3 voll. in all)
✓Editions of Syphilis Fracastoro;
✓English - Dutch Dict. Wely: (Van Goor's Handwoordenboeken)
✓Ellis: George Chapman
✓Embroidery Sept. 1935
✓Eliseeff: Elementary Japanese for University Students, 2 voll.
✓Edgar: English-Giarung Vocabulary
✓Edwards: Chinese Prose Literature, 2 voll.
✓Eitel: 3 Lectures on Buddhism 1884
✓Ettmayer: Das Wesen der Dialektbildung
✓Eisen: Mauthners Kritik der sprache
✓El Ktab des lois secretes de l'Amour
✓Epistolae et logistorici
✓Ethnologische Studien, 2 voll.
✓Edkins: Opium: Historical Note on the Poppy in China
✓Efendi: Cagataj-osmanisches Worterbuch
✓Aken: Voyages of Vertomannus A.D. 1503
Etienne
✓Errata to I. V. Giles & Pai Ping-chi: Japanese Personal Names, Peking, 1940

Damaged 1

16

資料 10（貼付ノート・Ashbee: Library Catalogue）

F

✓ Fagan: Life of Panizzi (Vol. 2)
✓ Fry: Art-History As an Academic Study
✓ Fletcher: The Witches' Pharmacopoeia
Fletcher: Books printed by Bodoni
✓ Funeral Discourse for Dr. Morrison Fletcher:
✓ Fanning: Voyages
✓ Fortune: Japan April 1944
✓ Fortune: Tea-districts of China
✓ Ferreira: Portuguese-English Dictionary (Diccionario: Portugues-Ingles)
✓ Franke: Eine Chinesische Tempelinschrift aus Idikutsahri bei Turfan
✓ Fernere zeitung auss Japon ...
✓ Friedman: Robert Grosseteste & the Jews
✓ Fanciullo a Scola
✓ Figueroa: Historia y ... relacion de las cosas que hizieron los Padres de la Compania de Jesus — los anos de 1607 y 1608
✓ Fischer: Reiseeindrucke aus Schantung
✓ Final Report Japanese Evacuation from the West Coast 1942
✓ Fuhrmann: & Danzel: Mexiko (3 voll.)
✓ Forster: Development of English Prose Between 1918 & 1939
✓ Fujikawa: History of Japanese Medicine (Germ.) (Geschichte der Medizin in Japan)
✓ Fujikawa: Nihonigakushi, ketteiban
✓ Fournier: on Typefounding
✓ Fournier: Manuel typographique (2 voll.)
✓ Fe~~r~~: ~~Le~~ L'Essence de la Science transcendante
× ✓ Fay: Notes on American Press of Eighteenth Century
✓ Frei: Interrogatif et indefini
✓ Fan: Dr. Johnson and Chinese Culture
Forty-third Chapter of the Three Kingdom Novel (2 voll)
✓ Fiske: The Dutch Colonies in America (2 voll.) & Quakers
✓ Freer Gallery of Art, Oriental Studies 1-2
× ✓ Faery Nights (Irish Fairy tales)
✓ Fanshawe: Lusiad (2nd edition) 1664
✓ Fischel: The Jews of Kurdistan a Hundred Yrs ago
✓ Filologiceskiya Zanyatiya Imperatricy Ekateriny II
✓ Frafi: Librorum Prohibitorum; Being Notes on 187 Curious & Uncommon Books 3 vols.
✓ Fonssagrives: Si-ling Annales du Musee Guimet
✓ Fukuyama: First Japanese Mission to America (1860)
✓ Foster: Supplementary Calendar ~~of Documents in~~ India Office Records
✓ Fujishima: Bouddhisme Japonais

Damaged!
Badly " 2

17

Freunden: Festgruss an Otto von Bohtlingk + Rudolf von Roth

Fonseca: Historical Sketch of Goa + Archaeological

Frei Luis de Sousa (School Text)

Fujisawa: Yoshida T. and R.L.Stevenson-1933

Field Museum Pamphlets, 25 voll.

Funke: Studien zur Gesch. der Sprachphilosophie. 1927

Field Museum Pamphlets, 12 voll. (~~extra~~)?

Fourmont: Meditationes Sinicae

Faceties de Pogge, 2 voll., (Liseux)

Finnish-English Dictionary (Suomalais-Englantilainen Sanakirja)

Festschrift V. Thomsen

Finn: Jews of China

Forsyth: Shantung

Foucher: L'art greco-bouddhique de Gandhara

Badly Damaged 3

# G

Giles: Some Truths about Opium

Giles: Freemasonry in China

Giles: From Swatow to Canton 1877

Gates: Landa's Yucatan 1549-79

Gates: Specimen of Dictionary

Gates Collection B-G of Middle American Literature 1

Gates Collection relating to Mexico and Central America

Gates: Maya Glyph Dictionary

Gates: Collection of Middle American Literature, Section A.

Gates: Aztec Herbal, English translation

Gates: Yucatan (Unbound copy) Before + After the Conquest

Gates: Distribution of the Several Branches of the Mayance Linguistic Stock

Gates: Perez Codex A Commentary upon the Maya-Tzental

Gates: De la Cruz-Badiano Aztec Herbal of 1552

Gates: The Spirit of the Hour in Archaeology

Gorer: The Revolutionary Ideas of the Marquis de Sade

Gibbings: Mosheim's Memoirs of the church in China

Grierson: The Poems of John Donne (2 voll.)

Gissing: Denzil Quarrier

Guignes: Viaggi (4 voll. in two)

Green: The Making of a Japanese Newspaper

Grajdanzev: Modern Korea - A Study of Social & Economic Changes under Jap. Rule

Gerr: Scientific and Technical Japanese

Gill: An Essay on Typography

Gates: Linguistic Concepts in Prehistoric America

Gates: El Sistema de Cronologia Azteca 18

Gates: An Outline Dictionary of Maya Glyphs - 1931

資料 10（貼付ノート・Ashbee: Library Catalogue）

√Giganov: Grammar of Tartar Language
√Gray: √Tercentenary of Hakluyt. an address on the occasion of the tercentenary of the death of Richard
√Gowland: Dolmens of Korea
√Gowland: Japanese pseudo-speise (Shiromé) & its Relation to the Purity of Jap. Notes on the copper & the Presence of Arsenic in Jap. Bronze
Gedenshtrom: Otryvkio Sibiri
√Golden Cockerel Press: Golden Asse of Lucius apuleius
√General Outlines of Education in Japan, 1884
√Giles: Sun Tzu on the Art of War
Grammatika altaiskago yazyka, '69
√Gabelentz: Die Sprachwissenschaft, (2nd ed.) 1901
√Grimaldi: Fang Sing Thou Kiai
√Gomboev: Altan Tobchi, etc.
√Goodland: Bibliography of Rites & Customs
√Gowland: Dolmens in Japan & Burial Mounds
√Grant: Books and Documents
√Gabelentz: Sze-schu, Schu-King, Schi-King
√Goodrich: Literary Inquisition of Chien-Lung
√Granet: La droite et la gauche, en Chine
√Grajdanzev: Formosa Today
√Golovnin's Captivity in Japan, 3 voll. (2nd ed. 1824)
√Golovnin's Captivity in Japan, 2 voll. 1818
√Grube: Metamorphosen der Gotter
√Giles: Historic China & other Sketches
√Gramatica de la lengua de Yap., 1888 - Capuchino:
√Goda Collection: Japanese Sword Fittings (none)
√Giles: Chinese Pictorial Art
√Gowland: Japanese Metallurgy
√Giles: San tzu ching
√Gorham: Tray Gardens
√Grey: Walks in City of Canton - 1875
√Geschichte der Sprachen d. vorderen Orients I-II. makas:
Gauthiot: Qq. termes techniques
√Grose's Classical Dict., 2nd ed. (A Classical Dict. of the Vulgar Tongue)
√Grigor'ev: Rossiya i Aziya
√Guntert: Grundfragen der Sprachwissenschaft
√Gardner: Western Books on China
√Guide to an exhibition of Japanese & Chinese Paintings principally from the Morrison Collection

√Gale: Cloud Dream of the Nine
√Golovnin: Voyage of the Sloop Diana (R)
√Gabelentz: Grammaire Mandchoue - 1833
√Ghaniev: Tatar-Russian Dictionary (Baku 1904)
√Giles: Six Centuries at Tunhuang
√Gale: Korean Folk Tales 1913
√Gabelentz: Essays on Mongolian and Manchu
√Gabelentz: Geschichte der grossen Liao
√Giles: Record of Buddhistic Kingdoms
√Grajdanzev: Formosa Today
√Gosse: T.L.Beddoes, 2 voll.
√Giles: Strange Tales from a Chinese Studio, 2 voll, 1st ed.
√Gronbech: Forstudier til tyrkisk lydhistorie 1902
√Giles: Glossary of Reference, 3rd ed.
√George Borrow Works, 16 voll. Works of
√Giles: Travels of Fa-hsien
Gunsaulus: Japanese Costume
√Gowland: Art of Casting Bronze in Japan - 1895
√Grose's Classical Dictionary, 1823 Egan:
√Grose's Provincial Glossary, 1811
√Giles: Note on Four Chinese Volumes sent for Identification
√Gabelentz: Thai-Kih-Thu 1876
√Gokhale: Pratityasamutpadasastra des Ullangha 19

資料 10（貼付ノート・Ashbee: Library Catalogue）

G

Garzoni: Grammatica della Lingua Kurda
Gualtieri: Della venuta de gli ambasciatori giaponesi 1586
Garcia ab Horto: Historia Aromatum
Grousset: Histoire de l'Extreme Orient (2 voll.)
Gesner: Mithridates (2nd edition)
Gardner: Philippine Folklore
Goudy: Typologia - Studies in Type Design & Type-Making
de Goeje: De muur van gog en magog
Getty: Chinese Seals — Notices of Found in Ireland
Golden Lotus (4 voll.) Egerton:
Gaelic Self-taught Maclaren's
Gladstone: On Books and the Housing of Them
Gay: Raretes Bibliographiques
Grot: Philological Studies of Catherine the Second
Gow: A.E. Housman
Gaekwad's oriental series, vol. 74
Gibbs: Chinese Imperial Names
Gingell: Ceremonial Usages of the Chinese
Grousset: Histoire de la Chine
Grunwedel: Altkutscha
Grew: Ten Years in Japan
Grabowsky: Ornamente bei den Naturvölkern

- 10 -

H

Huth: Die Inschriften von Tsaghan Baisin. 1894
Harlez: Chu-hsi
Harris: Voyages, 2 voll., folio
Hoernle: Ancient MSS from C. Asia - 1891-97
Hoernle: Antiquities from C. Asia
Hager: Monument de Yu
de Harlez: Religion nationale des tatares orientaux
Hirth: Tschau Ju-kua (Pamphlet)
de Harlez: Laotze — 1885

Damaged 3
Badly 1

History of Printing in China and Europe
Historia da expansao portuguesa no mundo 2 vols.
Hamerton: Intellectual Life
Hortus Suburbanus Calcuttensis
Heaslett: From a Japanese Prison, 1943
Historical Relations between Japan and Saghalien, 1920 Nakamura:
Historia gen. de ~~las Isl.~~ Philippinas 14 voll.
Hakluyt, 12 voll. Principal Navigations (Extra Series)
Hutchinson: Relations de la Compagnie franc
Heiberg: Geisteskrankheiten im klassischen Altertum
Haynes: Decline of Liberty in England
Hazlitt's Selected Essays
Hayn: 4 Bibliographien
Hanotaux: Bibliophiles
~~Huth: Inschriften von Tsaghen Baisin~~
Hirth: Keramische Gegenstände
History of Material Culture, 7 pamphlets
Hardy: Eastern Monachism
Hyacinth: San-czy-czin
Housman: Collected Poems of A.E.
Harcourt Smith: Cat. of various clocks, watches, automata, & other miscel. objects of European workmanship dating from the XVIIIth & the early XIXth centuries, in the Palace Museum & the Wu Ying Tien, Peking.

21

Hutchinson: Les premieres relations de la Compagnie française des Indes et du Siam au XVII Siecle.

Historia della China

Histoire de l'industrie de la peche maritime et fluviale au Japon 1900

Hippisley: Catalogue of Collection of Chinese Porcelain, 1890

Hills, Ford & Coutinho: A Portuguese Grammar

Hogben: Mathematics for the Million

Hogben: Interglossa

The Hongkong Almanack for 1846

Hargrave: The Earlier French Musicians (1632–1834)

Handbook of American Indian Languages (2 voll.)

Handbook of American Indians (2 voll.)

Hinder: Life and Labour in Shanghai

Humboldt: Fragmens de Geologie et de climatologie asiatique (2 voll. in one) 183

Hummel: Eminent Chinese of Ch'ing Period (2 voll.)

Huang: Lu Hsiang-Shan

Hustvedt: Ballad Books and Ballad Men

Hunter: The Literature of Papermaking 1390–1800

Hunter: Papermaking

Hunter: Papermaking by hand in India

Hubbard: British Fareastern Policy

Hulbert: Omjee the Wizard

Huish: Chinese Snuff Bottles of Stone, Porcelain, &c

Hume: Learned Societies & Printing Clubs

Hobson: British Museum Handbook of Pottery, Porcelain of Far East

Hobson: Chinese Pottery and Porcelain (2 voll.)

Housman: Name and Nature of Poetry

Holtom: Modern Japan and Shinto Nationalism

Hockin: a supplement to the Acc of Pelew Islands –1803

Hollingworth Papers Specimen Book

Historical and Statistical Abstract of the Colony of Hongkong 1807

Hirschfield: Sexual Anomalies & Perversions

Herbert: Limerick Printers & Printing

Henke: The Philosphy of Wang Yang Ming

Hellman: Four plays

Hannah: Tarawa

Hall's Voyages and Travels (6 voll. only)

Harington: The Metamorphosis of Aiax

Harrington: God Mammon and the Japanese

Hartwell: The Foochow Essays

Haas: Geschichte des christentums in Japan (2 voll.)

Haenisch: Dao Yuan-ch'ao Pi-shi, 1931

Hakluyt Society: History of the Two Tartar Conquerors of China

Hales: Milton's Areopagitica

Hagen: Aztec and Maya Papermakers

Hay: De rebus Iaponicis

Honey: Ceramic Art of China & other Countries of the Far East

H

Damaged 1

Badly " 1

22

資料 10（貼付ノート・Ashbee: Library Catalogue）

H

✓ Hart: The West Chamber
✓ Hart: Education in China
Harlez: Ecole philosophique moderne de la Chine (Sing-Li)
✓ Harlez: Le livre des esprits et des Immortels
✓ Hetherington: Pottery and Porcelain Factories of China
✓ Hetherington: Celadon Porcelain, its Story & Decorative Value

Histoire de Portugal – 1581.
✓ Hunter: Primitive Papermaking
✓ Hirth: Geschichte der Ostmongolen
✓ Hoffmann: Japanese Grammar, 2nd ed.
✓ Hirth Anniversary Volume
✓ Hyacinth: Istoriya pervyx chteyrex khanov
✓ de Harlez: Histoire de l'Empire de Kin
✓ Hunter: Turki text of Narratives of the Prophets
✓ Houtsma: Ein Turkisch-arabisches glossar 1894
✓ Hart: Japanese Art Work 1887
✓ Harada: Lesson of Japanese Architecture
✓ Housman: Shropshire Lad (Riccardi Press)
✓ Hetherington: Chinese Ceramic Glazes
✓ Hirth: Ancient Porcelain, 1888
✓ Hunter: Turki Texts
✓ Huart: Trois Actes Notariés Arabes de Yarkend
✓ Hashimoto: Kirishitan Kyogi no Kenkyu, 2 vols.

Damaged 1
Badly + none

– 9 –

✓ Hayn: Vier neue Curiositäten Bibliographieen – 1905
✓ Hayn: Bibliotheca erotica et curiosa Monacensis.
✓ Hughes: Chinese Philosophy in Classical Times
✓ Hirth: Native Sources for the History of Chinese Pictorial Art
✓ Huart: Conte bouddhique des deux freres
✓ Hatsukade: Bildungsideale in d. jap. Kultur und ihr Einfluss auf das Erziehungswesen in der Yedo-Zeit
✓ de Harlez: Reglements militaires de l'empereur Kia-King
✓ Haas: Dokument aus der jap. Inquisition
✓ Halloran's Journey to Japan, Loochoo, &c.
✓ Hughes: The Great Learning and the Mean-in-Action
✓ Hudson: Atlas of Far Eastern Politics
✓ Hyacinth: Kitai, 4 voll.
✓ Henry: Esquisse d'une Grammaire aleoute 1879
✓ Hirschfeld: Transvestitism, 2 voll.
✓ Hager: Pantheon chinois
✓ Hetherington: Early Ceramic Wares of China
✓ Hope: Temples of Nikko
✓ Henderson: Handbook of Japanese Grammar
✓ Hamilton: A New Acct of the East Indies, 2 voll.
✓ Hoffmann: Grammaire japonaise – 1861
✓ Histoire de la Chine, 13 voll., 4-to.
✓ Herring: Papermaking Ancient & Modern
✓ Houssaye: Monographie du the
✓ Hall's Voyage to Loochoo, 8vo.
✓ Hart: Marco Polo Venetian Adventurer:
✓ Hosie: Szechwan – its Products, industries & Resources
✓ Hirth: Scraps from a Collector's Notebook
✓ Haynes: Enemies of Liberty
✓ Hanakatsura
✓ Heyd: Histoire du Commerce du Levant, 2 voll.
✓ Hillier: List of Authorities of China
✓ Hager: Numismatique chinoise
✓ Hayashi: For His People

23

I

Road of Hist. E. Ysbrant Ides

✓Ides: The Three Years' Travels from Moscow to China

✓The Indian Mag., April 1903

Inoue-Tadou: Kirishitan gogaku no kenkyu

✓Inscription on the St. Louis Stele of 505 A.D.

✓Irish-English Dictionary (Irish Text Society)

✓Irish Franciscan Monthly July '40, June '40, May '40 (assisi)

✓Irish without Worry Collier:

I-Tsing: Records of the Buddhist Religion

✓Is Aboriginal Formosa A part of the Chinese Empire?, 1874

✓Imbault-Huart: Manuel de la langue coreenne 1889

✓Ivanovskii: Mandjurica, I - 1894

I-li (Probsthain), 2 voll. Steele:

✓Imbrie: Etymology Handbook of English-Japanese

✓Imbault-Huart: Anecdotes en chinois parle

✓Inscriptions de l'orkhon, folio

✓Ibn al-Muhanna: Arabic-Mongol-Turk. Glossary

✓Istoriya Sibiri, 2 voll.

✓Institut de sinologie de l'université Nationale de Pekin - 1925

✓In Memoriam Oskar Fanizza

✓Intorno ad una memoria di Guilio Klaproth

Imp. Ermitage, 1915

Izv. Vostoc. Otd. Imp. Arx. Ob. I, 2 voll.

✓Julien: Le Livre des Recompenses et des Peines

Jenner: Tsze Tien Piao Muh (A guide to the Dictionary)

✓Jespersen: Bone sprog - 1923.

✓Jami: Abode of Spring

✓Jaubert: Notice d'un manuscrit turc (J.A.) 1825

✓Julien: Tou-Kioue

✓Julien: Les deux cousines, 2 voll.

✓Julg: Marchen des Siddhi-Kur, Kalmuch text, 1866

~~Jean Second: Livre des Baisers~~

✓July and Inada: Sword and Same

✓Jespersen: Chapters on English

✓Japanese Education, 1879

✓Jews at K'ae-Fung-Foo 1851

✓Journal Bengal Asiatic Society, 1878-79. Vol XLVII Extra Vol XLVIII Pt. 2

✓Japanese View of Outer Mongolia Grajdanzev:

✓Japan in Yezo

Jesuit Linguistic Studies (J)

✓Julien: Histore de la porcelaine chinoise

✓Julien: Blanche et Bleue

✓Japanese Fairy World ; Griffis

✓Julien: Voyages des Pelerins bouddhistes, 3 voll. Hiouen-Thsang &

✓Julien: Avadanas, 3 voll.

Japan Society, London, Vol.I plus 2 voll. of Suppl.

✓Jenkins: Life of George Borrow

✓Jacobi: Printer's Vocabulary of Technical Terms, Phrases, etc

✓Jaeschke: Tibetan-English Dict. 1866

✓Julg: Mongolische Marchen-sammlung - 1868

✓Jahresb Frankfurter Vereins für Orientalische Sprachen - 1916.

✓Jespersen: Lehrbuch der Phonetik

✓John: On the Ancient Language of the Natives of Tenerife

Damaged 2
Badly 1

An Introduction to I-tsing's Record of the Buddhist Religion as practiced in India & the Malay Archipelago.

24

資料 10（貼付ノート・Ashbee: Library Catalogue）

Journal of the West Border Research Society, VIII
Supplement (Morse: Schedule of Physical
Anthropological Measurements & Observations
on Ten Ethnic Groups of Szechwan Province,
West China)

Joyce: Notes on the Physical Anthropology of Chinese
Turkestan & the Pamirs.

(None)

25

[illegible]

[illegible] de Julius Klaproth

[illegible] 2 vol

[illegible] 1943

[illegible]: Abode of Spring

[illegible] d'un manuscrit [illegible]

[illegible]

Julien: Les deux cousines, 2 voll.

[illegible], Kalmuch text, [illegible]

[illegible] and [illegible]

[illegible] Chapters of English

[illegible]

Journal Bengal Asiatic Society, 1878-79.

[illegible] View of Outer Mongolia

[illegible]

[illegible] Linguistic Studies (J)

Julien: Histoire [illegible] de la porcelaine chinoise

[illegible]

[illegible]

Julien: [illegible] bouddhistes, 3 voll.

[illegible], 3 voll.

[illegible], Vol. I plus 2 voll. of Suppl.

[illegible]

[illegible] Vocabulary

[illegible] Tibetan English Dict.

[illegible]

[illegible]

[illegible]

26

資料 10（貼付ノート・Ashbee: Library Catalogue）

J

✓Japanese Air Terms (2 voll.) Boyce;
✓Japanese Code of Criminal Procedure
Japan Society, New York: Chinese, Korean and Japanese Potteries
✓Japanese Women, Columbian Exposition, 1893
✓Jenkins: The Jesuits in China
✓Jespersen: Language, its Nature, Development and Origin
✓Jespersen: ^Rask ^Rasmus 1918
✓Jien Niimura:
✓Jizo
✓Jochelson: Archeological Investigations in Kamchatka
✓Jochelson: The Yakut
✓Jochelson: Peoples of Asiatic Russia
✓Johnson: Barnaby
3.
✓Johnson: Barnaby and Mr. O'Malley
✓Jones: Launay Innocencia
✓Jones: The Pastourelle - a Study of the Origin & Tradition of a Lyric Type
✓Jorgensen: Old Coins of China - a Guide to their Identification
✓Joyce: ~~Works~~ Ulysses
✓Jordanus: The Wonders of the East
✓Jenness: Report of the Canadian Arctic Expedition 1913-18

Damaged 1

27

Kaigaishinbunbetsushu, (2 voll.) + one Kaigai Shinbun (? "Batahya shinbun"?)

Kann: Currencies of China, 2. ed.

Karlgren: The Romanization of Chinese

Katanov: Otryvok iz odnoi tatarskoi letopisi o Kazani

Keeton: China, the Far East and the Future

Kelemen: Medieval American Art (2 voll.)

Kempis: Imitation of Christ (Elzevier edition)

Kenyon: Ancient Books and Modern Discoveries

King: Japan and Malaysia (2 voll.)

Kipling's Collected Poems

Kizer: The U.S.-Canadian Northwest

Knapp: George Borrow (2 voll.)

Konow: Memoirs the Asiatic Soc. of Bengal (Vol. 5 No. 2.)

Kozlov: Tibet i Dalailama

Kramp: Een nievw werk over China

Kuck: The Art of Japanese Gardens

Kuke debter, Istoriya Mongolov

- 11 -

Kowalewski: Dictionnaire Mongol-Russe-Francaise (3 vol. in 2)

Kluge: Beitrage zur mingrelischen Grammatik 1916

Kowalewskii: Mongolskaya Xrestomatiya, 2 voll.

Kotvič: Kalmyckiya Zagadki i poslovicy

Kohts: Erkenntnis Fahigkeiten des Schimpansen 1923

Kraus: Leben des japanischen Volkes, 2 voll.

~~Kirishiten Kyogi no Kenkyu, 2 voll.~~

Kirgiz-Russian Dict., 1903

Kotvie: Materialy dlya izuceniya tungusskix narecii

Kim: Die Aufmachung der mod. Zeitung in Ostasien

Karsch: Tribadie bei den Tieren

Kori: Kanawa the Incantation

Kaulen: Lingua mandshurica

Klaproth: Verzeichniss der chinesischen und mandshuischen Bucher und Handschriften, Berlin (Lacks Errata)

Kaempfer: History of Japan, 2 voll., large paper

Kern: Histoire du bouddhisme dans l'Inde, 2 voll.

~~Kaigaho no Kenkyu~~

Karlgren: Etudes sur la phonologie chinoise

~~Kowalewski Mongolian Dict., 3 voll. in 2~~

Kino: Japanese Expansion on the Asiatic Cont., Vol. I., II. III?

Konrad: Japonskaya Literatura, I.

Khanikoff: Memoire sur les Inscriptions musulmanes du Caucase

Kanokogi: Der Geist Japans

Kerner: N.E.Asia, 2 voll.

Kaempfer: Amoenitates exoticae

Badly Damaged 2

20

Lindgren: Shaman dress of the Dagurs, Solons & Numinchens in N.W. Manchuria
Laufer: East Asiatic Collection
Laufer: Introduction of Tobacco into Europe
Laufer: Chinese Baskets (Field Museum of Nat. Hist, 1925)
Lonchamp: Manuel du bibliophile francais, 2 voll. 1470-1920
Lonchamp: Manuel du bibliophile suisse
Lange: History of Materialism
~~Library of L.L.Bonaparte~~
Le Clert: Le papier, 2 voll, folio
Lloyd: Praises of Amida
Langles: Voyage dans l'Inde et à la Chine, 2 voll., 12mo
Lendoyro: Tagalog Language
Loewenstein: Swastika and Yin Yang
Lloyd: Creed of Half-Japan
de Lluys: Le Japon et Rome 1877
Laufer: Pottery of Han Dynasty
Lewis & Short: Latin Dict.
Le pi-pa-ki Ainé: ou L'histoire du Luth
Lindley: Fa Hian (The Pilgrimage of Fa Hian)
Le jardin parfume du cheikh Nefzaoui
Life of ~~Mrs.~~ Bird (Mrs Bishop) Stoddart:
Leyden: Memoirs of Baber
Life of Panizzi, Vol. I
Leland: Pidgin English
Lewis: Ranald McDonald 1824-1894
La Croze Thesaurus Tom 1&2. Lips. 1742-3.
Langles: Alphabet Tartare-Manchou, ~~4to~~ 1787
Le divan d'Amour
Locke: Ancient Quipu
Lecky: Hist. of European Morals, from Augustus to Charlemagne 2 voll.
Leskien: Handb. d. altbulg. Sprache 1922
Lettres persanes, Tome I.
Lettres edifiantes, 26 voll.
Library Cards
Lewy: Ban der europ. Sprachen
Letters rec. by East India Co, from its Servants in the East 6 voll. 1616
L'Anthropologie, 2 voll. Boule-Verneau
Le sutra en 42 articles
Laufer: Reindeer & its domestication
Lehtisalo: Vokalismus der ersten silbe im Samojedischen
Levi: Eastern Humanism
Laufer: Historical jottings on Amber in Asia
Lazareff Cat., 2 voll.
Ljungstedt: An Historical Sketch of the Portuguese Settlements in China
Langles: Voyages de Sino-bad le marin.
Lajard: Langage siffle des Canaries.
Levi: Fragment tokharien du Vinaya des Sarvastivadins.
Lit. sborik k 100-letiyo ... Kazan ... Univ.
Lefranc: Oeuvres de Francois Rabelais, 5 vol
La Belle Libraire
Lewy: Proceedings of the Royal Irish Academy

29

√Laufer: Jade
√Langles: Alphabet Mantchou, 1807
Linton: Sacrifice to the Morning Star
Luther: Ethische Anweisungen
√Laufer: Chinese-Hebrew Ms., a new source for the History of the Chinese Jews
√Laufer: History of Finger Prints
√Laufer: Language of the Yue-chi or Indo-Scythians

√Liu: Hsi 西夏國書字典音同一卷
√Lazarev: Aperçu historique du développement des Sciences exactes en Russie aux XVIII et XIX siècles - 1927
Leningrad Or. Inst.
X √Lenin Public Library Moscow, I.

Badly Damaged !

30

資料 10（貼付ノート・Ashbee: Library Catalogue）

Labarre: A Dictionary of Paper + Paper making terms
Lang: Shanghai considered socially
Langles: Des Livres tatars mantchoue de la Bibl. Nat.
La morale des Jesuites
Lantzeff: Siberia in the Seventeenth Century
Lataste: De Saurophthalme Scincoidien Originaire du Japon
Laufer: Beginnings of Porcelain in China (Field Mus. of Nat. Hist. Pub. #192)
Laufer: The Domestication of the Cormorant in China + Japan (F. M. of N. Hist. Vol. XLIII; #7)
Laures: Kirishitan Bunko
Leach: A Potter's Book
Leaçock: Montreal, Seaport and City
Legge: Christianity in China
Le Gallienne: Romance of Perfume
Lettera annale delle cose del Giapone (Milan edition)
Letters from Baker Street
Lewis: The Abolition of Man or Reflections on Education with Special Reference to the teaching of English in the Upper Forms of School
Lewis: Francois Villon
Lewis: The Monk (2 voll.)
Lewis: Ronsard
Li: Formation of the Chinese People
library cards
Library cards, 2 sets (3 separate pkgs.)
Lisiansky: A Voyage Round the World in the Yrs. 1803, 4, 5 & 6.
Lisboa: A China e os Chins 1888
Lockhart: The Life of Burns
The London Magazine Jan. '78
Lui: Secrets of Chinese Physicians
The Liberated Regions of China Behind the Enemy Lines Vol. I. (Mar. 45)

(none)

31

M

Man Unmask'd or the Island of Japan Nerthegood:

Matsuo: Haikai de Basho et de ses Disciples

Mansoor: The Story of Irish Orientalism

Marr & Briere: La Langue Georgienne

Maltese Grammar

Maffei: Selectarum epistolarum ex India (Venice edition)

Maya Society Quarterly, Vol. I

Martini: De bello tartarico (Antwerp edition)

Martini: Sinica historia (Munich edition)

Martini: De bello tartarico (Amsterdam edition)

Maillard: Traicte des Indulgences

MacDonald: Chronologie and Calendars

Mason: the Mohammedans of China

Margulies: the Artistic Possibilities of Literary Chinese

Matsubara: In Darkest Tokyo Schroeder, ed.:

Mansoor: Oriental Studies in Ireland & Irish Orientalists

Machiavelli: The Prince & the Discourses

Marakueff: ~~Chinese~~ Weights and Measures in China - 1930

Martin: Communism in China in Eleventh Century

Marco Polo, Latin edition ed. Muller ? Marcus Paulus - Haithon - Mercleri Chataja

Maffei: Opera (2 voll. 4to)

Matsokin: Summary of An Outline of the Morphology of Present Tense of Japanese Verb

Matsumoto: Beziehung zwischen Midado und Schogun vor 1868

Mattice: Lexicon of Bibliographical Cataloguing & Library Terms

Maupas: Grammaire et Syntaxe francoise (Bloys edition)

Mansion: A school ~~French~~ Grammar of Present Day French

March: Chinese Shadow-figure Plays & their making

The Maya Society and its Work

Mansfield: The Garden Party

Macfarlane: Sketches of Shanghai

Maudslay: A Glimpse of Guatemala

McCoy: Ten Escape from Tojo

McKerrow: An Introduction to Bibliography

McIlroy: Chamberlain's Japanese Grammar

McLeod: Japan & the ten lost tribes of israel, 2 voll.

Mckenney and Hall: A History of the Indian Tribes of North America (3 voll.)

McMurtrie: The Book - the Story of Printing & Bookmaking

Michaelis: A Dissertation on the Influence of Opinions on Language & of Language on Opinions

Middle American Research Records

Minayeff: Recherches sur le Bouddhisme

Minorsky: Marvazi on China, the Turks & India

Ming: Sosho Dictionary

Milne: the Stone Age in Japan

Milne: List of Japanese Minerals

Badly Damaged

32

- 14 -

Muir: Book Collecting as a Hobby in a series of letters to ...
Morris: Living with Lepchas
Muto: History of Anglo-Japanese Relations
Murdoch: History of Japan, Vol. II only
Middelton-Wake: Invention of Printing
Marsden: Travels of Marco Polo
Mason: Arabian Prophet (a Life of Mohammed from Chinese Sources)
Magic and Science in Western Yunnan HSU:
Morris: Traveller from Tokyo
Matsudaira: Culture of Kaki
McClean: Xavier Francis 1895
Milne: Sacred Edict of Kang-Hi
Medhurst: Shoo-King or the Historical Classic - 1846
Marlowe's Poems
Marsden: ~~Malayan~~ a Grammar of the Malayan Grammar
Melanges chinoise et bouddhiques, 4 voll. (lacks Vol. III Luzac)
Memoir of Raffles Sir T.
Milburn: Oriental Commerce, 2 voll., 4to.
Marshman: Works of Confucius, Vol. I
Marlowe: Edward II
Miscellanies Historical
Marlowe: Life and Dido
Marre: Gr. Tagalog
~~Manrique: Travels, 2 voll.~~
Murakami: Sinkan MSS (Memoirs of the Faculty of Literature & Politics, Taihoku Imp. Univ.)
Mole: Handbuch, 2 voll. der Sexualwissenschaften
Merhart: Bronzezeit am Jenissei
Map of the World 1506, British Museum
Missionary Success in Formosa, 2 voll. Campbell:
Murray's Handbook of Japan, 4th ed.
McGowan: Self-Immolation by Fire & on Avenging Habits of the Cobra
Moraes: Cartas do Japao
Marcuse: Handworterbuch der Sexualwissenschaft
Masson-Oursel: La Specificite de la Psychologie indienne, 1928
Man: Formosa
March: Standards of Pottery Description
Mollendorff: Manchu Literature
Melioranskii: Skazanie ob. edigel i toktanysy
Mongolo-Oiratskii epos
~~Memoir of Capt. W. Gile~~
March: China and Japan in Our Museums
Memorials of Rev. Douglas - 1877
Monumenta nipponica, Vol. V Part 1 - 1942
Medhurst: China - Its State & Prospects
Markham: Chinchona (Peruvian Bark)
Museum Journal, Dec. 1926.
Mirady-Nameh 1889 Le Comte Courteille:
Melanges russes, Tome III
Materialy dlya etnografii Rossii, Vol. 14
Materialy dlya ist. voiska Donskago
Meyeshof: Noms portugais de drogues
Mandrake Press (First List)
McIlroy: Chamberlain's Japanese Gr.

(None)

33

✓Memoir of Rev. S. Dyer Davies!
✓de Moges: Ambassade en Chine et au Japon
✓Morse: Traces of Early Race in Japan 1879
✓Marlowe: Faustus and Jew of Malta, 2 voll.
Marakuev: Russische Arbeiten ... Chin. Lexicographie

✓Martyrologium franciscanum sineuse
Sir John Mandervile, O.U.P.
✓Michael: Origin of Manchu Rule in China
✓Muto: Short History of Anglo-Japanese Relations
✓Memoirs of Benyowsky, 1904
✓Memoirs of Benyowsky, 1893 Oliver!
✓Marquart: Eransahr
✓Monboddo: Origin of Language, 6 voll.
✓Morse: Methods of Arrow Release
✓Milne: Retrospect of Ten Years of the Protestant Mission
✓Montgomery: History of Yaballaha III
✓Meyer: Grammatik der russischen sprache Historische
✓Marquart: Osteuropaische und ostasiatische streifzuge 1903
Moule: Christians in China Before the Year 1550. 2 voll.
✓Meadows: Translations from Manchou 1849
✓Marakuev: Der gefleckte Hirsch in der chinesischen Medizin
✓Memoires de Benyowsky, 2 voll., 1790 = (voyages of Benyowsky)
See F ✓Marco Polo (Argonaut)
✓Mickles: Lusiad (Bohn) Camoens'
✓Morrison: Malayan Postscript
✓Malinowski: Crime and Custom in Savage Society
✓Mechanic's Magazine, 12 Dec., '29
✓Morison: View of China
✓Morais: Seroes no Japao
✓Mir-Ali-Shir
✓McFadden: Bibliography of Pacific Area Maps
✓Mel'nikov: Materialy dlya istorii ... skopceskoi eresi
✓Miansarov: Bibliographia caucasica et transcaucasica
✓Montandon: Au pays des Ainou
✓Milloue: Bod-youl ou Tibet (Annales du Musée Guimet)
✓Mokogodaijiten, 3 voll.
✓Mezov: Sibirskaya Bibliografiya, I-III. 1903
✓Maybon: Theatre japonais (none)
✓Montandon: La civilisation ainou
✓Malan: San-tsze-king
✓Marnas: Religion de Jesus, 2 voll.
✓Morse: Catalogue Japanese Pottery
✓Morand: L'acupuncture
✓Mayers: Higher Authorities of China
✓Memoirs of W. Marsden
✓Marlowe: Tamburlaine the Great
✓Markham: a Memoir on the Indian Surveys
✓MacKinley: Tagalog Grammar (A Handbook & Gr. of the Tagalog Language, 1905)
× Mahler: Muhammadische Zeitrechnung
✓Morrison: Horae Sinicae (Translations from the Popular Literature with an essay on Civilization)
✓Meadows: Chinese and their Rebellions
Middendorff's Reise in den äussersten Norden und Osten Sibiriens, 3 vols.
× Wüstenfeld-Mahler: Vergleichungs-Tabellen II. Muhammedanischen u. christlichen Zeitrechnung

Meyerhof: Essai sur les noms portugais de drogues dérivés de l'arabe.

34

M

Moule: Nestorians in China
Morse: East India Company trading to China (5 voll.)
Mongolian Inscription (Wylie)
Morley: Study of Maya Hieroglyphs An introduction to the
Morley: Sherlock Holmes and Dr. Watson
Morley: Guide Book to Ruins of Quirigua
Moidrey: Confesseurs de la foi en Chine 1284-1862
Morison: Eustachio Celebrino da Udene
Monteiro: De l'influence portugaise au Japon
Mosheim: Memoirs of the Christian Church in China
Monkhouse: Chinese Porcelain A History & Description of
Montaigne's Essays (3 voll.) Florio:
Morrell: Voyages and Discoveries Narrative of Morrell's 1832
Muir: Book Collecting as a Hobby
Muller: Soghdiche Texte, I
Museum of Fine Arts, Boston: Catalogue of a special loan exhibition of Art Treasures from Japan
Muller: Ikkaku Sennin
The Muses Gardin for Delights Jones!
Meissner: Grammatik der japanischen schriftsprache (2 voll.)
Mesny's Chinese Miscellany, (4 voll.)
Mendozza: Dell' Historia della China (Venice edition)
Mencken: The American Language
Medicina Sinica (Cleyer) Frankfort 1682
Memoires de l'Academie Royale des Sciences des Lettres et des Beaux-Arts de Belgique. Tome XLI
McLeod. Illustrations to the Epitome of the Ancient History of Japan, 2nd edition.
Morris + Skeat: Chaucer
Memoirs of the Literature College, Imperial Univ, of Japan, No 1. 1887 (Chamberlain: The Language, Mythology, & Geographical Nomenclature of Japan viewed in the light of Aino Studies)
Batchelor: An Ainu Gr. &
Cat of Books relating to Yezo & the Ainus

Damaged!

35

N

Naito: Wall-paintings of Horyuji (2 voll.)
Nansen: The First Crossing of Greenland (2 voll.)
Nachod: Bibliography of Japan (2 voll.)
Neumann: Catechism of the Shamans
Nichols: Restoration of Ancient Bronzes + Cure of Malignant Patina (Field Museum of Natural History)
Normano and Gerbi: Japanese in South America
Norman: Soldier and Peasant in Japan + the Origins of Conscription
Nosaka: Labour Movement in Japan, 1921
Norris: History of Cataloguing
Nowiny z Iaponu y z Chiny

Nye: Morning of my Life in China 1873
Nachrichten, K. G. d. Wiss, Gott. phil-hist. 1910, 1
Nikkochizu (Guide map of Nikkosan, Japan)
Naliv Kine: Khokand Histoire du Khanat de
Nilsson: Primitive Time Reckoning
Nunn: Ecclesiastical Latin
Norman: Fighting Man of Japan, The Training + Exercises of the Samurai
Nihonbunten Kogi Wada!
Nihon to Portogaru
New-Castle Typ. Soc. 2 voll.
New-Castle Topogr. Soci., 1 vol.
Nioradze: Schamanismus bei den sibirischen Volkern
Nausester: Das Kind und die Form d. Sprache
Nihonjinko-mitsudo-zu
Novikov: Skifskaya istoriya, 3 in 1.
Notices et Extraits, vol. XI
Nonesuch Press Prospectus + Retrospectus 1929 + 1930 (2 vols)
Note Bibliographique (Academie Royale de Belgique)

Badly Damaged!

資料 10（貼付ノート・Ashbee: Library Catalogue）

✓Observatory of Zikawei
✓O Cuiv: Irish of West Muskerry, Co. Cork
✓Oliver: Korea, Forgotten Nation
✓Olschki: Marco Polo's Precursors
✓Omura: Dictionary of Legal Terms (English-Japanese Japanese-English)
✓O'Neill: A First Japanese Book -1874
✓O'Nolan: the New Era Grammar of Modern Irish
✓Onraet: Sixty Below
✓O'Halloran: Glamour of Limerick
✓Opuscules francoises des Hotmans
✓Osborn: A Cruise in Japanese Waters
✓Oxford Book of Ballads
The Oxford Book of English Verse
✓Oxford Book of Portuguese Verse
✓Our task in 1945 (Feb. 1945)
✓Olschki: Marco Polo il Milione - 1928 (unbound)

Orbeli: Musulmanskie izrazcy
Osorius: Histoire de Portugal (1581)
✓Ojedilla: Cristobal Acosta 1899
✓Otsuka: First Voyage of the English to Japan
✓Ocean of Story, 10 voll. Tawney & Penzer:
✓Os Lusiadas, (~~Moreno, Porto~~) de Luis de Camoes
✓"Outpost": Singapore Nightmare
✓Olearius: Voyages, 1719, folio
Otanike: Shinsaiikiki, 2 voll., folio
✓Observations, critiques sur le Japon et Philosophiques
✓Ostroumov: Tatar-Russian Dict. 1892
✓Osborn: Japanese Fragments
.Obrazcy mongol'skoi narodnoi literatury, I.
✓Olufsen: Bokhara Dialect, Turki Vocabulary 1905
✓Obrucev: Central Asia (R), 2 voll., 4to
✓Opyt grammatiki aleut skago yazyka, 1846 Veniaminov:
✓Ostrovskii: Votyaki
✓Oxford: Scaliger
✓Otto: Hauslehrerbestrebungen
✓Ogawa: Festivals ~~of~~ Yedo, Annual
✓Opisanie Korei, 3 voll. plus map
✓Otto: Kindesmundart
Ovidreff: Langue jap. litteraire

Damaged 1
Badly " 1

37

P

Pacific Affairs, Sept. 1943, Vol XVI, #3
Pai: Conversational Korean
Pallas: Meskwurdigkeiten, 3 voll.
Pallavicino: Opere scelte (Elzevier, 2 voll.)
Parsons: Notes in Japan
~~Davis: Ancient Chinese Paper Money as described in a Chinese work on Numismatics~~
Pamyati Kastrena
Paul of Aleppo: Travels of Macarius (2 voll.) Belfour:
Pauw: Recherches sur les Egyptiens et Chinois, 2 voll.
Peddie: Place Names in Imprints
Peking Gazette, 74, 77, 76, 73 (4 voll.)
Perry's Expedition Japan (1 vol. 8vo) & the China Seas Hawks:
Petrucci: Prodromo Apologetico di G. Petrucci
Phelps: Mount Omei
Philobiblon, Grolier Club (3 voll.)
Philobiblon, Inglis edition
Pineyro: Relacion del sucesso que tuvo nuestra santa fe en Japon los Reynos del - 1617
Pinto: Voyages and Adventures (1663) of Ferdinand Mendez Pinto.
Pollard: An Essay on Colophons
Preliminary Report on Expedition to N.W. Honduras (Smithson. Inst. 3445)
Preve: Tchemoulpo
Praz: The Romantic Agony
Priapeia veterum et recentiorum - 1798
Puini: Avalokitecvara sutra (Atsume Gusa)
Pumpelly: Geological Researches in China, Mongolia, & Japan
Smithsonian

Picture Frame (1)

Pfizmaier: Japanischen Volkspoesie, Über einige Eigenschaften
Partridge: Dictionary of R.A.F. Slang
Pomus: Buriat Mongolia
Pamyatniki Indiiskoi Filosofii I 1922
Pinto-Okamoto-Bernard: La Premiere Ambassade du Japon en Europe, 1582-1592

(none)

38

✓Persoz: Notice du Verb de Chine.
✓Piggott: The Elements of Sosho 17 -
✓Pumpelly: Explorations in Turkestan-Expedition of 1904, 2 vols.
✓Portogaru o tazuneru | Okamoto:
✓Pozdneev: Mongol'skaya Xrestomatiya
Panther: Marco Polo, 2 voll.
✓Peregrinacao de Pinto, 4 voll.
✓Purchas, 20 voll.
✓Pyke: Legibility of Print
✓Pokorny: Altkeltische gr.
✓Pelliot: Mongols et la papaute, 2 voll.
Pamphlet on Kondakov
Peking Catalogue of Clocks
Po etapam razvitiya .....
Pumpelly: Annan, 2 voll., 4to.
Panchatrentra (in Russian)
✓Putman: Books and their makers in the Middle Ages, 2 voll.
✓Penal Code of Japan 1882
✓Pfizmaier: Kritische Durchsicht der von Dawidow verfassten Wörtersammlung aus der Sprache der Ainos 1852
✓Paske-Smith: Japanese Traditions of Christianity
✓Pozdneev: Skazanie o xozdenii V. ... buza-baksi Shanu Malodorbotskago
✓Poppe: Altaisch und Urturkisch
✓Pruitt: Flight of an Empress
✓Practical Orthography of Tswana
✓Pekarskii: Russko-yak'utskii slovar'
Pinto: Peregmacao
✓Pfizmaier: Seelenzustande und Leidenschaften
✓Pypin: Istoriya russkoi etnograjii, 4 voll.
✓Poussin: The Way to Nirvana
✓Pozdneev: Mongoliya i Mongoly, 2 voll.
Potselnevskii: Turkmen Handbook
✓Phonetic Transcription and Transliteration - 1926
✓Pauthier: Le Livre de Marco Polo, 2 vols.
✓Putesestire na Seber ... 4to Miscellanies - Historical - 1857 - 1870
✓Protokoly Troitsk. Otd. Priam. Otd. I.R.G.O.
✓Pamphlets, 1 vol. buckram, red label.
Pamphlet on Ossetes
✓Putman: Censorship of the Church of Rome, 2 voll.
✓Pfizmaier: Alte Bewohner des heutigen Corea - 1868
36 Pfizmaier: 3 pamphlets (unbound)
✓Pelliot: Les mots à H initiale aujourd'hui amuie, dans le Mongol (Journal Asiatique Avril-Juin 1925)
✓Pozdneev: Ocerki byta Buddiiskix Monastyrei v Mongolii
✓Poole: Chronicles & Annals
✓Pfizmaier: Der Redner Tschang-I - 1860
✓ " : Bei Den Hiung-Nu's - 1864

Damaged 1

39

- 16 -

Publications of Protestant Missionaries -1867.
Pennell: Lithography and Lithographers
Pozdneev: Mongol'skaya letopis "Erdeniin erixe"
Pozdneev: Kalmyckaya Xrestomatiya, 1907
Pound: Ta Hio - The great Learning
Psalmanaazaar's Description of Formosa (Library of Impostors)
Potanin: Vostocnye Motivy - 1899
Pozdneev: Opyt sobraniya obrazcov manchurskoi literatury, I.
Paget: Human Speech
Priapeia, (Gaselee), 1890
Pinto: Peregrinacao, 1762 1938?
Parlement of Pratlers (Fanfrolico) Eliot:
Polish Science and Learning
Pamyai akad. A.N. Veselovskago, 1921 Damaged!
Pelliot: Comans (J.A.)
Pamyati V. Tomsena
Psichari: Language Question in Greece
Parker: Taoist Religion
Pitton de Tournefort: Voyage du Levant, 1718, 2 voll.
Paske-Smith: Western Barbarians in Japan & Formosa in Tokugawa Days
Paske-Smith: Glympse of the English House & English Life at Hirado 1613-23
Poppe: Xalxa-mongol'skii geroiceskii epos
Poppe: Materialy dlya issledovaniya tungusskogo yazyka, 1927
Pelikan: Skopcestvo, folio (1 plate missing)
Pierre Louys et l'histoire litteraire
Pfizmaier: Japanese Studies, VolS III, II, I quarto
Petrucci: La philosophie de la nature dans l'art d'extreme orient folio
Parker: A Thousand Years of the Tartars
Percival: Experiments on the Peruvian Bark
Penzer: ~~Burton~~ Annotated Bibliography of Sir Richard Burton
Poesia Medieval (Textos literarios)
Piggott: Garden of Japan
~~Pfizmaier: Japanese Studies, 4to, Vol. II~~
Pacific Area in American Research
Parker: Hospitals in China
Pritchard: Crucial Years of Anglo-Chinese Relations
Pierson: The Manyoshu, ~~vol.~~ Book 5
Plomer: Wynkyn de Worde Wynkyn & his contemporaries
~~Pfizmaier: Japanese Studies, Vol. I.~~
Penney: Japanese Popular Stories - 1890
Patkanov: Istoriya Mongolov - 1871 Malachi Abela
Pissoh: Sosho
Popov: Pantheon chinois, 1907
Pokotilov: Istoria vostocnyx mongolov
Parkinson: Trade in the Eastern Seas 1793-1813
Prestage: Portuguese Pioneers
Pages: Bibliographie japonaise
Piry: Erh-to-mei, 2 voll.
Paske-Smith: England and Japan (Extracted from the "History of Travayle")
Penzer: The Harem
~~Pfizmaier's Japanese Studies, 1 vol., 8vo. (making 2 in all)~~

Printed Books & Manuscripts on Japan (arranged chronologically) Maggs Bros.

See Back of Page - for further "P"s

40

Queen: Misadventures of Sherlock Holmes
Queri: Kraftbayrisch
Queiroz: Cartas de Inglaterra

Badly Damaged !

R

Radlov: Archaologische erforschung des Orchon-Beckens
Radlov: (Older Turkish Studies) Alttürkische Studien
Ratchford: Letters of Thomas J. Wise to John Henry Wrenn
The Red Gate Players Benton:
Redman: Shaw in and on Japan
Rein: Industries of Japan
Regamey: Japan in Art and Industry
Relation des Choises de Yucatan
Relazione della morte dell' ... di tournon
Rerum in Oriente Gestarum(Cologne '74)
Reynolds: The Voyage of the New Hazard
Reynolds: White sahibs in India
Rhode Island Imprints -1727-1800
de Rhodes: Histoire de la vie de cinq peres
Robinson collection: Oriental Numismatics
Robertson: Bibliography of the Philippine Islands
Rockhill: William of Rubruck The Journey of Friar
Rodriguez: Lettera di Giappone (Rome edition)
Ross: Both Ends of the Candle
Rosthorn: Tea Cultivation in Western Ssuch'uan
Rocher: La Province Chinoise du Yunnan (2 voll.)
Ryan: Jesuits under fire in the seige of Hongkong 1941
Rzepnicki historia Japonii
Rice: the Beginnings of Russian Icon Paintáng, 1938
Richthofen: Trade Route to S.W. China Recent Attempts to Find a ...
Restorations of the Mongolian Inscriptions (in folio) 41

✓Reflections, by a Lady 1778

✓Radloff: Das Kudatku Bilik, folio
✓Rundall: Memorials of Empire of Japon
✓Radloff: Kudatku Bilik, 4to
✓Remusat: Relation des royaumes bouddhiques
Rukopisi Turkestanskoi Publicnoi Biblioteki, 1889

Rondot: Vert de Chine
✓Rowse: On History - a Study of Present Tendencies
✓Radloff: Uigurische Sprachdenkmaler

✓Schjoth: Chinese Currency
✓Sibiriacoff: Zur Frage von den Aussere Verbindungen Sibiriens mit Europa
✓Sigler: Sycee Silver (Numismatic Notes & Monographs No 99)
Sinbirskii sbornik (imperfect)
✓Skelton: The Complete Poems of John Skelton Henderson
Skeat: Chaucer's Prologue
✓Smith: Japanese Goldfish - their Varieties & Cultivation
✓Smith: Profile by Gaslight - an Irregular Reading
✓Smith: William de Machlinia
✓Springfield Mill: 1807-1907 Riddle
✓Swinhoe: Natural History of Hainan

42

S

Shaw: Catalogue of Specimens of Cloth, 1787
Major Shaw's Journals with a memoir by Quincy
Sheehan: the Idiom of Living Irish
Shepherd: Australia's Interests and Policies in the Far East
Mary Shelley: Frankenstein
Shenstone: Men & Manners
Shirokogoroff: Psychomental complex of the Tungus
Shirokogoroff: Ethnical Unit and Milieu
Shirokogoroff: La theorie de l'ethnos
Shinjikan Shioya
Shorter Oxford Dictionary (2 voll.)
Short History of Ireland in Irish
Secundus: Basia (Nonesuch Press) Stanley, Thos.
Sennep: Un systeme negre de classification
Senstius: Malay Language
Staunion: Chinese Embassy to the Khan of the Tourgouth Tartars, 1821
Starrett: 221B, Studies in Sherlock Holmes
Stanton: the Triad Society
Stefansson: The Friendly Arctic
Stefansson: Arctic Manual
Stein: Explorations in Central Asia (Geog. Journal)
Stevens: Biblio. Essay on B. Franklin
Stevens: Bibles in the Caxton Exhibition 1877
St. Louis City Art Museum: Chinese Ceramics
St. Mark in Mongolian
The St. Paul's Magazine April '73
Stieda: Geschichte des buchhandels in Riga
Stiles: Bundling (Origin & History of Bundling)
Stopes: a Journal from Japan
Storia della fondazione de Cinesi (3 voll.)
Steinmetz: Japan and her People (2nd edition)
Stray Notes on Kioto, 2nd ed. & its environs 1880
Studies in Modern Irish (Parts 3-4) (Part 2) (3 voll.) O'Nolan
Summers: Lecture on the Chinese Language & Literature
Sunoo: Korean Textbook (Vol. 1 only)
Szczesniak: Notes on the Penetration of the Copernican Theory into China (17th – 19th centuries)
" : the Penetration of Copernican Theory into Japan
Szinnyei: Ungarische sprachlehre
Stories of Benjamin David Benjamin & Messrs ed. Sassoon & Co
Smithsonian Miscel Collections, Vol. 97, No. 1 (Archeological Expedition to Northwestern Honduras, 1936 by Strong, Kidder & Paul, Jr.)
Steele: The Logomachy "The 43rd chapter of the Three Kingdom Novel San-go-chi" (2 vols)

Damaged 1
Badly " 1

43

Rondot: Vert de Chine
Rowse: On History - a study of present tendencies
Radloff: Uigurische Sprachdenkmaler
Reuter: Anlautsvokale im Tocharischen
Richthofen: Letters on Provinces of China
Ross: Polyglot List of Birds in Turki, Manchu & Chinese
Rety: La jolie papetiere
Ruwet: Religion des Lamas
Ross: Chinese Foreign Policy - 1877 ?
Rabelais, 3 voll. (English ed.) Gargantua and Pantagruel
Ruskaya letopis, 8 voll., 4to.
R.G.S: Alphabets of Foreign Languages transcribed into English / Gleichen & Reynolds
Ryley: Ralph Fitch, England's Pioneer to India
Radloff: Chuastuanit, 1909
Rochet: Proverbes mantchoux et mongols
Rudnev: Materialy po govoram vostočnoi mongolii
Rudnev: Xori-buryatskii govor 1913-14
Riggs: Armeno-Turkish Grammar 1856 Damaged 3
Richthofen's Letters 1870-72
Read: Prelude to Chemistry
Rosny: Feuilles de momidzi
Rahder: Japanologische Verkenningen
Ross: Corea, its History, Manners & Customs
Revon: De arte florali
Remusat: Recherches sur les Langues tartares 1820 Tome Ier
Reade: Registrum librorum eroticorum, 2 voll.
Remondino: Circumcision
Rosenberg: O mirosozercanii sobremennogo
Redin: Painyati G.B. de Rossi
Raquette: English-Turki Dictionary 1927
Rentskii: Lyndi bozi i skopcy, '72
Rotta: La filosofia del linguaggio nella patristica e nella Scolastica
Rahder: Glossary of the Dasabhumikasutra
Regnault: Medecine et pharmacie
Roth: Jewish contribution to Civilization
Russian Orientalia, 1 vol. so lettered 1899-1915
Reumuth: Logische Beschaffenheit der Kindlichen sprachanfange
Remusat: Sciences naturelles chez les peuples de l'Asie orientale
Rosny: L'epouse d' outre-tombe
Remusat: Doctrine Samaneenne
Ryerson Collection of Japanese Illustrated Books
~~Rabelais ed. Lefranc, 5 voll.~~
Remusat: Miroir des langues mandchoue et Mongole
Rose Innes's Dictionary of Chinese-Japanese Characters & Compounds
Relacoes entre Portugueses e japoneses
Ribeiro's Ceilao
Ramstedt: Abhandlungen zur Mongolischen Philologie
Royle: Fibrous Plants of India
Raffles: Report on Japan to the Secret Committee of the English East India Co
Radloff: Morpholojie der Turksprachen
Riasanovsky: Fundamental Principles of Mongol Law
Rockhill: Diplomatic Audiences & Intercourse with Korea
Ribeiro: Andam Faunos Pelos Bosques
Remusat: Melanges, 5 voll (consisting of 2 melanges & 2 nouveaux mel. & one Posthumous)
Raffles: Java, 2 voll.
Ribeiro: Filhas de Babilonia
see Ross: Dialogues in Eastern Turki
Remusat: Iu-Kiao-li, 4 voll. ou Les deux cousines
Rytschkow: Historie von Kasan
Rosny: Catalogue de la Biotheque jap. de Nordenskiold
Robinson: Genius of Hebrew Grammar
Ramstedt: Mongolica
Russian-Tartar Dictionary, 4to.

資料 10（貼付ノート・Ashbee: Library Catalogue）

S

✓Shaw: Catalogue of Specimens of Cloth, 1787

✓Major Shaw's Journals with a memoir by Quincey

✓Sheehan: The Idiom of Living Irish

✓Shepherd: Australia's Interests and Policies in the Far East

Mary Shelley: Frankenstein

✓Shenstone: Men & Manners

✗ ✓Shirokogoroff: Psychomental complex of the Tungus

✓Shirokogoroff: Ethnical Unit and Milieu

✓Shirokogoroff: La theorie de l'ethnos

✓Shinjikan Shioya

✓Shorter Oxford Dictionary (2 voll.)

Short History of Ireland in Irish

✓Secundus: Basia (Nonesuch Press) Stanley, Bros.

✓Sennep: Un systeme negre de classification ... linguistique

✓Senstius: Malay Language A Survey of Aids for the teaching of the

✓Staunion: Chinese Embassy to the Khan of the Tourgouth Tartars, 1821

✓Starrett: 221B, Studies in Sherlock Holmes

✓Stanton: The Triad Society

✓Stefansson: The Friendly Arctic

✓Stefansson: Arctic Manual

✓Stein: Explorations in Central Asia (Geog. Journal)

✓Stevens: Biblio. Essay on B. Franklin

✓Stevens: Bibles in the Caxton Exhibition 1877

✓St. Louis City Art Museum: Cat. of the Samuel C Davis Collection of Chinese Ceramics

St. Mark in Mongolian

The St. Paul's Magazine April '73

✓Stieda: Geschichte des buchhandels in Riga

✓Stiles: Bundling (Origin & History of Bundling)

✓Stopes: A Journal from Japan

✓Storia della fondazione de Cinesi (3 voll.)

✓Steinmetz: Japan and her People (2nd edition)

✓Stray Notes on Kioto, 2nd ed. & its environs – 1880

✓Studies in Modern Irish (Parts 3-4) (Part 2) (3 voll.) O'Nolan

✓Summers: Lecture on the Chinese Language & Literature

✓Sunoo: Korean Textbook (Vol. 1 only)

✓Szczesniak: Notes on the Penetration of the Copernican Theory into China (17th – 19th centuries)

✓ " : The Penetration of Copernican Theory into Japan

✓Szinnyei: Ungarische sprachlehre

✓Stories of Benjamin David Benjamin & Messrs E.D. Sassoon & Co

✓Smithsonian Miscel Collections, Vol. 97, No. 1 (Archeological Expedition to Northwestern Honduras, 1936 by Strong, Kidder & Paul, Jr.

✓Steele: The Logomachy "The 43rd chapter of the Three Kingdom Novel Sangokushi" (2 vols)

Damaged Badly 1 1

43

S

Sade: Idee sur les romans
Safford: the Chamorro language of Guam
Sandwell: The Canadian Peoples
Sansom: Historical Grammar of Japanese
Sansom: Japan
Sahagun: Ancient Mexico
Sakanishi: A Handful of Sand
Sakanishi: Songs of a Cowherd
Satomi: Altjapanischer Idealismus und seine Entwicklung
Saville: Reports on the Maya Indians of Yucatan (Indian Notes + Monographs Vol IX, #3)
Sayer: Pidgin English
Scarron: Le Virgile travesti
Schall: Chinesische Mission
Schmidt: Mongolian Grammar (French, 2 voll.)
Schmidt: Mongolische Grammatik
Schjoth: Chinese Currency
Sibiriacoff: Zur Frage von den Ausseren Verbindungen Sibiriens mit Europa
Sigler: Sycee Silver (Numismatic Notes + Monographs – No 99)
Sinbirskii sbornik (imperfect)
Skelton: the Completed Poems of John Skelton Henderson:
Skeat: Chaucer's Prologue
Smith: Japanese Goldfish – their Varieties & Cultivation
Smith: Profile by Gaslight – an irregular readers
Smith: William de Machlinia
Springfield Mill: 1807-1907 Riddle.
Swinhoe: Natural History of Hainan

42

資料 10（貼付ノート・Ashbee: Library Catalogue）

S

✓Shaw: Catalogue of Specimens of Cloth, 1787
✓Major Shaw's Journals with a memoir by Quincey
✓Sheehan: the Idiom of Living Irish
✓Shepherd: Australia's Interests and Policies in the Far East
Mary Shelley: Frankenstein
✓Shenstone: Men & Manners
✗ ✓Shirokogoroff: Psychomental complex of the Tungus
✓Shirokogoroff: Ethnical Unit and Milieu
✓Shirokogoroff: La theorie de l'ethnos
✓Shinjikan Shioya

Damaged 1
Badly " 1

✓Shorter Oxford Dictionary (2 voll.)
Short History of Ireland in Irish
✓Secundus: Basia (Nonesuch Press) Stanley Thos.
✓Sennep: Un systeme negre de classification
✓Senstius: Malay Language a Survey of Aids for the Teaching of the
✓Staunion: Chinese Embassy to the Khan of the Tourgouth Tartars, 1821
✓Starrett: 221B, Studies in Sherlock Holmes
✓Stanton: the Triad Society
✓Stefansson: The Friendly Arctic
✓Stefansson: Arctic Manual
✓Stein: Explorations in Central Asia (Geog. Journal)
✓Stevens: Biblio. Essay on B. Franklin
✓Stevens: Bibles in the Caxton Exhibition 1877
✓St. Louis City Art Museum: Cat. of the Samuel C Davis Collection of Chinese Ceramics
St. Mark in Mongolian
The St. Paul's Magazine April '73
✓Stieda: Geschichte des buchhandels in Riga
✓Stiles: Bundling (Origin & History of Bundling)
✓Stopes: A Journal from Japan
✓Storia della fondazione de Cinesi (3 voll.)
✓Steinmetz: Japan and her People (2nd edition)
✓Stray Notes on Kioto, & its environs 2nd ed. (1880)
✓Studies in Modern Irish (Parts 3-4) (Part 2) (3 voll.) O'Nolan
✓Summers: Lecture on the Chinese Language & Literature
✓Sunoo: Korean Textbook (Vol. 1 only)
✓Szczesniak: Notes on the Penetration of the Copernican Theory into China (17th, 19th centuries)
✓ " : the Penetration of Copernican Theory into Japan
✓Szinnyei: Ungarische sprachlehre
✓Stories of Benjamin David Benjamin & Messrs E.D. Sassoon & Co
✓Smithsonian Miscel Collections, Vol. 97, No. 1 (Archeological Expedition to Northwestern Honduras, 1936 by Strong, Kidder & Paul, Jr.
✓Steele: The Logomachy "The 43rd chapter of the Three Kingdom Novel San-go-[illegible] (2 vols)

43

S×

✓Specimen of Japanese Wastepaper & Imitations of Leather Patterns (2 vols)

✓Senaveratne: Chino-Sinhalese Relations in the Early & Middle Ages

✓Senaveratne: Some Notes on the Chinese References

✓Sicardo: Christianaad de Japon

- 21 -

✓Sonderabdruck aus "Ungarische Jahrbucher".

Schmidt: Izucerie Kitaya
Semenov: Zur Frage .....
✓Singh: History of Khokand
✓Staunton: Notices of China, 2nd ed.
✓Stopes: Plays of Old Japan The "No".
Semenov: Pamyatriki ariiskoi Kultunz
✓Skrine & Ross: Heart of Asia
✓Segenbringende Reisaehren, 3 voll. Langegg: (Midzuho-Gusa)
✓Szinnyei: Herkunft der Ungarn
Sristed: Life of Burton
✓Semenov: Contradictions dans les avis sur la metempsychose dans les oeuvres de Nasir-i-Khosrau et chez les Ismailiens de Pamir
✓Saddharmapandarikasutra, yellow silk, oblong
✓Schuchardt: Miscellanea linguistica
✓Stopes: Contraception
✓Sade: La Philosophie dans le Boudoir 1875
✓Shaw: Gr. Eastern Turki language 1 vol.
✓Sanchez: De Matrimonio, folio
✓Schiefner: Jukagirische Sprache (Melanges Asiatiques) (2 copies)
Semenov: La religion du Satan
Scerbatsky: Filosofskoe ucenie buddizma
✓Schuchardt: Deutsch gegen Franzosisch und Englisch
✓Scherk: Psychologie der Eunuchoiden
✓Schiefner: Thusch-Sprache
✓Schiefner: Tibetan Tales
✓Sermão de S. Antonio - 1940
Sulejman: Cagatai Worterbuch
✓Stopes: Preliminary Notes on Various Technical Aspects of the Control of Conception
✓Sanzyezin

Shin-sai Ikiki (Hsin Hsi Yu Ki) 2 vols.

(none)

44

資料 10（貼付ノート・Ashbee: Library Catalogue）

- 20 -

Schneider: Systematische Unweisungen (Martin Luther

✓Schott: Vocabularium Sinicum
✓Saussure: L'horometrie des Chinois (et le Systeme Cosmologique)
✓St. Aulaire: Chinese Running Hand writing (Groeneveldt)
✓Satow: Japanese Chronological Tables 1874
✓Sanceau: Indies Adventure
✓Semeonoff: Key to Russian Grammar
✓Schuchardt: Primitiae linguae vasconum 1923
✓Soper: Buddhist Architecture in Japan
X ✓Serindia, 5 voll. (Vol III damaged)
✓Siebold: Japan and the Comity of Nations
✓Suski: Conj. of Japanese Verbs
✓Schmidt: Forschungen Mongolen und Tibeter
✓Skold: Ungarische Endbetonung
✓Sun tzu: Principles of War — Badly Damaged!
✓Stanton: Chinese Drama
✓Siren: Walls and Gates of Peking
~~Schmidt: Mongolian Dictionary~~
✓Siebold: Mariner's Guide to Japan
✓Seebohm: Birds of Japanese Empire
✓Semeonoff: A new Russian Grammar
✓Stevens: East India Co. The Court Records of the 1599-1603
✓Spizelius: De re litteraria Sinensium Commentarius
✓Straelen: New Diplomacy in Far East
✓Standish: Three Bamboos
✓Sedillot: Hist. des sciences mathematiques, 2 voll.
✓Summers: Vampire — His Kith & Kin
✓Smith ; China (A narrative of an exploratory visit to each of the Consular Cities of China) 1844-46
✓Sbornik Dogovorov Rossiis Kitaen 1689-1881
✓Siebold: Bibliotheca japonica, Lib. IV (Lui Ho) 1838
✓Siebold: Thesaurus, ~~the~~ Literarum Ideographicarum
Staat van alle Volkeren, I
✓Stein: Memoir on the Ancient Geography of Kashmir
✓Simon: Bibliotheca Bacchica, vol. I
✓Shitaijii
✓Sainson: Memoires sur l'Annam
✓Schurhammer: Disputationen des P. Cosme de Torres S.J. mit den Buddhisten in Yamaguchi im Jahre 1551
✓Stone: Story of Phallicism, 2 voll.
✓Smith: Visit to China 1857
Semenov: Annan (Pamphl.)
✓Sauval: Chronique scandaleuse
✓Sbornik Trudov Orxonskoi exped. I-V in 2 voll.
✓Semenov: Materialy dlya izucheniya ... tadzikov Central'noi Azii ... 1900-1901 nareciya Gornyx
✓Sternberg: Gilyak, 4to.
✓Six Early Printed Maps (Brit. Museum)
Stem-Szanacatalogue
✓Stadelmann: Laotse und die Biologie
✓Studer: Anglo-N. Lapidaries
✓Smith: Japan (Ten Weeks in Japan) 1861.
✓Saussure: La serie septenaire, Cosmologique et Planetaire
✓Schmidt: Mongolisch-Deutsch-Russisches Worterbuch
✓2 Sbornik Trudov Orxonskoi Ekspedicii I

45

Second: Le Livre des Baisers
Schefer: Histoire de l'Asie centrale, texte persan
Semenov: ~~Tadjik~~ GrammaTIKA Tadzikskogo YAZYKA, 1927
Saussure: Origines de l'astronomie chinoise
Sinica Franciscana, I
Schleicher: Zur vergleichenden Sprachengeschichte - 1848
Sansom: Living in Tokyo
Schmidt: Kamasutram
Scarborough: Chinese Proverbs
Soubeiran: Matiere medicale chez les Chinois
Satow: English-Japanese Dictionary of the Spoken Language
Sade: Les 120 journees de Sodome ou l'ecole du Libertinage par le Marquis de Sade
Stein: Archaeological Work N-W. Frontier Province, 1905
Shuck: Portfolio Chinensis or A Collection of Authentic Chinese State Papers
Shchukin: Poezdka v Yakutske, '44
Smith & Mikami: History of Japanese Mathematics
Sade: Dialogue entre un pretre et un moribond
Stejneger: Birds of Kuril Islands
Satow: Jesuit Mission ~~Pass~~ Press in Japan
Schmidt: Geschichte der Ostmongolen
Sahlin: Cesar Chesneau deu Marsais
Symonds: Wine Women and Song (Medieval Latin Students' Songs)
Seikakokushojitenondo
Schmidt: Eine mongolische Quadratinschrift aus der Regierungszeit der mongolischen Dynastie Juan in China.
Saussure: Systeme cosmologique sino-iranien.
Schmidt: Bogda gesser Khan, Übersetzung
Sleeman: Ramaseeana (Papers on Thuggee)
Selections from Nippon Seishin Library
Schmidt: Epic of Bogda Gesser Khan, Mongol text
Schleicher: Die Darwinsche Theorie u.d. Sprachwissenschaft
Shcherbatskoi: Pamyatniki Indiiskoi filosofii, I
Schiefner: Betrage zur Kenntniss der tungusischen mundarten
Stekel: Fetischismus
Segalen: Steles (Collection Coreenne) "Kokinhiroku"
Sir J. Suckling's Works, 3rd ed.
Schmidt: Die Sprachfamilien der Erde, Atlas 1926
Staunton: Miscellaneous Notices rel. to China, '22
Stcherbatsky: Buddhist Nirvana Conception of
Stael-Holstein: Kacyapaparivarta
Schmidt: Sprachfamilien der Erde, text und Sprachenkreise
Saussure: Origine Babylonienne de l'astronomie chinoise
Strallen: A missionary in the Market

(none)

46

資料 10（貼付ノート・Ashbee: Library Catalogue）

✓Takekoshi: Economic Aspects of Japan (3 voll.)
✓Tamagna: Italy's Interests and Policies in the Far East
✓Tartar-Russian Vocabulary, Kazan'76 (1876)
✓Taylor: Catalog of Books on China in the Essex Institute
✓Taylor: A Visit to India, China and Japan
Teillo: Relation (French edition)
✓Telepnef: Paracelsus

✓Thomas &Konow: Two Medieval Documents from Tun-Huang
✓Thompson: Guam and its People
✓Thompson: People of the Serpent
✓Thompson et al: How the Jap Army Fights (2 copies)
✓Thompson: Civilization of the Mayas (Field M. of Nat Hist. Anthropology Leaflet 25)
✓Thompson: A Blue and White Nankin Porcelain, a Catalogue of
✓Thompson: Materials of Medieaval Painting
✓Thorne: St. George & the Octopus
✓Thornton: Chronology of Librarianship
Three Tales by Pushkin
✓Thunberg: Voyages (2 voll. quarto) de C. P. Thunberg au Japon
Tracey Woodward Collection of Japan (Sale Catalogue)
X ✓ Transactions of the Oriental Ceramics Scoeity Vol. 19
Trigault: De Christiana Expeditione apud Sinas (Paris edit.)
✓Tronson: Voyage of the Barracuta to Japan, Kamtschatka, Siberia, China, etc
✓Tomes: The Americans in Japan - 1860
Toren: Voyages

✓Tourist Library, 13: Kimono - Japanese Dress
✓Timperley: Some Contrasts between China and Japan in the Light of History (China Society)
✓Tir na Deo, Irish fairy tales
✓Titsingh: Illustrations of Japan
✓Tschepe: Der T'ai-Schan
✓Tschichold: Chinesische farbendrucke der gegenwart
✓ " Neue chinesische farbendrucke aus der zehnbambushalle
✓Tschichold: Geschichte der schrift in bildern
✓Turrettini: San-ze-king, Texte avec les versions - 1876
✓Tursellini: Vita Fr. Xavierii (Zannetti edition)
✓Tsen: Histoire de la poesie Chinoise
✓Tsuchii: Kirishitan Gogaku no Kenkyu

Badly Damaged !

47

Tatar Grammar, '01
✓Tarrent: Hongkong, Part I, 1861
✓Ten Years of Japanese Burrowing
Talko-Hryncewicz: Etnologii Azyi srodkowej, '10
Tebenkov: Drevneishiya Snosheniya Rusi
✓Tourist Library # 21 ~~...~~ Japanese Buddhism
✓Thomsen: Inscriptions de l'Orkhon, with portr., etc.
✓Tolnai: Ungarisches Lesebuch mit Glossar
✓Tavares: Epitome de gramatica portuguesa
✓The ~~..~~ Bulls
✓Tezkereh-i-Evlia, 2 voll., folio
✓Tsurayuki: Log of a Japanese Journey (Harris translator)
✓Tanizaki: Puis que je l'aime
✓Three Turki MSS from Kashgar
✓Trigault: Rei Christ apud Japonios
✓Trans. Oriental Ceramic Soc., 17 voll. (18 not yet purchased)
Turselin: La Vie de F. Xavier, 1612
✓Tolkowsky: Hesperides
Tikov: Gr. de la langue darkwa
✓Tchoubinof: ~~Georgien Dict., 4to.~~ Dictionnaire Georgian-Russe-Francais
Trudy Muzeya Paleogr. I. & III, 2 voll.
✓Thoms: Chinese Courtship
✓Taraporewala: Contamination in Language
✓Thompson: Diary of Richard Cocks, 2 vols

22

✓Test on Far East & Pacific Area (2 copies)
Tucci: Apologie du taoisme
✓Thomsen: Samlede Afhandlinger, 3 voll.
✓Ta-ssi-yang-kuo I, 1
✓Tonkoisho, folio, chitsu (+ a copy in 8vo)
✓Thomsen: Turcica
✓Trudy Bibliogr. Kom. Byvs, pri SNKTSSR 1-3
✓Trudy Troick 10-15
✓Trudy Troick 4-9
✓Trudy Troickosavsko-kyaxtinskago otd. I-II, III 2-3
✓Transliteration of ~~Russian~~ Slavonic (Brit. Acad.)
✓Trudy Troick .... III, 1
✓Taschenbuch fur Buchersammler, 3 voll.
Turkemistan, 1928
~~.........~~
See SX Ten Thousand Cases Birth Control
✓Thomas: Affectionate Pair
✓Travels of Sebastien Manrique 1629-1643, 2 vols

Toda: The Ryerson Collection of Japanese & Chinese Illustrated Books

(none)

48

資料 10（貼付ノート・Ashbee: Library Catalogue）

Ulrich:& Kup: Books and Printing: Selected List of Periodicals 1800-1942

Updike: Printing Types (2 voll.), Their History forms & Use

Unger: Hamanns Sprachtheorie
Utilite de la flagellation, '01
Um auto de Gil-Vicente (school text) Garrett:
Ueda's Dict , 5 voll. Ueda & Matsui: Dai-Nippon Kokugo Jiten
Une Famille Tongouse
Useful Plants of Japan
Uspenskii: Oceski z ist. Trapezunsk. imperii
Uzatel' k Aktam ..., 1838
Uhlenbeck: Over een mogelijke Verwantschap van het Baskisch met de Palaeo-Kaukasische Talen
Verbal Discussions during Peace Negotiations, Tientsin 1895
Venezianischer Dirnenspiegel
Verbickii: Altaiskie inorodcy
Vuilleumier: Symbolism of Chinese Imp. Ritual Robes
Van Straelen: A Missionary in the War-net
Varthema's Itinerary (ditto)
Volpicelli: Chinese Phonology 1896
Vignali: Cazzaria
Vladimircov: Obrazcy Mongolskoi narodnoi slovesnosti
Vamberry: Pinto
Verhandelingen van het genootschap van Batavie, 18th part.
Vostocnye zapiski, I, 1927, 8vo.
Vienna Ac. Verzeichnis, 2 voll.
Vimalapracnottararatnamala versio tibetica, folio
Vostocnyya Zametki, 1895, folio
Vitale: Pekinese Rhymes
Vareni Regni Japoniae et Siam
Venn: Life of Xavier 1862 (The Missionary Life & Labours of Francis Xavier)
Voyages Towards N.W. (Hakluyt Soc.)
Vegetation of Mt. Fuji Hayata:
Vostocnye zapiski, I, 8vo.
Voyage of John Saris to Japan (Hakluyt)
Vindel's Biblioteca Oriental, 2 voll.
Valentyn: Oud en Nieuw Oost-Indien, 5 voll.
Voyages of M. Frobisher (Argonaut)
Vitale: Grammaire Mongole-Dialecte des Khalkhas
Voyage du Levant, 2 vols

Voiage and Travaile of Syr John Maundeville

- 23 -

Voigt: Hortus Suburbanus Calcuttensis (Cat. of the Plants which have been cultivated in the Hon. East India Co's Botanical Garden, Calcutta)
Vamberry: Story of My Struggles
Vida de S. Francisco de Xavier, 4 voll.
Vamberry: Cagataische Sprachstudien 1867
Vatin: Minuskii Krai
Valenziani: Kan-kan-yau-rai
Vamberry: Uigurische Sprachmonumente
Viana: Afonso de Albuquerque
Vogeler: Die Freiheit der Liebe in der Kommunistischen Gesellschaft
Von Zach: Erganzungen
Vladimircov: Buddizm v Tibete
Vsemirnaya Literatura, 2 voll, 8vo
Visite aux temples de Pekin
Voprosy reseniya. 1918
Version turque der Bakhtiar Nameh
Vladimircov: Obrazcy mongol'skoi narodnoi slovesnosti, 1926
Verzeichnis der von der Kaiserlichen Akademie der Wissenschaften in Wien
Vareni Descripto Regni Japoniae E.. Regni chinen Descripto ... 1649

Tatar Grammar, '01
✓Tarrant: Hongkong, Part I, 1861
✓Ten Years of Japanese Burrowing
Talko-Hryncewicz: Etnologii Azyi srodkowej, '10
Tebenkov: Drevneishiya Snosheniya Rusi
✓Tourist Library # 21 Japanese Buddhism
✓Thomsen: Inscriptions de l'Orkhon, with portr., etc.
✓Tolnai: Ungarisches Lesebuch mit Glossar
✓Tavares: Epitome de gramatica portuguesa
✓The Bulls
✓Tezkereh-i-Evlia, 2 voll., folio
✓Tsurayuki: Log of a Japanese Journey (Harris translator)
✓Tanizaki: Puis que je l'aime
✓Three Turki MSS from Kashgar
✓Trigault: Rei Christ apud Japonios
✓Trans. Oriental Ceramic Soc., 17 voll. (18 not yet purchased)
Turselin: La Vie de F. Xavier, 1612
✓Tolkowsky: Hesperides
Tikov: Gr. de la langue darkwa
✓Tchoubinof: ~~Georgian Dict., 4to.~~ Dictionnaire Georgian-Russe-Français
Trudy Muzeya Paleogr. I. & III, 2 voll.
✓Thoms: Chinese Courtship
✓Taraporewala: Contamination in Language
✓Thompson: Diary of Richard Cocks, 2 vols

22

✓Ttext on Far East & Pacific Area (2 copies)
✓Tucci: Apologie du taoisme
✓Thomsen: Samlede Afhandlinger, 3 voll.
✓Ta-ssi-yang-kuo I, 1
✓Tonkoisho, folio, chitsu (+ a copy in 8vo)
✓Thomsen: Turcica
✓Trudy Bibliogr. Kom. Byvs.pri SNKTSSR 1-3
✓Trudy Troick 10-15
✓Trudy Troick 4-9
✓Trudy Troickosavsko-kyaxtinskago otd. I-II, III 2-3
✓Transliteration of ~~Russia~~ Slavonic (Brit. Acad.)
✓Trudy Troick .... III, 1
✓Taschenbuch fur Buchersammler, 3 voll.
Turkemistan, 1928
~~Tonkoisho, folio~~.
see Sx ✓Ten Thousand Cases Birth Control
✓Thomas: Affectionate Pair.
✓Travels of Sebastien Manrique 1629-1643, 2 vols
Toda: The Ryerson Collection of Japanese & Chinese Illustrated Books
(none)

43

Damaged 2
Badly 1

✓Vaillant: Aztecs of Mexico
Valette: Dutch Grammar (2 voll.)
✓Van Buren: Labour in Japan 1881
✓Vandenbosch: Dutch East Indies
✓Van der Meulen: Poolsch herbata

✓Van Gulik: The Ch'an Master Tung-Kao 1944
✓van Mook: The Netherlands Indies and Japan - Battle on Paper 1940-41
✓Vassalli: Grammatica della Lingua Maltese
✓Vendryes: Language, a Linguistic Introduction to History
✓Verlaine: Sagesse
✓Victoria and Albert Museum: Chinese Porcelain Periods of Kang Hsi Yung Cheng & Chien Lung
✓Villon: Oeuvres, ed. Foulet
✓Voyage to Olof Toree

Voiage and Travaile of Syr John Maundeville - 1932

- 23 -

Voigt: Hortus Suburbanus Calcuttensis (Cat. of the Plants which have been cultivated in the Hon. East India Co's Botanical Garden, Calcutta)
✓Vamberry: Story of My Struggles
Vida de S. Francisco de Xavier, 4 voll.
✓Vamberry: Cagataische Sprach Studien 1867
Vatin: Minuskii Krai
✓Valenziani: Kan-ka-mau-rai
✓Vamberry: Uigurische Sprachmonumente
✓Viana: Afonso de Albuquerque
✓Vogeler: Die Freiheit der Liebe in der Kommunistischen Gesellschaft
Von Zach: Erganzungen
Vladimircov: Buddizm v Tibete
✓Vsemirnaya Literatura, 2 voll, 8vo
✓Visite aux temples de Pekin
✓Voprosy i reseniya. 1918
Version turque der Bakhtiar Nameh
✓Vladimircov: Obrazcy mongol'skoi narodnoi slovesnosti, 1926 49
Verzeichnis der von der Kaiserlichen Akademie der Wissenschaften in Wien
Vareni Descripto Regni Japoniae E... Regni chinen Descripto ... 1649

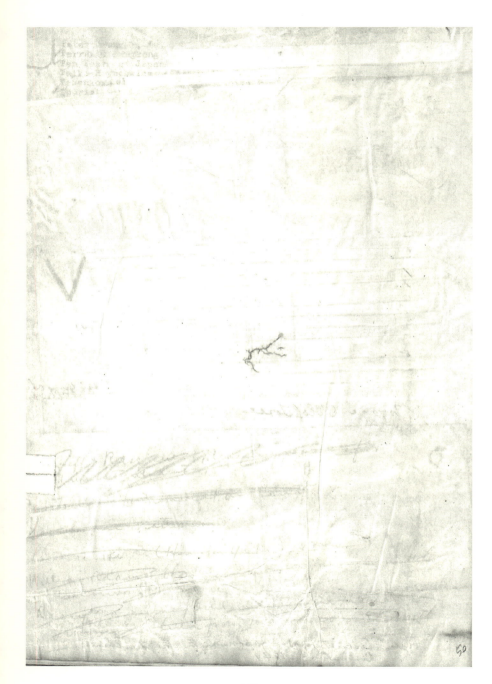

資料 10（貼付ノート・Ashbee: Library Catalogue）

W

Waddell: Mediaeval Latin Lyrics
Waddell: Peter Abelard
Waddell: The Uttermost Isles
Wagner: Kaiserreich China
Wakefield: The Traveller in Asia - 1817
Walters Collection: Oriental 1884
Ward: the Origin of Cosmetic Dentistry
Warriner: Cruise of the U.S. frigate Potomac
Watkins: Anthology of American Negro Literature
Watt: The Commercial Products of India (1 voll.)
Watters: Essays on the Chinese Language 1889
Wayman: E.S. Morse
Weingreen: A Practical Grammar of Classical Hebrew
van Wely: English Dictionary (Dutch-English part)
Whatman: Specimen book
Whiteway: The Rise of Portuguese Power in India 1497-1550
Whitney: Colloquial Hungarian
Wilkins: Mathematical and Philosophical Works (2 voll.) of the Rt. Rev. John Wilkins
Williams: Chinese Observations of Comets
Williams: Tibet and her Neighbours
Williams: A Key into the Language of America
Willis: Bibliophily or Booklove
Wilmot: Collected Works of John Wilmot Earl of Rochester Hayward: Nonesuch Press
Wilson: an A/c of the Pelew Islands Keate: 1783
Wilson: The Miraculous Birth of Language
Winterich: Early American Books and Printing
Writings of A.K. Coomaraswamy
Wroth: History of Printing in colonial Maryland - 1922
Whittaker: Bach's Contatas
Wu: Prehistoric Pottery in China
Wyndam-Quin: Notes on History of Adare
The Works of Robert Burns (8 voll.)

Damaged 3

51

Wessels: Early Jesuit Travellers in Central Asia 1603-1721
Winkler: La langue basque et les langues ouralo-altaiques - 1917
Williamson: Book of Famille Rose
Works of Tourneur (Fanfrolico) Nicoll:
Weston: Playground of Far East
Webster: Kan Ying Pien, Shanghai 1918
Waley: Monkey
Whitaker: Eastern Turki 1904
Williams: Ilocano Grammatik der
Wahnelt: Kindersprache u. Altersmundarten
Wylie: Une Inscription Mongole (J.A.)
White: Chinese Jews, 3 voll.
Woolf: 3 Tibetan Mystery Plays
Winiwarter: Kiyonaga et Choki
Wiedemann: Gr. der wotjakischen sprache
Wenstrom: Swedish-English Dict.
Wright and Sinclair: History of Later Latin Literature
Wickersham: ~~Alaskan~~ Bibliography of Alaskan Literature 1724-1924
Weil: Tatarische Texte
Wells: Perspective in Chinese Painting
Wylie: Ethnography of the Han
Wylie: Publications of Protestant Missionaries
Weig: Chinesische Familiennamen
What is an Index?
Wenkstern: Bibliography of Japan, 2 voll.
Warner: Japanese Sculpture of Suiko Period
Watchdog: Japanese and the Pacific Problems
William Adams (brochure)
Wang: Chinesische klassische Oper. und Kultur-Geschichte
Wiener Beitrage zur Kunst Asiens, 2 voll.
Wingfield: Curse of Koshiu
Wylie: Nestorian Tablet of Segan Foo
Wright: Existing legal situation as it relates to conflict in Far East
Williams: Relations with Chinese Empire - 1877
Wilhelm & Gundert: Chinesische Literatur, Japanische Literatur
Wang: Histoire anecdotique chinoise - [illegible]
Wm. Adams, the Pilot-major of Gillingham who Discovered Japan

Warren: An Index to "A Guide to the Study of Book Plates"
Warren: Study of Book-plates, 2 voll.

Waley: The Poet Li Po

(none)

52

資料 10（貼付ノート・Ashbee: Library Catalogue）

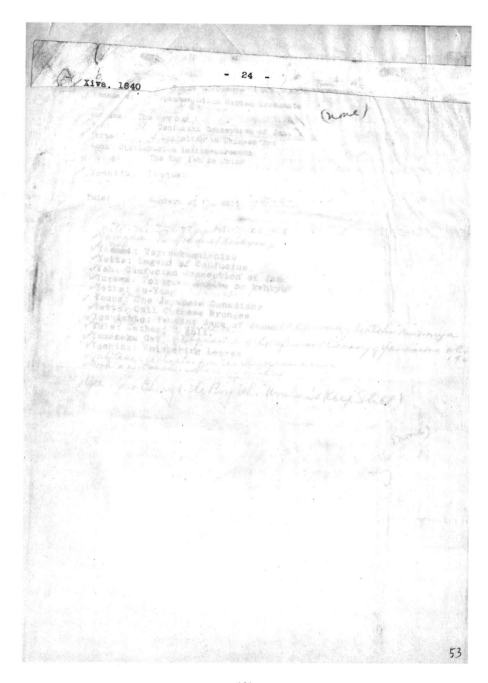

\- 24 -

Xiva. 1840

(none)

Yule: [illegible]

Yetts: Legend of Confucius
Yah: Confucian Conception of [illegible]
Yetts: [illegible]
Young: The Japanese Canadians
Yetts: Cull Chinese Bronzes
Yule: Cathay [illegible]
Yoshida: Whispering Leaves

53

Works of Tourneux (Pan-folios) N. [illegible]
Weston: Playground of Far East
Watsta[illegible]: Ken [illegible] Press, Shanghai 1918
Waley: Monkey
Whitaker: Eastern Pathways
Williams: Tibetan [illegible]
Wenzel: Kindersprache u. Altersmundarten
Wylie: Une Inscription Mongole (J.A.)
White: Chinese Jews, 3 voll.
Woolf: 3 Tibetan Mystery Plays
Wilkinson: Playmate at Choki
Wiedemann: Gr. der [illegible] Sprache
[illegible]
Wright and Sinclair: History of Later Latin Literature
Winterschmm: Bibliography [illegible]
Weber: Tatarische Texte [illegible]
Wylie: Perspective in Chinese Painting
Wylie: Ethnography of the Han
Wylie: Publications of Protestant Missionaries
Wolff: Chinesische Familiennamen
What is an Index?
Wenckstern: Bibliography of Japan, 2 voll.
Warner: Japanese Sculpture of Suiko Period
Watchdog: Japanese and the Pacific Problems
William Adams (brochure).
Wang: Chinesische Oper.
Wiener Beiträge zur Kunst Asiens, 2 voll.
Wingfield: Curse of Koshiu
Wylie: Nestorian Tablet
Wright: Existing legal situation as it relates to conflict in Far East
Williams: Relations with Chinese Empire
Wilhelm & Gundert: Chinesische Literatur
Wang: Histoire anecdotique chinoise

Warner: Study of Book-plates, 2 voll.

54

資料 10（貼付ノート・Ashbee: Library Catalogue）

Yamada: Nihonkogohokogi
Yamada: Nihonbunpokogi
Yamada: Nihonbunporon
Yamanaka: Catalogue of Otsuye (see Japanese Caricatures)
Yamanaka: Japanese Stone Garden Ornaments
Yashima: The New Sun
Yeh: The Confucian Conception of Jen
Yetts: Symbolism in Chinese Art
Youn: Dictionarium latino-coreanum
Young: The English in China
Yoshida: Lacquer

Yule: Wonders of the East

Yule: Memoir of Capt. W. Gill, R.E.
Yamada: Kenpohono/Kenkyu
Yanai: Toyodokushichizu
Yetts: Legend of Confucius
Yeh: Confucian Conception of Jen
Yuzawa: Tokugawa Gogaku no kenkyu
Yetts: An-Yang: a Retrospect
Young: The Japanese Canadians
Yetts: Cull Chinese Bronzes
Yoshimoto: Peasant Sage of Japan (The Life + Work of Sontoku Ninomiya
Yule: Cathay, & the Way Thither 4 Voll.
Yamanaka Cat. (Liquidation of the Reference Library of Yamanaka & Co. Inc. 1944)
Yoshida: Whispering Leaves
Yoshitake: A chapter from the Uiger-un Lalai
Yoshida: Amakusaban Kinkushu
Yee: Lo Cheng (The Boy Who Wouldn't Keep Still)

(none)

55

Z

✓ Zaehnsdorf: Short History of Book Binding

Zamcarano: Mongolian Mss. of the Seventeenth Century

✓ Zottoli, 4 voll.

✓ Zottoli: Cursus litteraturae sinicae (Vol.5 only)

✓ Zimmermann: Altchinesische porzellane im alten serai

Zt. Fur Vergl. Rechtsw., Vol. 43, Nos. 1-2

✓ Zurla: Marco Polo, Vol. I.

✓ Zweig: The Buried Candelabrum

✓ Zeitschrift fur vergleichende Rechtswissenschaft, XLIII Band, Heft 1 u 2.

✓ Zi: Practique des examens litteraires en Chine

✓ Zamcarano: Buryat Proizvedeniya Naradnoi Slovestnosti, 1913-8

✓ Zorell: Georgische Bibelubersetzung

✓ Zenker: Chinesische Philosophie

Zilal i Ilkan

✓ Zwick: Handb. der westmongolischen sprache

✓ Zwick: Westmongolische grammatik

Zlatokuznecy Dagestana

✓ Zapiski of Astraxani, '84

✓ Zapiski o sibiri, 1837

✓ Zach: Einige Ergänzungen zu Sacharow's Mandzursko-Russki Slowarj. 1911

✓ de Zacharko: La syntax Kirghize de P. M. Melioranski

Damaged 2

56

資料 10（貼付ノート・Ashbee: Library Catalogue）

Damaged Mark ✓ /
Badly " " ✓ ×

Damaged books = 36
Badly " " = 24
Total 60

In making your claim I would suggest that you include a margin of say 5 "damaged" & 10 "badly damaged" for the Russian, Sanskrit & Mongolian etc Books which have not been checked off.

57

D
2
1
1
2
1
1
1
2
1
1
3
1
1
2
1
1
1
1
1
3
1
2
3
2
36
BD
1
1
1
2
2
3
1
1
1
2
1
1
1
1
1
1
1
1
1
24
58

**資料 10**（貼付ノート・Ashbee: Library Catalogue）

Catalogues & Book Lists

Harvard Un. Press

1. Aids to the Study of Jap. & Chinese
2. Fall 1944 (2 copies)
3. The Loeb Classical Library
4. Complete Cat. For 1944

Orientalia Inc.

No. 126 – 1943-44
" 127 – 1944-45 | 2 copies

Francis Edwards.

1. Cat. 671
2. " 673
3. " 675
4. " 676 (2 copies)
5. " 677
6. " 678

Luzac & Co

1. Cat. of the Library of the Late A. G. Ellis, M.A. (Part III)
2. Vols LVI – #1, 2, 3, 4.
3. Luzac's Oriental List & Book Review Quarterly. Vols. LVI – Jan-Dec 1945; LV – Jan-Dec. 1944.

59

Americana

1. Americana & Voyages.
2. Americana Cat. No. CLXX
3. Americana Nos 166, 171, 172
4. Americana Advertiser

Grafton & Co

Nos. 245, 246, 247, 249, 250, 253, 254, 256.

Maggs Bros. Ltd

Cat 739 (Vol. 2 Part VII)
Cat #746 (Vol 2 Part IX)

Franz C. Feger

Hispanic American Hist, Travels, Descriptions (2 copies)

Bernard Quaritch Ltd

Nos 621, 622, 623 & 624 (1944)

60

"Education for Responsible Living"
More Bargains in Better Books
J.D. & Jane Perkins

1 Chinese, Jap., Korean & Russian Lang Texts
2 Special List of Books on the Far East
3 List #20 - Jap. Grs. Textbooks & Dictionaries
4 List #21 - Tourist Library
5 List #34 - Books on Oriental Religion, Religious Art & Philosophy
6 List #36 - Economics & Business
7 List #37 - Chinese Grs. Textbooks & Dictionaries
8 List #38 - History & Law of the Orient
9 List 39 - Miscll. Oriental Texts
10 List #42 - Oriental Art
11 List #43 - Books on Gardens, Flowers & Flower Arrangement
12 List #44 - Oriental Lang. List
13 " #46 - Oriental Lit & Translations into English

61

資料 10（貼付ノート・Ashbee: Library Catalogue）

List #47 – Oriental Customs & Manners
" #48 – Miscel. List of Oriental Lang. Texts
" #49 – Theatre Music & Dance
#50 – Oriental Periodicals
#51 – Books on the Far East
#52 – Pacific Area Lib Duplicates
#53 – Woodblock Prints

62

Davis & Orioli

Cat. Nos 118, 119, 120, 121, 122 & 123.

Oxford Univ. Press

1. Books for Fall 1944
2. New Books - May 1944
3. General Cat. 1943

Ifan Kyrle Fletcher

Cat 78 (1945)
Cat 61 (1944)

1. Swiss Books thru 5 Centuries
2. Books of Switzerland
3. Robinson Ltd:

Rare Books & M.S.S Cat #78

Sotheby & Co:

Cat. of Valuable Printed Books 1945

Myers & Co Ltd

Cat. of Scarce & Interesting Old & Modern Books

63

資料 10（貼付ノート・Ashbee: Library Catalogue）

Harry A Levinson

Choice Books & MSS., Cat #19 (1944)

Philip C Duschnes

Books – Cat #67

Rosenthal Ltd

"Rare Books" – Cat # VI

British Museum

Catalogues, Guide Books + Other Publications (Oct 1945–)

~~Royal Inst.~~ of Inter Affairs

Check List

Modern Library

Loeb Classical Library

64

1.

Binyon: Spirit of Man in Asian Art
Major Shaw: Journals
Housman: Name and Nature of Poetry
Gow: A.E. Housman
Allen: Japan and the Expedition thereto of the U.S.
Copinger: The Elzevier Press
Butler: Hudibras
Duff: Early Printed Books
Elton: The Great Book Collectors
Regamey: Japan in Art and Industry
Oxford Book of Ballads
Tschepe: Der T'ai-Schan
Henke: Philosphy of Wang Yang Ming
van Mook: Netherlands Indies and Japan
Normano and Gerbi: Japanese in South America
Ball: Cultivation and Manufacture of Tea in China
Christian: Modern Burma
Li: Formation of the Chinese People
Cordier: Conflit entre la France & la Chine
Chesterton: Collected Poems
Taylor: Catalog of Books on China in the Essex Institute
Lewis: Ronsard
Hunter: Papermaking
Norris: History of Cataloguing
Cowley: Bibliographical Description and Cataloguing
Mencken: The American Language
Cox: The Poems of Sappho
Museum of Fine Arts, Boston: Catalogue of a special loan exhibition of Art Treasures from Japan
Jenkins: The Jesuits in China
Robinson collection: Oriental Numismatics
Historical and Statistical Abstract of the Colony of Hongkong
Fanning: Voyages
Whiteway: The Rise of Portuguese Power in India 1497-1550
Final Report Japanese Evacuation from the West Coast 1942
Lantzeff: Siberia in the Seventeenth Century
Morrell: Voyages and Discoveries
Rockhill: William of Rubruck
Beazley: Carpini and Rubruquis
Ellis: Sonnets & Folk Songs
Bickerstaffe: Araki the Daimio
MacDonald: Chronologie and Calendars
Peddie: Place Names in Imprints
Young: The English in China
Anderson: Japanese Wood Engravings
Belloc: Avril
Gill: An Essay on Typography

65

2.

Moule: Nestorians in China
Bushnell: The World's Earliest Libraries
Dennett: Americans in Eastern Asia
Wilkins: Mathematical and Philosophical Works (2 voll.)
Holtom: Modern Japan and Shinto Nationalism
McMurtrie: The Book
Wu: Prehistoric Pottery in China
Harington: The Metamorphosis of Aiax
Catalogue des Russica (2 voll.)
Garcia ab Horto: Historia Aromatum
Gay: Raretes Bibliographiques
Sakanishi: Songs of a Cowherd
Lisboa: A China e os Chins
Fanciullo a Scola
Schall: Chinesische Mission
Dulaurier: Les Mongols d'apres les Historiens Armeniens
Onraet: Sixty Below
O'Halloran: Glamour of Limerick
Garzoni: Grammatica della Lingua Kurda
Taylor: Visit to India, China and Japan
Zt. Fur Vergl. Rechtsw., Vol. 43, Nos. 1-2
Watters: Essays on the Chinese Language
De Guignes: Voyages a Peking (3 voll. text, 1 vol. atlas)
Ryan: Jesuits under fire in the seige of Hongkong
Thornton: Chronology of Librarianship
Jones: The Pastourelle
Ides: Three Years' Travels from Moscow to China
Thunberg: Voyages (2 voll. quarto)
Carpenter: Emerson and Asia
Waddell: Peter Abelard
Ross: Both Ends of the Candle
Stefansson: Arctic Manual
Osborn: A Cruise in Japanese Waters
Skelton: Completed Poems
Ellis: Kanga Creek
The Muses Gardin for Delights
Kizer: U.S.-Canadian Northwest
Curtis: History of Ireland
Jespersen: Rask
Ferreira: Portuguese-English Dictionary
Bates: Intertraffic
Gaelic Self-taught
Carus: The Canon of Reason and Virtue
Giles: Freemasonry in China
Hinder: Life and Labour in Shanghai
Thompson: People of the Serpent
Day: Songs of D'urfey

66

Stanton: Triad Society
Monkhouse: Chinese Porcelain
Winterich: Early American Books and Printing
Reynolds: Voyage of the New Hazard
Goudy: Typologia
Zamcarano: Mongolian Mss. of the Seventeenth Century
Thompson: Blue and White Nankin Porcelain
Hummel: Eminent Chinese of Ch'ing Period (2 voll.)
Erdberg: Chinese Influence on European Garden Structures
Naito: Wall-paintings of Horyuji (2 voll.)
Morison: Eustachio Celebrino da Udene
Anderson: Japanese Wood Engravings (8vo.)
Radlov: Older Turkish Studies
Wilmot: Works, Nonesuch Press
Langles: Des Livres tatars de la Bibl. Nat.
Williams: Chinese Observations of Comets
Kelemen: Medieval American Art (2 voll.)
Getty: Chinese Seals
Sade: Idee sur les romans
Morse: East India Company trading to China (5 voll.)
Updike: Printing Types (2 voll.)
Biot: Villes de la Chine
Fortune: Tea-districts of China
Haas: Geschichte des christentums in Japan (2 voll.)
Morley: Study of Maya Hieroglyphs
Stopes: Journal from Japan
Knapp: George Borrow (2 voll.)
Hubbard: British Fareastern Policy
Philobiblon, Inglis edition
Tsen: Histoire de la poesie Chinoise
Catalogue of the Caxton Exhibition
Clark: Indian Sign Language
Grajdanzef: Modern Korea
March: Chinese Shadow-figure Plays
Robertson: Bibliography of the Philippine Islands
Vaillant: Aztecs of Mexico
O'Nolan: New Era Grammar of Modern Irish
Ratchford: Letters of Thomas J. Wise to John Henry Wrenn
Hart: The West Chamber
Hustvedt: Ballad Books and Ballad Men
Whitney: Colloquial Hungarian
Gorer: The Revolutionary Ideas of the Marquis de Sade
Staunton: Chinese Embassy to the Khan of the Tourgouth Tartars
Diary of a Journey overland through the Maritime Provinces of China, from Manchao to Canton
Bazin: Academie Imperiale de Peking
Catalogue of Chinese Books in the Asiatic Department, St. Petersburg

67

資料 10（貼付ノート・Ashbee: Library Catalogue）

6.

Yule: Wonders of the East
Hakluyt Society: Tartar Conquerors of China
The Maya Society and its Work
Moidrey: Confesseurs de la foi en Chine
Tronson: Voyage of the Barracuta
Weingreen: Grammar of Classical Hebrew
Gates: Aztec Herbal, English translation
Minorsky: Marvazi on China
Vandenbosch: Dutch East Indies
Bushell: Oriental Ceramic Art, text volume, 8vo.
Castren: Burjatische sprachlehre
Safford: Chamorro language of Guam
Baker Street Inventory
Appointment in Baker Street
Baker Street and Beyond
Baker Street Four-Wheeler
Jochelson: The Yakut
Gibbings: Mosheim's Memoirs of the church in China
Hobson: Chinese Pottery and Porcelain (2 voll.)
Marr & Briere: La Langue Georgienne
Victoria and Albert Museum: Chinese Porcelain
Harrington: God Mammon and the Japanese
Relazione della morte dell' ... di tournon
Maffei: Selectarum epistolarum ex India (Venice edition)
Warriner: Cruise of the frigate Potomac
Albertinus: Historische relation ... im konigreich Iapon ...
Martini: Sinica historia (Munich edition)
Hay: De rebus Iaponicis
Queen: Misadventures of Sherlock Holmes
Tursellini: Vita Fr. Xavierii (Zannetti edition)
Toren: Voyages
Gesner: Mithridates (2nd edition)
Dellon: Nouvelle relation d'un Voyage aux Indes orientales
" : Inquisition de Goa (3 voll.)
Boode: Notes for collectors of Chinese Antiques
Olschki: Marco Polo's Precursors
Fournier: Manuel typographique (2 voll.)
Brand: Travels to China (Amsterdam edition, French)
Nosaka: Labour Movement in Japan
Storia della congregazione de Cinesi (3 voll.)
Doyle: The True Conan Doyle
Telepnef: Paracelsus
Wilson: The Miraculous Birth of language
Leach: A Potter's Book
Bizonfy: Hungarian Dictionary
Japanese Air Terms (2 voll.)
Trigault: De Christiana Expeditione apud Sinas (Paris edit.)
Van der Meulen: Poolsch herbata

68

Bayer: Museum Sinicum
Alpini: Medicina aegyptorum
Martini: De bello tartarico (Amsterdam edition)
Kempis: Imitation of Christ (Elzevier edition)
Bontius: De medicina Indorum (Leiden edition)
Boispreaux: La vie de Pierre Aretin
King: Japan and Malaysia (2 voll.)
Rodriguez: Lettera di Giappone (Rome edition)
Martini: De bello tartarico (Antwerp edition)
Fernere zeitung auss Japon ...
Teillo: Relation (French edition)
Boym: Briefve Relation
Alcune lettere delle cose del Giappone (Milan edition)
Lettera annale delle cose del Giapone (Milan edition)
Bouvet: Portrait de l'empereur de la Chine (Paris edition)
Gualtieri: Della venuta de gli ambasciatori giaponesi
Rhodes: Histoire de la vie de cinq peres
Guignes: Viaggi (4 voll. in two)
La morale des Jesuites
Constable's Miscellany (Voll. 1-3)
Steinmetz: Japan and her People (2nd edition)
Wakefield: The Traveller in Asia
Huish: Chinese Snuff Bottles
Legge: Christianity in China
Cunningham: History of the Szechuen Riots
Yamanaka: Catalogue of Otsuye
Doyle: The True Conan Doyle
Swinhoe: Natural History of Hainan
Wyndam-Quin: Notes on History of Adare
Rosthorn: Tea Cultivation in Western Ssuch'uan
Lewis: Abolition of Man
Forster: Development of English Prose
Brinton: On the Words Anahuac and Nahuatl
Stieda: Geschichte des buchhandels in Riga
Redman: Shaw in and on Japan
Collis: New Sources for Life of Empress Dowager Tz'u Hsi
Lang: Shanghai considered socially
Szczesniak: Notes on Penetration of Copernican Theory into China
" : Penetration of Copernican Theory into Japan
Omura: Dictionary of Legal Terms
St. Mark in Mongolian
Mason: Mohammedans of China
Schmidt: Mongolian Grammar (French, 2 voll.)
Fletcher: Books printed by Bodoni
Mansoor: Oriental Studies in Ireland
Gates: Perez Codex
Zaehnsdorf: Short History of Book Binding

69

8.

Tourist Library, 13: Kimono - Japanese Dress
Grousset: Histoire de la Chine
Lockhart: The Life of Burns
Borton: Japan since 1931
Tamagna: Italy's Interests and Policies in the Far East
Corson: Introduction to the Works of John Milton
Leacock: Montreal, Seaport and City
Hogben: Mathematics for the Million
Starrett: 221B, Studies in Sherlock Holmes
Lewis: The Monk (2 voll.)
Donne: A Sermon of Valediction
Willis: Bibliophily or Booklove
Baudelaire: Les Fleurs du Mal
Nansen: The First Crossing of Greenland (2 voll.)
Parsons: Notes in Japan
~~Davis: Ancient Chinese Paper Money as described in a Chinese work on Numismatics~~
Grew: Ten Years in Japan
Sahagun: Ancient Mexico
Vendryes: Language, a Linguistic Introduction to History
Sandwell: The Canadian Peoples
Thompson et al: How the Jap Army Fights (2 copies)
Cressey: China's Geographic Foundations
Jespersen: Language, its Nature, Development and Origin
Hills, Ford & Coutinho: A Portuguese Grammar
Shenstone: Men & Manners
Dunn: Grammar of the Portuguese Language
Grierson: The Poems of John Donne (2 voll.)
Jones: Innocencia
Mansfield: The Garden Party
Gladstone: On Books and the Housing of Them
Williams: A Key into the Language of America
The Oxford Book of English Verse
The Hongkong Almanack for 1846
Hippisley: Catalogue of Collection of Chinese Porcelain, 1890
Gates: Collection of Middle American Literature, Section A.
Minayeff: Recherches sur le Bouddhisme
The Works of Robert Burns (8 voll.)

90

9.

Browne: Religio Medici, MacMillan edit.
Labarre: A Dictionary of Paper
Cordier: Bibliotheca Japonica
Laures: Kirishitan Bunko
Aretino: Ragionamenti
Mendozza: Dell' Historia della China (Venice edition)
Pei: Conversational Korean
Bisson: American Policy in the Far East
Skeat: Chaucer's Prologue
Pamyati Kastrena
Epistolae indicae, epistolae Japanicae (2 voll. in one Louvain edition)
Handbook of American Indians (2 voll.)
Puini: Avalokitecvara sutra (Atsume Gusa)
Bibliography of Brosset
Kozlov: Tibet i Dalailama
Harlez: Le livre des esprits
Pineyro: Relacion del sucesso que tuvo nuestra fe en Japon
Peking Gazette, 74, 77, 76, 73 (4 voll.)
Takekoshi: Economic Aspects of Japan (3 voll.)
Kuke debter, Istoriya Mongolov
Hirschfield: Anomalies
Timperley: Contrasts between China and Japan (China Society)
Whatman: Specimen book
Mary Shelley: Frankenstein
Bronte: Wuthering Heights
Carroll: Alice in Wonderland
Sansom: Historical Grammar of Japanese
Kipling's Collected Poems
Fanshawe: Lusiad (2nd edition)
Tartar-Russian Vocabulary, Kazan'76
Golden Lotus (4 voll.)
Harlez: Ecole philosophique moderne de la Chine (Sing-Li)
Morley: Sherlock Holmes and Dr. Watson
Priapeia veterum et recentiorum
Stefansson: Friendly Arctic
Grousset: Histoire de l'Extreme Orient (2 voll.)

71

資料 10（貼付ノート・Ashbee: Library Catalogue）

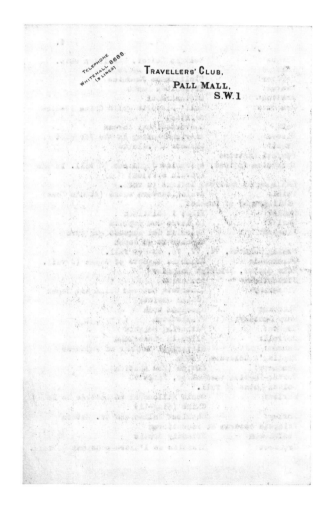

TELEPHONE
WHITEHALL 8688.
(3 LINES)

TRAVELLERS' CLUB,
PALL MALL,
S.W.1

10.

Watt: Commercial Products of India (1 voll.)
Mckenney and Hall: Indian Tribes of North America (3 voll.)
Letters from Baker Street
Laufer: Beginnings of Porcelain in China
St. Louis City Art Museum: Chinese Ceramics
Fagan: Life of Panizzi (Vol. 2)
Tir na Deo, Irish fairy tales
Belmar: Zapoteca-serrana y Zapoteca del Valle
Faery Nights (Irish Fairy tales)
Shepherd: Australia's Interests in the Far East
Handbook of American Indian Languages (2 voll.)
Charlevoix: Histoire du Japon (4to, 2 voll.)
Montaigne's Essays (3 voll.)
Watkins: Anthology of American Negro Literature
Machiavelli: The Prince
Gates Collection B-G
Gates Collection relating to Mexico and Central America
Relation des Choises de Yucatan
Inoue-Tadou: Kirishitan gogaku no kenkyu
Mongolian Inscription (Wylie)
Thompson: Civilization of the Mayas
Meissner: Grammatik der japanischen schriftsprache (2 voll.)
De Ricci: Editions originales de Ronsard
Transactions of the Oriental Ceramics Scoeity Vol. 19
Pinto: Voyages and Adventures ('63)
Macfarlane: Sketches of Shanghai
Maudsley: Glimpse of Guatemala
Blades: William Caxton (1st edit., 2 voll.)
Zottoli: Cursus litteraturae sinicae (Vol.5 only)
Pallavicino: Opere scelte (Elzevier, 2 voll.)
Camoens: Lusiadas, '76
Ferr: 18 L'Essence de la Science transcendante
Documents preserved in the National Museum of Peiping
A Baker Street Song Book
Forty-third Chapter of the Three Kingdom Novel (2 voll)
Yamanaka: Japanese Stone Garden Ornaments

72

資料 10（貼付ノート・Ashbee: Library Catalogue）

TELEPHONE
WHITEHALL 8688.
(3 LINES)

TRAVELLERS' CLUB,
PALL MALL,
S.W.1

11.

Rodger: History of Silk
Collis: Courts of the Shan Princes
Karlgren: Romanization of Chinese
Hart: Education in China
Epitome of History of Pellew Islands
Van Gulik: The Ch'an Master Tung-Kao 1944
Criterion Miscellany No. 5
Yeh: Confucian Conception of Jen
Gardner: Philippine Folklore
Margulies: Artistic Possibilities of Chinese
Irish Franciscan Monthly July'40, June '40, May '40
Tracey Woodward Collection of Japan (Sale Catalogue)
Fujikawa: Nihonigakushi, kaiteihan
Secundus: Basia (Nonesuch Press)
Maffei: Opera (2 voll. 4to)
Sansom: Japan
Allen: History of Georgia
Acostae HistoriamRerum in Oriente Gestarum (Paris '72)
Rerum in Oriente Gestarum(Cologne '74)
The Chinese and Japanese Repositories (Voll.1-3, 2 Voll.)
Perry's Japan (1 vol. 8vo)
Le Gallienne: Romance of Perfume
Ulrich:& Kup: Books and Printing: Selected List of Periodicals
Phelps: Mount Omei
Dyn 1-6 (1 vol.)
Radlov: Archaologische erforschung des Orchon-Beckens
Hales: Milton's Areopagitica
Japanese Code of Criminal Procedure
Chen: Taxation in China in Tsing Dynasty
Oliver: Korea, Forgotten Nation
McIlroy: Chamberlain's Japanese Grammar
Neumann: Catechism of the Shamans
Davidson: Hebrew Grammar
Sakanishi: A Handful of Sand
Irish-English Dictionary (Irish Text Society)
Turrettini: San-ze-king
Hall's Voyages and Travels (6 voll. only)
Alcock's Specimens of Japanese Papers (2 voll.)

93

資料 10（貼付ノート・Ashbee: Library Catalogue）

TELEPHONE
WHITEHALL 8688
(3 LINES)

TRAVELLERS' CLUB,
PALL MALL,
S.W.1

12.

| | |
|---|---|
| Yamada: | Nihonbunpokoji |
| Beal: | Suhkililihkiu |
| Saville: | Reports on the Maya Indians |
| Beal: | Two Chinese Buddhist Inscriptions found at Buddha Gaya |
| Waddell: | The Uttermost Isles |
| Figueroa: | Historia ... los anos de 1607 y 1608 |
| Herbert: | Limerick Printers |
| Stein: | Explorations in Central Asia (Geog. Journal) |
| Kuck: | Art of Japanese Gardens |
| Hulbert: | Omjee the Wizard |
| Gissing: | Denzil Quarrier |
| Deshayes: | La Ceremonie du the au Japon |
| Freer Gallery of Art, Oriental Studies 1-2 | |
| Nichols: | Restoration of Ancient Bronzes |
| Beal: | Origin of the Spiritual Activity Developed in Buddhism |
| Martin: | Communism in China in Eleventh Century |
| Laufer: | Domestication of the Cormorant |
| The Red Gate Players | |
| Jochelson: | Peoples of Asiatic Russia |
| Chinese Medical Journal, March 1933 | |
| Fletcher: | The Witches' Pharmacopoeia |
| Goeje: | De muur van gog en magog |
| Ball: | Is Buddhism a preparation for Christianity? |
| Coushnir: | Chinese coins without currency |
| Collocott: | Tongan astronomy |
| Bowditch: | Mayan Nomenclature |
| Rice: | Beginnings of Russian Icon Painting |
| Bolton: | Language used to Domestic Animals |
| Fischel: | The Jews of Kurdistan |
| Green: | Making of a Japanese Newspaper |
| Katanov: | Otryvok iz odnoi tatarskoi letopisi o Kazani |
| R.W.Chambers: | 1874-1942 |
| Fan: | Dr. Johnson and Chinese Culture |

74

資料 10（貼付ノート・Ashbee: Library Catalogue）

TELEPHONE
WHITEHALL 8688.
(3 LINES)

TRAVELLERS' CLUB,
PALL MALL,
S.W.1

13.

| | |
|---|---|
| Ward: | Origin of Cosmetic Dentistry |
| Yetts: | Symbolism in Chinese Art |
| Britton: | Fifty Sheng inscriptions |
| Monteiro: | De l'influence portugeise au Japon |
| Dumezil: | Introduction a la grammaire des langues caucasiennes |
| " | Le verbe caucasien |
| Williams: | Tibet and her Neighbours |
| Shirokogoroff: | Ethnical Unit and Milieu |
| Hetherington: | Pottery and Porcelain Factories of China |
| Dawes: | The Ancients their Music |
| Sunoo: | Korean Textbook (Vol. 1 only) |
| Mattice: | Lexicon of Bibliographical Terms |
| Carrington: | Beauty |
| Gates: | Specimen of Dictionary |
| Shirokogoroff: | La theorie de l'ethnos |
| Van Buren: | Labour in Japan |
| Baudelaire: | La Beaute, Corydon Press |

Inscription on the St. Louis Stele of 505
Writings of A.K. Coomaraswamy

| | |
|---|---|
| Gates: | Distribution of the Mayance Stock |

Springfield Mill: 1807-1907

| | |
|---|---|
| Konow: | Memoirs Asiatic Soc. of Bengal (Vol. 5 No. 2.) |
| Gates: | Spirit of the Hour |
| Hetherington: | Celadon Porcelain |
| Shaw: | Catalogue of Specimens of Cloth '87 |
| Jorgensen: | Old Coins of China |
| Seyer: | Pidgin English |
| Whittaker: | Bach's Contatas |

Short History of Ireland in Irish
Irish without Worry

| | |
|---|---|
| Hargrave: | Earlier French Musicians |
| Hellman: | Four plays |
| Cordier: | Bibliotheca Sinica (5 voll.) |
| Nachod: | Bibliography of Japan (2 voll.) |
| McKerrow: | Introduction to Bibliography |

Hollingworth Papers Specimen Book

| | |
|---|---|
| Gingell: | Ceremonial Usages of the Chinese |

Shinjikan

75

資料 10（貼付ノート・Ashbee: Library Catalogue）

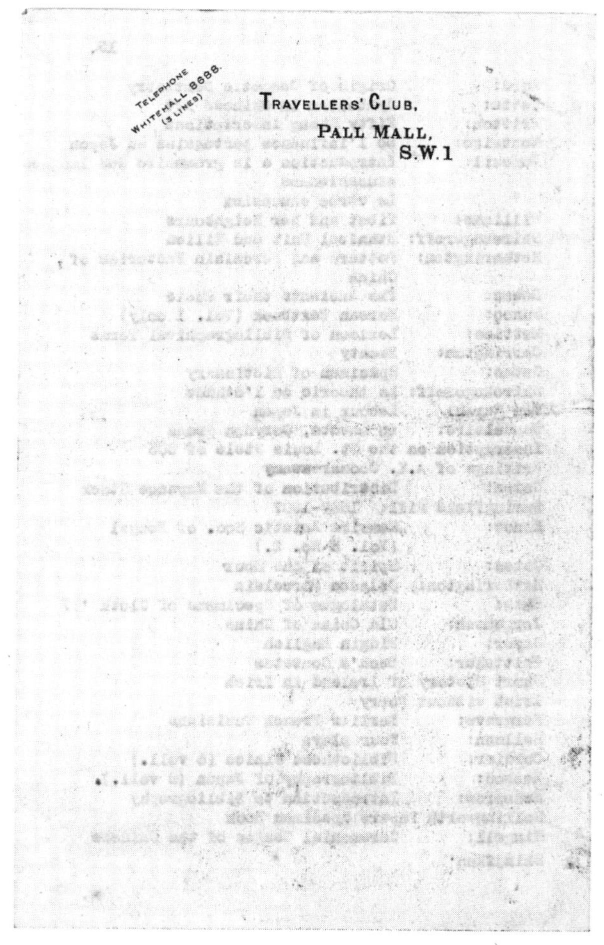

TELEPHONE
WHITEHALL 8688.
(3 LINES)

TRAVELLERS' CLUB,
PALL MALL,
S.W.1

14.

Andrews: Bibliopegy in the U.S.
Concise Oxford Dictionary
Yamada: Nihonbunporon
Jien
Valette: Dutch Grammar (2 voll.)
Wely: English Dictionary (Dutch-English part)
Chase: Tyranny of Words
Claremont Oriental Studies, Part 5
Medicina Sinica (Cleyer) Frankfort '82
Complete Sherlock Holmes
Smith: Profile by Gaslight
Lewis: Francois Villon
Joyce: Works
Reynolds: White ~~xkxi~~ sahibs in India
Hogben: Interglossa
Rocher: La Province Chinoise du Yunnan (2 voll.)
Keeton: China, the Far East and the Future
Classics: (Chinese M. of I. )
Catalogue of Swiss Books (2 voll.)
Tschichold: Chinesische farbendrucke der gegenwart
" Neue chinesische farbendrucke aus der zehnbambushalle
Shorter Oxford Dictionary (2 voll.)
Library cards, 2 sets
Boym: Flora sinensis (incomplete facsimile)
Covarrubias: Atlas
Scarron: Le Virgile travesti
Maupas: Grammaire et Syntaxe francoise (Bloys edition)
Epistolai indicai, Louvain'66
Opuscules francoises des Hotmans
Marco Polo, Latin edition ed. Muller
Kaigaishinbunbetsushu, (2 voll.)
Batabiyashimbun (6 voll.)
Three Tales by Pushkin
Pacific Affairs, Sept. 1943
Sinbirskii sbornik (imperfect)
Fiske: Dutch Colonies in America (2 voll.)
Preliminary Report on Expedition to N.W. Honduras (Smithson. Inst. 3445)
Ey: Portuguese Grammar (2 voll.)
Thorne: St. George
Apollinaire: L'Oeuvre des conteurs allemands
Studies in Modern Irish (Parts 3-4) (Part 2) (3 voll.)
Yamada: Nihonkogohokogi
Catalogue Chinese Maritime Customs, Collection, Philadelphia '76
Morley: Guide Book to Ruins of Quirigua
Beyer: Shell Ornament Sets
Hannah: Tarawa

96

資料 10（貼付ノート・Ashbee: Library Catalogue）

15.

Dorn: Beitrag zur geschichte der georgier, I
Stories of Benjamin David Benjamin
Szinnyei: Ungarische sprachlehre
Al giocc cinese chiamato il rompicapo
Mansion: French Grammar
Maillard: Traicte des Indulgences

Beazley: Dawn of modern geography, 3 voll.
Bretschneider: Botanicon sinicum, 3 voll.
library cards
Zettoli, 4 voll.
Frei: Interrogatif et indefini
Boxer: Portuguese embassy to Japan
Youn: Dictionarium latino-coreanum
Dubray: F. Rops, Scheur
Petrucci: Prodromo
Kann: Currencies of China, 2. ed.
Gaekwad's oriental series, vol. 74
Auboyer: Influences au kondo du Horyuji
McLeod : Japan & ten lost tribes of israel, 2 voll.
Wagner: Kaiserreich China
Rein: Industries of Japan
Grunwedel: Altkutscha
Delepierre: Philobiblon
Hume: Learned Societies
Edwards: Lives of founders of British Museum
Lisiansky: voyage round the world
Fortune, Japan No.
Asakawa: Early Institutional life of Japan
Rhode Island Imprints
Canadian Arctic Expedition Report 15 B
Bergerstein: Untersuchung der von den Chinesen benutzten holztafelchen
Pallas: Merkwurdigkeiten (3 voll.)
Matsubara: In Darkest Tokyo
Fischer: Reiseeindrucke aus Schantung
Müller: Ikkaku sennin
Funeral Discourse for Morrison, Ds.
Richthofen: Trade Routes to Southwestern China
Anderson: Memo. on Chinese Currency. 77

TRAVELLERS' CLUB,
PALL MALL,
S.W.1

16.

Latoste: Scincoïdien originaire du japon
Chino-Sinhalese relations (2 voll.)
Hartwell: Foochow Essays
The Indian Magazine, April 1903
Kramp: Een nieuw werk over China
Preve: Tchemoulpo
Sibiriacoff: Aussere verbindungen Sibiriens
mit ~~Europ~~ Europa.
Bushell: Mongolian capital of Shangtu
Matsuo: Miki
Yoshida: Lacquer
Chamberlain: Ainu Language and Folklore
Milne: List of Japanese Minerals
O'Neill: A First Japanese Book
Histoire de la peche au Japon
Thomas & Konow: Two Medieval Documents
Giles: Some Truths about Opium
Middle American Research Records.
Summers: Lecture on the Chinese Language
Berendt: Alphabet for the Mexican languages
Gates: Yucatan (unbound copy)
Villon: Oeuvres, ed. Foulet
D'Avezac: Mappemonde turka
Bergen: Sages of Shantung
Gennep: Un systeme negre de classification
Bang: Vom Köktürkischen zum osmanischen 1917
The St. Paul's Magazine April '73

98

資料 10（貼付ノート・Ashbee: Library Catalogue）

17.

The London Magazine, January '78
Fujikawa: History of Japanese Medicine (Ger.)
Matsumoto: Beziehung zweischen Mikado und Schogun
Dickens: Guide to Sericulture
Jones: Americans in Japan
Stray Notes on Kioto (2nd ed.)
Milne: Stone Age in Japan
Dickens: Megalithes du japon
Japanese Women, Columbian exposition
Satomi: Altjapanischer idealismus
Bishop: Historical Geography of Early Japan.
Matsokin: Morphology of Present Tense of Japanese Verb
The Observatory of Zi-ka-wei
Zurla: Marco Polo (Vol. I)
Jizo
Pauw: Egyptiens et Chinois (2 voll.)
Blades Exhibition
Cole: Index to Bibliographical Papers

79

TELEPHONE
WHITEHALL 8688.
(3 LINES)
TRAVELLERS' CLUB,
PALL MALL,
S.W.1

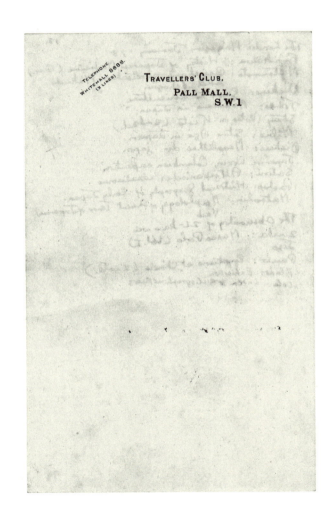

資料 10（貼付ノート・Ashbee: Library Catalogue）

Adam: Grammaire Mandchou
Antonii: Panormitae Hermaphr. ed. Forberg
Aungervy le Society. Voyages of Vertomannus
Aubert: La petite pantoufle
Allen: Korean Tales
Arber: Herbals
Alcock: Art and Art Industry in Japan
Ananga-Ranga
Aston: Grammar of Spoken Japanese, 4th ed.
Atkinson: Travels in the Amoor
Ament: Begriff der Kindersprache
Andreae: Bibliotheca sinologica
Articles in Formosan
Adami: Ungarische Sprachkunst
Atkinson: Oriental and Western Siberia
Ars Asiatica, Vol. III
Armeff: Books of the Ancients
Arnold: Islamic Book
Arberry: British Orientalists
Akademik S.F.Oldenburg, 1934
Amyot: Dictionnaire Mantchou
Anesaki: Buddhist Art
Ambassades vers l'Empereur du Japon, 2 voll., 12 mo
Adamson: Camoens, 2 voll.
Alexeev: Kitaiskaya Poema
Adam: Gr. de la langue tongouze
Amakusaban Kinkushu
A Model Japanese Villa
Ars Asiatica, I.
Adler: Dialectic
American Anthropologist 34, 4.
Art Chretien Chinois
Apollinaire: Sade
Albuquergue, 4 voll.
Aziatskiya Rossiya, 3 voll., 4 to., Atlas, folio
Ament: Deutung der ersten Kinderworte
Altaiskii Almanax
Arch. franc historici conspectus chronologicus
Alepseev: Japanese Gold and Silver Coins
Alfaric: Vie chretienne due Bouddha
Alaska Historical Museum
Andreev: Yazgulemskii Yazyk
Authors and Printer's Dict.
Anadyrskii Krai, 1893.
Art Militaire Chinois (Uncoloured)

Brosset: Arakel de Tauriz, Registre Chronologique
Brosset: Rapport sur l'ouvrage intitule Numizmaticeskie fakty
Bibliotheca Lindesiana: Cat. of Chinese Books
Bedevian: Polyglottic Dict. of Plant Names

80

Bang & Marquart: Ostturkische Dialektstudien
Becker: Feudal Kamakura
Brief Summary of Do Ka Zang
Brockelmann: Mittelurkischer Wortschatz
Blochet Histoire des Mongols (texte)
Blades: Enemies of Books, 2nd ed.
Burton: Catallus
Brown: Pilgrims Progress (Cambridge English Classics)
Beal: Travels of Buddhist Pilgrims
Bibliographie des oeuvres de H. Cordrer
Beveridge: Babur Nama in Engl., 2 voll.
Bayer: De Horis Sinicis
Boxer: Affair of the Madre de Deus
Bibliotheca Curiosa Monacensis
Binyon: Flight of the Dragon
Bhuyan: Early British Relations with Assam
Binyon: Chinese Art and Buddhism
Blochet: Babar Nama
Bretschneider: Chinese Silkworm Trees
Bunakov: Oracle Bones from Honan
Blochet: Introd. a l'histoire des Mongols
Bartold: Istoriya izuceniya Vostoka
Bartold: Turkestan down to the Mongol Invasion
Bonaparte: Documents de l'epoque Mongole
Budenz: Az ugor nyelvek osszehasonlito alaktana
Bonneau: Curiosa
Bohtingk: Spracheder Jakuten
Balfour: Huang Tsze
Birdwood: Report of Old Records of India Office
Baranov: Kitaiskii noyi gor
Burford's Canton
Bullock: Etajima
Brooks: Account of Weights
Beveridge: Babar Nama, Turkitext
Beal: Romantic History of Buddha
Benyowsky's Travels, 2 voll., 4to.
Brodrick: Little China
Burton's Camoens, 6 voll.
Ball: Macao
Browne's Religio Medici (tall 4to.)
Bailey: Lucretius on the Nature of Things
Bowring: Flowery Scroll
Blake: Grammar of Tagolog
Biot: Etoiles jilantes
Ball: The Pitt of the Classics
Brit. Museum: Japanese Books, 2 voll., 4to.
Balfour: Waifs and Strays from Far East
Ballagi: Hungarian Dict.
Buck: Sun Yat Sen
Baber Nama 1857
Busbeq: Episbolae

81

資料10（貼付ノート・Ashbee: Library Catalogue）

\- 3 -

Bauer: Woman
Brookes: Intern. Rivalry in Pacific Islands
Braithwaite: Life of Sogoro
Bouillard: Attitudes des Buddhas
Bloch: German Interests in Far East
Bellows German Dict.
Blochet: Babar Nama
Bacon: Advancement of Learning
Bickerstaffe: Araki the daimio
Berjeau: Calcoen, Dutch Narrative
Bretschneider: Mediaeval Geography
Bingham: Founding of T'ang Dynasty
Balfour: Leaves from my Chinese Scrapbook
Benneville: Yotsuya Kaidan
Beveridge: Notes on MSS of Babar
Bang: Turkische Namen einiger Grosskatzen
Bulletin de la Maison franco-jap. I
Ballagi: Pocket Hungarian Dict.
Bang: Kokturkische Inschrift
Braga: Camoens, 2 voll., ms.
Boguras: Koryak Texts
Bruce: Humanness of Chu hsi
Bacof: Ecriture cursive tibetaine
Bang: Turkische Bruchstucke
Beveridge Babar Nama (Pamphlet)

Browne's, Sir T. Works, Bohn, 3 voll.
Brown, I.: Books of Words

Comerford's Journal
Coxe: Russian Discoveries, 2nd. ed.
Catalogue of Philatelic Library of Earl of Crawford
Camoens: Passion of Christ
Chavannes: Les religieux eminents
Christopher: Palaeography and Archives
Courteille: Memoires de Baber, 2 voll. in 1.
Covell: Under the Seal of Sesshu
Catalogue Turkestan Public Library (R)
Clifton: Fortune Telling by Japanese Swords
Codex Cumanicus
Cornish: Borderlands of Language in Europe
Cahen: Livre de comptes

82

Bauer: Woman
Brookes: Intern. Rivalry in Pacific Islands
Braithwaite: Life of Sogoro
Bouillard: Attitudes des Buddhas
Bloch: German Interests in Far East
Bellows German Dict.
Blochet: Babar Nama
Bacon: Advancement of Learning
Bickerstaffe: Araki the daimio
Berjeau: Galcoen, Dutch Narrative
Bretschneider: Mediaeval Geography
Bingham: Founding of T'ang Dynasty
Balfour: Leaves from my Chinese Scrapbook
Benneville: Yotsuya Kaidan
Beveridge: Notes on MSS of Babar
Bang: Turkische Namen einiger Grosskatzen
Bulletin de la Maison franco-jap. I
Ballagi: Pocket Hungarian Dict.
Bang: Kokturkische Inschrift
Braga: Camoens, 2 voll., ms.
Boguras: Koryak Texts
Bruce: Humanness of Chu hsi
Bacof: Ecriture cursive tibetaine
Bang: Turkische Bruchstucke
Beveridge Babar Nama (Pamphlet)
Bramsen: Coins of Japan
Bibliographie clerico-galante
Bloch: Leben ungerer Zeit
Batchelor: Ainu Fireside Stones
Bang: Turcica
Boas Anniversary Volume
Brit. Museum Japanese and Chinese Paintings
Bouxat: Pamphlet
Bute: Ancient Language of T
Bishop of Victoria: Lewchew

Comerford's Journal
Coxe: Russian Discoveries, 2nd. ed.
Catalogue of Philatelic Library of Earl of Crawford
Camoens: Passion of Christ
Chavannes: Les religieux eminents
Christopher: Palaeography and Archives
Courteille: Memoires de Baber, 2 voll. in 1.
Covell: Under the Seal of Sesshu
Catalogue Turkestan Public Library (R)
Clifton: Fortune Telling by Japanese Swords
Codex Cumanicus
Cornish: Borderlands of Language in Europe
Cahen: Livre de comptes

82

- 4 -

Cordier: Narrative of Recent Events in Tongking
Cordier: La France en Chine, Vol. I only
Courteille: Dictionnaire turk-oriental
Castren: Ostjakische Sprachlehre
Conrady: Indochinesische Causativ-denominativ-bildung
Catalogue of Mollendorff Manchu Library
Castagne: Congres de turkologie de Bakon
Campbell: List of Birds Collected in Corea
Cardim: Notes on Port.-English Grammar
Campbell: Recent Journey in N. Korea
Catalogue of Lockhart Library
Churchill: Beach-la-Mar
Catalogue of Chinese Works in Bodleian Library
Contributions on Folklore, 3 voll.
Clement: Article on the Poppy
Chamberlain: Japanese Poetry.
Charpentier: W. of Rubruk & Roger Bacon
Courant: L'Asie Centrale
Cahen: Histoire des relations de la Russie
Chrestomatia arcaica   Textos literarios
Chamberlain: Romanized Japanese Reader
Couvreur: Dictionnaire classique, folio
Catolikku Daijiten, I.
Chukaminkoku Shinchizu
Chalfant: Early Chinese Writing
Cordier: Quelques donnees nouvelles
Catalogue titles and index entries
Castren: Tungusische Sprachlehre
Cordier: Merveilles de l'Asie
Camus: Voyages de Thevenot
Campbell: Journey in N. Korea
Collis: Land of the Great Image
Catalogue of Drujon
Chamberlain: Japanese Written Grammar
Ceylon and the Hollanders 1658-1796
Centenaire de l'Ecole des Langues orientales
Chater Collection Catalogue, 4to.
Clark: Formosa
Carlo: Paleografia Espanola, 2 voll.
Curtius: Jap. Spraakkunst
Costumes of China
Chamberlain: Moji no Shirube
Civil Code of Japan, 2 voll.
Castagne: Congres de turkolozie
Catholic Native Episcopacy in China
Culin: Chinese in America
Chavannes: Expression des voeux
Cat. Rostor Museum
Clark: Abbey of St. Gall
Campos: History of Portuguese in Bengal

83

- 5 -

Carus: T'ai Shang Kan Ying P'ien
Courant: Le presse periodique japonaise
Compar. Tables of Christian and Muham. Dates
Chavannes: T'ai chan
Conder: Notes on Japanese Architecture

Calthrop: Book of War
Chardin's, Sir T.: Travels in Persia (Argonaut)
Couto: Da Asia, 24 voll.
Campbell: Arabian Medicine, 2 voll.
Cocks: Diary, 2 voll.

Deeters: Kharthwelische Verbum
Dickins: Japanese Odes
Douglas: Birds and Beasts of GR Anthology
Dandolo: Art of Rearing Silkworms
Dautremer: Nikko passe et present
Duhren: Neue Forschungen
Dennys: Folklore of China
Douglas: Paneros
Dahlgren: Debuts de la cartographie du Japon
Dickins: Old Bamboo Hewer's Story, '88
Drevnayya Rossiiskaya Bibliotheka, 20 voll.
de Corbeil: Lettres sur l'histoire philos. des langues, 1820
de Landes: Glossaire er.
Diccionario do Povo, No 4.
Duhren: de Sade und seine Zest
da Costa: Uma Carta nautica portuguesa
d'Arcy: Hao-Rhieon-tchouan
Duhren: Sade u. seine Zeit
Dulaure: Des cultes qui ont precede l'idolatrie
Duhren: R. de la Bretonne
Diwan Lughat, 3 voll.
Davis: Han Koong Tsew, '29
Donisthorpe: Loveliest of Friends
d'Auteroche: Voyagien Siberie, 3 voll.
Descriptio Regii Japoniae (Armsterdam)
Derbend-Nameh
Davis: San-yu-low

84

- 5 -

Carus: T'ai Shang Kan Ying P'ien
Courant: Le presse periodique japonaise
Compar. Tables of Christian and Muham. Dates
Chavannes: T'ai chan
Conder: Notes on Japanese Architecture
Conferences Musee Guimet 1903-04
Closter-documente
Chinese Hist., 4 voll., 12 mo
Camoes: Liricas School Texts
Couling: Luminous Religion
Catalogue de la Litterature mondiale, 2 voll., 4to.
Comptes rendus ... exploration du N. de la Mong.
Caucasus polyglottus, I.
Collinson: Soul of Grammar
Chavannes: Les livres chinois
Coxwell: Siberian Folk Tales
Chavannes: La Sculpture

Deeters: Kharthwelische Verbum
Dickins: Japanese Odes
Douglas: Birds and Beasts of GR Anthology
Dandolo: Art of Rearing Silkworms
Dautremer: Nikko passe et present
Duhren: Neue Forschungen
Dennys: Folklore of China
Douglas: Paneros
Dahlgren: Debuts de la cartographie du Japon
Dickins: Old Bamboo Hewer's Story, '88
Drevnayya Rossiiskaya Bibliotheka, 20 voll.
de Corbeil: Lettres sur l'histoire philos. des langues, 1820
de Landes: Glossaire er.
Diccionario do Povo, No 4.
Duhren: de Sade und seine Zest
da Costa: Uma Carta nautica portuguesa
d'Arcy: Hao-Rhieon-tchouan
Duhren: Sade u. seine Zeit
Dulaure: Des cultes qui ont precede l'idolatrie
Duhren: R. de la Bretonne
Diwan Lughat, 3 voll.
Davis: Han Koong Tsew, '29
Donisthorpe: Loveliest of Friends
d'Auteroche: Voyagien Siberie, 3 voll.
Descriptio Regii Japoniae (Armsterdam)
Derbend-Nameh
Davis: San-yu-low

84

Diosy: Yamato-damashi-i
Dictionary of English Book Collections
Danvers: Portuguese in India, 2 voll.
da Orta: Simples and Drugs of India
Dickins: Chushingura
Dickins: Old Bamboo Hewer's Story
de Korne: Fellowship of Goodness
Douglas: South Wind
Dingwall: Kakiemon Designs
Douglas: Fortunate Union
Davidson: Formosa Past and Present
Dorfler: Ahron ben Elia
Dandin: Sigillographie sino-annamite
Dalgado: Glossano luso-asiatico, 2 voll.
Davis: Fortunate Union, 2 voll.
Donner: Zur Phonetik des samojed
du Halde: China, 2 voll. folio
Dagestan, 1847
Davis: Chinese Miscellanies
J. de la Societe finno-origienne, 37.

Exercises in Yokohama Dialect, '79
Erdmann: Muhammed's Geburt u. Abrahah's Untergang
Epic of Bogdo-khan Janggar, Kalmuck text.
Elferink: Het oordeel
Ecke: Twin Pagodas of Zayton
Emelyanov: Grammatika votyackogo yazyka
Etnograficeskii Sbornik, Vol. I.
Eastern Art, 4 parts plus 2 voll. (3 voll. in all)
Editions of Syphilis
English - Dutch Dict.
Ellis: George Chapman
Embroidery Sept. 1935
Eliseeff: Elementary Japanese, 2 voll.
Edgar: English-Giarung Voc.
Edwards: Chinese Prose Literature, 2 voll.
Eitel: 3 Lectures on Buddhism
Ettmayer: Das Wesen der Dialektbldung
Eisen: Mauthners Kritik der spr.
El Ktab des lois secretes
Epistolae et logistorici
Ettnologische Studien, 2 voll.
Edkins: opium

Fonssagrives: Si-ling
Fukuyama: First Japanese Mission to America
Foster: Supplementary Calendar of Documents in India Office
Fujishima: Bouddhisme Japonais

85

Fonseca: Historical Sketch of Goa
Frei Luis de Sousa (School Text)
Fujisawa: Yoshida T. and R.L.Stevenson
Field Museum Pamphlets, 25 voll.
Funke: Studien zur Gesch. der Sprachphilos
Field Museum Pamphlets, 12 voll. (extra)
Fourmont: Meditationes Sinicae
Faceties de Pogge, 2 voll., Liseux
Finnish-English Dictionary
Festschrift V. Thomsen
Finn: Jews of China
Forsyth: Shantung
Foucher: L'art greco-bouddhique, 3 voll.
Florenz: White Aster
Frois: Premiere Ambassade (Pinto)
Foster: John Company
Florenz: Japanese Poems
Figueiredo: Portuguese Dict., 2 voll.
Faber: Eine Staatslehre .... Mencius
Forster: Report of Mission to Yarkund
Foster: East India House
Franke: Ackerbau u. Seidengewinnung in China
Fenellosa: Noh
Foster: Guide to India Office Records
Fillos de Pairs, 2 voll.
Fenollosa: Blossoms from a Japanese Garden
Fehlinger: Geschlectsleben der Natur volker
Farnell: Myttologic Study

Gale: Cloud Dream of the Nine
Golovnin: Voyage of the Sloop Diana (R)
Gabelentz: Grammaire Mandchoue
Ghaniev: Tatar-Russian Dictionary (Baku)
Giles: Six Centuries at Tunhuang
Gale: Korean Folk Tales
Gabelentz: Essays on Mongolian and Manchu
Gabelentz: Geschichte der grossen Liao
Giles: Record of Buddhistic Kingdoms
Grajdanzev: Formosa Today
Gosse: T.L.Beddoes, 2 voll.
Giles: Strange Tales from a Chinese Studio, 2 voll, 1st ed.
Gronbech: Forstudier til tyrkisk lydhistorie
Giles: Glossary of Reference, 3rd ed.
George Borrow: Works, 16 voll.
Giles: Travels of Fa-hsien
Gunsaulus: Japanese Costume
Gowland: Art of Casting Bronze in Japan
Grose's Classical Dictionary, '23
Grose's Provincial Glossary, '11
Giles: Note on Four Chinese Volumes

86

Gray: Tercentenary of Hakluyt
Gowland: Dolmens of Korea
Gowland: Japanese pseudo-speise
Gedenshtrom: Otryvkio Sibiri
Golden Cockerel Press: Golden ASSC
General Outlines of Education in Japan, 1884
Giles: Sun Tzu
Grammatika altaiskago yazyka, '69
Gabelentz: Die Sprachwissenschaft, 2nd ed.
Grimaldi: Fang sing thou Riai
Gomboev: Altan Tobchi
Goodland: Bibliography of Rites
Gowland: Dolmens in Japan
Grant: Books and Documents
Gabelentz: Sge-schu
Goodrich: Literary Inquisition
Granet: La droite et la gauche
Grajdanzev: Formosa Today
Golovnin's Captivity in Japan, 3 voll.
Golovnin's Captivity in Japan, 2 voll.
Grube: Metamorphosen der Sotter
Giles: Historic China
Gramatica de la lengua de Yap., '88
Goda Collection, Japanese Sword Fittings
Giles: Chinese Pictorial Art
Gowland: Japanese Metallurgy
Giles: San tzu ching
Gorham: Tray Gardens
Gray: Walks in City of Canton
Geschichte der Sprachen d. vorderen Orients
Gauthiot: Qq. termes techniques
Grose's Classical Dict., 2nd ed.
Grigor'ev: Rossiya i Aziya
Guntert: Grundfragen der Sprach w.
Gardner: Western Books on China

Hunter: Primitive Papermaking
Hirth: Geschichte der Ostmongolen
Hoffmann: Japanese Grammar, 2nd ed.
Hirth Anniversary Volume
Hyacinth: Istoriya pervyx chteyrex khanov
Harlez: Histoire de l'Empire de Kin
Hunter: Turk. text of Narratives of the Prophets
Houtsma: Turkisch-arabisches glossar
Hart: Japanese Art Work
Harada: Lesson of Japanese Architecture
Housman: Shropshire Lad (Riccardi Press)
Hetherington: Chinese Ceramic Glazes
Hirth: Ancient Porcelain
Hunter: Turk. Texts

87

Hughes: Chinese Philosophy in Classical Times
Hirth: Native Sources of Chinese Pictorial Art
Huart: Conte bouddhique des deux freres
Hatsukade: Biloungsideale in d. jap. Kultur
Harlez: Reglemento militaires
Haas: Dokument aus der jap. Inquisition
Halloran's Journey to Japan and Loochoo
Hughes: The Great Learning and the Mean-in-Action
Hudson: Atlas of Far Eastern Politics
Hyacinth: Kitai, 4 voll.
Henry: Grammaire alecute
Hirschfeld: Transvestismus, 2 voll.
Hager: Pantheon chinois
Hetherington: Early Ceramic Wares
Hope: Temples of Nikko
Henderson: Japanese Grammar
Hamilton: New Acct of the East Indies, 2 voll.
Hoffmann: Grammaire japonaise
Histoire de la Chine, 13 voll., 4-to.
Herring: Papermaking
Houssaye: Monographie du the
Hall's Voyage to Loochoo, 8vo.
Hart: Marco Polo
Hosie: Szechwan
Hirth: Scraps from Collector's Notebook
Haynes: Enemies of Liberty
Hanakatsura
Heyd: Commerce on Levant, 2 voll.
Hillier: List of Authorities of China
Hager: Numismatique chinoise
Hayashi: For His People
History of Printing in China and Europe
Historia da expansao portuguesa no mund, 2
Hamerton: Intellectual Life
Hortus Suburbanus Calcuttensis
Heaslett: From a Japanese Prison
Historical Relations between Japan and Saghalien
Historia gen. de las Isl. Philipp., 14 voll.
Hakluyt, 12 voll.
Hutchinson: Relations de la Compagnie franc
Heiberg: Geisteskranken
Haynes: Decline of Liberty in England
Hazlitt's Essays
Hayn: 4 Bibliographien
Hanotaux: Bibliophiles
Hirth: Inschriften von Tsaghan Baisin
Hirth: Keramische Gegenstande
History of Material Culture, 7pamphlets
Hardy: Eastern Monachism
Hyacinth: San-czy-czin
Housman: Collected Poems

88

Harlez: Chu-hsi
Harris: Voyages, 2 voll., folio
Hoemle: Ancient MSS from C. Asia
Hoemle: Antiquities from C. Asia
Hager: Monument de Yu
Harlez: Religion des tatares orientaux
Hirth: Tschan Ju-kua (Pamphlet)
Harlez: Laotze

Is Aboriginal Formosa  A past of the Chinese Empire
Imbault-Huart: Manuel de la langue coreenne
Ivanovskii: Mandjurica, I
I-li (Probsttain), 2 voll.
Imbrie: Etymology
Imbault-Huart: Anecdotes en chinois parle
Inscriptions de l'orkhon, folio
Ibn al-Muhanna: Arabic-Mongol-Turk. Gloss.
Istoriya Sibiri, 2 voll.
Institut de sinologie de Pekin
In Memoriam Panizza
Intorno ad una memoria di guilio Klaproth
Imp. Ermitage, 1915
Izv. Vostoc. Otd. Imp. Arx. Ob. I, 2 voll.

Jespersen: Bome sprog
Jami: Abode of Spring
Janburt: Notice d'un manuscrit ture (J.A.)
Julien: Tou-Rioue
Julien: Les deux consines, 2 voll.
Julg: Marchen des Siddhi-Kur, Kalmuch text, '66
Jean Second: Livre des Baisers
Joly and Inada: Sword and Same
Jespersen: Chapters on English
Japanese Education '77
Jews at K'ae-jung-joo
Journal Bengal Asiatic Society, '78-79
Japanese View of Outer Mongolia
Japan in Yezo
Jesuit Linguistic Studies (J)
Julien: Histore de la porcelaine chinoise
Julien: Blanche et Bleue
Japanese Fairy World
Julien: Voyages des Pelerins bouddhistes, 3 voll.
Julien: Avadanas, 3 voll.
Japan Society, London, Vol.I  plus 2 voll. of Suppl.
Jenkins: Life of Borrow
Jacobi: Printer's Vocabulary
Jaeschke: Tibetan-English Dict.
Julg: Mongolische Marchen-sammlung
Jahresb Frankfurter Vereins, 1 vol.
Jespersen: Lehrbuch der Phonetik

81

- 11 -

Kluge: Beitrage zur mingrelischen Grammatik
Kowalewskii: Mongolskaya Xrestomatiya, 2 voll.
Kotvie: Kalmyckiya Zagadki i poslovicy
Kohts: Erkenntnis Fahigkeiten des Schimpansen
Kraus: Leben des japanischen Volkes, 2 voll.
Kirishitan Kyogi no Kankyu, 2 voll.
Kirgiz-Russian Dict., 1903
Kotvie: Materialy dlya izuceniya tungusskix narecii
Kim: Die Aufmachung der mod. Zeitung in Ostasien
Karsch: Tribadie bei den Tieren
Kori: Kanawa the Incantation
Kaulen: Lingua mandshurica
Klaproth: Verzeiniss der chinesischen Bucher, Berlin (Lacks Errata)
Kaempfer: History of Japan, 2 voll., large paper
Kern: Histoire du bouddhisme dans l'Inde, 2 voll.
Keigoho no Kenkyu
Karlgren: Etudes sur la phonologie chinoise
Kow alewsk: Mongolian Dict., 3 voll. in 2
Kino: Japanese Expansion on Asiatic Cont., Vol. I.
Konrad: Japonskaya Literatura, I.
Khamkoff: Inscriptions musulmanesdn Caucase
Kanokogi: Geist Japans
Kerner: N.E.Asia, 2 voll.
Kaempfer:Amoenitates exotical
Kuno: Japanese Expansion, Vol. II.
Kasem-Beg: Turkish Grammar
Koops: Historical Account .... Paper
Katendyke's Dagboek
Kaempfer's Japan, 8vo.
Koda: Leaving the Hermitage
Kagawa: Before the Dawn
Koch: Kastratensekte
Klementz and Radlov: Turfan Exped.
Karpor: Turkmen
Karutz: Volker Nord und mittel Asiens
Keteti Szemle IX
Kashetsin: Buddizm
Klautke: Nutzpflanzen Chinas
Kern: Index to Versp. Geschnfter
Korzybski: Manhood of Humanity
Kattagani Badaxsan
Klaproth: Voyages au Caucase, 2 voll.
Kultur-Kuriosa, 3 voll.

Laufer: Jade
Langles: Alphabet Mantchou, '07
Linton: Sacrifice to the Morning Star
Luther: Ethische Anweisungen
Laufer: Chinese-Hebrew Ms.
Laufer: History of Finger Prints

90

Lindgren: Shaman dress of the Dagurs
Laufer: East Asiatic Collection
Laufer: Introduction of Tobacco into Europe
Laufer: Chinese Baskets
Lonchamp: Manuel du bibliophile francais, 2 voll.
Lonchamp: Manuel du bibliophile suisse
Lange: History of Materialism
Library of L.L.Bonaparte
Le Clert: Le papier, 2 voll, folio
Lloyd: Praises of Amida
Langles: Voyage dansl Inde, 2 voll., 12mo
Lendoyro: Tagalog Language
Loewenstein: Swastika and Yin Yang
Lloyd: Creed of Half-Japan
Lluys: Le Japon et Rome
Laufer: Pottery of Han Dynasty
Lewis & Short: Latin Dict.
Le pi-pa-ki
Lindley: Fa Hian
Le jardin parfume
Life of Mrs. Bird
Leyden: Memoirs of Baber
Life of Panizzi, Vol. I
Leland: Pidgin English
Lewis: Ranald McDonald
La Croze Thesaurus
Langles: Alphabet Manchou, 4to.
Le divand Amour
Locke: Ancient Quipu
Lecky: Hist. of European Morals, 2 voll.
Leskien: Handb. d. altbulg Sprache
Lettres persanes
Lettres edifiantes, 26 voll.
Library Cards
Lewy: Ban der europ. Sprachen
Letters rec. by East India Co., 6 voll.
L'Anthropologie, 2 voll.
Le sutra en 42 articles
Laufer: Reindeer
Lehtisalo: Vokalismus im Samojedischen
Levi: Eastern Humanism
Laufer: Amber in Asia
Lazareff Cat., 2 voll.
Ljungstedt: Portugese Settlements in China
Langles: Voyages de Sino-bad
Lajard: Langage siffle
Levi: Fragment tokharien
Lit. sborik k 100-letiyo ... Kazan ... Univ.

91

Lazarev: Sciences exactes en Russie
Leningrad Or. Inst.
Lenin Public Library Moscow, I.

Martyrologium franciscanum sineuse
Sir John Mandervile, O.U.P.
Michael: Origin of Manchu Rule in China
Muto: Short History of Anglo-Japanese Relations
Memoirs of Benyowsky, 1904
Memoirs of Benyowsky, '93
Marquart: Eransahr
Monboddo: Origin of Language, 6 voll.
Morse: Methods of Arrow Release
Milne: Retrospect of Ten Years of the Protestant Mission
Montgomery: History of Yaballaha III
Meyer: Grammatik der russischen sprache
Marquart: Osteuropaische streifzuge
Moule: Christians in China, 2 voll.
Meadows: Translations from Mandchou
Marakuev: Der gefleckte Hirschin der chines Medizin
Memoires de Benyowsky, 2 voll., 1790
Marco Polo (Argonaut)
Mickle's Lusiad (Bohn)
Morrison: Malayan Postscript
Malinowski: Crime and Custom in Savage Society
Mechanic's Magazine, 12 Dec., '29
Morison: View of China
Morals: Seroes no Japao
Mir-Ali-Shir
McFadden: Bibliography of Pacific Area Maps
Mel'nikov: Materialy dlya istorii ... skopceskoi eresii
Miansarov: Bibliographia caucasica
Montandon: Au pays des Ainou
Milloue: Bod-youl ou Tibet
Mokogodaijiten, 3 voll.
Mezov: Sibirskiya Bibliografiya
Maybon: Theatre japonais
Montandon: La civilisation ainou
Malan: San-tsze-king
Marnas: Religion de Jesus, 2 voll.
Morse: Catalogue Japanese Pottery
Morand: L'acupuncture
Mayers: Higher Authorities of China
Memoirs of W. Marsden
Marlowe: Tamburlaine
Markham: Indian Surveys
MacKinley: Tagalog Grammar
Mahler: Muhammadische Zeitrechnung
Morrison: Horae Sinicae
Meadows: Chinese and their Rebellions

92

Muir: Book Collecting
Morris: Living with Lepahas
Muto: History of Anglo-Japanese Relations
Murdoch: History of Japan, Vol. II only
Middelton-Wake: Invention of Printing
Marsden: Marco Polo
Mason: Arabian Prophet
Magic and Science in Western Yunnan
Morris: Traveller from Tokyo
Matsudaira: Culture of Kaki
McClean: Xavier
Milne: Sacred Edict
Medhurst's Shoo-Ring
Marlowe's Poems
Marsden's Malayan Grammar
Melanges chinoise et bouddhiques, 4 voll. (lacks Vol. III Luzac)
Memoir of Raffles
Milburn: Oriental Commerce, 2 voll., 4to.
Marshman: Works of Confucius, Vol. I
Marlowe: Edward II
Miscellanies Historical
Marlowe: Life and Dido
Marre: Gr. Tagalog
Manrique: Travels, 2 voll.
Murakami: Sinkan MSS
Mole: Handbuch, 2 voll.
Merhart: Bronzezeitam Jenissei
Map of the World 1506, British Museum
Missionary Success in Formosa, 2 voll.
Murray's Handbook of Japan, 4th ed.
McGowan: Self-Immolation by Fire
Moraes: Cartas do Japao
Marcuse: Handworterbuch
Masson-Oursel: Psychologie indienne
Man: Formosa
March: Pottery Description
Mollendorff: Manchu Literature
Melioranskii: Skazanie ob. edigel i toktanysy
Mongolo-Oiratskii epos
Memoir of Capt. W. Gile
March: China and Japan in Our Museums
Memorials of Rev. Douglas
Monumenta nipponica, V Part 1
Medhurst: China
Markham: Chinchona
Museum Journal, Dec. '26
Mirady-Nameh
Melanges russes, III
Materialy dlya etnografii Rossii, Vol. 14
Materialy dlya ist voiska Donskago
Meyeshof: Noms portugais de drogues

93

- 15 -

Memoir of Rev. S. Dyer
Moges: Ambassade en Chine
Morse: Traces of Early Race in Japan
Marlowe: Faustus and Jew of Malta, 2 voll.
Marakuev: Russische Arbeiten ... Chin. Lexicographie

Nye: Morning of my Life in China
Nachnchten K. G. d. Wiss. Gott. phil-hist. 1910, 1
Nikkochizu
Naliv Rine: Khokand
Nilsson: Primitive Time Reckoning
Nunn: Ecclesiastical Latin
Norman: Fighting Man of Japan
Nihonbunten Kogi
Nihon to Portogaru
New Castle Typ. Soc. 2 voll.
New Castle Topogr. Soci., 1 vol.
Nioradze: Schamanismus
Nausester: Das Kind und die Form d. Sprache
Nihonjinko-mitsudo-zu
Novikov: Skifskaya istoriya, 3 in 1.
Notices et Extraits, vol. XI

Orbeli: Musulmanskie izrazcy
Osorius: Histoire de Portugal (1581)
Olmedilla: Cristobal Acosta
Otsuka: First Voyage of the English
Ocean of Story, 10 voll.
Os Lusiadas, Maranus, Porto
"Outpost": Singapore Nightmare
Olearius: Voyages, 1719, folio
Otanike: Shinsaiikiki, 2 voll., folio
Observations, critiques sur le Japon
Ostroumov: Tatar-Russian Dict.
Osborn: Japanese Fragments
Obraziy mongol'skoi narodnoi literatury, I.
Olufsen: Bokhara Dialect
Obrucev: Central Asia (R), 2 voll., 4to
Opyt grammatiki aleut skago yazyka
Ostrovskii: Votyaki
Oxford: Scaliger
Otto: Hauslehrerbestrebungen
Ogawa: Festivals of Yedo
Opisanie Korei, 3 voll. plus map
Otto: Kindesmundart
Ovidreff: Langue jap. litteraire

Partridge: Dictionary of R.A.F. Slang
Pomus: Buriat Mongolia

94

Pennell: Lithography and Lithographers
Pozdneev: Mongol'skaya letopis "Erdeniin erixe"
Pozdneev: Kalmyckaya Xrestomatiya
Pound: Ta Hio
Psalmanaazaar's Formosa (Library of Impostors)
Potanin: Vostochnye Motivy
Pozdneev: Opyt sobraniya mandjurskoi literatury, I.
Paget: Human Speech
Priapeia, (Gaselee), 1890
Pinto: Peregrinacao, 1762
Parlement of Prattlers (Fanfrolico)
Polish Science and Learning
Pamyai akad. A.N. Veselovskago, 1921
Pelliot: Comans (J.A.)
Pamyati V. Tomsena
Psichari: Language Question in Greece
Parker: Taoist Religion
Pitton de Tournefort: Voyage du Levant, 1718, 2 voll.
Paske-Smith: Western Barbarians in Japan
Paske-Smith: Glympse of the English House
Poppe: Xalxa-mongol'skii geroiceskii epos
Poppe: Materialy dlya issled tungusskogo yazyka
Pelikan: Skopcestvo, folio (1 plate missing)
Pierre Louys et l'histoire litteraire
Pfizmaier: Japanese Studies, Vol. III, quarto
Petrucci: La philosophie de la nature, folio
Parker: Thousand Years of the Tartars
Percival: Experiments on Peruvian Bark
Penzer: Burton Bibliography
Poesta Medieval (Textos literarios)
Piggott: Garden of Japan
Pfizmaier: Japanese Studies, 4to, Vol. II
Pacific Area in American Research
Parker: Hospitals in China
Pritchard: Crucial Years of Anglo-Chinese Relations
Pierson: Manyoshu, vol. 5
Plomer: W. de Worde
Pfizmaier: Japanese Studies, Vol. I.
Penney: Japanese Popular Stories
Patkanov: Istoriya Mongolov
Pissoh: Sosho
Popov: Pantheon chinois
Pokotilov: Istoria vostocnyx mongolov
Parkinson: Trade in the Eastern Seas
Prestage: Portuguese Pioneers
Pages: Bibliographie japonaise
Piry: Erh-ton-mei, 2 voll.
Parke-Smith: England and Japan
Penzer: Harem
Pfizmaier's Japanese Studies, 1 vol., 8vo. (making 2 in all)

95

- 17 -

Portogaru o tazuneru
Pozdneev: Mongol'skaya Xrestomatiya
Panther: Marco Polo, 2 voll.
Peregrinacdo de Pinto, 4 voll.
Purchas, 20 voll.
Pyke: Legibility of Print
Pokomy: Aetivische gr.
Pelliot: Mongols et la papaute, 2 voll.
Pamphlet on Kondakov
Peking Catalogue of Clocks
Po etapam razvitiya .....
Pumpelly: Annan, 2 voll., 4to.
Panchatrentra (in Russian)
Putman: Books in the Middle Ages, 2 voll.
Penal Code of Japan
Pfizmaier: Aino Wortersammlung
Paske-Smith: Japanese Traditions of Xtianity
Pozdneev: Skazanie o xozdenii ... baza-baksi
Poppe: Altaisch und Urturkisch
Pruitt: Flight of an Empress
Practical Orthography of Tswana
Pekarskii: Russko-yak'utskii slovar'
Pinto: Peregmacao
Pfizmaier: Seelenzustande und Leidenschaften
Pypin: Istoriya russkoi etnograjii, 4 voll.
Poussin: Nirvana
Pozdneev: Mongoliya: Mongoly, 2 voll.
Potselnevskii: Turkmen Handbook
Phonetic Transcription and Transliteration

Putesestire na Seber ... 4to
Protokoly ......
Pamphlets, 1 vol.      buckram, red label.
Pamphlet on Ossetes
Putman: Censorship of Church of Rome, 2 voll.
Pfizmaier: alte Bewohner des heutrgen Corea
Pfizmaier: 3 pamphlets (unbound)

Queri: Kraftbayrisch

Radlov! Kudatku Bilik, folio
Rundall: Memorials of Empire of Japon
Radlov: Kudatku Bilik, 4to
Remusat: Relation des royaumes bouddhiques

96

Ryley: Ralph Fitch
Radlov: Chuastuanit
Rochet: Proverbes mantchoux et mongols
Rudnev: Materialy po govoram vostochnor mongolii
Rudnev: Xori-buryatskii govor
Riggs: Anneno-Turkish Grammar
Richthofen's Letters '70-72
Read: Prelude to Chemistry
Rosny: Feuilles de momidzi
Rahder: Japanologische Verkenningen
Ross: Corea
Revon: De arte florali
Remusat: Langues tartares
Reade: Registrum librorum, 2 voll.
Remandino: Circumcision
Rosenberg: O mirosozercanii sobremennogo
Redin: Painyati G.B. de Rossi
Raquette: English-Turki Dictionary
Rentskii: Lyndi bozi i skopcy, '72
Rotta: La filosofia del linguaggio rella patristica
Rahder: Glossary of the Dasabhumikasutra
Regnault: Medecine et pharmacie
Roth: Jewish contribution to Civilization
Russian Orientalia, 1 vol. so lettered
Reumuth: Lozische Beschaffenhert der Kindlichen sprachanfange
Remusat: Sciences naturelles chez les peuples de l'Asie orientale
Rosny: L'epouse d' outre-tombe
Remusat: Doctrine Samaneenne
Ryerson Collection of Japanese Illustrated Books
Rabelais ed. Lefranc, 5 voll.
Remusat: Miroir des langues mandchoue
Rose Inne's Dictionary
Relacoes entre Portugueses e japoneses
Ribeiro's Ceilao
Ramstedt: Abhandlungen
Royle: Fibrous Plants of India
Raffles: Report on Japan
Radlov: Morpholojie der Turksprachen
Riasanovsky: Principles of Mongol Law
Rockhill: Diplomatic Audiences
Ribeiro: Andam Faunos
Remusat: Melanges, 5 voll.
Raffles: Java, 2 voll.
Ribeiro: Filhasde Babilonca
Ross: Dialogues in Eastern Turki
Remusat: Iu-Riao-li, 4 voll.
Rytschkov: Historie von Kasan
Rosny: Biotheque jap. de Nordenskiold
Robinson: Genius of Hebrew Grammar
Ramstedt: Mongolica
Russian-Tartar Dictionary, 4to.

97

Rondot: Vert de Chine
Rowse: On History
Radlov: Nigurische Sprachdenkmaler
Reuter: Anlautsvokalein Tochanschen
Richthofen: Letters on Provinces of China
Ross: Polyglott List of Birds
Rety: La jolie papetiere
Ruwet: Religion des Lamas
Ross: Chinese Foreign Policy
Rabellais, 3 voll. (English ed.)
Ruskaya letopis, 8 voll., 4to.
R.G.S: Alphabets of Foreign Languages

Schefer: Histoire de l'Asie centrale, texte persan
Semenov: Tadjik Grammar
Sanssure: Origines de l'astronomie chinoise
Sinica Franciscana, I
Schleicher: Zur vergleichenden Sprachengeschichte
Sansom: Living in Tokyo
Schmidt: Kamasutram
Scarborough: Chinese Proverbs
Soubeiran: Matiere medicale chez les Chinois
Satow: English-Japanese Dictionary
Sade: Les 120 journees
Stein: Archaeological Work N-W. Frontier, 1905
Shuck: Portfolio Chinensis
Shchukin: Poezdka v Yakutske, '44
Smith & Mikami: History of Japanese Mathematics
Sade: Dialogue entre un pretre et un moribond
Stejneger: Birds of Kuril Islands
Satow: Jesuit Mission Puss
Schmidt: Geschichte der Ostmongolen
Sahlin: Cesar Chesneau deu Marsais
Symonds: Wine Women and Song
Seikakokushojitenondo
Schmidt: Eine mongolische Quadratinschrift
Sanssure: Systeme cosmologique sino-iranien
Schmidt: Bogda gesser Chan, ubersetzung
Sleeman: Ramaseeana
Selections from Nippon Seishin Library
Schmidt: Epic of Bogda Gesser Khan, Mongol text
Schleicher: Die darw inische Theorie u.d. Sprachwissenschaft
Shcherbatskoi: Pamyatniki Indiiskoi filosofii, I
Schiefner: Betrage zur Kenntruiss der tungus mundarten
Stekel: Fetischismus
Segalen: Steles (Collection coreenne)
Sir J. Suckling's Works, 3rd ed.
Schmidt: Die Sprachfamilien der Erde, Atlas
Staunton: Miscellaneous Notices rel. to China, '22
Stcherbatsky: Buddhist Nirvana
Stael-Holstein: Kacyapaparivarta
Schmidt: Sprachfamilien der Erde, text

98

Schott: Voabularium Sinicum
Sanssure: L'horometrie des Chinois
St. Aulaire: Chinese Running Hand
Satow: Japa ese Chronological Tables
Sancean: Indies Adventure
Semeonoff: Key to Russian Grammar
Schuchardt: Primitiae linguae vasconum
Soper: Buddhist Architecture in Japan
Serindia, 5 voll.
Siebold: Japan and Comity of Nations
Suski: Conj. of Japanese Verbs
Schmidt: Forschungen ... Mongolen
Skold: Ungarische Endbetonung
Sun tzu: Principles of War
Stanton: Chinese Drama
Siren: Walls and Gates of Peking
Schmidt: Mongolian Dictionary
Siebold: Mariner's Guide to Japan
Seebolm: Birds of Japanese Empire
Semeonoff: Russian Grammar
Stevens: East India Co.
Spitzelius: De re litterania Sinensium
Straelen: New Diplomacy in Far East
Standish: Three Bamboos
Sedillot: Hist. des sciences mathematiques,, 2 voll.
Summers: Vampire
Smith ; China
Sbornik dogovorov Rossiis Kitaen
Siebold: Bibliotheca japonica, lit. IV
Siebold: Thesaurus, 4to.
Staat van alle Volkere, I
Stein: Ancient Geography of Kashmir
Simon: Bibliothea bacchica, vol. I
Shitaijii
Sainson: Memoires sur l'Annam
Schurhammer: Disputationen
Stone: Story of Phallicism, 2 voll.
Smith: Visit to China
Semenov: Annan (Pamphl.)
Sauval: Chronique scandaleuse
Sbornik Orxonskoi exped. 1-V in 2 voll.
Semenov: Materialy dlya ... tadzikov ... 4to
Sternberg: Gilyak, 4to.
Six Early Printed Maps (Brit. Museum)
Stem-Szanacatalogue
Stadelmann: Laotse undd. Biologie
Studes: Anglo-N. Lafidanes
Smith: Japan
Sanssure: La sene septenaire

99

Schmidt: Izucerie Kitaya
Semenov: Zur Frage .....
Singh: History of Khokand
Staunton: Notices of China, 2nd ed.
Stopes: Plays of Old Japan
Semenov: Pamyatriki ariiskoi Kultunz
Skrine & Ross: Heart of Asia
Segenbringende Reisaehren, 3 voll.
Szinnyei: Herkunft der Ungarn
Sristed: Life of Burton
Semenov: Contradictions dans les avis ...
Saddharmapandarikasutra , yellow silk, oblong
Schuchardt: Miscellanea linguistica
Stopes: Contraception
Sade: Philosophy
Shaw: Gr. Eastern Turki, 1 vol.
Sanchez: De Matrimonio, folio
Schiefner: Yukagirische Sprache
Semenov: La religion du Satan
Scerbatsky: Filosofskoe ucenie buddizma
Schuchardt: Deutschgegen Frauzosisch
Scherk: Psychologie der Eunuchoiden
Schiefner: Tusch-Sprache
Schiefner: Tibetan Tales
Sermao de S. Antonio
Sulejman: Cagataj Worterbuch

Tatar Grammar, '01
Tarrant: Hongkong, Part I
Ten Years of Japanese Burrowing
Talko-Hryncewicz: Etnologii Azyi srodkowej, '10
Tebenkov: Drevneishiya Snosheniya Rusi
Tourist Library, 21st vol.
Thomsen: Inscriptions d'Orkhon, with portr., etc.
Tolnai: Ungarisches Lesebuch
Tavares: Epitome de gramatica portuguesa
Thexo Bulls
Tezkereh-i-Evlia, 2 voll., folio
Tsurayuki: Log of a Japanese Journey
Tanizaki: Puis que je l'aime
Three Turki MSS from Kashgar
Trigault: Rei Christ apud Japonios
Trans. Oriental Ceramic Soc., 17 voll. (18 not yet purchased)
Turselin: La Vie de F. Xavier, 1612
Tolkowsky: Hesperides
Tikov: Gr. de la langue darkwa
Tchonbinov: Georgian Dict., 4to.
Trudy Muzeya Paleogr. I. & III, 2 voll.
Thorn: Chinese Courtship

100

Tucci: Apologie du taoisme
Thomsen: Samlede Ajhandlinger, 3 voll.
Ta-ssi-yang-kuo I, 1
Tonkoisho, folio, chitsu
Thomsen: Turcica
Trudy Bibliogr. Kom. Byvs pri SNKTSSR 1-3
Trudy Troick 10-15
Trudy Troick 4-9
Trudy Troickosavsko-kyaxtinskago otd. I-II, III 2-3
Transliteration of Russia (Brit. Acad.)
Trudy Troick .... III, 1
Taschenbuch fur Buchersammler, 3 voll.
Turkemistan, 1928
Tonkoisho, 8vo.
Ten Thousand Cases Birth Control
Thorns: Affectionate Pair

Unger: Hamanns Sprachtheone
Utilite de la flagellation, '01
Um auto de gil Vicente (school text)
Ueda's Dict. , 5 voll.
Une Famille Tongouse
Useful Plants of Japan
Uspenskii: Oceski z ist. Trapezunsk. imperii
Uzatel'R Aktam ..., 1838

Venezianischer Dirnenspiegel
Verbickii: Altaiskie inorodcy
Vuilleumier: Symbolism of Chinese Imp. Robes
Van Straelen: A Missionary in the War-net
Varthema's Itinerary (ditto)
Volpicelli: Chinese Phonology
Vignali: Cazzaria
Vladimircov: Obrazcy Mongolskoi narodnoi slovesnosti
Vamberry: Pinto
Verhandelingen van het genootschap van Batavia, 18th part.
Vostocnye zapiski, I, 1927, 8vo.
Vienna Ac. Verzeichnis, 2 voll.
Vimalapracnottaratnamala versio tibetica, folio
Vostocnyya Zametki, 1895, folio
Vitale: Pekinese Rhymes
Vareni Regni Japoniae et Siam
Venn: Life of Xavier
Voyages Towards N.W. (Hakluyt Soc.)
Vegetation of Mt. Fuji
Vostocnye zapiski, I, 8vo.
Voyage of Saris to Japan (Hakluyt)
Vindel's Biblioteca Oriental, 2 voll.
Valentyn: Oud en Nieuer Oost. Indien, 5 voll.
Voyages of M. Frobisher (Argonaut)
Vitale: Grammaire Mongole

101

- 23 -

Vamberry: Story of My Struggles
Vida de Xavier, 4 voll.
Vamberry: Caghataische Studien
Vatin: Minuskii Krai
Valenziani: Kan-kan-wau-rai
Vamberry: Uigurische Sprachmonumente
Viana: Albuquerque
Vogeler: Die Freiheit der Liebe
Von Zach: Erganzungen
Vladimircov: Buddizm v Tibete
Vsemirnaya Literatura, 2 voll, 8vo
Visite auz temples de Pekin
Voprosy: reseniya
Version turque der Bakhtiar Nameh
Vladimircov: Obraczy mongol'skoi slovesnosti, paper

Warren: Study of Book-plates, 2 voll.

Waley: Monkey
Whitaker: Eastern Turki
Williams: Ilocano Grammar (G)
Wahnelt: Kindersprache u. Altersmundarten
Wylie: Une Inscription Mongole (J.A.)
White: Chinese Jews, 3 voll.
Woolf: 3 Tibetan Mystery Plays
Winiwarter: Kiyonaga et Choki
Wiedemann: Gr. der wotjakischen sprache
Wenstrom: Swedish-English Dict.
Wright and Sinclair: History of Later Latin Literature
Wickersham: Alaskan Bibliography
Weil: Tatarische Texte
Wells: Perspective in Chinese Painting
Wylie: Ethnography of the Han
Wylie: Publications of Protestant Missionaries
Weig: Chinesische Familiennamen
What is an Index?
Wenkstem: Bibliography of Japan, 2 voll.
Warner: Japanese Sculpture of Suiko Period
Watchdog: Japanese and the Pacific Problems
William Adams (brochure)
Wang: Chinesische Oper.
Wiener Beitrage zur Kunst Asiens, 2 voll.
Wingfield: Curse of Koshiu
Wylie: Nestorian Tablet
Wright: Existing legal situation as it relates to conflict in Far East
Williams: Relations with Chinese Empire
Wilhelm & Gundert: Chinesische Literatur
Wang: Histoire anecdorique chinoise

102

Vamberry: Story of My Struggles
Vida de Xavier, 4 voll.
Vamberry: Caghataische Studien
Vatin: Minuskii Krai
Valenziani: Kan-kan-wau-rai
Vamberry: Uigurische Sprachmonumente
Viana: Albuquerque
Vogeler: Die Freiheit der Liebe
Von Zach: Erganzungen
Vladimircov: Buddizm v Tibete
Vsemirnaya Literatura, 2 voll, 8vo
Visite auz temples de Pekin
Voprosy: reseniya
Version turque der Bakhtiar Nameh
Vladimircov: Obraczy mongol'skoi slovesnosti, paper

Winkler: La langue basque et les langues ouralo-altaiques
Williamson: Book of Famille Rose
Works of Tourneur (Fanfrolico)
Weston: Playground of Far East
Webster: Kan Ying Pien, Shanghai 1918
Waley: Monkey
Whitaker: Eastern Turki
Williams: Ilocano Grammar (G)
Wahnelt: Kindersprache u. Altersmundarten
Wylie: Une Inscription Mongole (J.A.)
White: Chinese Jews, 3 voll.
Woolf: 3 Tibetan Mystery Plays
Winiwarter: Kiyonaga et Choki
Wiedemann: Gr. der wotjakischen sprache
Wenstrom: Swedish-English Dict.
Wright and Sinclair: History of Later Latin Literature
Wickersham: Alaskan Bibliography
Weil: Tatarische Texte
Wells: Perspective in Chinese Painting
Wylie: Ethnography of the Han
Wylie: Publications of Protestant Missionaries
Weig: Chinesische Familiennamen
What is an Index?
Wenkstem: Bibliography of Japan, 2 voll.
Warner: Japanese Sculpture of Suiko Period
Watchdog: Japanese and the Pacific Problems
William Adams (brochure)
Wang: Chinesische Oper.
Wiener Beitrage zur Kunst Asiens, 2 voll.
Wingfield: Curse of Koshiu
Wylie: Nestorian Tablet
Wright: Existing legal situation as it relates to conflict in Far East
Williams: Relations with Chinese Empire
Wilhelm & Gundert: Chinesische Literatur
Wang: Histoire anecdorique chinoise

102

Xiva, 1840

Yauchi: Toyodokushichizu
Yetts: Legend of Confucius
Yeh: Confucian Conception of Jen
Yuzawa: Tokugawa gogaku no kenkyu
Yetts: An-Yang
Young: The Japanese Canadians
Yetts: Cull Chinese Bronzes
Yoshimoto: Peasant Sage of Japan
Yule: Cathay, 4 voll.
Yamanaka Cat.
Yoshida: Whispering Leaves

Zi: Practique des examens litteraires en Chine
Zamcarano: Buryat Texts
Zorell: Georgische Bibelubersetzung
Zenker: Chinesische Philosophie
Zilal i Ilkan
Zwick: Handb. der westmongolischen sprache
Zwick: Westmongolische grammatik
Zlatokuznecy Dagestana
Zapiski of Astraxani, '84
Zapiskio sibiri, 1837

\- - - - - - - -

103

Sicardo: Christiandad del Japon — 1 —
Radlov: Kudatku Bilik, folio
Hunter: Primitive Papermaking
Is Aboriginal Formosa a part of the Chinese Empire?
Venezianischer Dirnenspiegel
Comerford's Journal.
Brosset: Arakel de Tauriz, Registre chronologique
Schefer: Histoire de l'Asie centrale, texte persan
Lo Cheng the boy who wouldn't keep still
Martyrologium franciscanum sinense
Rundall: Memorials of Empire of Japan
Semenov: Tadjik Grammar
Adam: Grammaire mandchou
Gale: Cloud Dream of the Nine
Coxe: Russian Discoveries, 2nd ed.
Antonii Panormitae Hermaphr. ed. Forberg
Catalogue of Philatelic Library of Earl of Crawford.
Jespersen: Böme sprog
Brosset: Rapport sur l'ouvrage intitulé Numizmatičeskie fakty
Orbeli: Musulmanskie izrazcy
Camoens: Passion of Christ
Aungervyle Society: Voyages of Vertomannus
Partridge: Dictionary of R.A.F. Slang
Saussure: Origines de l'astronomie chinoise
Radlov: Kudatku Bilik, 4to
Golovnin: Voyage of the Sloop Diana (R)
Verbickii: Altaiskie inorodcy
Queri: Kraftbayrisch
Rémusat: Relation des royaumes bouddhiques
Nye: Morning of my Life in China
Winkler: La langue basque et les langues ouralo-altaïques
Vuilleumier: Symbolism of Chinese Imp. Robes
Pozdneev: Buriat Mongolia
Hirth: Geschichte der Ostmongolen 104

Jaubert: Notice d'un manuscrit turc (J.A.) -2-
Deeters: Kharthwelische Verbum
Yanchi: Toyodokushichizu
Pennell: Lithography & Lithographers
Sir John Mandeville, O.U.P.
Michael: Origin of Manchu Rule in China
Sinica Franciscana, I
Hoffmann: Japanese Grammar, 2nd ed.
Bibliotheca Lindesiana: Cat. of Chinese Books
Gabelentz: Grammaire mandchoue
Whitney: Index of Chinese Characters in Hepburn's Dict.
Chavannes: les religieux éminents
Hirth Anniversary Volume
Osorius: Histoire de Portugal (1581)
van Straelen: A Missionary in the War-net
Schleicher: Zur vergleichenden Sprachengeschichte
Jami: Abode of Spring
Muto: Short History of Anglo-Japanese Relations
Ghaniev: Tatar-Russian Dictionary (Baku)
Exercises in Yokohama Dialect, '79
Bedevian: Polyglottic Dict. of Plant Names
Sansom: Living in Tokyo
Erdmann: Muhammed's Geburt u. Abrahah's Untergang
Christopher: Palaeography and Archives
Schmidt: Kamasutram
Giles: Six Centuries at Tunhuang
Memoirs of Benyowsky, 1904
Scarborough: Chinese Proverbs
Gale: Korean Folk Tales
Ryley: Ralph Fitch
Memoirs of Benyowsky, '93
Soubeiran: Matière médicale chez les Chinois
Bang & Marquart: Osttürkische Dialektstudien
Kluge: Beiträge zur mingrelischen Grammatik
Fanshawe: Lusiad, 1st ed.
Marquart: Eranšahr 105
11 Fonssagrives: Si-ling

-3-

Monboddo: Origin of Language, 6 voll.
Unger: Hamanns Sprachtheorie
Pozdneev: Mongol'skaya letopis "Erdeniin erixe"
Morse: Methods of Arrow Release
Gabelentz: Essays on Mongolian & Manchu
Courteille: Memoires de Baber, 2 voll. in 1
Dickins: Japse Odes
Radlov: Chuastuanit
Pozdneev: Kalmyckaya Xrestomatiya
Aubert: La petite pantoufle
Kowalewskii: Mongolskaya Xrestomatiya, 2 voll.
Hyacinth: Istoriya pervyx chetyrex khanov
Harlez: Histoire de l'Empire de Kin
Gabelentz: Geschichte der grossen Liao
Becker: Feudal Kamakura
Rochet: Proverbes mantchoux et mongols
Imbault-Huart: Manuel de la langue coréenne
Hunter: Turki Text of Narratives of the Prophets
Covell: Under the Seal of Sesshu
Douglas: Birds & Beasts of GK Anthology
Pound: Ta Hio
Olmedilla: Cristobal Acosta
Zi: Pratique des examens littéraires en Chine
Catalogue Turkestan Public Library (R)
Brief Summary of Do Ka Zang
Psalmanaazaar's Formosa (Library of Impostors)
Rudnev: materialy po govoram vostochnoi mongolii
Epic of Bogdo-khan Janggar, Kalmuck text
Pozdneev: Očerki byta buddiiskix monastyreï
Zamcarano: Buryat Texts
Rudnev: Xori-buryatskii govor
Julien: Tou-Kioue
Tatar Grammar, '01
Dandolo: Art of Rearing Silkworms
106 Potanin: Vostochnye motivy 106

資料 10（貼付ノート・Ashbee: Library Catalogue）

—4—

Brockelmann: Mitteltürkischer Wortschatz
Kotvič: Kalmyckiya zagadki i poslovicy
Giles: Record of Buddhistic Kingdoms
Riggs: Armeno-Turkish Grammar
Satow: English-Japanese Dictionary
Clifton: Fortune Telling by Japse Swords
Milne: Retrospect of Ten Years of the Protestant Mission
Julien: Les deux cousines, 2 voll.
Sade: Les 120 journées
Fukuyama: First Japse Mission to America
Williamson: Book of Famille Rose
Works of Tourneur (Fanfrolico)
Montgomery: History of Yaballaha III
Allen: Korean Tales
Sir J. Chardin's Travels in Persia (Argonaut)
Varthema's Itinerary (ditto)
Kohts: Erkenntnis Fähigkeiten des Schimpansen
Codex Cumanicus
Dautremer: Nikko passé et présent
Pantusov: Ghazat dar mulk i chîn
Houtsma: Türkisch-arabisches Glossar
Pozdneev: Narodnyya pêsni Mongolov
Patkanov: Cygany
Grajdanzev: Formosa Today
Blochet: Histoire des Mongols (texte)
Joly & Inada: Sword and Samé
Volpicelli: Chinese Phonology
Gosse: T. L. Beddoes, 2 voll.
Cornish: Borderlands of Language in Europe
Hart: Japse Art Work
Kraus: Leben des japanischen Volkes, 2 voll.
Diosy: Yamato-damashi-i
Giles: Strange Tales from a Chinese Studio, 2 voll., 1st ed.
Weston: Playground of Far East
141 Calthrop: Book of War 107

—5—

Richthofen's Letters '70–'72
Harada: Lesson of Japanese Architecture
Stein: Archaeological Work N.-W. Frontier, 1905
Blades: Enemies of Books, 2nd ed.
Webster: Kan Ying Pien, Shanghai 1918
Meyer: Grammatik der russischen Sprache
Kirishitan kyôgi no kenkyu, 2 voll.
Cahen: Livre de comptes
Marquart: Osteuropäische Streifzüge
Grønbech: Forstudier til tyrkisk lydhistorie
Dühren: Neue Forschungen
Read: Prelude to Chemistry
Elferink: Het oordeel
Giles: Glossary of Reference, 3rd ed.
Shuck: Portfolio Chinensis
Vignali: Cazzaria
Foster: Supplementary Calendar of Documents in India Office
Fujishima: Bouddhisme japonais
Shchukin: Poězdka v Yakutskě, '44
Rosny: Feuilles de Momidzi
Fonseca: Historical Sketch of Goa
Ecke: Twin Pagodas of Zayton
Housman: Shropshire Lad (Riccardi Press)
Burton: Catullus
Moule: Christians in China, 2 voll.
Waley: Monkey
Hetherington: Chinese Ceramic Glazes
Smith & Mikami: History of Japse Mathematics
Laufer: Jade
Arber: Herbals
Langlès: Alphabet Mantchou, '07
Jülg: Märchen des Siddhi-Kur, Kalmuck text, '66
Dennys: Folklore of China
175 Sade: Dialogue entre un prêtre et un moribond

108

6

X Cordier: Narrative of Recent Events in Tongking
⊘ Rahder: Japanologische Verkenningen
• Meadows: Translations from Manchu
/ Alcock: Art & Art Industry in Japan
⊘ Ross: Corea
X Cordier: La France en Chine, vol. I only
\ Stejneger: Birds of Kuril Islands
△ Hirth: Ancient Porcelain
X Douglas: Paneros
⊘ Revon: De arte florali
X Dahlgren: Débuts de la cartographie du Japon
△ Hunter: Turki Texts
• Marakuev: Der gefleckte Hirsch in der chines. Medizin
X Courteille: Dictionnaire turk-oriental
• Mémoires de Benyovsky, 2 voll., 1790
X Dickins: Old Bamboo Hewer's Story, '88
/ Brown: Pilgrim's Progress (Cambridge English Classics)
/ Beal: Travels of Buddhist Pilgrims
+ Whitaker: Eastern Turki
\ Tarrant: Hongkong, part I
/ Bibliographie des oeuvres de H. Cordier
△ Otsuka: First Voyage of the English
△ Pozdneev: Opyt sobraniya mandjurskoi literatury, I
+ Williams: Ilocano Grammar (G)
⊘ Rémusat: Langues tartares
\ Satow: Jesuit Mission Press
△ Ocean of Story, 10 voll.
△ George Borrow: Works, 16 voll.
/ Beveridge: Babur Nama in Engl., 2 voll.
\ Schmidt: Geschichte der Ostmongolen
⊘ Reade: Registrum librorum, 2 voll.
X Drevnayya Rossiiskaya Bibliotheka, 20 voll.
△ Paget: Human Speech
X de Corbeil: Lettres sur l'histoire philos. des langues, 1820
21° X Castrén: Ostjakische Sprachlehre

109

7

Priapeia, (Gaselee), 1890
de Landes: glossaire ér.
Sahlin: César Chesneau du Marsais
Bayer: De Horis Sinicis
Marco Polo (Argonaut)
Pinto: Peregrinaçao, 1762
Ananga-Ranga
Giles: Travels of Fa-hsien
Hughes: Chinese Philosophy in Classical Times
Aston: Grammar of Spoken Japanese, 4th ed.
Remondino: Circumcision
Os Lusiadas, Maranus, Pórto
Conrady: Indochinesische Causativ-denominativ-bildung
Emelyanov: Grammatika votyackogo yazyka
Vladimircov: Obrazcy mongolskoi narodnoi slovesnosti
Boxer: Affairs of the Madre de Deus
Jean Second: Livre des Baisers
Kirgiz-Russian Dict., 1903
Diccionario do Povo, Nº 4.
Mickle's Lusiad (Bohn)
Frei Luis de Sousa (school text)
Bibliotheca Curiosa Monacensis
Binyon: Flight of the Dragon
Symonds: Wine Women & Song
Dühren: de Sade und ~~sein~~ seine Zeit
Parlement of Prattlers (Fanfrolico)
Morrison: Malayan Postscript
Gunsaulus: Japanese Costume
id.: Gods & Heroes of Japan
Linton: Sacrifice to the Morning Star
Polish Science & Learning
Rosenberg: O mirosozercanii sobremennogo buddizma na dal'nem Vostoke, 1919
242 Kotvic: Materialy dlya izučeniya tungusskix narečii

110

-8-

Gowland: Art of Casting Bronze in Japan
Seikakokushojitenondō
Pamyati akad. A.N. Veselovskago, 1921
Atkinson: Travels in the Amoor
Malinowski: Crime & Custom in Savage Society
Grose's Classical Dictionary, '23
Grose's Provincial Glossary, '11
Utilité de la flagellation, '01
Ten Years of Japanese Burrowing
Bhuyan: Early British Relations with Assam
Hirth: Native Sources of Chinese Pictorial Art
Catalogue of Möllendorff Manchu Library
Kim: Die Aufmachung der mod. Zeitung in Ostasien
Ament: Begriff der Kindersprache
Wahnelt: Kindersprache u. Altersmundarten
Pelliot: Comans (J.A.)
Modi: Astōdan
Karsch: Tribadie bei den Tieren
Luther: Ethische Anweisungen
Huart: Conte bouddhique des deux frères
Castagné: Congrès de turkologie de Bakou
Nachrichten K. G. d. Wiss. Gött. phil.-hist. 1910, 1
Campbell: List of Birds collected in Corea
Kori: Kanawa the Incantation
Fujisawa: Yoshida T. & R.L. Stevenson
Giles: Note on 4 Chinese Volumes
Laufer: Chinese-Hebrew Ms.
Laufer: History of Finger Prints
Binyon: Chinese Art & Buddhism
Blochet: Babar Nama
Bretschneider: Chinese Silkworm Trees
Hatsukade: Bildungsideale in d. jap. Kultur
Cardim: Notes on Port.-English Grammar
Campbell: Recent Journey in N. Korea
Wylie: Une inscription mongole (J.A.)
278 Schmidt: Eine mongolische Quadratschrift

Harlez: Règlements militaires — 9
Pamyati V. Tomsena
Talko-Hryncewicz: Etnologii Azyi środkowej, 10
Gray: Tercentenary of Hakluyt
Psichari: Language Question in Greece
Mechanics' Magazine, 12 Dec., '29
Parker: Taoist Religion
Haas: Dokument aus der jap. Inquisition
Saussure: Système cosmologique sino-iranien
Gowland: Dolmens of Korea
Gowland: Japse pseudo-speise
Lindgren: Shaman dress of the Dagurs
Tebenkov: Drevneïskiya Snosheniya Rusi
Rêdin: Pamyati G.B. de Rossi
Pitton de Tournefort: Voyage du Levant, 1718, 2 voll.
Jespersen: Chapters on English
White: Chinese Jews, 3 voll.
Catalogue of Lockhart Library
Schmidt: Bogda Gesser Chan, übersetzung
Gedenshtrom: Otryvki o Sibiri
Paske-Smith: Western Barbarians in Japan
300 Churchill: Beach-la-Mar
Golden Cockerel Press: Golden Asse
Woolf: 3 Tibetan Mystery Plays
Sleeman: Ramaseeana
Winiwarter: Kiyonaga et Choki
Paske-Smith: Glympse of the English House
Tourist Library, 21st vol.
Selections from Nippon Seishin Library
Poppe: xalxa-mongol'skii geroičeskii epos
Catalogue of Chinese Works in Bodleian Library
Morison: View of China
"Outpost": Singapore Nightmare
Halloran's Journey to Japan & Loochoo
Moraes: Serões no Japão
314 Hughes: The Great Learning & the Mean-in-Action 112

— 10 —

Hudson: Atlas of Far Eastern Politics
da Costa: Uma carta náutica portuguesa
Schmidt: Epic of Bogda Gesser Khan, mongol text
General Outlines of Education in Japan, 1884
Mir-Ali-Shir
Vambery: Pinto
McFadden: Bibliography of Pacific Area Maps
Verhandelingen van het Genootschap van Batavia, 18th part.
d'Arcy: Hao-Khieou-tchouan
Thomson: Inscriptions d'Orkhon, with portr., etc
Andreae: Bibliotheca sinologica
Giles: Sun Tzŭ
Bunakov: Oracle Bones from Honan
Grammatika altaiskago yazyka, '69
Articles in Formosan
Laufer: East Asiatic Collection
Raquette: English-Turki Dictionary
Blochet: Introd. à l'histoire des Mongols
Dühren: Sade u. seine Zeit
Schleicher: Die darwinische Theorie u. d. Sprachwissenschaft
Shcherbatskoi: Pamyatniki Indiiskoi filosofii, I
Gabelentz: Thai-kih-thu
Vostočnye zapiski, I, 1927, 8vo
Gabelentz: Die Sprachwissenschaft, 2nd ed.
Wiedemann: Gr. der wotjakischen Sprache
Rentskii: Lyudi bož'i i skopcy, '72
Field Museum Pamphlets, 25 voll.
Poppe: materialy dlya issled. tungusskogo yazyka
Ádámi: Ungarische Sprachkunst
Rotta: La filosofia del linguaggio nella patristica
Kaulen: Lingua mandshurica
Mel'nikov: materialy dlya istorii ... skopčeskoï eresii
Bartol'd: Istoriya izučeniya Vostoka
349 Hyacinth: Kitai, 4 voll. 113

-11-

Dulaure: Des cultes qui ont précédé l'idolatrie
Ivanovskii: Mandjurica, I
Henry: Grammaire aléoute
Barthold: Turkestan down to the Mongol Invasion
Veniaminov: Opyt grammatiki aleutsko-lisevskago yazyka
Funke: Studien zur Gesch. der Sprachphilos.
Atkinson: Oriental + Western Siberia
Dühren: R. de la Bretonne
Field Museum Pamphlets, 12 voll. (extra)
Miansarov: Bibliographia caucasica
Vienna Ac., Verzeichnis, 2 voll.
Vimalapragnottaratnamala versio tibetica, folio
Vostočnyya Zametki, 1895, folio
Schiefner: Beiträge zur Kenntniss der tungus. Mundarten
Pelikan: Skopčestvo, folio (1 plate missing)
Bonaparte: Documents de l'époque mongole
Klaproth: Verzeichniss der chinesischen Bücher, Berlin [lacks errata!]
Olearius: Voyages, 1719, folio
Stekel: Fetischismus
Segalen: Stèles (Collection coréenne)
Hirschfeld: Transvestismus, 2 voll.
Sir J. Suckling's Works, 3rd ed.
Divan Lughat, 3 voll.
Budenz: Az ugor nyelvek összehasonlitó alaktana
Montandon: Au pays des Aïnou
Etnografičeskii sbornik, vol. I.
Laufer: Introduction of tobacco into Europe
Laufer: Chinese Baskets
Schmidt: Die Sprachfamilien der Erde, Atlas
Rukovodstvo turecko-tatarskago aderbidžanskago narečie, 1857
379 Contributions on folklore, 3 voll. 114

資料 10（貼付ノート・Ashbee: Library Catalogue）

-12-

△ Pierre Louÿs et l'histoire littéraire
\ Tolnai: Ungarisches Lesebuch
x Clementi: Article on the Poppy
x Davis: Han Koong Tsew, '29
/ Ars Asiatica, vol. III
⊗ Kaempfer: History of Japan, 2 voll., large paper
/ Arnett: Books of the Ancients
o Fourmont: Meditationes Sinicae
\ Staunton: Miscellaneous Notices rel. to China, '22
\ Stcherbatsky: Buddhist Nirvana
\ Staël-Holstein: Kaçyapaparivarta
// Vitale: Pekinese Rhymes
x Chamberlain: Japanese Poetry
// Um auto de Gil Vicente (school text)
⊙ Rahder: Glossary of the Dasabhumikasutra
⊙ Regnault: Medecine et pharmacie
△ Pfizmaier: Japanese Studies, vol. III, quarto
o Journal West China Border Research Soc., vol. VIII, Suppl.
△ Petrucci: La philosophie de la nature, folio
△ Hager: Panthéon chinois
400 △ Ōtanike: Shinsaiikiki, 2 voll., folio
△ Grimaldi: Fang sing thou Kiai
⊙ Roth: Jewish Contribution to Civilisation
/ J. Brown: Books of Words
\ Schmidt: Sprachfamilien der Erde, text
△ Gomboev: Altan Tobchi
x Charpentier: W. of Rubruk & Roger Bacon
o Facéties de Pogge, 2 voll., Liseux
† Wenström: Swedish-English Dict.
⊗ Kern: Histoire du bouddhisme dans l'Inde, 2 voll.
• Milloué: Bod-youl ou Tibet
\ Tavares: Epitome de gramatica portuguesa
o Finnish-English Dictionary
413 ⊗ Lonchamp: Manuel du bibliophile français, 2 voll.

115

-13-

Lonchamp: Manuel du bibliophile suisse
Bonneau: Curiosa
Wright & Sinclair: History of Later Latin Literature
Lange: History of Materialism
Russian Orientalia, 1 vol. so lettered
Festschrift V. Thomsen
Parker: Thousand Years of the Tartars
Wickersham: Alaskan Bibliography
Yetts: Legend of Confucius
Yeh: Confucian Conception of Jên
Reumuth: Logische Beschaffenheit der kindlichen Sprachanfänge
Schott: Vocabularium Sinicum
Saussure: L'horométrie des Chinois
Percival: Experiments on Peruvian Bark
St Aulaire: Chinese Running Hand
Remusat: Sciences naturelles chez les peuples de l'Asie orientale
Courant: L'Asie centrale
Satow: Japanese Chronological Tables
Hetherington: Early Ceramic Wares
Arnold: Islamic Book
Mōkogodaijiten 3 voll.
Cahen: Histoire des relations de la Russie
Penzer: Burton Bibliography
I-li (Probsthain), 2 voll.
Mežov: Sibirskiya Bibliografiya
The 10 Bulls
Chrestomatia arcaica } Textos literarios
Poesia medieval }
Hope: Temples of Nikko
Keigohō no kenkyū
Library of L. L. Bonaparte
Arberry: British Orientalists
446 Sanceau: Indies Adventure 116

— 114 —

Le Clert: Le papier, 2 voll., folio
Lloyd: Praises of Amida
Donisthorpe: Lost list of Friends
Finn: Jews of China
Semenoff: Key to Russian Grammar
Chamberlain: Romanized Japse Reader
Rémusat: Doctrine Samanéenne
Forsyth: Shantung
Maybon: Théâtre japonais
Japanese Education 77
Observations critiques sur le Japon
Rosny: L'épouse d'outre-tombe
Böhtlingk: Sprache der Jakuten
Tezkereh-i-Evliâ, 2 voll., folio
Couvreur: Dictionnaire classique, folio
Catolikku daijiten, I.
Karlgren: Etudes sur la phonologie chinoise
d'Auteroche: Voyage en Sibérie, 3 voll
Kowalewski: Mongolian dict., 3 voll. in 2
Foucher: L'art gréco-bouddhique, 3 voll.
Schuchardt: Primitiae linguae vasconum
Soper: Buddhist Architecture in Japan
Goodland: Bibliography of Rites
Eastern Art, 4 parts + 2 voll. (3 voll in all)
Montandon: La civilisation aïnou
Vareni Regni Japoniae et Siam
Chūkaminkoku shinchizu
Balfour: Huang Tsze
Langlès: Voyage dans l'Inde, 2 voll., 12mo
Serindia, 5 voll.
Chalfant: Early Chinese Writing
Kuno: Japse Expansion on Asiatic Cont., vol. I
Siebold: Japan & Comity of Nations
Susk: Conj. of Japse Verbs
48 Schmidt: Forschungen in Mongolen 117

-15-

/ Birdwood: Report of Old Records of India Office
⊗ Konrad: Japonskaya Literatura, I.
\ Tsurayuki: Log of a Japse Journey
\ Tanizaki: Puisque je l'aime
× Cordier: Quelques données nouvelles
• Nikkōchizu
\ Sköld: Ungarische Endbetonung
/ Akademik S. F. Ol'denburg, 1934
• Malan: San-tsze-king
• Marnas: Religion de Jésus, 2 voll.
△ Henderson: Japse Grammar
○ Florenz: White Aster
ø Jensat Kae-jung-joo
\ Sun tzu: Principles of War
○ Hamilton: New Acct of the East Indies, 2 voll.
△ Piggott: Garden of Japan
ø Journal Bengal Asiatic Society, '78-79
• Morse: Catalogue Japse Pottery
500 △ Pfizmaier: Japse Studies, 4to, vol. II
• Morand: L'acupuncture
⊗ Lendoyro: Tagalog Language
× Catalogue titles & index entries
○ Hoffmann: Grammaire japonaise
× Descriptio Regii japonicae (Amsterdam)
/ Amyot: Dictionnaire mantchou
△ Pacific Area in American Research
ø Japse View of Outer Mongolia
⊙ Ryerson Collection of Japse Illustrated Books
• Mayers: Higher Authorities of China
\ Stanton: Chinese Drama
\ Sirén: Walls & Gates of Peking
σ Yuzawa: Tokugawa gogaku no Kenkyū
⊗ Loewenstein: Swastika & Yin yang
△ Parker: Hospitals in China
⊙ Rabelais, ed. Lefranc, 5 voll.
517 • Memoir of W. Marsden

118

-16-

518 Baranov: Kitaiskii nogi goo
Gowland: Dolmens in Japan
Pritchard: Crucial Years of Anglo-Chinese Relations
Person: Maggōshin, vol. 5.
Burford's Canton
Marlowe: Tamburlaine
Markham: Indian Surveys
Ostroumov: Tatar-Russian Dict.
Castrén: Tungusische Sprachlehre
MacKinlay: Tagalog Grammar
Plomer: W. de Worde
Anesaki: Buddhist Art
? Histoire de la Chine, 13 vols., 4to
Three Turki Mss from Kashgar
Derbend-Nāmeh
Pfizmaier: Japanese Studies, vol. I.
Cordier: Merveilles de l'Asie
Schmidt: Mongolian Dict.
Rémusat: Miroir des langues mandchoue
Siebold: Mariner's Guide to Japan
Zorell: Georgische Bibelübersetzung
Herring: Paper-making
Houssaye: Monographie du thé
Japan in Jezo
Mahler: Muhammadische Zeitrechnung
Seebohm: Birds of Japan Empire
Grant: Books & Documents
Semenoff: Russian Grammar
Gabelentz: Sse-schu
Hall's Voyage to Loochoo, 8vo
Poole: Chronicles & Annals
Venn: Life of Xavier
Goodrich: Literary Inquisition
552 Davis: San-yu-low
Pfizmaier's Japanese Studies, 1 vol., 8vo

119

-17-

553 o Frois: Première Ambassade (Pinto)
× Camus: Voyages de Thévenot
/ Bullock: Etajima
o Yetts: An-Yang
• Morrison: Horae Sinicae
\ Stevens: East India Co.
× Dictionary of English Book Collectors
△ Granet: La Droite et la gauche
+ Weil: Tatarische Texte
O Editions of Syphilis
Jesuit Linguistic Studies (J).
o English-Dutch Dict.
† Wells: Perspective in Chinese Painting
△ Penney: Japse Popular Stories
\ Spitzelius: De re litteraria Sinensium
o Foster: John Company
/ Brooks: Account of Weights
△ Patkanov: Istoriya Mongolov
O Rose Innes' Dict.
/ Voyages towards N.W. (Hakluyt Soc.)
/ Ambassades vers l'Empereur du Japon, 2 voll, 12mo
/ Adamson: Camoens, 2 voll.
× Couto: Da Asia, 24 voll.
/ Beveridge: Babar Nama, Turki Text
• Meadows: Chinese & their Rebellions
O Relações entre Portugueses e Japoneses
△ Piggott: Sosho
× Campbell: Journey in N. Korea
Index to Indian Antiquary, 2 voll.
/ Beal: Romantic History of Buddha
⊗ Lloyd: Creed of Half Japan
⊗ Khanikoff: Inscriptions musulmanes du Caucase
• Muir: Book collecting
\ Straelen: New Diplomacy in Far East
587 △ Hart: Marco Polo 120

資料 10（貼付ノート・Ashbee: Library Catalogue）

18

588 Popov : Panthéon chinois
Benyowsky's Travels, 2 voll., 4to
Alexeev: Kitaïskaya Poema
Collis: Land of the Great Image
Adam: Gr. de la langue tongouze
Imbrie: Etymology
Danvers: Portuguese in India, 2 voll.
Lluys: Le Japon et Rome.
Brodrick: Little China
Ribeiro's Ceilão
Young: The Japse Canadians
Wylie: Ethnography of the Han
601 Burton's Camoens, 6 voll.
Morris: Living with Lepchas
Vegetation of Mt Fuji
Norman: Fighting Man of Japan
Ball: Macao
Amakusaban Kinkushu
Laufer: Pottery of Han Dynasty
Julien: Histoire de la porcelaine chinoise
Ramstedt: Abhandlungen
Browne's Religio Medici (tall 4to)
Nalivkine: Khokand.
Catalogue Drujon
Lewis & Short: Latin Dict
Wylie: Publications of Protestant Missionaries
Chamberlain: Japanese Written Grammar
Julien: Blanche et Bleue
Pokotilov: Istoria vostočnyx mongolov
Le pi-pa-ki
Japse Fairy World
Bailey: Lucretius on the nature of things
Nilsson: Primitive Time Reckoning
Standish: 3. Bamboo
672 Nunn: Ecclesiastical Latin

121

673 — 19 —

⊗ Lindley: Fa Hian
/ Bowring: Flowery Scroll
△ Parkinson: Trade in the Eastern Seas
△ Hosie: Szechwan
/ Blake: Grammar of Tagalog
⊗ Le jardin parfumé
△ Grajdanzev: Formosa Today
△ Hirth: Scraps from Collector's Notebook
⊗ Kanokogi: Geist Japans
\ Sédillot: Hist. des sciences mathématiques, 2 voll.
// Vostočnye zapiski, I, 8vo
// Voyage of Saris to Japan (Hakluyt)
X Dickins: Old Bamboo Hewer's Story
△ Prestage: Portuguese Pioneers
⊗ Life of Mrs Bird
• Muto: History of Anglo-Japse Relations
⊗ Kerner: N.E. Asia, 2 voll.
• Nihonbunten kōgi
⊙ Royle: Fibrous Plants of India
△ Haynes: Enemies of Liberty
⊗ Kaempfer: Amoenitates exoticae
X da Orta: Simples + drugs of India
X Ceylon & the Hollanders 1658–1796
• Murdoch: History of Japan, vol. II only
X Centenaire de l'Ecole des Langues orientales
/ Biot: Etoiles filantes
/ Ball: The Pitt of the Classics
\ Summers: Vampire
⊗ Kuno: Japanese Expansion, vol. II
⊗ Kasem-Beg: Turkish grammar
⊙ Raffles: Report on Japan
\ Smith: China
X Dickins: Chushingura
△ Hanakatsura
[65] \ Sbornik dogovorov Rossii s Kitaem 122

658 — 20 —

Radlov: Morphologie der Türksprachen
Pagès: Bibliographie japonaise
Siebold: Bibliotheca japonica, lib. IV
A Model Japse Villa
Leyden: Memoirs of Baber
Middleton-Wake: Invention of Printing
Heyd: Commerce du Levant, 2 voll.
Brit. Museum: Japanese Books, 2 voll., 4to
Riasanovsky: Principles of Mongol Law
Marsden: Marco Polo
Chater Collection catalogue, 4to.
Hillier: List of Authorities of China
Hager: Numismatique chinoise
de Kome: Fellowship of Goodness
Piry: Erh-tou-mei, 2 voll.
Maslon: Arabian Prophet
Koops: Historical Account... Paper
Kattendyke's Dagboek
Weig: chinesische Familiennamen
Florenz: Japse Poems
Vindel's Biblioteca Oriental, 2 voll.
Ars Asiatica, I
Siebold: Thesaurus, 4to
Figueiredo: Portuguese Dict., 2 voll.
Gokhale: Pratityasamutpadaśastra
? Valentyn: Oud en Nieuw Oost-Indiën, 5 voll.
Lipz, Panizzi, vol. I
Balfour: Waifs & Strays from Far East
Clark: Formosa
Magic & Science in Western Yunnan
Hayashi: For His People
Parke-Smith: England & Japan
700 Rockhill: Diplomatic Audiences
Douglas: South Wind
702 Staat van alle Volkere, I. 123

7'3 Penzer: Harem -21-
Leland: Pidgin English
Morris: Traveller from Tokyo
Adler: Dialectic
Voyages of M. Frobisher (Argonaut)
Lewis: Ranald McDonald
Carlo: Paleografia Española, 2 voll.
Matsudaira: Culture of Kaki
McClean: Xavier
History of Printing in China & Europe
Ballagi: Hungarian Dict.
Historia da expansão portuguesa no mundo, 2 voll.
Milne: Sacred Edict
Medhurst's Shoo-King
La Croze Thesaurus
Pfizmaier's Japse Studies, 1 voll., 8vo (making 2 voll)
Stein: Ancient Geography of Kashmir
Hamerton: Intellectual Life
Marlowe's Poems
Ribeiro: Andam Faunos
Osborn: Japse Fragments
Portugam o tazunero
Golownin's Captivity in Japan, 3 voll.
" " " ", 2 voll.
Ellis: George Chapman
Faber: Eine Staatslehre ... Mencius
Buck: Sun yat sen
Simon: Bibliotheca bacchica, vol. I.
Curtius: Jap. Spraakkunst.
Grube: Metamorphosen der Götter
Kaempfer's Japan, 8vo ?
Giles: Historic China
Koda: Leaving the Hermitage
Shitaijii
Rémusat: Mélanges, 5 voll.
738 Trigault: Rei Christ. apud Japonios 124

-22-

739 ○ Embroidery Sept. 1935
// Ueda's | Dict., 5 voll.
\ Trans. Oriental Ceramic Soc., 17 voll. (18. not yet purchased)
⊗ Raffles' Java, 2 voll.
⊗ Langlès: Alphabet mantchou, 4to
△ Pozdnéev: mongol'skaya Xrestomatiya
× Dingwall: Kakiemon Designs
/ Art Militaire chinois (uncoloured)
△ Obrazcy mongol'skoĭ narodnoĭ literatury, I.
△ Hortus Suburbanus Calcuttensis
✕ I-tsing: Records of Buddhist Kingdoms
† What is an Index?
† Wenkstern: Bibliography of Japan, 2 voll.
/ Baber Nama 1857
△ Hearlett: From a Japse Prison
\ Sainson: Mémoires sur l'Annam
⊗ Le divand Amour
\ Schurhammer: Disputationen
// Une Famille Tongouse
\ Turselin: La Vie de F. Xavier, 1612
△ Historical Relations between Japan & Saghalien
△ Gramatica de la lengua de Yap, 188
△ Gōda Collection, Japse Sword Fittings
⊗ Ribeiro: Filhas de Babilonia
△ Olufsen: Bokhara Dialect
• Marsden's Malayan Grammar
• Mélanges chinois et bouddhiques, 4 voll. (lacks vol. III Luzac)
• Memoir of Raffles
// Vitale: Grammaire mongole
⊗ Ross: Dialogues in Eastern Turki
/ Busbeq: Epistolae
// Vambery: Story of my Struggles
⊗ Locke: Ancient Quipu
✕ Costumes of China
773 • Milburn: Oriental Commerce, 2 voll., 4to

125

—23—

774 . Eliseeff: Elementary Japse, 2 voll.
X Chamberlain: Moji no Shimbe
Tolkowsky: Hesperides
Lecky: Hist. of European Morals, 2 voll.
Bauer: Woman
X Campbell: Arabian Medicine, 2 voll.
• Marshman: Works of Confucius; vol. I.
Takakusu: I-tsing (dissertation)
X Douglas: Fortunate Union
+ Warner: Japse Sculpture of Suiko Period
X Civil Code of Japan, 2 voll.
• Marlowe: Edward II
Brookes: Intern. Rivalry in Pacific Islands
X Davidson: Formosa past & present
• Miscellanies Historical
• Marlowe: Life & Dido
• Marre: Gr. Tagalog
Leskien: Handb. d. altbulg. Sprache
Forster: Report of Mission to Yarkand ✓
Pauthier: Marco Polo, 2 voll.
Yetts: Cull Chinese Bronzes
Julien: Livre des Récompenses et des peines
Stone: Story of Phallicism, 2 voll.
Edgar: English-Giarung Voc.
Rémusat: Iu-kiao-li, 4 voll.
Historia gen. de las Isl. Philipp., 14 voll.
800 Sir T. Browne's Works, Bohn, 3 voll.
X Castagné: Congrès de turkologie
Gibs: Chinese Pictorial Art
Julien: Voyages des Pèlerins bouddhistes, 3 voll.
Yoshimoto: Peasant Sage of Japan
Rytschkov: Historie von Kasan
Lettres persanes
Lettres édifiantes, 26 voll.
808 Vida de Xavier, 4 voll. 126

資料 10（貼付ノート・Ashbee: Library Catalogue）

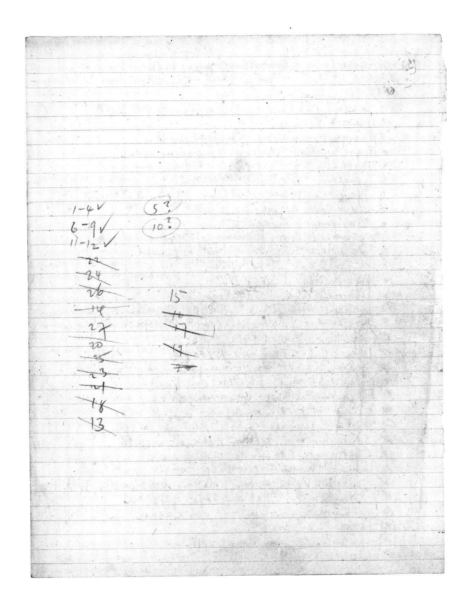

1-4 ✓
6-9 ✓
11-12 ✓
22
24
26
14
27
20
25
23
21
18
13

5?
10?

15
16
17
19
20

849 Peregrinação de Pinto, 4 voll. — 24 —
Julien: Avadânas, 3 voll.
Rosny: Biothèque jap. de Nordenskiöld
Library lands
Yule: Cathay, 4 voll.
Cocks: Diary, 2 voll.
Manrique: Travels, 2 voll.
Hakluyt, 12 voll.
Purchas, 20 voll.
Edwards: Chinese Prose Literature, 2 voll.
Smith: Visit to China
Braithwaite: Life of Sogoro
Murakami: Sinkan MSS.
Bouillard: Attitudes des Buddhas
Gowland: Japse Metallurgy
Hutchinson: Relations de la Compagnie franç
Lewy: Bau der europ. Sprachen
Bloch: German interests in Far East
Eitel: 3 Lectures on Buddhism
Semenov: Annan (pamphl.)
Robinson: Genius of Hebrew Grammar
Pyke: Legibility of Print
Heiberg: Geisteskranken
Dörfler: Ahron ben Elia
Jitenhyōmoku
Sauval: Chronique scandaleuse
Japan Society, London, vol. I- + 2 voll. of Suppl.
Dumdin: Sigillographie sino-annamite
Moll: Handbuch, 2 voll.
Dalgado: Glossario luso-asiatico, 2 voll.
Letters rec. by East India Co., 6 voll.
Sbornik Orkonskoi exped. I-V in 2 voll.
Vambéry: Caghataische Studien
Merhart: Bronzezeit am Jenissei 127
843 Ramstedt: Mongolica

34844 ○ Ettmayer: Das Wesen der Dialektbildung
\ Semenov: Materialy dlya...tadžikov. – 4to
\ Sternberg: Gilyak, 4to
⊖ Obručev: Central Asia (R), 2 voll., 4to
• Map of the World 1506 ⎫
\ Six Early Printed Maps ⎭ Brit Museum
• Nihon to Portogaru
• Missionary Success in Formosa, 2 voll.
† Watchdog: Japanese & the Pacific Problems
• Murray's Handbook of Japan, 4th ed
△ Giles: San tzu ching
△ Haynes: Decline of Liberty in England
• Newcastle Typ. Soc. 2 voll.
⌐ Bellows German Dict
× Davis Fortunate Union 2 voll.
⌐ Blochet: Babar Nama
⊖ Opyt grammatiki aleutskago yazyka
X Catholic Native Episcopacy in China
⊗ L'Anthropologie 2 voll.
⊗ Le sûtra en 42 articles
• McGowan: Self-Immolation by Fire
• Moraes: Cartas do Japão
⊗ Laufer: Reindeer
σ Yamanaka Cat.
• Marcuse: Handwörterbuch
⊖ Pokorny: Altirische Gr.
† William Adams (brochure)
• Newcastle Typogr. Soc., 1 vol.
† Xiva, 1840
⊗ Lehtisalo: Vokalismus im Samojedischen
X Donner: Zur Phonetik des Samojed.
⊖ Ostrovskii: Votyaki
\ Stein-Szama Catalogue
σ Zenker: Chinesische Philosophie
X du Halde: China, 2 voll. folio
⊗ Russian-Tartar Dict, 4to
850 △ Hazlitt's Essays

128

25

881 Masson-Oursel: Psychologie indienne
Bacon: Advancement of learning
Hayn: 4 Bibliographien
Kagawa: Before the Dawn
Pelliot: Mongols et la papauté, 2 voll.
pamphlet on Kondakov
Levi: Eastern Humanism
Wang: Chinesische Oper
Stadelmann: Laotse und d. Biologie
Peking Catalogue of Clocks
Studer: Anglo-N. Lapidaries
American Anthropologist 34, 4
Useful Plants of Japan
Hanotaux: Bibliophiles
Jenkins: Life of Borrow
Smith: Japan
Bickerstaffe: Araki the daimio
Foster: East India House
Mair: Formosa
900 Morch: Pottery Description
Jacobi: Printer's Vocabulary
Nioradze: Schamanismus
Saussure: La série septénaire
Rondot: vert de Chine
Art chrétien chinois
Koch: Kastratensekte
Culin: Chinese in America
Berjeau: Calcoen, Dutch Narrative....
Hopkins: The six Scripts
Huth: Inschriften von Tsaghan Baišin
Klementz & Radlov: Turfan Exped.
Chavannes: Expression des voeux
Schmidt: Izučenie Kitaya
Laufer: Amber in Asia
915 Waley: Li Po 129

33[916] • Möllendorff: Manchu Literature
• Meliorauskii: Skazanie ob edigel i toktamyšy
/ Apollinaire: Sade
△ Oxford: Scaliger
× Jikov: Gr. de la langue darkwa
• Nausester: Das Kind und die Form d. Sprache
○ Eisen: Mauthners Kritik der Spr.
△ Hirth: Keramische Gegenstände
/ Bang: Monographien zur türk. Sprachgesch.
/ Vatin: Minuskii Krai
× Cat. Rostov Museum
/ Bibliografiya Vostoka I
⊗ Karpov: Turkmen
+ Imp. R. Istor. Obšč. 1866–1916
△ Po etapam razvitiya ....
• Mongolo-Oiratskii epos
+ Inostrancev: Xunnu
+ Ist. svedenie Voiska Donskago, 1886
△ Pumpelly: Annau, 2 voll., 4to
/ Böhtlingk Festgabe
\ Tchoubinov: Georgian Dict, 4to
○ Gorham: Tray Gardens
/ Bartol'd: Ist. Turkestana (pamphlet)
⊗ Karutz: Völker Nord- und Mittel Asiens
? + Joyce: Anthropology of Chinese Turkestan
? / Albuquerque, 4 vol.
\ Trudy muzeya paleogr. I + III, 2 voll.
+ Wiener Beiträge zur Kunst Asiens, 2 voll.
× Dagestan, 1847
△ Panchatantra (in Russian)
/ Bang: Manichaeische Hymnen
\ Semenov: Zur Frage....
△ Putnam: Books in the Middle Ages, 2 vol.
△ History of Material Culture, 7 pamphlets
⊗ Lazareff Cat., 2 vol.
957 / Aziatskaya Rossiya, 3 vol. 4to, Atlas, folio 130

952 Valenziani: Kan-kan-wau-rai
Zilal i Ilkan
Jaeschke: Tibetan-English Dict.
Davis: Chinese Miscellanies
Imbault-Huart: Anecdotes en chinois parlé
Keleti Szemle IX
Ament: Deutung der ersten Kinderworte
Altaiskii almanax } 2
8 pamphlets
Thom: Chinese Courtship
Kashetsin: Buddizm
Singh: History of Khokand
Penal Code of Japan
Pfizmaier: Aino Wörtersammlung
Arch. franc. historici conspectus chronologicus
Rowse: On history
Parke-Smith: Japse Traditions of Xtianity
Clark: Abbey of St Gall
Campos: History of Portuguese in Bengal
Franke: Ackerbau u. Seidengewinnung in China
Bretschneider: Mediaeval Geography
Carus: T'ai Shang Kan Ying | P'ien
Staunton: Notices of China, 2nd ed.
Stopes: Plays of Old Japan
Alepseev: Japanese Gold & Silver Coins
Jülg: Mongolische Märchen-sammlung
Fenollosa: Noh
Pozdneev: Skazanie o xoždenii ... bāza-bakši
Bingham: Founding of T'ang dynasty
Hardy: Eastern Monachism
Memoir of Capt W Gill
Ljungstedt: Portuguese Settlements in China
J. de la Société finno-ougrienne q 37.
~~NHH~~ Nihonjinkōmitsudozu
980 Semenov: Pamyatniki ariiskoi Kultury 131

-27-

986 Poppe: Altaisch und Urtürkisch
Courant: La presse périodique japonaise
Foster: Guide to India Office Records
Gray: Walks in City of Canton
Compar. Tables of Christian & Muham. Dates
Pruitt: Flight of an Empress
Chavannes: T'ai chan
Zwick: Handb. der westmongolischen Sprache
Conder: Notes on Japse Architecture
Radlov: Uigurische Sprachdenkmäler
Hyacinth: San-czy-czin
Vambery: Uigurische Sprachmonumente
Housman: Collected Poems
March: China & Japan in der Museum
1000 Conférences Musée Guimet 1903-04
Balfour: Leaves from my Chinese Scrapbook
Skrine & Ross: Heart of Asia
Tucci: Apologie du Taoisme
Zwick: Westmongolische Grammatik
Inscriptions de l'Orkhon, folio
Segenbringende Reisaehren, 3 voll.
Klautke: Nutzpflanzen Chinas
Memorials of Rev. Douglas
Thomsen: Samlede Afhandlinger, 3 voll.
Practical Orthography of Ts'wana
Szinnyei: Herkunft der Ungarn
Monumenta nipponica, V part 1
Medhurst: China
Langlès: Voyages de Sind-bâd
Harlez - Chu-hsi
Geschichte der Sprachen d. vorderen Orients
Markham: Chinchona
Stisted: Life of Burton
Blumeville: Yotsuya Kaidan
1020 Wingfield: Curse of Koshiu

132

1021 Warren: Study of Bookplates, 2 voll. 28
Pfizmaier: Seelenzustände und Leidenschaften
Lajard: Langage sifflé
Lévi: Fragment tokharien
Museum Journal, Dec. 26
Zlatokuznecy Dagestana
Reuter: Anlautsvokale im Tocharischen
Semenov: Contradictions dans les avis ...
Beveridge: Notes on MSS of Babar
Bang: Türkische Namen einiger Grosskatzen
Otto: Hauslehrerbestrebungen
Bulletin de la Maison franco-jap. I
Ta-ssi-yang-kuo I, 1
Tonkōisho, folio, chitsu
Saddharmapundarikasutra, yellow silk, oblong
Harris: Voyages, 2 voll., folio
Pypin: Istoriya russkoi etnografii, 4 voll.
Schuchardt: Miscellanea linguistica
Thomsen: Turcica
Stopes: Contraception
Richthofen: Letters on Provinces of China
Hoernlé: Ancient MSS from C. Asia
" : Antiquities from C. Asia
Poussin: Nirvana
Ballagi: Pocket Hungarian Dict.
El Kitab des lois secrètes
Ross: Polyglott List of Birds
Bang: Köktürkische Inschrift
Trudy Bibliogr. Kom. Byvš pri SNKTSSR 1-3
Hagen: Monument de Yu
Braga: Camoens, 2 voll., ms.
Closter-Documente
Sage: Philosophy
Bogoras: Koryak Texts
Pozdneev: Mongoliya i Mongoly, 2 voll.
1056 Ozawa: Festivals of Yedo 133

32

1052 Bruce: Humanness of Chu hsi
Bacot: Ecriture cursive tibétaine
Gauthiot: Qq. termes techniques
Alfaric: Vie chrétienne du Bouddha
Bang: Türkische Bruchstücke
Beveridge Babar Nama (pamphlet)
Bramsen: Coins of Japan
Viana: Albuquerque
Jahresb. Frankfurter Vereins, 1 vol.
Filles de Papis, 2 voll.
Chinese Hist., 4 voll., 12mo
Bibliographie clérico-galante
Bloch: Leben unserer Zeit
Novikov: Skifskaya istoriya, 3 vol
Trudy Troick. 10–15
" " 4–9
Ibn al-Muhannā: Arabic-Mongol-Turk. gloss.
Istoriya Sibiri, 2 voll.
Kern: Index to Versp. Geschriften
Shaw: Gr. Eastern Turki, 1 vol.
Korzybski: Manhood of Humanity
Saval: Spanish Gr., 2 voll.
Grose's Classical Dict, 2nd ed.
"On to the city of God"
Batchelor: Ainu Fireside Stories
Fenollosa: Blossoms from a Japanese Garden
Zapiski ob Astraxani, '84
Pekarskii: Russko-yakutskii slovar'
Vogeler: Die Freiheit der Liebe
Camões: Liricas } school texts
Pinto: Peregrinacão
Conling: Luminous Religion
Catalogue de la Littérature mondiale, 2 voll., 4to
Kattagan i Badaxšan
1091 Sanchez: De Matrimonio, folio

134

-29-

1092 (X) Klaproth: voyages au Caucase, 2 voll.
Institut de sinologie de Pékin
Potseluevskii: Turkmen Handbook
In Memoriam, Panizza
Réty: La jolie papetière
Rucker: Religion des Lamas
Mirâdj - Nâmeh
Grigor'ev: Rossiya i Aziya
1100 Trudy Troickosavsko-kyaxtinskago Otd. I-II, III 2-3
Alaska Historical Museum
(X) Kultur-Kuriosa, 3 voll.
Phonetic Transcription + Transliteration
Opisanie Koreï, 3 voll + map
Bang: Turcica
Mélanges russes, III
Transliteration of Russian (Brit Acad)
von Zach: Ergänzungen
X Collinson: Some of grammar
Schiefner: Jukagirische Sprache
(X) Lit. Sbornik k 100-lětiyu ... Kazan... Univ.
Putešestvie na Sěber... 4to
Fehlinger: Geschlechtsleben der Naturvölker
Semenov: La religion du Satan
Trudy Troick.... III, 1
Protokoly " ....
Boas Anniversary Vol.
materialy dlya etnografii Rossii, vol. 14
X Chavannes: Les livres chinois
Taschenbuch für Büchersammler, 3 voll.
X Coxwell: Siberian Folktales
Ščerbatsky: Filosofskoe učenie buddizma
Vladimircov: Buddizm v Tibete
Pamphlets, 1 vol. buckram, red label
Harlez: Religion des Tatares orientaux
1126 Zapiski o Sibiri, 1837

135

-3 1127 Andreev: yazgulëmskii yazyk
Turkemistan, 1928
Lazarev: Sciences exactes en Russie
V semirnaya Literatura, 2 voll., 8vo
Donner: Bei den Samojeden
Comptes rendus... exploration du N. de la Mong.
Authors + Printers Dict
Otto: Kindesmandart
Materialy dlya ist. voïska Donskago
Epistolae et logistorici
Tonkōisho, 8vo
pamphlet on Ossetes
Farnell: Mythologic Study
Caucasus polyglottus, I
Hirth: Tschau Ju-kua (pamphlet)
Brit Museum Japanese + Chinese Paintings
Intorno ad una memoria di Giulio Klaproth
Laufer: Language of Yüe-chi
Meyerhof: Noms portugais de drogues
Ovidieff: Langue jap. littéraire
Leningrad Or. Inst., 28
Schuchardt: Deutsch gegen Französisch
Bonrat: pamphlet
Scherk: Psychologie des Eunuchoiden
Ten Thousand Cases Birth Control
Verbal discussions during peace Negotiations
Ethnologische Studien, 2 voll.
Bute: Ancient Language of Teneriffe?
Schiefner: Tusch-Sprache
Anadyrskii krai, 1893
Memoir of Rev. S. Dyer
Wylie: Nestorian Tablet
Imp. Ermitage, 1915
Wright: Existing legal situation as it relates to conflict in Far East
1161 Visite aux temples de Pékin 136

—30—

1162 • Moges: Ambassade en Chine
△ Gündert: Grundfragen der Sprachw.
o Yoshida: Whispering Leaves
\ Thoms: Affectionate Pair
/ Bishop of Victoria: Lewchew
\ Schiefner: Tibetan Tales
\ Sermão de S. António
o Edkins: Opium
△ Putnam: Censorship of Church of Rome, 2 voll.
△ Pfizmaier: alte Bewohner des heutigen Corea
• Morse: Traces of Early Race in Japan
△ Harlez: Laotze
△ Pfizmaier: 3 pamphlets (unbound)
+ Williams: Relations with Chinese Empire
o Ross: Chinese Foreign Policy
† Wilhelm + Gundert: Chinesische Literatur
• Notices et Extraits, vol. XI
• Marlowe: Faustus & Jew of Malta, 2 voll.
// Voprosy i recenziya
o Rabelais, 3 voll. (English ed.)
o Russkaya lĕtopis', 8 voll., 4to
o Lenin Public Library Moscow, I
// Uspenskii: Očerki iz ist. Trapezunsk. imperii
• Marakuev: Russische Arbeiten — Chin. Lexicographie
\ Sulejman: Čagătaj Wörterbuch
o Izv. Vostoč. Otd. Imp. Arx. Ob. I, 2 voll.
o Jespersen: Lehrbuch der Phonetik
x Chavannes: La Sculpture
o R.G.S.: Alphabets of Foreign Languages
// Ukazatel' k Aktam ..., 1838
// Version turque du Bakhtiar Nameh
† Wang: Histoire anecdotique chinoise
// Vladimircov: Obrazcy mongol'skoi slovesnosti, paper
1195 △ Gardner: Western Books on China

137

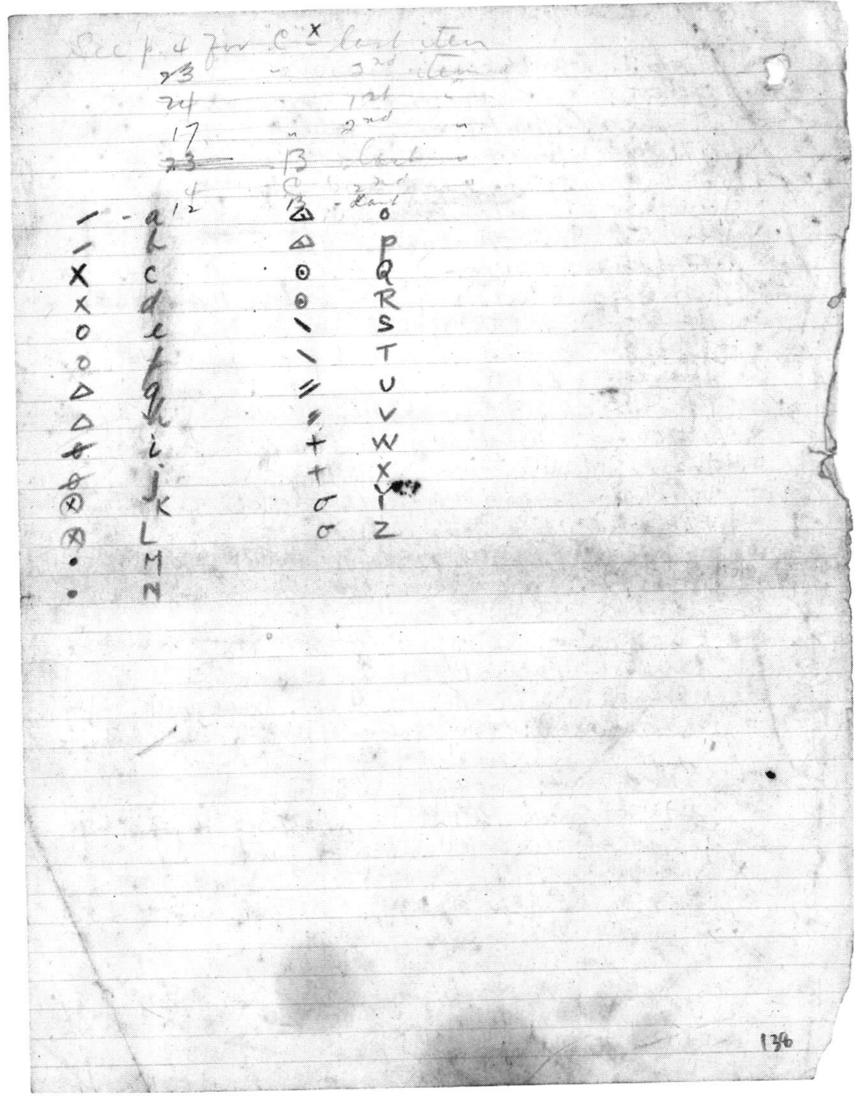

# 資料11（貼付ノート・Transaction of the Asiatic Society of Japan）

資料 11（貼付ノート・Transaction of the Asiatic Society of Japan）

資料11（貼付ノート・Transaction of the Asiatic Society of Japan）

Transaction of the Asiatic Society of Japan
18 bound vols.

vol. 1—2
3—4
5—6
7, | 8,
9, | 10,
11—12,
13—14,
15—16
17？ ナシ
18 19
20
21—22

23—24
25—26
27—28
29—30

22 4 冊

General Index 1—23

Vol. X. Supplement (Index & Chamberlain's Kojiki)

parts

| vol. | part | vol. | part |
|---|---|---|---|
| — ? | — ? | 34 | 1—4 |
| $2^{\times2}$ | — | 35 | 1—5 (missing 2—5) |
| 3 | 1 1884, $2^{\times2}$ 1884 | 36 | 2—$3^{\times2}$ |
| 3 | 1 (1905) | 37 | $1^{\times2}$ |
| 4？ | 2 1875 | 38 | $3^{\times2}$, $4^{\times2}$ $5^{\times2}$ |
| 7 | 1 | 31 | — (2 copies) |
| 9 | 3 | 39 | — |
| 11 | 1—2 | 40？ ナシ | — |
| 12 | 1—3 | 41 | $1^{\times2}$—5 |
| 13 | 1—$2^{\times2}$ | 42 | 1—2 |
| 14 | $1^{\times3}$—2 (part 1, 1 copy only) | 43 | 1—2 |
| 16 | 2—3 | 44 | 1—2 |
| 18 | 1—2 | 45 | 1—2 |
| 19 | 1—3 | 46 | 1—2 |
| 20 | 1—2 (part 1 missing) | 47 | — |
| 22 | 2 | 48 | — |
| 27 | $2^{\times2}$—$3^{\times2}$ (2—3 モウ一部) | 49 | $1^{\times2}$—$2^{\times2}$ |
| 29 | $1^{\times2}$—$2^{\times2}$ (1—2 モウ一部) | 56 | — |
| 30 | 1—3 | | |
| 32 | — $\times2$ (2 copies o.k.) | | |
| 33 | $1^{\times2}$—$2^{\times2}$ (4 copies o.k.) | | |

224冊

Journal of the China Branch of the R. A. S.
(56 bound vols.)

vol

2, 5, 8–9 12–14 16, 18, 23—29
31—69

parts

17, $19^{1}$ $20^{2-6}$ $21^{1,2,5,6}$ $22^{1,3}$ $25^{2}$
$31^{1-3}$

Index to vollume 1—54.

24. Lg(F) Meillet - Histoire des Grecque et Latine.

193. Rp(D) Mittheilungen der Deutschen Gesellschaft für Natur- und Völqkerkunde ostasiens :-

1) G. Hütterott - Das Japanische Schwert
2) Freiherr von Zedtwitz - Japanische Musikstücke
3) P. Meyet - Ein Besuch in Corea

161. Nv R. H. Mottram - Europa's beast, London, 1930.

20. Lg(D) Meissner - Japanische Umgangssprache.

104. Es Mr Monumenta Serica - Journel of Oriental Studies of the Catholic University of Peking, Henri Vetch, Peiping, 1935-38, 3 vols.

14. Lg Y, Matsumiya - Exercises in Japanese conversation, Tokyo.

97. Ml(F) V. Madsen et V. Thomen - Anatomie Mandchoue, Bibliotheque Royal, Copenhagen, 1919.

135. Cal W. A. Mason - A history of the art of writing, Macmillan, N. Y., 1928.

108. Fi Munro - Coins of Japan, Yokohama, 1904.

(✓) Marlowe; The Tragical Story of Dr. Faustus, edited by F. S. Boas; Methuen & Co., London.

(✓) Matsukata, Masayoshi; Report on the Post-Bellum Financial Administration in Japan 1896-1900, Government Press, Tokio, 1900.

(✓) Map of Japan and Adjacent Regions, 1937.

(✓) Mathews, R. H., Europa's Beast, 1930

資料11（貼付ノート・Transaction of the Asiatic Society of Japan）

324. Bb Merryweather, F. S. Bibliomania in the Middle Ages, The Woodstock Press, London, 1933

528. Jy Midzukami, H., A Collection of Japanese Proverbs and Sayings, The Kairyudo Press, Tokyo, 1940

833. Po Milford, H.S., The Oxford Book Of Regency Verse, The Clarendon Press, Oxford, 1928

813. Ta Miller, I.L., The Chinese Girl, Peiyang Press, Tientsin, 1932

522. Gr Millman, R. M., The Verb of the Japanese Written Language, Kyo Bun Kwan, Tokyo, 10th Yr. of Taisho

1043. St Mills, E.H.F., The Tragedy Of Ab Qui And Other Modern Chinese Stories, George Routledge & Son, London, 1930

1158. Po Milton, Paradise Lost, Ginn & Co., Boston, 1879

644. Pc Minakawa, M., Four No- Plays, (2 copies) Sekibundo, Tokyo, 1934

15. At Minamoto, H. and Henderson, H. G., An Illustrated History of Japanese Art, Hoshino Shoten, Kyoto, 10th Yr. of Showa 1935

1062. Tp Mitsui, T., An Outline History Of The Transportation And Communication Systems In Japan, Society for the Study of International Communication, Tokyo, 1925

1338. Fl (D) Mittheilungen Der Deutschen Gesellschaft Fur Natur-Und Volkerkunde Ostasieps,

939. Fl Mitteilungen der Deutschen Gesellschaft für Natur-Und Volkerhunde Ostasiens, 10 vols. 7-18 , 16 thin pamphlets, Tokyo,

715. La Miyake, M., An Outline of the Japanese Judiciary, The Japan Times & Mail, Tokyo, 1935

1093. By Miyamori, A., A Life Of Mr. Yukichi Fukuzawa, Maruya & Co., Tokyo, 1902

658. Dm Miyamori, A., Masterpieces Of Chikamatsu, The Japanese Shakespeare,
Kegan Paul, Trench, Trubner & Co. New York, 1926

564. Po Miyamori, A., An Anthology of Haiku Ancient and Modern, Maruzen, Tokyo, 1932

830. So (F) Miyaoka, T., Le Progres Des Institutions Liberales Au Japon, Imprimere De J. Dumoulin, Paris, 1921

1205. Jr Miyoshi, M., Journal Of The College Of Science, The Imperial University Of Tokyo, Tokyo, 1916

338. Tr M'Leod, J., Voyage of the Alceste to the Island of Lewchew, John Murray, London, 1818

1425. By Modern Industrial Technique In China, 燕京大学校, 3 vol

Part 1 林則徐 Lin Tse-Hsu, Pioneer Promoter of the Adoption of Western Means of Maritime Defense in China, 陳其田 , 1934

Part 2 曾国藩 Tseng Kuo-Fan, Pioneer Promoter of The Steamship In China, 陳其田 1935

Part 3 左宗棠 Tso Tsung T'ang, Pioneer Promoter of The Woollen Mill In China, 陳其田 , 1938

資料 11（貼付ノート・Transaction of the Asiatic Society of Japan）

1432. Ms　Moens, J.L., Çrivijiayá, Yāva en Katāha,
The Asiatic Review Vol. XXVIII No. 93, 1932

606. Gr　Möllendorff, P.G., A Manchu Grammar, The American
Presbyterian Mission Press, Shanghai, 1912

1459. At (D)　Monatsberichte über Kunstwissenschaft und Kunsthandel,
Fahrgang 2, 1-2,
Verlag der Vereingten Druckereien & Kunstanstalten, München,

771. Dc　Monier-Williams, M., A Sanskrit- English Dictionary,
The Clarendon Press, Oxford, 1899

961. Rn　Montague, Wm. P., Belief Unbound,
Yale University Press, New Heaven,

~~706. Es, Jr　Monumenta Serica : Journal of Oriental Studies of the
Catholic University of Peking,
Henri Vetch, Peiping,~~

778. Es　Monumenta Nipponica, (Vol. 4 Semi-Annual No. 2),
Sophia University, Tokyo, 1941

779. Es　Monumenta Nipponica, (Vol.4 Semi-Annual No. 1 ),
Sophia University, Tokyo, 1941

780. Es　Monumenta Nipponica, Vol. 1 -3,
Sophia University, Tokyo, 1938- 1940

1332. Jr　Moore, G., Journal Of The American Oriental Society , Vol. 21
First Half,
The American Oriental Society, Connecticut, 1902
(Index To The Journal of The American Oriental Society, Vols.
1-20)

~~88. Lt More Letters from Basil Hall Chamberlain to Lafcadio Hearn and Letters from M. Toyama, Y. Tsubouchi and Others, The Hokuseido Press, Tokyo, 1937~~

1088. Dc Morgan, E., Chinese New Terms Revised And Enlarged, Kelly & Walsh, Shanghai, 1932

448. Si Es Morgan, E., Tao the Great Luminant, Kelly & Walsh, Shanghai

517. Lg Mori, M. G., The Pronunciation of Japanese, The Herald-Sha, Tokyo, 1929

50. Bu Mori, M. G., Buddhism and Faith, Herald-Sha, Tokyo, 1928

976. Lg Morris, R., etc., Specimens Of Early English, 2 vols., The Clarendon Press, Oxford, 1926

598. Pa Morrison, A., The Painters of Japan, 2 vols., T.C.&.E.C. Jack, London, 1911

507. Cm Morse, H., The Gilds of China, Kelly & Walsh, Shanghai, 1932

24. Ar Morse, E. S., Iijima, I., etc., Shell Mounds of Omori and Hitachi, University of Tokyo, Tokyo, 1879

18. Jy Morse, E. S., Japanese Homes and their Surroundings, Harper & Bros., New York, 1889

189. Me Morse, W. R., Chinese Medicine, Paul B. Hoeber Inc., New York, 1938

370. Dl Jy Morse, E. S., Japan Day by Day, Kobunsha, Tokyo, 1936

201. Jr Mencken (H.L.) - The American Mercury - 107 (Nov. 1932) - 124 (Apr. 19[illegible])

資料 11（貼付ノート・Transaction of the Asiatic Society of Japan）

996. Dc Moseley, C.B., An English-Japanese Vocabulary Of Theological Biblical And Other Terms,
Methodist Publishing House (Kyo Bun Kwan), Tokyo, 1897

1301. Jy Mossman, S., New Japan,
John Murray, London, 1873

985. Lg Motti, P., Russian Conversation -Grammar,
David Nutt, London, 1901

407. Fi Moulton, H. G., Japan (An Economic and Financial Appraisal), The Brookings Institution, Washington, D.C., 1931

1176. Po Moult, T., The Best Poems of 1926,
Harcourt, Brace & Co., New York,

1101. Hy Mounsey, A.H., The Satsuma Rebellion,
John Murray, London, 1879

415. Lg Mullie, J., The Structural Principles of the Chinese Language, 2 vols., The Bureau of Engraving and Printing, Peiping, 1932

880. Mi Munro, N.G., Prehistoric Japan,
Yokohama, 1911

~~915. Ec Munro, N.G., Coins of Japan, (2 copies),~~
~~Box of Curios Printing And Publishing Co., Yokohama, 1904~~

one copy only

1209. Lt Murakami, N., ed., Letters Written By The English Residents In Japan,
The Sanko-sha, Tokyo, 1900

738. At Murakami, K., Representative Flower Arrangement Of Present- Day Japan, Vol. 3,
Nippon Flower Arrangement Society, Kyoto, 1879

1259. Ms Murakami, N., Diary of Richard Cocks, ( 2 copies ),
Sankosha, Tokyo, 1899

929. Dr Muramatsu, M., Glossary Of The Back Slang, 隱語彙集
Kinkodo, Tokyo, 1887

394. Hy Murdoch, J., A History of Japan, 3 vols., Kegan Paul,
Trench, Trubner & Co., London, 1925-1926

308. Bb Murray, D., Bibliography: Its Scope and Methods, James
Macelhose & Sons, Glasgow, 1917

785. Bn The Museum of Far Eastern Antiquites, Bulletin Nos., 1-12,
Stockholm, 1929 - 1940

145. Hy Muto, C., A Short History of Anglo-Japanese Relations, Hokuseido,
Tokyo, 1936

877. Tr Mutsu, I., Kamakura Fact & Legend,
Times Publishing Co., Tokyo, 1930

15. Gr Garfield Moilroy - Chamberlain's Japanese grammar.

1225A Mittheilungen der Deutschen Gesellschaft für
Nature-Und Volkerkunde Ostasien vols. 5

45. Fi(F) K. Matsuoka - L'étalon de change or en Extrême-Orient.

61. Lg(F) Meillet et Marcel Cohen - Les langues du monde.

資料11（貼付ノート・Transaction of the Asiatic Society of Japan）

435. Cl Nachod, O., Geschichte von Japan die Übernahme der Chinesischen Kultur, 2 vols., Verlag Asia Major, Leipzig, 19[illegible]

~~175. Dp Nachod, O., Die Beziehungen der Niederlandise Ostindische Kompagnie zu Japan, Rob. Friese, Leipzig, 1897~~

436. Hy Nachod, O., Geschichte von Japan, die Urzeit, Friedrich Andreas Perthes Aktiengesellschaft, Gotha, 1906

1300. Dp (F) Nagaoka, H., Histoire Des Relations Du Japon avec L'Europe, (2 copies), Henri Jouve, Paris, 1905

1039. Dc Naitō, N., A New Dictionary Of Nautical Terms, Yūhodo, Tokyo, 1917

736. At Nakahara, K., Selected Flower Arrangement Of The Ohara School, Nippon Flower Arrangement Society, Kyoto, 1937

328. Dc Nakamura, K. and others, Dictionary of English, Chinese and Japanese, 2 vols., Yamanouchi, F., Tokyo, 12th Yr. of Meiji

1243. Si Nakayama, K., Sinological Researches in Contemporary Japan, Japan Council of The Institute of Pacific Relations, 1931

1089. Nv Nakazato, K., Dai-Bosatsu Toge, Shunju Sha, Tokyo, 1927

1089. Dc Nash, V., Trindex, An Index to Three Dictionaries, Index Press, Yenching University, Peking

1097. Nv Natsume, S., Kokoro,(translated by Sato, I.), The Kokuseido Press, Tokyo, 1941

477. Jy Nehru, S. S., Money, Men and Women in Japan, Kokusai Shuppan Insatsusha, Tokyo, 1936

~~1008. Ta Netto, C., Papier Schmetterlinge aus Japan, (D) T.O. Weigel, Leipzig, 1888~~

1229. St (D) Netto, C., etc., Japanischen Humor, F.A. Brockhaus, Leipzig, 1901

1111. Dc A New Dictionary Of Military Terms, English-Japanese, Japanese English-English, Published by The Zu(To)nansha 圖南社, Tokyo, 1919

35. Ga Newsom, S., Japanese Garden Construction (日本庭園築造法), Domoto, Kumagawa & Perkins, Tokyo, 1939

100. Tr Newton, A. P., Travel and Travellers of the Middle Ages, Kegan Paul, Trench, Trubner & Co., London, 1930

1136. St Nicol, H., Microbes By The Million, The Penguin Books, London, 1939

942. Li Nicholson, R.A., A Literary History of The Arabs, T. Fisher Unwin, London, 1907

1427. Dc Nielsen, K., Lappisk Ordbok (Lapp Dictionary), 1. A-F, H. Aschehong & Co., Oslo, 1932

資料 11（貼付ノート・Transaction of the Asiatic Society of Japan）

~~899.~~ Ta The Nightless City,
An English Student Of Sociology, Maruya & Co., Yokohama,
1899

968. Rn Nisbet, The New Testament In Scots, 3 vols.,
William Blackwood & Co., Edinburgh, 1901, 1903, 1905

39. Ca Nishi, K., The Monthly Calendear of Floral Japan, Yoshikawa
Bookstore, Yokohama.

732. At Nishikawa, I., Floral Art Of Japan, Tourist Library:11.
Japanese Government Railways, Tokyo, 1938

895. In Nishimura, S., A Study of The Ancient Ships of Japan,
part 3, Ancient Rafts Of Japan, 日本古代の筏 ,
The Society of Naval Architects, Tokyo, 1922

894. In Nishimura, S., AStudy Of The Ancient Ships Of Japan,
日本古代船舶研究 , part 1-2 , The Kumano-no-Morota-Bune, or
The Massy-Paddle -Ship Of Kumano : The Hisago-Bune or The
Gourd-Ship,
The Society of Naval Architects, 造船協會 , Tokyo, 1920

471. Jy Nitobe, I., Western Influences in Modern Japan, The University
of Chicago Press, Chicago,

1074. Cl Nitobé, I., Bushido : The Soul Of Japan,
G.P.Putnams Sons, New York, 1905

1385. Fl 78 ~~Nitobe, I., Japanese Traits and Foreign Influences,
Kegan Paul, Trench, Trubner & Co., London, 1927~~

1168. Po Nobunaga, S., etc., Obiter Dicta On Japanese Odes,
Ginseisha, Tokyo, 1931

656. Pc Nogami, T., Masks Of Japan,
Kokusai Bunka Shinkokai, Tokyo, 1935

657. Pc Nogami, T., Masks Of Japan ( The Gigaku, Bugaku, and Noh Masks),
Kokusai Bunka Shinkokai, Tokyo, 1935

861. Pc Noguchi, Y., The Spirit Of Japanese Poetry,
John Murray, London, 1914

1038. Es Noguchi, Y., Seen & Unseen,
The Orientalia, New York, 1920

638. Pa Noguchi, Y., Hiroshige, 2 vols., 1chitsu,
Maruzen Co., Tokyo, 1940

1167. St Noguchi, Y., The American Diary Of A Japanese Girl,
Fuzanbo & Co., Tokyo,

642. Pt Noguchi, Y., The Ukiyoye Primitives, 1 vol, 1 chitsu,
(Privately Published) Tokyo,1933

650. Pt Noguchi, Y., Harunobu, 1 vol., 1 chitsu,
Yoshikawa, Yokohama, 1940

883. Pc The Noh Drama, (2 copies ),
Kokusai Bunka Shinkokai, Tokyo, 1937

884. Pc Noh Programme ; (Friday, August 6, 1937 ).
Kokusai Bunka Shinkokai, Tokyo, 1937

38. Cl Conrad Nielsen - Instituttet for Sammenlignende Kultur-forskning. (Serie B: Skrifter), Oslo, 1932.

464. Jy Norman, E. H., Japan's Emergence as a Modern State, Institute of Pacific Relations, New York, 1940

1224. Hy Notes On The History Of The Yoshiwara Of Yedo, Yokohama, 1894

1325. Jr Notes And Queries, (From The Journal Of The North China Branch Of The Royal Asiatic Society, Vol. 48, 1917)

87. At Nasu - The fundaments of Japanese archery, 2 vols.

✓ 78. Jy Dp Nitobé - Japanese traits & foreign influences, Kegan Paul, London, 1927.

~~414. Jy 78 Nitobe, I., Japanese Traits and Foreign Influences, Kegan Paul, French, Trabner & Co., London, 1927~~

905. Gr (F) Kr. Nyrop, Grammaire Historique De La Langue Francaise, 6 vols., Alphouse Picard & Fils, Paris,

✓ 94. Td Dp Osker Nachod - Die Beziehungen der Niederländischen Ostindischen Kompagnie zu Japan in Siebzehn Jahrhundert, Rob. Fries, Leipzig, 1897.

✓ 100. Cu(D) O. Netto - Papier-Schmetteringe aus Japan ( 日本紙蝶々 ), Weigel, Leipzig, 1888.

(✓) Nusay Munis; Tanka (Poesias Japonesas de
Theo D. Horiguchi

(✓) Nagai Kafu; Le Jardin des Pivoines; Au
Sans Pareil, Paris; 1927.

(✓) Nam-Hoa Tu-Dien (南華字典)

✓ nouvel Orient vol. 4.

459. Po Obata, S., The Works of Li-Po, the Chinese Poet, Hokuseido Press, Tokyo, 1936

233. Ct The Official Catagloue issued by the Kyoto Commercial Museum, 1910

347. Li Ogden, C. K., Bentham's Theory of Fictions, Kegan Paul, Trench, Trubner & Co., London, 1932

348. Li Ogden, C. K. and Richards, I. A., The Meaning of Meaning, Kegan Paul, Trench, Trubner & Co., London, 1930

867. Ms Ogden, C.K., Debabelization, Kegan Paul, London, 1931

735. At Ohara, [illegible]., Selected Flower Arrangement Of The Ohara School, Vol. 2, Nippon Flower Arrangement Society, Kyoto, 1938

733. At Ohashi, S., Japanese Floral Arrangement, Gei-en-sha, Osaka, (Yamanaka Co., New York) 1936

555. Lg Ojima, K., The National Language Readers of Japan, 13 vols., Sankosha, Tokyo, 1929-39

1401. Lg Ojima, K., The National Language Readers Of Japan, 6 vols., Sanko-sha, Tokyo, 1929-1932 (vols. 1, 4-8)

1404. Lg Ojima, K., What Is The Japanese Language ?, Sanko-sha, Tokyo, 1929

227. Zo Okada, Y., A Catalogue of Vertebrates of Japan, Maruzen Co., Tokyo, 1938

1443. Zo. Okada, Y., Amphibia And Replilia Of Jehol, Report Of The First Scientific Expedition To Manchoukuo, Waseda University, Tokyo, 1935

756. At Okakura, K., The Heart Of Heaven, Nippon - Bijutsuin, Tokyo, 1922

863. At Okakura, K., The Book Of Tea, Angus & Robertson, Australia, 1932

1030. So Okakura, Y., The Life And Thought Of Japan, J.M.Dent & Sons, London, 1913

1204. La Okamatsu, S., Provisional Report On Investigation Of Laws And Customs In The Island Of Formosa, The 'Kobe Herald' Office, Kobe

392. Pu Oriental Pamphlets ( Various articles bound in 2 vols.)

393. Pu Lg Oriental and Linguistic Pamphlets bound in 1 volume.

899. Jr Ostasiatische Zeitschrift, 4 copies, Verlag von Walter de Gruyter, Berlin, 193

1238. Pt Oswald, J.C., A History Of Printing, D.Appleton & Co., New York, 1928

240. By Otani, R., etc., Tadataka Ino, The Japanese Land-Surveyor, The Yamato Society, Tokyo, 1932

資料 11（貼付ノート・Transaction of the Asiatic Society of Japan）

898. Jr Otto Kummel, Ostasialische Zeitischrift, 4 copies, Oesterheld & Co., Verlag, Berlin,

349. Ps Oursel-Masson, P., Comparative Philosophy, Kegan Paul, Trench, Trubner & Co., London, 1926

1102. Nv Ozaki, K., The Gold Demon : Konjiki Yasha, 3 vols., (Rewritten in English by A.M. Lloyd ), The Yurakusha, Tokyo, 1905

56. Lg K. Ojima - National language readers of Japan, Vol I & supplement, Vol. IV-VIII, Sankosha, Tokyo, 1929-39, Total 7 vols.

8. Dc Okakura - Kenkyusha's New English-Japanese dictionary.

2. The Original Letters of the English Pilot William Adams, (written from Japan) Between A.D 1611 and 1617 ) Japan Gazette Office, Yokohama, 1896

資料 11（貼付ノート・Transaction of the Asiatic Society of Japan）

1298. Dc (F) Pagés, L., Dictionnaire Japonais Français,
Fermin Didot Freres, Paris, 1868

671. Rn (F) Pagés, L., Histoire De La Religion Chretienne, 2 vols.,
Charles Dounial, Paris, 1869

695. Bb (F) Pages, L., Bibliographia Japonaise Ou Catalogue Des
Ouvrages Relatifs Au Japon,
Benjamin Daprat, Paris, 1859

927. By (F) Pages, L., Benjamin Duprat, Bibliographie Japonaise : Ou
Catalogue Des Ouvrages Relatifs Au Japon,
Librairie De L'Institut Impérial De France, Paris, 1859

896. Gr (F) Pagès, L. Benjamin Duprat, Essai De Grammaire Japonaise,
Libraire de L'Institut Imperial de France, Paris, 1861

553. Lg Palmer, H. E., The Principles of Romanization, Maruzen,
Tokyo, 1931

1058. Ta Paris, J., Kimono,
W. Collins Sons & Co., London,

964. Po Paris, J., A Japanese Don Juan And Other Poems,
W. Collins Sons & Co., London, 1926

513. Dc Parker, C. K., A Dictionary of Japanese Compound Verbs,
Maruzen Co., Tokyo, 1939

1258. Rn Paske-Smith, M., Japanese Traditions Of Christianity,
J.L. Thompson & Co., Kobe, 1930

704. Rn Paske- Smith, M., Japanese Traditions Of Christianity,
Thompson & Co., Kobe, 1930

849. Lg (F) Paulham, F., La Double Fonction Du Langage,
Librairie Felix Alcan, Paris, 1929

915. Lg Pedersen, H., Språkvetenskapen Under Nittonde Århundradet,
P. A. Norstedt & Soners, Stockholm,

901. Tr (F) Pelliot, P., Le Premier Voyage De L'Amphitrite Eu Chine,
Librairie Orientaliste, Paul Geuthner, Paris, 1930

181. By Pe. Joao de Loureiro (Missionario e Botânico José Maria Braga),
Escola Tipográfica do Orfanato, Macau, 1938

668. Hy (F) Pere De Charlevoix, Histoire Du Japon, 6 vols.,
Rollin, Paris, 1754

676. Pc (F) Peri, N., Cinq Nô,
Editions Bossard, Paris, 1921

652. Pc (D) Perzyński, F., Japanische Masken, 2 vols.,
Verlag Von Walter De Gruyter & Co., Berlin, 1925

1416. Li (F) Petillou, C., Allusions Litteraires, 3 parts(No. 8, 13, 33)
Impérimerie de la Mission Catholique, Changhai, 1909-1921

62. Pa Petrucci, R., Chinese Painters, Brentans' Publishers, New York,
1920

680. Rn (F) Pfister, L., Notices Sur Les Jesuites De L'Ancienne
Mission De Chine, 2 vols.,
Imprimere De La Mission Catholique, Chang-hai, 1934

66. Tr Cu Sammal Purchas - Purchas, his pilgrim in Japan.

3. Dc M. Alderton Pink - A dictionary of correct English.

889. Lg (D) Pfizmaier, A., Die Poetischen Ausdrücke der Japanischen Sprache,
In Commission Bei Karl Gerold's Sohn, Wien, 1873

890. Lg (D) Pfizmaier, A., Die Poetischen Ausdrucke der Japanischen Sprache,
In Commission Bei Karl Gerold's Sohn, Wien, 1874

~~333. Ms Pfoundes, C., Fuso-Mimi Bukuro: A Budget of Japanese Notes, The Japan Mail, Yokohama, 1875~~

592. Po Pierson, Dr. J. L., The Manyôśû, 4 vols., E. J. Brill, Leyden, 1929-1936

1228. At Piggott, F.T., The Music And Musical Instruments Of Japan, Kelly & Walsh, Yokohama, 1909

554. Ms Piggott, Capt. F.S.G., The Elements of Sosho, Kelly & Walsh, Yokohama, 2nd Year of Taisho

1164. Rn Pike, E.R., Slayers Of Superstition, Watts & Co., London, 1931

802. Fl, Lg Pilsudski, B., Materials For The Study Of The Ainu Language And Folklore,
Spolka Wydawnicza Polska, Cracow, 1912

1013. Gy (F) Planchet, J.M., L'Empire Chinois, 2 vols.,
Imprimerie Des Nazaristes, Pékin, 1926

1014. Tr Planchet, J.M., Souvenirs D'Un Voyage Dans La Tartarico Et Le Thibet, 2 vols.,
Imprimerie des Nazaristes, Pékin, 1924

1458. Hy (P) A Plano Colonial de Affonsa de Albuquerque, Lisboa, 1929

210. Po Plants from China, Formosa, 3 vols. (The Journal of the Linnean Society), 1886-1905

1095. Ta Plomer, W., Paper Houses, The Hogarth Press, London, 1929

1344. Fl (D) Ploss, H., Das Weih in der Natur-und Völkerkunde, 3 vols., Neufeld & Henius Verlag, Berlin, 1927

526. Lg Pocket Handbook of Colloquial Japanese, Nippon-no-Romazi-Sya, Tokyo, 3rd Year of Showa

955. Po The Poetical Works of Robert Herrick, 4 vols., The Cressent Press, London, 1928

117. B Pompe van Meerdervoort, J. L. C., Vijf Jaren in Japan 1857-1863, 2 vols., Leiden, 1867-68

690. Jy Ponsonby-Fane, R., The Imperial Family Of Japan, Japan Chronicle, Kobe, 1915

633. Rn Ponsonby-Fane, R., Suminoe No Ohokami, Kyoto, 1935

628. Rn Ponsonby-Fane, R., Kashima Jinguki, Kyoto, 1937

625. Rn Ponsonby - Fane, R., Divine Spirits Of Shinto And Hirota Jinja, Kyoto, 1934

~~1331. Dp Pergament, M.J., The Diplomatic Quarter In Peking, China Booksellers, Peking, 1927~~

資料 11（貼付ノート・Transaction of the Asiatic Society of Japan）

578. Na Porter, W. N., The Tosa Dairy, Henry Frowde, London, 1912

581. Li Porter, W. N., The Miscellany of a Japanese Priest (Tsure-Zure Gusa), Humphrey Milford, London, 1914

453. Pi Postage Stamps of Manchoukuo, The Manchoukuo Postal Society, Hsinking, 1940

(F)
57[illegible]. At Poupées Japonaises, K.B.S., Tokyo

114. Bu Pratt, J. B., The Pilgrimage of Buddhism and a Buddhist Pilgrimage, The Macmillan Co., New York, 1928

255. In Preservation of Leather Bookbindings, Leaflet No. 69, The United States Department of Agriculture, Washington, D.C.

444. Rs Pretschneider, E.; Mediaeval Researches (From Eastern Asiatic Sources), 2 vols., Kegan Paul, Trench, Trubner & Co., London, 1910; reprinted and published by Buntenkaku, Peiping, 1937.

953. Pt Price, F.W., tr., Sun Yat-Sen, San Min Chu I : The Three Principles Of The People , The Commercial Press, Shanghai, 1928

235. In Priest, A. and Simmons, P., Chinese Textiles (An Introduction to the Study of their History, Sources, Technique, Symbolism, and Use), The Metropolitan Museum of Art, New York, 1934

[illegible]. Bu Prip-Moller, J., Chinese Buddhist Monasteries, O.U.P., London, etc., 1937

Pollard: Fine Books,

217. Rs Prishvin, M., Jen Sheng (The Root of Life), translated by George Walton and Philip Gibbons, Andrews Melrose, London, 1936

104. Hy Pritchard, E. H., Anglo-Chinese Relations during the 17th & 18th Centuries, University of Illinois, Urbana, 1929

1311. Bb (D) Professor Dr. F.W.K. Müller, (In Memoriam), Druck, Oskar Puchalt, Berlin, 1930

195. Nh Pryer, H., Butterflies of Japan, published by the Author in Yokohama; reprinted in Tokyo by the Shokubutsu Bunken Kanko-kai in the 10th Yr. of Showa

1320. Pt Perkins, P.D., The Paper Industry and Printing in Japan, Japan Reference Library, New York, 1940

68. Hy Peter Pratt - History of Japan, 1822.

205. Rn Alekcie Pojatniev - About Jesus Christ in Kamik language, Translated from Greek, St. Petersburg, 1887.

17. Dc Hy Gy E. Papinot - Dictionary of history and geography of Japan.

123. La Dp M. J. Pergament - The diplomatic quater in Peking, China Booksellers, Peking, 1927.

86. Cu Le C. Pfoundes - Fu-so Mimi Bukuro ( 扶桑耳袋 ), a budget of Japanese notes, Japan Mail, Yokohama, 1875.

資料 11（貼付ノート・Transaction of the Asiatic Society of Japan）

1256. Ct Quaritch, B., A Catalogue Of Books, London, 1860

309. Bb Quarterly Bulletin of Chinese Bibliography, 9 vols., The Chinese National Committee on Intellectual Co-operation, Shanghai, 1934-1941

310. Bb Quarterly Bulletin of Chinese Bibliography Title Page, one envelope

~~1352. Ms 136 The Queen's Book Of The Red Cross, Hodder & Stoughton, 1939~~

399. Tr Quennell, P., A Superficial Journey through Tokyo and Peking, Faber & Faber Ltd., London

1288. Pt Quigley, H.S., Japanese Government And Politics, The Century Co., London, 1932

834. Po Quiller - Couch, A., The Oxford Book Of Ballads, The Clarendon Press, Oxford, 1927

136. Ms . The Queen's Book of the Red Cross, Hodder & Stoughton, London, 1939.

1123. Gy 183 Radloff, W., Atlas der Alterthümer der Mongolie,
(D) (In the Russian language), 1892

720. Do (D) Radloff, W., Die Alttürkischen Inschriften Der Mongolei, (Vol.1-3) 2 vols., St. Petersburg, 1895

590. Lg 15 Radloff, W., Versuch Eines Wörterbuches der Türk-Dialecte, Dc 4 vols., St. Petersbourg, 1893-1911

1214. Rn (F) Rahder, J., La Gnose Bouddhique, Librairie D'Amérique Et D'Orient, Paris, 1937

1048. Ta Rancat, T., The Honourable Picnic, John Lane, London, 1931

360. Dc Raguet, E. et Ono, T., Dictionnaire Francais-Japonais, San-saisha, Tokyo, 1905

379. Jy Rathgen, K., Staat und Kultur der Japaner (Monographien zur Weltgeschichte XXVII), Verlag von Klasing, Leipzig, 1907

200. Bo Read, B. E. and Liu, J. C., Plantae Medicinalis Sinensis (本草新註), Peking Union Medical University in collaboration with the Peking Laboratory of Natural History, Peking, 1927

201. Bo Read, B. E., Botanical, Chemical and Pharmacological Reference List to Chinese Materia Medica, Peking Union Medical College, Peking, 1923

202. Bo Read, B. E., Chinese Medical Plants from the Pen Ts'ao Kang Mu (本草綱目), Peking Natural History Bulletin, Peking, 1936

資料 11（貼付ノート・Transaction of the Asiatic Society of Japan）

243. Me Read, B. E., Chinese Materia Medica - Animal Drugs, Peking Natural History Bulletin, Peking, 1931

244. Me Read, B. E., Chinese Materia Medica - Dragon and Snake Drugs, The Peking Natural History Bulletin, Peking

245. Me Read, B. E., Chinese Materia Medica - Turtle and Shellfish Drugs, The Peking Natural History Bulletin, Peking, 1937

246. Me Read, B. E., Chinese Materia Medica; Avian Drugs, The Peking Natural History Bulletin, Peking, 1932

247. Me Read, B. E. and Pak, G., Minerals and Stones (A Compendium of Minerals and Stones used in Chinese Medicine from the Pen Ts'ao Kang Mu), The Peking Natural History Bulletin, Peking, 1936

251. Me Read, B. E. and Liu, J. C., A Review of the Scientific Work done on Chinese Materia Medica, Peking Union Medical College, Peking

190. Nh Read, B. E., Common Food Fishes of Shanghai, The North China Branch of the Royal Asiatic Society, Shanghai, 1939

178. Rp Read, B., Shanghai Foods, The Chinese Medical Association, Shanghai. 1937

1239. Rn (F) Recherches Sur Les Superstitions En Chine, 5 bands, Imprimerie De T'ou-se-we, Chang-hai, 1912-1938

1525. Dp The Record of Townsend Harris in Japan

1079. Le Redesdale, L., Tales Of Old Japan, Macmillan & Co., London, 1928

1173. Ay Rhys, E., etc., chosen, A Century of English Essays an Anthology, J.M.Dent & Sons, London, 1925

166. Bu Reichelt, K. L., Truth and Tradition in Chinese Buddhism (佛教源流攷), The Commercial Press, Shanghai, 1934

1303. Jy (D) Rein, J.J., Japan, 2 vols., Verlag von Wilhelm Engelmann, Leipzig, 1886

424. Hy Jy Reischauer, R. K., Early Japanese History, 2 vols., Princeton University Press, Princeton, 1937

158. Bu Reischauer, A. K., Studies in Japanese Buddhism, The Macmillan Co., New York, 1925

一十目録ニ見エズガ No.[illegible] と No.224 ノ間ニ (Book case 5 一番上棚左) ニ下記ノものあり
Remy, Ch., Notes Médicales sur le Japon, Libraires de la Faculté de Médecine, Paris, 1883 ?

490. Tr Renandot, E., Ancient Accounts of India and China (by two Mohammedan Travellers), translated from the Arabic, Sam Harding (Bible and Anchor on the Pavement), London, 1733

53. Py Renou, L., Les Maitres de la Philologie Védique, Paul Geuthner, Paris, 1928

1281. Dp The Report Of The League Commission On The Sino-Japanese Dispute, 1932

188. Mp Rand-Mc Nally - Handy atlas of the world, 1922.

1440. Rp Report Of The International Secretariat To The Pacific Council 1933-'36, Yosemite National Park, California, 1936

271. Rp Report on the Control of the Aborginies in Formosa, Bureau of Aborginial Affairs, The Government of Formosa, Taihoku, 1911

1199. Jr Report Of The Council Of The China Branch Of The Royal Asiatic Society, For The Year 1882, Journal, New Series, Vol.17 part 2, Noronha & Sons, Shanghai, 1884

1247. Rp, Ed Report Of The Minister of State for Education(56 th), The Department Of Education, Tokyo, 1934

1248. Rp, Ed Report Of The Minister of State for Education (59 th), The Department Of Education, Tokyo, 1938

1212. Bn Reprinted from the Bulletin Of The School Of Oriental Studies, Vol. 6 part 3

284. Rs Research Review of the Osaka Asiatic Society (No. 11 - Oct. 1933), The Osaka Asiatic Society. Osaka

1037. So Resident Orientals On The American Pacific Coast, Institute Of Pacific Relations, New York,

678. Bb (E) Retana, W.E., Aparato Bibliografico De La Historia General De Filipinas, 3 vols., Imprenta de la Sucesora de M. Minuesa de los Rios, Madrid, 1906

1179. Es Retrospect And Prospect,
Kawase & Sons., Kobe, 1928

647. Pt (F) Revon, M., Etude Sur Hokusai,
Société Française D'imprimerie Et De Librairie, Paris,
1896

332. La Riasanovsky, V. A., Customary Law of the Nomadic Tribes of
Siberia, Tientsin, 1938

1413. La Riasanovsky, V.A., Customary Law Of The Mangol Tribes, 3 parts,
Artistic Printinghouse, Harbin, 1929

352. Mo Richards, I. A., Mencius on the Mind, Kegan Paul, Trench,
Trubner & Co., London, 1932

1177. Ms Robertson, J.M., Ernest Renan,
Watts & Co., London, 1924

103. Na Rockhill, W. W., The Journey of William Rubruck, Hakluyt Society,
London, 1900

920. Lg (D) Rogge, C., Der Notstand Der Heutigen Sprachwissenschaft,
Max Hueber Verlag, München, 1929

688. Lg Romaji, No. 35 Maki Dai 8-9-Go,
Romaji-Hirome-Kai, Tokyo, 1940

810. Ta, Nv Romanne- James, O Toyo Writes Home,
Herbert Jenkins, London, 1926

~~1383. Fl~~ 132. ~~Rose, J., The Origin Of The Chinese People,
Oliphants, London, 1916~~

1336. Lg Rose-Innes, A., Conversational Japanese For Beginners, K.Yoshikawa & Co., Yokohama, 1926

1337. Dg Rose-Innes, A., Japanese Reading For Beginners, 5 vols., K.Yoshikawa & Co., Yokohama, 1930

1141. Lg Rose-Innes, A., Japanese Phrase-Book For Beginners And Tourists, Yoshikawa & Co., Yokohama,

1000. Dc Rose-Innes, A., Beginners' Dictionary Of Chinese-Japanese Characters, Yoshikawa Shoten, Yokohama, 1927

76. Bu Rosenberg, O., Introduction to the Study of Buddhism according to material preserved in Japan and China ( 名辞集 ), Faculty of Oriental Languages of the Imperial University of Petrograd, Tokyo, 1916

1389. Hy (F) Rosny, L., Histoire Des Dynasties Divines, 3 vols., Ernest Leroux, Editeur, Paris, 1887

783. Es, Rp (F) Rosny, M.L., Discours Et Rapports, 2 vols., Maisonneuve Et C, Libraire- Editeur, Paris, 1862-1878

279. Zo Rostovtzeff, Animal Style in South Russia and China, Princeton University Press, Princeton, 1929

758. Gr. (D) Roth, P.L., Han-Moun 漢文 Hilfsbuch Zur Grammatik der Koreanischen Sprache, Abtei , St. Benedikt, Tokwon, Korea, 1937

757. Lg (D) Roth, P.L., Grammatik der Koreanischen Sprache, Abtei St. Benedikt, Tokwon, Korea, 1936

1057. An, Jy (F) Rouveyre, Annuaire De La Société Des Études Japonaises, Libraire de la Société, Paris, 1881

~~256. By/30 Rouveyre, E., Connaissances Nécessaires a un Bibliophie, 5 vols., published by the editor, Paris~~

1058a Rouge (Gakujiten + Jiten), 2 vol.

1398. Rn Rowe, N.A., The Missionary Menace, Wishart & Co., 1932

36. At Rowland, B. Jr., Outline and Bibliographies of Oriental Art, 1 envelope, Harvard University Press, Cambridge, Mass., 1940

1099. So Rudd, H., Chinese Social Origine, The University Of Chicago Press, Chicago, 1928

1233. Po Rudyard Kipling's Verse, (Inclusive Edition 1885-1926), Hodder & Stoughton, London, 1931

639. At, Pt (D) Rumpf, F., Meister Des Japanischen Farbenholzschnittes, Walter De Gruyter & Co., Leipzig, 1924

21. Li (G) Rumpf, F., Das Ise Monogatari, Würfel Verlag, Berlin, 1932

80. At Pa Fritz Rumpf - Sharaku (写楽).

43. Lg(F) Ernest Renan - De l'origin du Language, Paris, 1925.

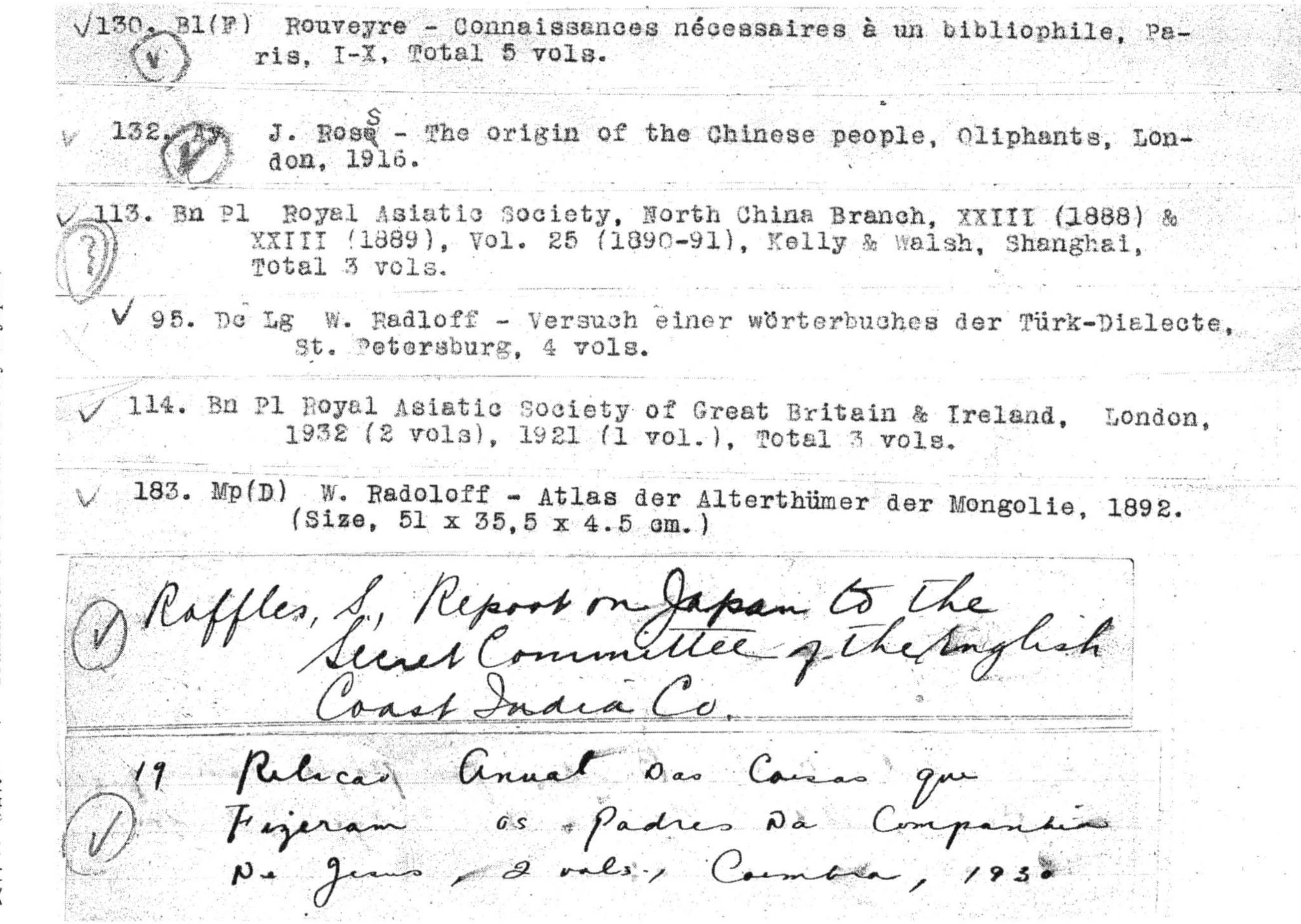

√130. Bl(F) Rouveyre - Connaissances nécessaires à un bibliophile, Paris, I-X, Total 5 vols.

√ 132. Ay J. Ross - The origin of the Chinese people, Oliphants, London, 1916.

√ 113. Bn Pl Royal Asiatic Society, North China Branch, XXIII (1888) & XXIII (1889), Vol. 25 (1890-91), Kelly & Walsh, Shanghai, Total 3 vols.

√ 95. Dc Lg W. Radloff - Versuch einer wörterbuches der Türk-Dialecte, St. Petersburg, 4 vols.

√ 114. Bn Pl Royal Asiatic Society of Great Britain & Ireland, London, 1932 (2 vols), 1921 (1 vol.), Total 3 vols.

√ 183. Mp(D) W. Radoloff - Atlas der Alterthümer der Mongolie, 1892. (Size, 51 x 35,5 x 4.5 cm.)

√ Raffles, S., Report on Japan to the Secret Committee of the English East India Co.

19 √ Relacao Annual das Coisas que Fizeram os Padres da Companhia de Jesus, 2 vols., Coimbra, 1930

Reprinted from the Annual Report of the Librarian of Congress (The Division of Orientalia) United States Government Printing Office, Washington, 1941

191. Lg Rose-Innes(A) - English-Japanese conversation dictionary Japanese phrase-book for beginners and tourist, Yoshikawa, Yokohama1935, 2 vols.

Read, B. E: Chinese Materia Medica - Insect Drugs. Peking Nat. Hist. Bulletin, 1941.

Report by Consul-General Hosie on the Province of Ssuch'uan (China No. 5 (1904).

A Review of Educational Work in Formosa, The Dept of Educational Affairs of Government-General of Formosa, 1916

Renan. A. De l'origine du langage, 1825

資料 11（貼付ノート・Transaction of the Asiatic Society of Japan）

1251. Tr Russell, L., America To Japan, G.P. Putnam's Sons, New York, 1915

843. Mo Russell, B., The Conquest Of Happiness, George Allen And Unwin, London, 1930

1449. (R) In the Russian Language, 1885

1450. (R) Russian Magazine, 4 parts, No.6-12, 1931

1451. (R) Russian Magazine, 4 parts, No. 7, 8, 9, 11, 12 1931 (5 parts)

461. Hy 将軍 征夷大将軍 幕府 (In the Russian language), 1916 (later)

1302. In the Russian Language 実用会話 1909 (later)

138. Ap(D) F. F. v. Peitzenstein - Das Weib, anthropologischen studien, 3 vols.

202. Nieder-Gr(D) Raveket (Hendk),- Gramatica of Nederdentsce Spraakkunst (低地ドイツ語文典 前編), Leyden, 1822.

203. Nieder-Gr(D) -,,- - Syntaxis of Nederdeutsche Woordvoecing (低地ドイツ語文典 後編), Leyden 1810.

29. Lg Rogets - Thésaurus of English words and phrases.

1368. Na Sachan, E. C., Alberuni's India, 2 vols., Kegan Paul, Trench
Trubner & Co., London, 1910

632. Rn The Sacred Scriptures Of Konkokyo,
Konkokyo Hombu, Okayama, 1933

~~627. Rn Sadler, A.L., Saka's Diary Of A Piligrim To Ise,
The Meiji Japan Society, Tokyo, 1940~~

577. Na Sadler, A. L., The Ten-Ft. Square Hut and Tales of the
Heike, Angus & Robertson Ltd., Sydney, 1928

661. Pc Sadler, A.L., Japanese Plays,
Angus & Robertson, Sydney, 1934

624. Ms Sadler, A.L., etc., Kocho (The Emperor Go=Mizuno-In's),
The Meiji Japan Society, Tokyo, 1922

1118. Li Saintsbury, G., A History Of English Prose Rhythm,
McMillan & Co., London, 1922

1175. Po Saintsbury, G., ed., John Dryden,
T. Fisher Unwin, London,

1150. By Saintsbury, G., John Dryden,
Ernest Benn, London,

259. Pu Saito, S., Bookplates in Japan, Meiji Shobo, Tokyo

689. Po Saito, H., A Voice Out Of The Serene, 雲上の一聲 : The
Poetical Works of His Late Majesty Meiji Tenno,
Tokyo, the First Year of Taisho

665. Rn, Cl — Saito, S., A Study of the Influence of Christianity Upon, Japanese Culture, The Japan Council of The Institute of Pacific Relation, Tokyo, 1931

651. Pc — Sakanishi, S., Kyogen, Marshall Jones Co., Boston, 1938

59. Pa — Sakanishi, S., The Spirit of the Brush, John Murray, London, 1939

659. Dm — Sakanishi, S., etc., A List Of Translation Of Japanese Drama Into English, French And German, 1 vol., 1 chitsu, American Council Of Learned Societies, Washington, 1935

154. Jr — Sakanishi, S., A Private Journal of John Glendy Sproston, U.S.N., Sophia University, Tokyo, 1940

~~274. Ps 112 Sakurazawa, N., Philosophie D'Extrème-Orient, Librairie Philosophique J. Vrin, Paris, 1931~~

~~395. Jy 70 Salwey, C. M., The Island Dependencies of Japan, Eugene L. Morice, London, 1913~~

1402. Es 70 — Salwey, C.M., The Island Dependencies Of Japan, Eugene L. Morice, London, 1913

1452. Rn (F) — Saṃtānāntrasiddhi Dharmakīrti Saṃtānāntra siddhitikā, (Bibliotheca Buddhica XIX), 1916

1033. Jr Samuel Coling, Edited, The New China Review, (4 vols.), (Nos. 1-24), unbound
Kelly & Walsh, Hongkong, 1919-1922

234. In Sanjonishi, K., Notes on Dyeing and Weaving in Ancient Japan,
Nippon Bunka Chuo Renmei, Tokyo, 1940

~~516. Gr Sansom, G. B., Historical Grammar of Japanese, 2 copies,
the Clarendon Press, Oxford, 1928~~

897. Hy Sarton, G., Introduction To The History Of Science, Vol. 1,
(From Homer To Omarkhyyam),
Published for The Carnegie Institution Of Washington by
The Williams & Wilkins Co., Baltimore, 1927

366. Hy Sansom, G. B., Japan (A Short Cultural History), Cresset
Press, London, 1931

1027. Nv Sasaki, U., tr., Kusamakura And Buncho,
Iwanami-Shoten, Tokyo, 1927

789. Ed Sasaki, H., Moral=Erziehung in Japan,
Akademische Verlagsgesellschaft, Leipzig, 1926

385. Rp Sashau, Dr. E., Mittheilungen des Seminers für orientalische
Sprachen au der Koniglichen Friederich Wilhelms, I-XVII,
Universität zu Berlin, Berlin, 1898-1914

941. Ta Sassoon, S., Memoirs Of An Infantry Officer,
Faber & Faber Ltd., London

資料 11（貼付ノート・Transaction of the Asiatic Society of Japan）

1431. Hy  Satow, E.M., tr., Kinse Shiriaku : A History Of Japan,
Japan Mail Office, 1873

743. Gr  Satow, E.M., List of Korean Geographical Names,
"Japan Mail" Office, Yokohama, 1884

1036. Lg  Satoh, H., etc., Anglo-Japanese Conversation Lessons,
Tokyo, 1896

926. Tr  Satow, E.M., The Voyage Of Captin John Saris To Japan,
1613,
Printed For The Haklnyt Society, London, 1900

862. Nv  Satow, E.M., Japan 1853 - 1864 : Genji Yume Monogatari,
Naigai Shuppan Kyokai, Tokyo, 1905

866. By  Satoh, H., Agitated Japan : The Life Of Baron Ii Kamon -
No - Kami Naosuke,
Maruya Co., Tokyo, 1896

1069. Lg (F)  Satow, E., Kuaiwa Hen Vingh-Cinq Exercices, 3 vols.,
Shiobido, Tokyo

1070. Ms  Sato, K., Amanojaku's Outspoken Comments,
Kenkyusha, Tokyo, 1930

1208. Dp  Satoh, H., Lord Hotta, The Picneer Diplomat Of Japan,
Hakubunkan, Tokyo, 1908

1299. Rn  Satow, E.M., The Jesuit Mission Press In Japan,
Privately Printed, Tokyo, 1888

20. Ob Taut, B., Houses and People of Japan, Sanseido, Tokyo, 12th Yr. of Showa

19. Ae Taut, B., Fundamentals of Japanese Architecture, K.B.S., Tokyo, 1936

538. Li Si Tchang Tchen-Ming, B., L'Ecriture Chinoise et Le Geste Humain, Librairie de T'ou-Sé-Wé, Changhai,

1417. Ms Tchang, M., Tombeau Des Liang, *Two copies* Impérimerie de la Mission Catholique, Changhai, 1912

216. Cu Tezuka, K., Japanese Food, Maruzen Company, Tokyo, 1936

~~12. Tr Terry, T. P., Terry's Guide to the Japanese Empire including Chosen and Taiwan, Houghton Mifflin Co., Boston, etc., 1933~~

1012. Gy Tibet, Rockhill, W.W., 1891 文殿閣書莊(影印), Peking, 1939

38. Ta Tibetan Tales (Derived from Indian Sources), Translated from the Tibetan of the Kahgyur by F. Anton von Schiefner, George Routledge & Sons, London

742. Jr T'ien Hsia, 天 下 , (Monthly) Vol. 1 - 6, The Sun Yat-sen Institute for the Advancement of Culture and Education, Nanking, 1935 - 1938

93. Hy Tien-Tsê Chang, Sino-Portuguese Trade from 1514 to 1644 (中葡通商研究), Late E. J. Brill & Co., Leyden, 1934

573. Lg Thesaurus Linguarum Orientalium, 4 vols., Francisci à Mesguien Meninski, Vienne; 1680

31[illegible]. Bb Thomas, E. C., The Love of Books: The Philobiblon of Richard de Bury, Chatto & Windus, London, 1925

794. Ed Thomas, A. F., Japan's National Education, Higher Normal School, 1933

686. Jy Thompson, A. M., Japan For A Week Britain For Ever, John Lane Co., London, 1911

232. Pa Thompson, D. V., The Materials of Medieval Painting, George Allen & Unwin Ltd., London, 1936

194. Bo Thunberg, C. P., Icones Plantarum Japonicarum, 1794; reprinted by the Shokubutsu Bunken Kankokai, Tokyo, in the 9th Year of Showa

252. Bo Thunberg, C. P., Flora Japonica, Lipsiae, 1784; Reprinted by the Shokubutsu Bunken Kankokai, Osaka, 8th Yr. of Showa

294. Pa Toda, K., The Ryerson Collection of Japanese and Chinese Illustrated Books, Art Institute of Chicago, Chicago, 1931

33. Pt Toda, K., Japanese Scroll Painting, The University of Chicago Press, Chicago, 1935

(F)
99. Bu Toki, H., Si-Do-In-Dzou (Gestes de L'officiant dans les ceremonies mystiques des Sectes Tendai et Singon)

1283. Tr Tokyo : Capital Of Japan, Tokyo Municipal Office, 1930

54. Is The Tombs of the Six Dynasties (六朝陵墓調査報告), The National Commission for the Preservation of Antiques, Nanking, 1935

681. Rn Satow, E.M., The Jesuit Mission Press In Japan, Keisei-sha-soten, Tokyo, 1888

86. Hy Satow, E. M., Kinsé Shiriaku (A History of Japan of Commodore Perry in 1853 to the Capture of Hakodate by the Mikado Forces in 1869), F. R. Wetmore & Co., Yokohama, 1876

987. Lg (D) Sauer, Schlüssel zur Italienischen Konversation-Grammatik, Julius Groos, Heidelberg, 1928

869. Rn Saunders, K., Buddhism, Ernest Benn, London, 1929

224. Ml (F) Savatier, Dr. L., Livres Kwa-Wi (Traduits du Japonais), Libraire de La Société Botanique de France, Paris, 1873

~~1405. Dc Schlegel, G., Nederlandsch-Chineesch Woordenbock, 4 vols., E.J. Brill, Leiden, 1886-1890~~

767. Pt (D) Schierlitz, E., Zur Technik Der Holztypendruche Aus Dem Wu-Ying-Tien In Peking, (Reprint from Vol. 1 Fasc. 1, Oct.,1935)

788. Ed (D) Schilling, K., Das Schulwesen der Jesuiten in Japan, Druck der Regensbergschen Buchdruckerei, Munster, 1931

1217. Dc (D) Schmidt, I.J., Mongolisch-Deutsch-Russisches Wörterbuch, St. Petersburg, 1835

資料11（貼付ノート・Transaction of the Asiatic Society of Japan）

1411. Hy (D) Schmidt, I.J., Geschichte der Ost-Mongolen und ihres Furstenhauses,
文殿閣書莊 , Peking, 民国26年

882. Es (D) Schmidt, W., Neue Wege Zur Erforschung Der Ethnologischen Stellung Japans,
Kokusai Bunka Shinkokai, Tokyo, 1935

608. Gr Schmidt, I. J., Grammatik Der Mongolischen Sprache,
St.- Petersburg, 1891

904. By (F) Schrijinem, J., Essai de Bibliographic de Geograpic Linguistique Generale,
N.V. Dekker & van de Vegten J. W. van Leeuwen, Nimegue, 1933

165. Bu Schulemann, G., Die Geschichte der Dalailamas, Carl Winter's Universitätsbuchhandlung, Heidelberg, 1911

476. In Schumpeter, E. B., The Industrialization of Japan and Manchukuo, The Macmillan Company, New York, 1940

613. Rn Schurhammer, G., Shinto,
Kurt Schroeder Bonn, 1923

1046. Ta Scidmore, E.R., Jinrikisha Days In Japan,
Harper & Brothers, New York,

1146. Ar Scott, W., The Antiquary,
J.M.Dent & Sons, London, 1923

1394. Li Scott, W., Old Mortality,
J.M.Dent & Sons, London, 1932

1172. Ms Scott, W., Kenilworth,
J.M.Dent & Sons, London, 1923

741. Sc Scott, J., English- Corean Dictionary,
Church Of England Mission Press, Corea, 1891

70. Sp Sculptural Forms in Terra Cotta from Chinese Tombs, The Toledo
Museum of Art, Toledo, Ohio

965. Ta Seabrook, W.B., The Magic Island,
The Literary Guild Of America, New York, 1929

646. Pt (D) Seidlitz, W., Geschichte Der Japanischen Farbenholzsch-
nitts,
Verlag Von Wolfgang Jess, Dresden, 1921

1399. Po Selected Poems Of Francis Thompson,
Jonathan Cape, London, 1929

472. Mr Selections from Inazo Nitobe's Writings, The Nitobe Memorial
Fund, Tokyo, 1936

672. Mr (F) Senart, etc., Mémoires Concernant L'asie Orientale,
Ernest Lerout, Paris, 1913

1343. In Sericultural Industry in Japan,
The Japan Sericultural Association, Tokyo, 1910

212. Zo Serrurier, L., Encyclopédie Japonaise (頭書増補訓蒙図彙大成),
E. J. Brill, Leyde, 1875

693. Bb (F) Serrurier, L., Bibliothèque Japonaise,
Imprimerie ci- devant E. J. Brill, Leyde, 1896

928. Gr (F) Serrus, Ch., Le Parallelisme Logico-Grammatical,
Librairie Felix Alcan, Paris, 1933

1063. Le The Seven Deities Of Good Luck Santaro,
The Taisho Eibunsha, Tokyo, 1925

95. Bu Shacklock, F., Some Aspects of the Influence of Western Philosophy
Upon Japanese Buddhism, Kyo Bun Kwan, Tokyo, 14th Yr. of Showa

842. Cu Shaw, G., Osaka Sketches,
The Hokuseido Press, Tokyo, 1926

855. Jy Shaw, G., Japanese Scrap- Book,
The Hokuseido Press, Tokyo, 1932

177. Rp Shaw, N., Silk (Replies from Commissioners of Customs to
Inspector General's Circular No. 103), The Maritime Customs
China, Shanghai, 1917

1112. Lg Sheba, S., Japanese in 3 Weeks,
The Japan Times & Mail, Tokyo, 1930

1124. Pa Shibui, K., Idéalisme Et Réalisme Dans L'Estampe Erotique
Primitif Du Japon,
Des Ateliers Photo-Mécaniques, Otsuka, M., 6 Plates and
8 sheets, 64 pages of catalogue in the 1st part, 1926,
62 plates & 3 sheets 24 pages of catalogue, 1928

462. Hy Shimmi, K., Die Geschichte der Dukeherrschaft in Japan, Braus-Riggenbach, Basel, 1939

814. Cu Shimomura, J., Life Of The Japanese Women Of To-Day, Kenkyusha, Tokyo, 1930

532. Dc Shinoda, M., Kotaba no Hayashi, Maruzen & Co., Tokyo, 1895

1100. Ta Shioya, S., Chushingura, An Exposition, The Hokuseido Press, Tokyo, 1940

856. Nv Shioya, S., tr., Namiko : A realistic novel by Kenjiro Tokutomi, The Yurakusha, Tokyo, 1905

268. Sc Shirokogoroff, S. M., Anthropology of Eastern China and Kwangtung Province, The Commercial Press, Shanghai, 1925

1347. So Shirokogoroff, S.M., Social Organisation Of The Manchus, Shanghai, 1924 (Royal Asiatic Society (North China Branch) Extra Volume 3)

1200. Sc Shirokogoroff, S.M., Anthropology Of Northern China, Shanghai, 1923 (Royal Asiatic Society : North China Branch Extra Vol. 2)

241. Jy A Short Bibliography on Japan, K.B.S., Tokyo, 1934

364. Es Shryock, J. K., The Study of Human Abilities (The Jen Wu Cbif of Liu Shao), American Oriental Society, New Heaven, 1937

449. Te Shryock, J. K., The Origin and Development of the States Cult of Confucius, The Century Co., New York and London

120. Nh Siebold, Ph. Fr. de, De Historiae Naturalis in Japonica Statu (日本博物志), 2 vols., Ikubundo, 12th Yr. of Showa 1939

121. Ct Siebold, Ph. Fr. de, Catalogue de la Bibliotèque Apportèe au Japon par Siebold, Ikubundo, Tokyo, 11th Yr. of Showa 1936

832. Cu Siebold, H., Studien Uber Die Aino, Verlag Von Paul Parey, Berlin, 1881

191. Nh Siebold, Ph. Fr. de., conjunctis studiis Temmnick et Schegel, Fauna Japonica, 4 vols., Lugduni Batavorum, 1833; Reprinted in Tokyo by the Shokubutsu Bunken Kankokai in the 9th Yr. of Showa 1934

198. Bo Siebold, P. F. de. and Zuccarini, J. G., Flora Japonica, 1826; reprinted in Tokyo by the Shokubutsu Bunken Kankokai in the 7th Yr. of Showa 1932

199. Bo Siebold, P. F. de, Synopsis Plantarum Oeconomicarum per Universum Regnum Japonicum, Batavia, 1830; reprinted in Tokyo by the Shokubutsu Bunken Kankokai in the 8th Yr. of Showa 1933

334. G Siguret, J., Territories et Populations des Confins du Yunnan, Henri Vetch, Peiping, 1937

1435. Zo Silkworms In India, Indian Museum Notes Issued By Trustees Vol.1, No.3, Calcutta, 1890

336. Tr Simon, E.M.H., Riukiu-Inseln, R. Voigtländers Verlag, Leipzig, 1914

857. Cu Sinclair, G.W., Tokyo People, Keibunkan, Tokyo, 1925

584. Cu Singer, K., The Life of Ancient Japan, Iwanami Shoten, Tokyo, 1939

1291. Bo Sinnott, E.W., Botany Principles And Problems, McGraw-Hill Book Co., New York, 1935

29 Pa Sirén, O., The Chinese on the Art of Painting, Henri Vetch, Peiping, 1936

977. Li Skeat, W., Specimens Of English Literature, The Clarendon Press, Oxford, 1930

398. Na Sladen, D., Queer Things About Japan, Anthony Treherne & Co., London, 1903

1426. Lg (F) Smedt, A., & Mostaert, A., Dictionaire Monguor-Francais, Imprimerie de l'Université Catholique, Peiping, 1933

1174. Lg Smith, L.P., Words And Idioms In The English Language, Constable & Co., London, 1928

1285. Po Smith, J.C., etc., The Poetical Works of Edmund Spenser, Oxford University Press, London, 1929

907. Lg  Smith, J.A., S.P.E. Tract No. xxxlv Interlanguage, T.C. Macaulay, Artifical Languages, Clarendon Press, 1930

454. Cu So  Smith, A. H., Village Life in Chiná (A Study in Sociology), Oliphant, Anderson and Ferrier, Edinburgh and London

455. Si  Smith, A. H., Chinese Characteristics, Fleming H. Revell Co., New York

674. Pri  The Smithsonian Institution, Report Of The U.S. National Museum, Government Printing Office, Washington, 1893

274. Gy  Snow, H. J., Notes on the Kuril Islands, John Murray, London, 1897

1092. Ms  Snyder, H.M., The Ma-Jung Manual, Houghton Møfflin Co., Boston, 1923

491. Na  Sokolsky, G. E., The Tinder Box of Asia, Doubleday, Doren & Co., New York, 1932

75. Bu  Soothill, W. E., etc., A Dictionary of Chinese Buddhist Terms, Kegan Paul, Trench, Trubner & Co., London, 1937

1289. Sta  The Special Population Census Of Formosa, Report of The Committee of the Formosan Special Census Investigation, 1909

221. Bo  Spörry, H., Bambus in Japan, Zürcher & Furrer, Zürich, 1903

1447. Rs (R) スパルウヰン , In the Russian Language "Japanese Army", △
3 parts,
東洋学院 , 浦鹽斯德, 1909

1448. Lg (R) スパルウヰン , Practical Japanese Conversation In the
Russian Language,
浦鹽斯德, 1910

1055. Cl (D) Sprauger, E., Kulturprobleme Im Gegenwärtigen Japan Und
Dentschland,
Nichidoku Bunka Kyokai, Tokyo, 1938

1387. Fl (D) Ssetsen, S., Geschichte Der Ost-Mongolen und Ihres
Fürstenhauses,
St. Petersburg, 1829

768. Cu Stael- Holstein, On The Sexagenary Cycle Of The Tibetans,
(Reprint from Vol. 1, Fasc. 2,1935( 2 copies),

765. Es, Jr Stael- Holstein, Monvmenta Serica, 6 vols.,
Henri Vetch, Peiping, 1935- 1941

1184. St Stanley, A., The Bedside Book,
Victor Gollancz, London, 1932

816. Cu Straelen, H., The Japanese Women Looking Forward,
Kyo Bun Kwan, Tokyo, 1940

1076. Tr Starr, F., A Diary, The American On The Tokaido,
Dai Nippon Tosho Kabushiki Kaisha, Tokyo, 1916

1330. Rn Starr, F., Korean Buddhism,
(Reprinted from The Journal of Race Development, Vol. 9,
No. 1, July, 1918)

831. Cu Starr, F., The Ainu Group,
The Open Court Publishing Co., Chicago, 1904

746. Rn Starr, F., Korean Buddhism,
Marshall Jones Co., Boston, 1918

812. Cu, At (D) Stratz, C.H., Die Korperformen In Kunst Und Leben Der Japaner,
Verlag Von Ferdinand Enke, Stuttgart, 1904

480. Jy Stead, A., Japan by the Japanese, William Heinemann, London,
1904

466. Jy Stead, A., Japanese Patriotism, John Lane the Bodley Head,
London

~~1126. Pa~~ 185 ~~Stein, A., The Thousand Buddhas : Ancient Paintings From
Tun-Huang, 33+15 plates, with An Introductory Essay by Binyon, L.
Bernard Quaritch, London, 1921~~

935. Hy Stein, M.A., Ruins Of Desert Cathary, 2 vols.,
Macmillan & Co., London, 1912

~~772. Tr~~ 98 ~~Stein, A., Innermost Asia, 4 vols., (Vol. 1-2 = Text,
Vol. 3 Plates & Plans, Vol. 4 Maps)
The Clarendon Press, Oxford, 1928~~

773. At Stein, A., Archaeological Reconnaissances,
Macmillan & Co., London,

726. Ps Stein, M.A., Ancient Khotan, 2 vols.,
The Clarendon Press, Oxford, 1907

923. Lg Steinhal, H., Geschichte Der Sprachwissenschaft Bei Den
Griechen Und Romern, (2 vols. bound together),
Ferd. Dummlers Verlagsbuchhandlung, Berlin, 1890-1891

924. Lg Steinthal, H., Die Mande-Neger-Sprachen,
Ferd. Dummlers, Berlin

925. Lg Steinthal, H., 1881 and Misteli, F., 1893, Abriss Der
Sprachwissenschaft, Ferd. Dummlers, Berlin

139. Bu Steinilber-Oberlin, E., etc., Les Sectes Bouddhiques Japonaises,
G. Crés et Cie, Paris

353. Ps Stephen, L., English Thought in the Eighteenth Century,
2 vols., Smith Elder & Co., London, 1876

643. Pt Stewart, B., Subjects Portrayed In Japanese Colour-
Prints,
Kegan Paul & Co., London, 1922

1006. Gr Stolz-Schmalz, Lateinische Grammatik,
C.H. Beck'sche Verlag, Munchen, 1928

995. Gr Stolz-Schmalz, Lateinische Grammatik II,
C.H. Beck'sche Verlagsbuchhandlung, Munchen, 1928

612. Pt Strange, E.F., Tools And Materials Illustrating The Japanese
Method Of Colour- Printing,
The Authority Of The Board Of Education, London, 1924

資料 11（貼付ノート・Transaction of the Asiatic Society of Japan）

1169. Po Strong, L.A., ed., Eighty Poems : An Anthology, Basil Blackwell, Oxford, 1924

219. Bo Me Stuart, Rev. G. A., Chinese Materia Medica, Presbyterian Mission Press, Shanghai, 1928

534. Lg The Study of the Japanese Language, British Association of Japan, 1935

486. Si Sung, J. Z. D., The Symbols of Yi King (or the Symbols of the Chinese Logic of Changes), The China Modern Education Co., Shanghai, 1934

487. Si Sung, Z. D., The Text of Yi King (Chinese original with English translation), The China Modern Education Co., Shanghai, 1935

1090. Hy Sugematsu, The Identity Of The Great Conqueror Genghis Khan, W.H. & L.Collingridge, London, 1879

828. Pc Sugiyama, M., ~~etc.~~ + Fujima K. An Outline History Of The Japanese Dance, Kokusai Bunka Shinkokai, Tokyo, 1937

361. Ms Summers, Rev. J., The Phoenix, 3 vols., "The Phoenix", London, 1870-1873

160. Bu Suzuki, D. T., Essays in Zen Buddhism, Luzac & Co., London, 2 vols., 1927 and 1933.

168. Bu Suzuki, D. T., Zen Buddhism and its Influence on Japanese Culture, The Eastern Buddhist Society, Kyoto, 1938

170. Bu Suzuki, D. T., The Lanka-Vatara Sutra, George Routledge & Sons Ltd., London, 1932

171. Bu Suzuki, D. T., Studies in the Lankavatara Sutra, George Routledge & Sons Ltd., London, 1930

1148. St Synge, J.M., Deirdre Of The Sorrows, George Allen & Unwin, Londom, 1924

629. Jy Synopsis Of The Ceremonies Of Ascension To The Throne Of H.M. The Emperor Of Japan,

1147. St Swift, J., Gulliver's Travels, Humphrey Milford Oxford University Press, London, 1925

1180. St Swinburne, A.C., Thomas Middleton, T.Fisher Unwin, London,

65. Es Mr Sophia University - Monumenta Nipponica, Vol V, semi-annual No. 1 (1942).

~~1007. Ty.~~ (D) 145 ~~Siebold, Fr., Nippon Archiv Zur Beschreibung von Japan, 5 vols., Bei Dem Verfassen, Leyden, 1852~~

6054 Schrenck, L. V., Die Völker des Amur-Landes, Gedruckt auf Verfügung der Kaiserlichen Academie der Wissenschaften

145. Jy Av(D) Siebold - Nippon, Archiv zur Beschreibung, Heft 1, 5, 11-12, 13-14, 17-20, Leiden, 1832, Total 5 vols.

81. So S. M. Shirokogoroff - Social organization of the Manchus (Royal Asiatic Society), Shanghai, 1924.

[illegible]0. Pt C. M. Salwey - The island dependencies of Japan, Eugène L. Morice, London, 1913.

131. Rs(D) Bruno Schindler & c.- Asia Major, Verlag der Asia Major, Lipsiae, 1924-7, 4 vols.

146. Jy Av(L) Siebold - Catalogus librorum et manuscriptorum Japonicorum, Lugduni-Batavorum, 1845.

112. Ps(F) Sakurazawa - Philosophie d'extrème orient, Libraire Philosophique, Paris, 1931.

107. Tr Sadler - Saka's diary of a pilgrim to Ise ( 伊勢大神參詣記 ), Meiji Japan Society, Tokyo, 1940.

31. Dc(H) G. Schlegel - Nederlandisch-Chineesch Woordenboek ( 荷華文語類參 ), J. E Brill, Leiden, 1886-1890.

10. Gr Sanson - Historical grammar of Japanese, The Clarendon Press, Oxford, 1928.

98. Ta Gy Stein - Innermost Asia, The Clarendon Press, Oxford, 1928, 4 vols.

139. Hy Gy(D) Leopold v. Schrenck - Die Völker des Amur Landes.

18. Ds 札幌教區宣教師團－獨和辭典，光明社

(✓) Seki & Katakura; English-Japanese Dictionary of Paper-Making Terms (Eiwa Seishi Jiten), 3rd edition.

(✓) Sastri, H. Krishna; South Indian Images of Gods & Goddesses; Madras Gov. Press; 1916

(✓) Sweet, H.; A primer of Spoken English, 1911

(✓) The Student's Practical Dictionary (Urdu-English), 1900

資料11（貼付ノート・Transaction of the Asiatic Society of Japan）

1321A (ca) Keleti Szemle (Revue Orientale) 9 bound vols. Vol 1, 2, 3, 13, 14, 15, 16, 17, 20 Kúnos Ignácz + etc., Otto Harrassowitz 1900 — 1927: + one part 9 vols. (1905)

Sindel, R. W., Bamboo for papermaking Marchant, Singer, London, 1909 ✓

✓ 7 Soulié, G. l'Histoire de la Chine, de l'antiquité jusqu'en, Payot. Paris, 1929

71. Es J. A. B. Scherer - Japan, whither ?

21. Gr Sloman - A Latin grammar.

118. Es Scherer - America, pageants & personalities.

91. En Po A. von Staël-Holsten - Sanskrit hymn translated with Chinese characters.

122. Hy(D) I. J. Schmidt - Geschichte der Ost-Mongolien.

1. Dc E. M. Satow - English-Japanese dictionary of the spoken language, Sanseido, 4th edition.

2. Dc E.M. Satow — English-Japanese Dictionary of the spoken language, Sanseido, 4th edition.

853. Bo Tada, S., Romazigaki Manyosyu,
Maruzen Co., Tokyo, 1934

973. Dp Taft, H.W., Japan And America : A Journey And A Political
Survey,
Macmillân Co., New York, 1932

709. Rn Tagawa, D., Church and State in Modern Japan,
Kyo Bun Kwan, Tokyo, 1939

682. Rn Takahashi, M., Catalogue Of Special Books On Christian
Missions,
Tenri Central Library, Nara, Japan, 1932

1294. Ml (D) Takaki, T., Die Hygieneschen Verhältnisse der Insel Formosa,
Druck Von C.C. Meinhold & Sohne, Dresden, 1911

914. Lg Takaki, Y., Japanese Studies In The Universities And
Colleges Of The United States : Survey for 1934 ,
Institute Of Pacific Relations, Honolulu, 1935

229. Zo Takatsuka, Prince N., Japanese Birds, Board of Tourist Industry,
Tokyo, 1941

230. Bo Takeda, H., Alpine Flowers of Japan, Sanseido, Tokyo, 1938

272. Gu Takekoshi, Y., Japanese Rule in Formosa, Longmans, Green &
Co., London, 1907

786. By Takekoshi, Y., Prince Saionji,
Ritsumeikan University, Kyoto, 1933

1268. Rn Takakusu, J., A Pali Chrestomathy,
Kinkodo & Co., Tokyo, 1900

138. Ea Takakusu, J. et Watanabe, K., Hobogirin (Dictionnaire Encyclopédique du Bouddhisme), 2 vols. and supplement, Maison-Franco-Japonaise, Tokyo, 1929-1931

1395. Dc Takenobu, Y., The Japan Year Book, 1926,
The Japan Year Book Office, Tokyo, 1926

173. At Taki, S., Japanese Fine Art, Fuzambo for the National Committee on the Intellectual Cooperation of the League of Nations Association of Japan, Tokyo, 1931

~~1820. Cu 7/ Tamura, N., The Japanese Bride, Harper & Brothers Publishers, New York, 1893~~

115. Ga Tamura, T., Art of the Landscape Garden in Japan, K.B.S., Tokyo, 1935

557. Lg Tanakadate, A., La Phonetique Japonaise, published by the author, Tokyo, 1936
(F)

1273. Dc Taranzano, C., Vocabulaire Des Science Mathematiques,
(F) Physiquee Et Naturelles, 2 vols.,
Imprimerie De La Mission Catholique, Sien- Hsien, 1936

132. Taranzano, R. P. C., Ouvrages du P. H. Bernard sur l'Extrême-Orient, Hautes Études, Tientsin, 1939

1279. Dc Taranzano, C., Supplément Au Vocarulaire Français-Chinois
(F) Des Sciences, 2
Imprimerie De La Mission Catholique, Sien-Hsien, 1920

1287. Ta Tomita, K., etc., Japanese Treasure Tales, Yamanaka & Co., Osaka

1098. Lg Tomita, G., Stranger's Handbook Of The Japanese Language, Kelly & Walsh, Yokohama, 1893

1117. Hy Toynbee, R.J., A Study Of History, Oxford University Press, London, 1939

1077. Nv Toyoda, M., The Composition Class, The Herald Of Asia, Tokyo, 1938

782. Li Toyoda, M., Shakespeare In Japan : An Historical Survey, Iwanami Shoten, Tokyo, 1940

282. Jr The Transactions of the Asiatic Society of Japan, 19 vols. (Second Series - I-IV, VI-XIX, and Vol. I - Reprints, Dec. 1925), Kyo Bun Kwan, Tokyo supplement to vol I - Dec 1926 Vol XVIII - Dec 1939

744. Es Transactions Of The Korea Branch Of The Royal Asiatic Society, 朝鮮, Vol. 23-30, Y.M.C.A. Press, Seoul, Korea, 1934 - 1940

745. Es Transactions Of The Korea Branch Of The R.A.S., Vol.1 - 23., Hon. Librarian, Seoul, Korea, 1900-1934

1328. Rp Transactions of the Korea Branch of the Royal Asiatic Society 朝鮮, 4 vols., (Vols. 10 & 11, two Copies) Christian Literature Society Of Korea, 1919-1920

1323. Rp Transactions Of The Asiatic Society Of Japan, 6 vols., Kelly & Walsh, Yokohama, 1906- 1912

1187. Jr Transactions Of The Asiatic Society Of Japan, Second Series
Supplement To Vol.1, December, 1924

1188. Jr Transactions Of The Asiatic Society Of Japan, (binded),
Vol. No. 12, 18, 19, 31, 34, 35, 45, 46, 47, 48, 49, 50,
1883-1922,
Kelly & Walsh, Yokohama

1189. Jr Transactions Of The Asiatic Society Of Japan, (unbinded),
Vol. No. 2, 3, 7, 14, 20, 27, 29, 30, 32, 16, 33, 35, 38,
1882-1911,
Kelly & Walsh, Yokohama

1190. Jr Transactions Of The Asiatic Society Of Japan, (unbinded),
Vol. 50,
Keio-gijiku, Tokyo, 1922

1191. Jr Transactions Of The Asiatic Society Of Japan, Vols., 1-30
( except Vols. 17, 18), 28 vols.,
Kelly & Co., Yokohama, 1895-1901

1192. Jr Transactions Of The Asiatic Society Of Japan, Vol. 8 part 1-
2 to Vol. 14 part 1-2, Vol.11,
Mieklijohn & Co., Yokohama,

1372. Jr Transactions Of The Asiatic Society Of Japan, (Extracted
from the), Vol. 17, part 1,
(Parker, E.H.)

1373. Jr Transactions Of The Asiatic Society Of Japan, (Extracted
from the), Vol. 18, part 1,
(Batchelor, J.)

Transactions of the Asiatic Society of Japan - vol 18 1939
(Second Series)

1359. Rp — Transactions Of The Asiatic Society Of Japan, Vol. 24, (Ainu Words As Illustrative Of Customs And Matters Pathological, Psychological And Religious)

1195. Jr — Transactions Of The Asiatic Society Of Japan, Vol. No. 3, 9, 10, 18, 19(2 copies), 30, 32, 33, 34, 36, 37(2 copies), 38(2 copies), 41, 49, 23 parts, Kelly & Walsh, Yokohama, 1875-1922

442. Rs — Transactions of the Asiatic Society of Japan (Supplement of Vol. XXXII - The Japanese Chronology), Kelly & Walsh, Tokyo, 1910

1241. Cal, At (D) — Trautz, F.M., Eine Buddhistisch Kunsthandschrift der Japanischen Fujiwara-Zeit, Die Reichsdruckerei, Berlin, 1926

11. At Ar — Treasures of the 7th & 8th Centuries Excavated in Japan (天平地宝), The Imperial Household Museum, Tokyo, 1937

109. Dp — Treat, P. J., Diplomatic Relations Between the United States and Japan 1853-1895, 2 vols., Stanford University Press, Stanford, 1932

980. Lg — Trofimov, M.V., The Pronunciation Of Russian, The University Press, Cambridge, 1923

1156. St — Trollope, A., Barchester Tower, J.M.Dent & Sons, London, 1938

422. Si Hy — Tschepe, A., Histoire du Royaume de T's In, Mission Catholique, Changhai, 1923

資料 11（貼付ノート・Transaction of the Asiatic Society of Japan）

799. Dm (K) Tsiang Un-Kai, K'ouen K'iu, 崑曲, Le Théatre Chinois Ancien,
Librairie Ernest Leroux, Paris, 1932

~~43. At 93 Tsuda, N., Handbook of Japanese Art, Sanseido, Tokyo, 19[illegible]~~

22. Ga Tsuda, N., Gardens in Japan, 21 plates, K. B.S., Tokyo, 1935

44. Pa Tsuda, N., Ideals of Japanese Painting, Sanseido, Tokyo, 1940

~~1384. Li 63 Tsuchida, K., Contemporary Thought Of Japan And China, Williams And Norgate, London, 1929~~

1016. By Tsudzuki, K., An Episode From The Life Of Count Inouye, by the Author, Tokyo, 1912

1044. Cl Tsurumi, Y., Present day Japan,
Columbia University Press, New York, 1926

1464. Rn Tucci, G., The Nyāyamukha Of Dignāga, The Oldest Buddhist Text On Logic,
In Kommission bei O Harrassowitz, Heidelberg, 1930

597. (R) Ms Tureckiya Legendy o Svyatoĭ Sofŭ, Smirnov, Petersburg, 1898

292. Cu Tun Li-Ch'en and Bodde, D., Annual Customs and Festivals in Peking, Henri Vetch, Peking, 1936

500. Ps T'ang-Su des Ceu-Tsi (Ein Beitrag zur Kenntnis der Chinesischen Philosophie), Verlag Asia Major, Leipzig, 1932

156. (R) Two volumes in the Russian Language

1316. Rp T'ien Hsia, 17 vols.
Published under the auspices of the Sun Yat-sen Institute fo
for the Advancement of Culture and Education, Kelly &
Walsh, Shanghai, 1938-1940

1317. Rp T'ien Hsia, 天下,
Reprint from August, 1936

184. Sct The Tibetan, Mongolian & Manchurian Buddhist scriptures, 6 vols.

85. At Pa Katsuki Takahashi - Wall paintings of Hôryuji temple.

9. Dc Takenobu - New Japanese-English dictionary (新和英大辭典), Kenkyusha.

99. Dc Lg Meninski - Thesaurus Ling. Orientalium, Turcicae, Arabicae, Persicae, 4 vols.

160. Nv A. Trollope - Barcherter Towers, London, 1938.

103. Pri The Times - Printing in 20th Century, London, 1929.

74. Cu Ta Naomi Tamura - The Japanese bride, Harper & Brothers, N.Y., 1893.

190. Jr Transaction of the Asiatic Society of Japan, Tokyo, odd Volumes (unbound), 1872-1912, 57 vols (3 packages).

✓ 105. Tr Gy Terry's - Guide to the Japanese Empire including Japan, Korea & Formose, Houghton Mifflin, Boston, 1933.

✓ 93. At Noritake Tsuda - Hand-book of Japanese art, Sanseido, Tokyo, 1938.

✓ 63. Li Kyoson Tsuchida - Contemporary thought of Japan and China, Williams & Norgate, London, 1929.

✓ 185. Pa The thousand Buddhas (Paintings recoversd by A. Stoin & with essey by L. Binyon) - Ancient paintings from the cave-temples of Tun-Huang (敦煌), Bernard Quaritch, London, 1921. (Contained in a box). Collection by the Orchou-Expedition.

(✓) Tiếng anh cho người Việt-Nam, Imprimerie Trung-Bac Tân-Van, Hanoi, 1941

854. Ca Uenoda, S., Calender Of Annual Events In Tokyo, Kyo Bun Kwan, Tokyo, 1931

805. Pc Umemoto, R., Introduction to The Classic Dance of Japan, Sanseido Co., Tokyo, 1935

655. Rn Underwood, A.C., Shintoism, The Epworth Press, London, 1934

751. Lg Underwood, H.G., An Introduction To The Korean Spoken Language, Kelly & Walsh, Yokohama, 1890

260. By Ushikubo, D. J. R., Life of Kôyetsu, published by the Author,

96. Bu Utsuki, N., The Shin Sect (A School of Mahayana Buddhism), Bureau of Buddhist Books, Kyoto, 1937

401. Jy Uyehara, Y., Songs for Children Sung in Japan, Hokuseido Press, Tokyo, 1940

40A Ukiyoe Naishi 2 vols, Shibui, K., Taihokaku, Tokyo 1933

126. Tr(P) Vida de João de Barros, Indice geral das quatro Decada da Sua Asia, Lisboa, 1778.

127. Tr(P) -,,- Decada un decima da Asia, Lisboa, 1778.

128. Tr(P) -,,- Indice geral des Decados de Couto, Lisboa, 1778.

Vincent, Benjamin: Haydn's Dictionary of Dates relating to all ages & Nations; Edward Moxon & Co., London, 1866

1163. Po A. E. Vale And Other Poems,
Macmillan & Co., London, 1931

1181. St Vechten, V., Nigger Heaven,
Alfred A. Knopf, London, 1928

893. Do (E) Villamor, I., La Antique Escritura Filipina,
Manila, Islus Filipinas, 1922

1094. Ta Vines, S., Yofuku Or Japan In Trousers,
Wishart & Co., London, 1931

137. Fl Visser, M. W. de, The Dragon in China and Japan, Johannes
Müller, Amsterdam, 1913

1002 von Möllendorff, P. G., A Manchu Grammar with
Analysed Text, Printed at the American Presbyterian
Mission Press, Shanghai, 1892.

519. Li Lt Voruz, E., Style Épistolaire Japonais, Tokyo, 5th Year of Taisho 1916

711. Pn (P) Voss, G.S., etc., Kirishito- ki und Sayo-Yoroku,
Sophia University, Tokyo, 1940

712. Si, Jy (P) Vinaza, Escritos De Los Portugueses Y Castellanos
referentes a las lenguas de China Y El Japón ( Congre
so Internacional De Orientalistas),
Lisboa, 1892

146. Voyages de Thunberg, 4 vols., Paris, 1796

147. Rp Vries, M. G., Reize Naar Japan in 1643, Frederick Muller, Amsterdam, 1858

340. Tr Voyages de Francois Bérnier, 2 vols., Paul Marret, Amsterdam, 1709

27. Dc Sc A vocabulary of chemical terms (化學語彙).

23. Dc Vigario Apostologio Japoniae- Lexicon Latino-Iaponicum.

28. Hy Lg Vendryes - A linguistic introduction to history.

200. Rs Van Gulik (R. H.) - Hayagriva - The mantrayānic aspect of horse - Cult in China nad Japan. (With 14 illustrations), E.J. Brill, Leiden, 1935.

180. Dc Bo Gerth Van Wijk - Dictionary of plant-names, Martinno Nijhoff, The Hague, 1911.

187. Dc(R) В.В. Вельяминовъ-Зерновъ-Словарь Джагатайско-Турецкій(チャガタイ語-トルコ語辞典)
V.V. Velyaminov-Zernov - Slovar Dzagataisko-Turetskij, St. Petersburg, 1868.

106. Hy Wada, T., American Foreign Policy Towards Japan during the 19th Century, The Toyo Bunko, Tokyo, 1928

950. Ta Waddll, H., The Wandering Scholars, Constable & Co., London, 1926

161. Bu Waddell, L. A., The Buddhism of Tibet (Lamaism), W. Heffer & Sons Ltd., Cambridge, 1934

183. Sc Waddington, C. H., The Scientific Attitude, The Penguin Books, Harmondsworth, 1941.

576. Po Wakameda, T., Early Japanese Poets (Complete translation of the Kokinshu), The Yuhodo, Tokyo, 4th Yr. of Showa

937. Pa Waley, A., An Introduction To The Study Of Chinese Painting, Ernest Benn, London, 1923

594. Po Waley, A., Japanese Poetry (The "Uta"), The Clarendon Press, Oxford, 1919

1050. Tr Waley, A., Ch'ang-Ch'un, The Travels Of An Alchemist, George Routledge & Sons, London, 1931

494. Te Si Waley, A., The Way and Its Power (A Study of the Tao Tê Ching and its Place in Chinese Thought), Houghton Mifflin Company, Boston, 1935

546. Li Na Waley, A., The Pillow Book of Sei Shonagon, George Allen Unwin Ltd., London, 1929

1465. Rn (D) Walleser, M., Jahrbuch des Instituts für Buddhismus-Kunde, vol.1., U
Universitats-Buchhaudlung, Heidelberg, 1930

1194. Jr Walter, N., etc., The Asiatic Society Of Japan : Index to Chamberlain's Kojiki, (Vol. X, Supplement),
Tokyo, 1906

419. (F) Ps Wang Tch'ang Tche, Le Philosophie Morale de Wang Yang-Ming, Librairie de Tou-sè-Wé, Changhai, 1936

913. Tr Ward, F.K., The Land Of The Blue Poppy : Travels Of A Naturalist In Eastern Tibet,
University Press, Cambridge, 1913

774. Pa Warner, L., Buddhist Wall-Paintings,
Harvard University Press, Cambridge, Massachusetts, 1938

113. Sp Warner, L., The Craft of Japanese Sculpture, McFarlane, Warde, McFarlane, New York, 1936

684. Pc Watanabe, Y., Bunraku : Japanese Puppet Play,
Japan Photo Service, Tokyo, 1939

579. Li Watanabe, T., The Treasury of Japanese Literature, Juppo Kaku, Tokyo, 8th Year of Showa

675. Pc Watey, A., The No Plays Of Japan,
George Allen & Unwin, London, 1921

資料11（貼付ノート・Transaction of the Asiatic Society of Japan）

179. Cm Watson, E., The Principal Articles of Chinese Commerce (The Maritime Customs - China), Statistical Department of the Inspectorate General of Customs, Shanghai, 1930

1060. Rn Watters, I., The Eighteen Lohan Of Chinese Buddhist Temples, Kelly & Walsh, Shanghai, 1925

162. Tr Watters, T., etc., On Yuan Chwang's Travels in India 629-645 A.D., 2 vols., Royal Asiatic Society, London, 1904-1905.

434. Wedembybr, A., Japanische Frühgeschichte, Deutsche Gesellschaft fur Natur-u. Völkerkunde Ostasiens, Tokyo, 1930

1152. Lg Weekley, E., Saxo Grammaticus, Kegan Paul, Trench, Trubner & Co., London, 1930

1166. Te Wells, H.G., The Mind In The Making, Jonathan Cape, London, 1928

7. 267. Rs Werner, E. T. C., Chinese Weapons, The Royal Asiatic Society, Shanghai, 1932

52. Dc Werner, E. T. C., A Dictionary of Chinese Mythology, Kelly & Walsh Ltd., Shanghai, 1932

445. Cl Werner, E. C. T., A History of Chinese Civilization, The Shanghai Times, Shanghai, 1940

427. Ps Werner, E. T. C., The Chinese Idea of the Second Self, The Shanghai Times, Shanghai, 1932

~~1230. At 83 Wertheimber, L., A Muramasa Blade, Ticknor And Company, Boston, 1887~~

1396. Dc 4.5 West, M., The New Method English Dictionary,
Longmans, Green & Co., London, 1936

351. Mo Westermarck, E., The Origin and Development of the Moral Ideas, 2 vols., Macmillan & Co., London, 1924 and 1926

1120. Pa Wheelwright, W.B., Printing Papers,
The University of Chicago Press, 1936

1129. St Wherry, E., The Wanderer On A Thousand Hills,
Penguin Books, London, 1940

26. Pa White, W. C., Tomb Tile Pictures of Ancient China, The University of Toronto Press, Toronto, 1939

80. Tr White, W. C., Tombs of Old Lo-Yang, Kelly & Walsh, Ltd., Shanghai, 1934

404. Li Whitehouse, W., Ochikubo Monogatari, or the Tale of the Lady Ochikubo, J. L. Thompson & Co., Kobe, 1934

1162. St Whither Civilization,
Kawase & Sons, Kobe, 1934

172. Gr Whitney, W. D., A Sanskrit Grammar, Breitkopf & Härtel, Leipzig, 1924

851. Dr Whitney, W.N., A Concise Dictionary Of The Principal Roads,
Maruya & Co., Tokyo, 1889

1028. Cu Whymant, N., The Chinse-Japanese Puzzle,
Victor Gollancz, London, 1932

323. Pri Wibong, F. B., Printing Ink, Harper Bros., New York, 1926

375. Ps Wieger, L., Textes Philosophiques (Confusiisme Taoisme Buddhisme), Hien-Lieu, 1930

376. Hy Si Wieger, L. La Chine (A Travers les Ages), Hien-Lieu, 1924

377. Lg Wieger, L., Charactères Chinois, Hien-Lieu, 1932

374. Hy Wieger, L., Textes Historiques (Histoire Politique de la Chine depuis l'origine jusqu'en 1929), 2 vols., Hien-Lieu, 1929

134. Dp Wildes, H. E., Aliens in the East (A New History of Japan's Foreign Intercourse), University of Pennsylvania, Philadelphia, 1937

77. Cu Wilhelm, R., The Secret of the Golden Flower (A Chinese Book of Life – 太乙金華宗旨 ), Kegan Paul, Trench, Trubner & Co., London, 1931

447. Si Cu Wilkinson, H. P., The Family in Classical China, Kelly & Walsh, Shanghai, 1926

508. Si Williams, S. W., The Middle Kingdom, Charles Scribner's Sons, New York, 1883

25. At Williams, C. A. S., Outlines of Chinese Symbolism and Art Motives ( 中国表記図譜 ), Kelly & Walsh Ltd., Shanghai, 1932

83. Tr Williamson, J. A., The Voyages of the Cabots and the Discovery of North America under Henry VII and Henry VIII, The Argonaut Press, London, 1929

402. Na Willoughby-Meade, G., Chinese Ghouls and Goblins, Constable & Co., London, 1928

1456. Lg Winstedt, R.O., The Malay School Series, No.2, Fraser & Neave,

~~330. H. Witsen, N., Noord en Oost Tartarye, 2 vols., M. Schalekamp,~~ Amsterdam, 1785

1139. St Wodehouse, P.G., Sam The Sudden, Methuen & Co., London, 1939

1134. St Wodehouse, P.G., Blandings Castle, Bernhard Tauchnitz, Leipzig, 1936

1135. St Wodehouse, P.G., Lord Emsworth And Others, Bernhard Tauchnitz, Leipzig, 1938

1133. St Wodehouse, P.G., Summer Lightning, Bernhard Tauchnitz, Leipzig, 1931

167. Lg Wolfenden, S. N., Tibeto-Burman Linguistic Morphology, The Royal Asiatic Society, London, 1929.

203. Me Wong, K. C. and Lieu-Teh, W., History of Chinese Medicine, Tientsin Press Ltd., Tientsin

13. Pi Woodward, A. M. T., The Postage Stamps of Japan and Dependencies (大日本及全属国ノ郵便切手 ), 2 vols., Harris Publications Ltd., London, 1928

1080. Es Working the Miracle of The Twentieth Century, (By a Japanese), Rimpo Kyokai, Tokyo, 1938

389. Dp Wright, S. T., China's Struggle for Tariff Autonomy 1843-1938, Kelly & Walsh, Shanghai, 1938

295. Pri Wroth, L. C., A History of the Printed Book, The Limited Editions Club, New York, 1938

931. Lg (D) Wundt, W., Völkerpsychologie eine Untersuchung der Entwicklungsgesetze von Sprache, Mythus und Sitte, 2 vols Alfred Kroner Verlag, Stuttgart, 1921-1922

962. Lg Wyld, H.C., A Short History Of English, John Murray, London, 1927

944. Lg Wyld, H.C., A History Of Modern Colloquial English, T. Fisher Unwin Ltd., London, 1919

250. Li At Wylie, A., Notes on Chinese Literature (On the Progressive Advancement of the Art), The French Bookstore, Peking, 1939

417. Si Rs Wylie, A., Chinese Researches, Shanghai, 1897; reprinted and published by Buntenkaku, Peiping, 1936

34. De H. C. Wyld - The universal English dictionary.

35. De H. C. Wyld - The Universal English dictionary.

150. Nv P. G. Wodehouse - A gentleman of leisure.

163. Nv Wodehouse - Mr. Mulliner speaking, N. Y., 1930.

153. Nv Wodehouse - Carry on, Jeeves, New York, 1927.

115. Nv P. G. Wodehouse - A century of Humour.

159. Li H. F. Wood - A collection of British authors, "The passenger from Scotland Yard", Leipzig, 1888.

✓ The War in the Far East, the Military Correspondent of the Times, John Murray, London, 1905.

✓ 83. Ed Ad Louis Wertheimber - Muramasa blade, a story of feudalism in old Japan, Ticker & co., Boston, 1887.

✓ 4. Lg Dc Michael West - New method of English dictionary, Longmans, Green & Co., London, 1936. ~~(2 copies another in 1960)~~

✓ 5. Lg Dc Michale West - New Method of English dictionary, Longmans, Green & Co., London, 1940.

140. Gy(H) Nicholaas Witsen - Noord en oost Tartaryen, Gewesten, Azien en Europa, Amsterdam, 1785, 2 vols.

Wright: Trade & Tariffs of Certain Pacific Countries

Wilkinson, R. J.; A Malay-English Dict; Kelly & Walsh Ltd., Singapore; 1901.

資料11（貼付ノート・Transaction of the Asiatic Society of Japan）

823. Cu Yamada, W., The Social Status Of Japanese Women,
Kokusai Bunka Shinkokai, Tokyo, 1935

1015. Hy Yamada, M., Ghenkō : The Mongal Invasion Of Japan,
Smith Elder & Co., London, 1916

451. Pi Yamamoto, Y., Japanese Postage Stamps, Board of Tourist
Industry, Tokyo, 1940

1246. Fl Yanagi, S., Folk-Crafts In Japan,
K.B.S., Tokyo, 1936

558. Cal Yang Yu-Hsun, La Calligraphie Chinoise depuis les Han,
Librairie Orientaliste Paul Geuthner, Paris, 1937

281. So Jr The Yenching Journal of Social Studies, 2 vols., Yenching
University, Peking, 1938 and 1939

1358. Fl Yoe, Shway, The Burman, His Life And Nations,
Macmillan & Co., London, 1910

411. La Young, C. W., Japanese Jurisdiction in the South Manchurian
Railway Areas, John Hopkins Press, Baltimore, 1931

412. La Young, C. W., The International Legal Status of the
Kwantung Leased Territory, John Hopkins Press, Baltimore,
1931

413. Pt Young, C. W., Japan's Special Position in Manchuria (Its
Assertion, Legal Interpretation and Present Meaning),
John Hopkins Press, Baltimore, 1931

474. Jy Young, M., Japan under Taisho Tenno 1912-1926, George Allen & Unwin, London, 1928

837. Rn, Cl The Young East : Buddhism and Japanese Culture, The International Buddhist Society, Tokyo, 1938

838. Rn, Cl The Young East : Autumn, The International Buddhist Society, Tokyo, 1935

839. Rn, Cl The Young East : Autumn, The International Buddhist Society, Tokyo, 1936

840. Rn, Cl The Young East : Winter, The International Buddhist Society, Tokyo, 1936

1104. Nv **Young Forever And Five Other Novelettes by Contemporary Japanese Authors, Translated into English by Members of The Japan Writers Society, The Hokuseido Press, Tokyo, 1941**

648. Pt Yoshida, H., Japanese Wood- Block Printing, The Sanseido Co., Tokyo,1939

524. Lg **Yoshitake, S., The Phonetic System of Ancient Japanese, The Royal Asiatic Society, London, 1934**

213. Sc Yoshino, Y., The Japanese Abacus, Kyobunkwan, Tokyo, 1937

1242. Es Yoshitake, S., Ex Actorum Orientalium Volumire 13 Excerptum, The Royal Asiatic Society, London, 1934

資料 11（貼付ノート・Transaction of the Asiatic Society of Japan）

850. Lg Yuasa, M., How To Write And Read Japanese Correctly, Okazakiya Shoten, Tokyo, 1929

498. Ps Yu-lan Fung, Chuang Tzŭ (Exposition of the Philosophy of Kuo Hsiang), The Commercial Press, Shanghai, 1933

437. Tr Yule, Sir H., Travels of Marco Polo, 2 vols, John Murray, London

297. Bb Yü, P. Y. and Gillis, I. V., Title Index to the Ssŭ K'u Ch'üan Shu, Peiping, 1934

[illegible] Es(F) Kikou Yamada - Japan, dernière heure.

67. Cu Shway Yoe - The Burman, his life & nations, Macmillan, London, 1910.

168. Es Hy Sir Henry Yule - Cathay and the way thither, being a collection of medieval notice of China, London, 1915, 5 vols.

(Vol. I in 2 copies)

資料 11（貼付ノート・Transaction of the Asiatic Society of Japan）

363. Dc Zach, E., Lexicographische Beiträge, ~~4 vols.~~, Peking, 1902-1906

607. Dc Zakharoff, I., Complete Manchu - Russian Dictionary, Henri Vetch, The French Bookstore, Peking, 1939

423. Si Cu Zi, E., Pratique des Examens Militaires en Chine, Imprimerie de la Mission Catholique, Changhai, 1896

資料 11（貼付ノート・Transaction of the Asiatic Society of Japan）

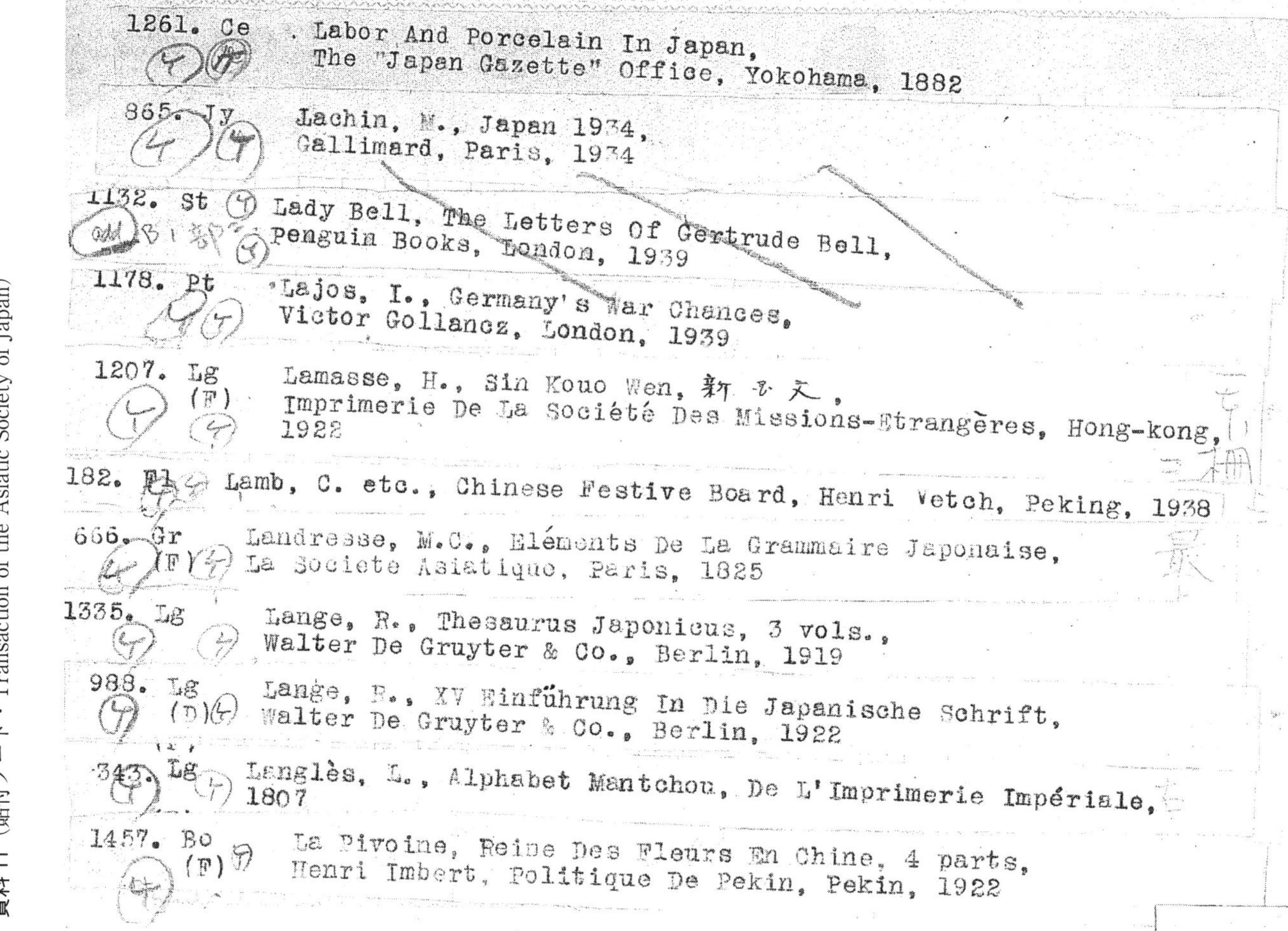

1261. Ce . Labor And Porcelain In Japan,
The "Japan Gazette" Office, Yokohama, 1882

865. Jy Jachin, M., Japan 1934,
Gallimard, Paris, 1934

1132. St Lady Bell, The Letters Of Gertrude Bell,
Penguin Books, London, 1939

1178. Pt Lajos, I., Germany's War Chances,
Victor Gollancz, London, 1939

1207. Lg (F) Lamasse, H., Sin Kouo Wen, 新 [illegible] 文,
Imprimerie De La Société Des Missions-Etrangères, Hong-kong,
1922

182. Fl Lamb, C. etc., Chinese Festive Board, Henri Vetch, Peking, 1938

666. Gr (F) Landresse, M.C., Eléments De La Grammaire Japonaise,
La Societe Asiatique, Paris, 1825

1335. Lg Lange, R., Thesaurus Japonicus, 3 vols.,
Walter De Gruyter & Co., Berlin, 1919

988. Lg (D) Lange, R., XV Einführung In Die Japanische Schrift,
Walter De Gruyter & Co., Berlin, 1922

343. Lg Langlès, L., Alphabet Mantchou, De L'Imprimerie Impériale,
1807

1457. Bo (F) La Pivoine, Reine Des Fleurs En Chine, 4 parts,
Henri Imbert, Politique De Pekin, Pekin, 1922

1455. Ps　Laplace, P. S., Essai Philosophique Sur Les Probabilités, 2 vols., Gauthier-Villars Et C^ie, Editeure, Paris, 1921

696. Dc (I)　Laponiae, V. A., Lexicon Latino- Japonicum, Typis & C. De Propaganda Fide, Romae, 1870

1032. Cu (F)　La Poupée Japonaise, Kokusai Bunka Shinkokai, Tokyo,

1351. Ta (F)　Larguier, L., L'Après-Midi Chez L'Antiquaire, L'Edition, Paris, 1922

184. Es　Laskins, C. H., Renaissance of the Twelfth Century, Harvard University Press, Cambridge, 1928

185. Sc　Laskins, C. H., Mediaeval Science, Harvard University Press, Cambridge, 1927

492. Fl　Lattimore, O., The Mongols of Manchuria, George Allen & Unwin, London

286. Pri　Laufer, B., Paper Printing in Ancient China, The Caxton Club, Chicago, 1931

2. Pa (V)　Laufer, B., T'ang, Sung and Yüan Paintings Belonging to Various Chinese Collectors, G. Van Oest & Co., Paris, etc., 1924

47. Sp　Laufer, B., Chinese Grave-Sculptures of the Han Period, E. L. Morice, London, 1911

687. Jd　Laures, T., An Ancient Document on the Early Intercomrse between Japan and the Philippine Islands, Cultura Social, Manila, 1941

204. Nh Hy　Laufer, B., Sino-Iranica (Chinese Contributions to the History of Civilization in Ancient Iran), Field Museum of Natural History, Chicago, 1919

1280. Rn　Laures, J., Kirishitan Bunko : A Manual of Books and Documents on the Early Christian Mission in Japan, Sophia University, Tokyo, 1940

718. La (F)　Leang K'i-Tch'ao, La Conception De La Loi Et Les Théories Des Légestes A La Veille Des Ts'In, China Booksellers, Pekin, 1926

1305. Jy　Leavenworth, C.S., The Loochoo Islands, "North-China Herald", Shanghai, 1905

1467. Rn (R)　Ŀébi, S., Sphutārthā Abhidharmarkā-Çavyakhya The Work Of Yacomitra First Koçasthāna, In Russia, 1918

775. At, Cl (D)　Le Coq, Bilderatlas Zur Kunst und Kullurgeschichte Mittelasien, Dietrich Reimer, Berlin, 1925

1021. Ca　Lee, F.H., Tokyo Calendar, Hokuseido Press, Tokyo, 1934

418. Ps　Le Gall, S., Le Philosophe Tchou Hi, sa Doctrine, son Influence, Mission Catholique, Changhai, 1923

1322. Li Legge, J., The Chinese Classics, vols. 1-8,
Wen Tien Ko, Peking, 1939
1 論語大学中庸, 2 孟子, 3 尚書上, 4 尚書下,
5 詩経上, 6 詩経下, 7 春秋左傳上, 8 春秋左傳下,

~~1393. Te (7) Legge, J., The Four Books,
The Chinese Books Company, Shanghai, 1930~~

488. Po Legge, J., The Book of Poetry (Chinese Text with English translation), The Chinese Book Co., Shanghai

1035. Te Legge, J., etc., English-Japanese Confucian Analects,
Fumikodo Shoten, Tokyo, 1932

362. Si/(?) Legge, J., The Chinese Classics, 4 vols:
Vol. I: Confucian Analects, etc., The Clarendon Press, Oxford, 1893
" II: The Work of Mencius, The Clarendon Press, London, 1895
" III: The Shoo King or the Book of Historical Documents, Trubner & Co., London, 1865
" IV: The She King or the Book of Poetry, Henry Frowde, London

B.C. 12 最下位

989. Lg (D) Lehrbücher Des Seminars Für Orientalische Sprachen zu Berlin,
Walter De Gruyter & Co., Berlin, 1922

841. Cu (F) Les Caracteres Ou Les Moeurs De Ce Siecle,
Rene Hilsum, Editeur A Paris, 1896

~~187. Lt/167 Letters from Basil Hall Chamberlain to Lafcadio Hearn, Compiled by Kazuo Koizumi, Hokuseido Press, Tokyo, 1936~~

資料 11（貼付ノート・Transaction of the Asiatic Society of Japan）

1442. De Levy, C., Dictionnaire Coréen-Français, Les Missionnaires de Corée,
Imprimeur+Libraire, Yokohama, 1880

1407. Ar Leyden, E.J., Annual Bibliography Of Indian Archaeology For The Year 1926 Kern Institute,
Brill, Leyden, 1928

441. Jr Hy Lin Yutang, A History of the Press and Public Opinion in China, Kelly & Walsh, Shanghai, 1937

560. Lg Liggins, Rev. J., Familiar Phrases in English and Romanized Japanese, London Mission Press, Shanghai, 1860

225. Bo Linnaei Genera Plantarum Holmiae, 1754; Reprinted by the Shokubutsu Bunken Kankokai, Tokyo, 1939

1314. Rp The Library Of Congress, 18 vols.,
Government Printing Office, Washington, 1928-1939

1408. Me List Of Chinese Medicines,
Shanghai, 1889

1312. Lg Lockhart, L.W., Word Economy,
Kegan Paul, London, 1931

660. Dm Lombard, F.A., An Outline History Of The Japanese Drama,
George Allen & Unwin, London, 1928

~~798. Ed Lombard, F.A., Pre-[Meiji] [Education] In Japan,
Kyo Bun Kwan, Tokyo, 1914~~

543. By Lorenzen, A., Hitomaro, L. Friederichsen & Co., Hamburg, 1927

24. Do Lowell, P., Chosön : The Land Of The Morning Calm, Ticknor And Company, Boston, 1886

1025. Gy Lowell, P., Noto : An Unexplored Corner Of Japan, Houghton Mifflin & Co., Boston

1049. Ps Lowell, P., The Soul Of The Far East, The Macmillan Co., New York, 1920

836. By Ludovici, A.M., Nietzsche His Life and Works, Dodge Publishing Co., New York,

1415. Ta Yule & Cordier, Cathay And The Way Thither, 4 vols., 文殿閣書莊, Peking, 1938-1939 ?

1151. St Lyall, A., It Isn't Done, Kegan Paul, Trench, Trubner &cCo., London, 1930

700. Po Lloyd, A., Imperial Songs, The Kinkodo Publishing Co., Tokyo, 1905

Los Franciscanos in Japan

173. Et Te James Legge - The Four Books ( 英華四書 ), The Chinese Books Co., Shanghai, 1930.

77. Ed Lombard - Pre-Meiji education in Japan, Kyobunkan, Tokio, Tokyo, 1914.

101. Bn Pl(F) - La Societé Académique Indo-Chinoise - Bulletin, Au siège de la Societé, Paris, 1878-1890, 6 vols.

39. Dc Ram Narain Lal - The student's practical dictionary of Hindustani-Urdu-English (Persia), 1940

102. Mr(F) L'Académie des Sciences de l'Urss, 1928-30 (classe des humanités), 2 vols.

206. Hy(Siamese) The list of Chau Phaya in Ratana Kosintra, Bamrung Nukulkit, 2461 (Tai Era), 1918, A.D.

59. Lg Rudolf Lange - A text book of colloquial Japanese, revised English edition by C. Noss, Kyobunkan.

12. Dc(F) Jam Lemaréchal - Dictionnaire Japonais-Français.

22. Dc Lewis - A Latin dictionary for schools.

42. Lg Linguistic Society of America, vol IV, 1928. vols 4 [illegible] 1-6, 1-3 5 6 are [illegible]

6. Lg Lyell - Slang, phrase and idiom in English.

Henry Lester Institute of Medical Research, Annual Reports; 6 vols: 1934, 1935, 1936, 1937-38, 1939, 1940.

~~Henry Lester Institute of Medical Research~~

Liste des Publications et Tables du Bulletin (1901-1915) (Ecole Française d'Extrême-Orient); Imprimerie d'Extrême-Orient, Hanoi, 1917.

1429. Ms. O Institute, vols. 54.
Imprensa Da Universidade, Coimbra, 1907

資料 11（貼付ノート・Transaction of the Asiatic Society of Japan）

資料11（貼付ノート・Transaction of the Asiatic Society of Japan）

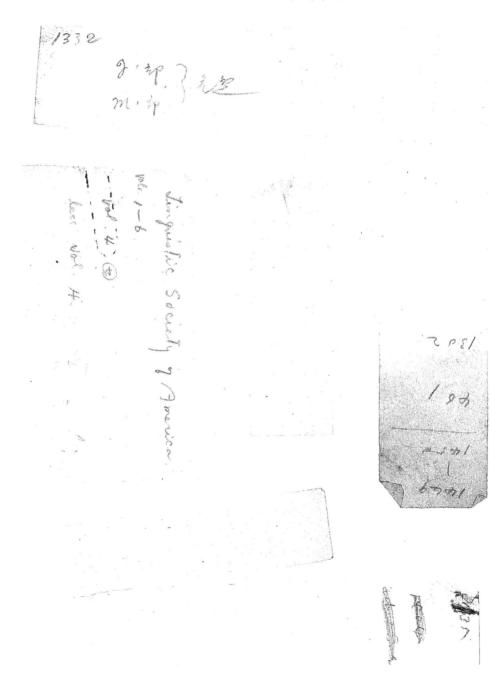

Radlov + Malov: Suvarṇaprabhāsa,
(Bibliotheca Buddhica XVII)
6 vols St Petersburg
circa 1915

# 資料12（目録・List of 364 missing or imperfect books）

資料 12（目録・List of 364 missing or imperfect books）

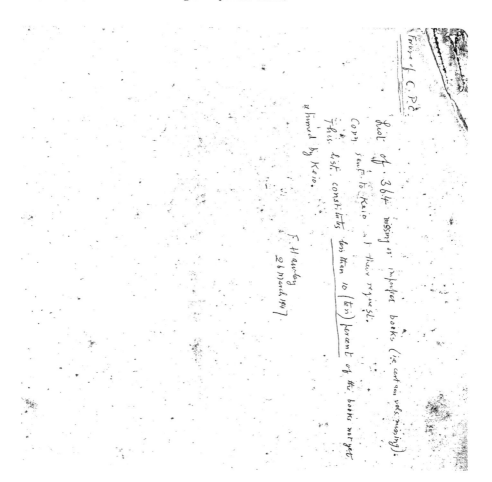

Folio of C.P.C.

List of 364 missing or imperfect books (i.e. certain vols. missing).

Copy sent to Keio at their request.

This list constitutes less than 10 (ten) percent of the books not yet returned by Keio.

F. Hawley

26 March 1947

| 書名 | 冊數 | 缺及未還 |
| --- | --- | --- |
| 1 賀茂眞淵全集 東京 吉川弘文館 昭和二年—七年 賀茂百樹著 | 十二冊 | 八。九。十一。十二 共四冊 |
| 2 官刻 東醫寶鑑 享保九年 | 二十五冊 桐箱入 | 十六冊目及 桐箱 |
| 3 琉球處分 | 三冊 | 三冊目（琉球處分提綱） |
| 4 大増訂 國史大辭典 八代國治編 東京 吉川弘文館 昭和二年 | 六冊 | 三冊目（す〜と） |
| 5 植物名實圖考 小野職愨重修 | 四十八冊 六帙 | 第六帙目（第十三巻之第十九巻） |
| 6 類聚古集 大正三年 | 四帙 | 第三帙目 |
| 7 謠曲通解 大和田建樹 東京 博文館 明治二十五年 | 八冊二帙 | 第一帙目（第一巻之第四巻）四冊 |
| 8 謠曲文解 勝野嘉一郎編 東京 江島伊兵衛 明治三十九年—四十年 | 二冊 | 前編 一冊 |

10 今昔物語　明治二十九年　二冊　下冊

11 藤陰山房叢書（写本）　二十七冊　第四冊目しかあらず　第一之第三。欠　第五之第二十七　計二十六冊　は慶應にあり。

12 植物名實圖攷　商務院書館　（洋本）　二冊　第二冊目（圖の方）

13 國譯本草綱目　東京　春陽堂　昭和四年－八年　白井光太郎外　十五冊　第十冊

14 假名の日本書紀　東京　大同館書店　大正九年　植松安　二冊　下巻

15 太平御覧　涵芬樓刊　百三十六冊　第百三十冊目

16 格致鏡原
合本 十六冊 第九冊之第十六冊
(初印本 )(背の番号は十七之三十二となってゐる。)

17 日本農民建築
東京 聚樂社 昭和九年－十五年 石原憲治
十四冊 第十二冊目之第十四冊
(共三冊)

18 國文註釋全書
國學院 明治四十年－四十三年
二十冊 二十冊共

19 八史經籍志
文政八年
二帙十七冊 二帙 十七冊

20 平家物語についての研究
平家物語考 一冊 明治四十四年
平家物語の語法 上・下 二冊 大正三年
文部省
三冊 三冊共

21 大同類聚方 (寫本)
二十三冊 一冊(三〇七七号)
第九十四巻之第九十五巻

22 漢魏叢書 九十六種
涵芬樓刊
四十冊四帙 四十冊 四帙

23 廣東新語 木天閣版
八冊二帙 八冊 二帙

以上

No. 4

| | 書名 | 冊数 | 缺々未還 |
|---|---|---|---|
| 24 | 廈門音系　羅常培　上海　国立中央研究院　民国十九年 | 一冊 | 一冊 |
| 25 | 愛書趣味　一号～二十六号（附目録二枚） | 二十六冊及目録二枚 | 二十六冊 附目録二枚 |
| 26 | アイヌ語を通じて観たるアイヌの族姓　他　国語漢文研究会　東京　明治書院　明治四十四年 | 一冊 | 一冊 |
| 27 | 足利学校秘本書目　日本書誌学会編輯　昭和八年 | 二冊一帙 | 二冊一帙 |
| 28 | あた[illegible]小[illegible]ちしかみざいく　中島種二　京都　河原書店　昭和十年 | 三冊 | 三冊 |
| 29 | アリンス國辞彙　宮武外骨　東京　半狂堂　昭和四年 | 一冊 | 一冊 |

30 足利学校事蹟考（全） 川上廣樹 明治十三年 一冊 一冊
（此の書二部有り、帙入のもの
のみ寄る。）

31 淺野家の有恒社と株式会社 関彪編者 大正十三年 一冊 一冊

32 アクセントと方言 服部四郎 一冊 一冊
東京 明治書院

33 足利学校遺蹟考 一冊 一冊
足利学校遺蹟図書館編、発行
大正十一年

34 亜細亜研究 渡部薫太郎編 一冊 一冊
大阪東洋学会 昭和七年

35 愛日樓印譜 溝上與三郎 一冊 一冊
大正十四年

No.5

**資料 12**（目録・List of 364 missing or imperfect books）

n.b.

36 世阿彌舞踊讀本
藤蔭桂樹
東京 河出書房 昭和十三年
一冊 一冊

37 相阿彌四季山水畫
秋山光夫編
一帖一帙 一帖一帙

38 足利学校沿革誌
足利学校遺蹟圖書館編幷行
大正六年
一冊 一冊

39 足利学校遺蹟沿革
足利学校遺蹟圖書館編幷行
明治四十四年
一冊 一冊

40 天草版金句集の研究
（東洋文庫論叢 第二十四）
吉田澄夫
東洋文庫 昭和十三年
一冊 一冊

41 奄美大島民謡大観 文英吉 鹿児島県南島文化研究社 昭和八年 一冊 一冊

42 賣春婦異名集（全） 宮武外骨 東京成光館 昭和八年 一冊 一冊

43 賣扇庵扇譜 宮脇新兵衛 京都芸艸堂 大正六年 一冊 一冊

44 番椒圖說 伊藤介稿 明治十五年 一冊 一冊

45 美術研究
第一号―第十二号（一組）
第一号―第七十二号（一組）
同第三十八号―第四十五号は二部づつ。
又英文の説明書、二・三枚づつ各冊に添附。
九十二冊

九十二冊 外に
英文の説明書、各冊に
二・三枚づつ添附。

No.7

no.8

46 美味珍味　食草抱　一冊　一冊
東京　九ノ内出版社　昭和八年

47 文房四譜　和紙研究会編　二冊一帙　二冊一帙
京都　便利堂　昭和十六年　（此の書　二部有り。一部のみ帰る。）

48 文求堂書目　田中慶太郎編・発行　一冊　一冊
昭和八年

49 玫瑰花冠記録　一冊一帙　一冊一帙
明治二年

50 文藝（合本）　一冊　一冊
自昭和八年十二月至昭和九年三月
改造社
（フランク・ホーレー論文記載）

51 佛教辞典（梵漢対訳）　一冊　一冊
荻原雲来
丙午出版社　昭和二年

52 文学に現はれたる我が国民思想の研究　津田左右吉
東京　洛陽堂　大正八年―十年
四冊　四冊

53 佛教大辞典　望月信亨
東京佛教大辞典発行会
昭和十一年―十二年
七冊　七冊

54 文章讀本　谷崎潤一郎
一冊　一冊

55 文法集成　本多亀三
東京　弘文館　明治四十三年
一冊　一冊

56 文学　岩波書店発行
(イ) 第二より第七巻迄　五十五冊
(ロ) 第二巻第十二号　一冊
(ハ) 第一号より第二十号迄　二十冊
(ニ) 第一巻―第六巻　揃い　六十六冊
全百四十二冊
百四十二冊　百四十二冊

No.9

No. 10

| | 書名 | 冊数 | 缺乃未還 |
|---|---|---|---|
| 57 | 大明三藏聖教目録 及び補正索引 南條文雄 東京 南條博士記念刊行会 昭和四年 | 二冊 | 二冊 |
| 58 | 動安居士文集 帝王韻記附 その解説 朝鮮古典刊行会編・発行 昭和十四年 | 三冊一帙 | 三冊一帙 |
| 59 | 土木工学用語集 紫藤龍児 土木学会 昭和十一年 | 一冊 | 一冊 |
| 60 | 大日光中禅寺写真帳 鈴木常観 中禅寺寺務所 昭和十五年 | 一冊 | 一冊 |
| 61 | 道家の思想と其の展開 津田左右吉 岩波書店 昭和十四年 | 一冊 | 一冊 |
| 62 | 新作 都々逸小唄 | 一冊 | 一冊 |

No.11

63 大東輿地圖、大東輿地圖索引
京城帝国大学法文学部　昭和十一年　二冊一函　二冊一函

64 大広益會玉篇
慶長九年　五冊一帙函入　五冊一帙函入

65 大般若波羅蜜多経第四十四巻
（ホノルル目録番号第九五三）　一巻　一巻

66 大同石仏寺　木下杢太郎
東京座右宝　昭和十六年　一冊　一冊

67 大西郷遺訓　小谷保太郎編著
政教社　大正十五年　一冊　一冊

68 永楽大典　東洋文庫編・発行　五冊
昭和五年　解説一冊　一帙　解説一冊

69 江戸時代語研究（雑誌）
第一巻第一号―第四号
第二巻第一号（二部）　六冊　六冊
松川弘太郎
江戸株詠会
昭和十一年

No.12

70 燕京大学学報 第一期—第二十七期（全揃） 二十七冊 二十七冊

71 英和雙解隠語彙集 村松守義 金港堂 明治二十年 一冊 一冊

72 燕京大学圖書館目録初稿 鄧嗣禹編 燕京大学圖書館 一九三五年 一冊 一冊

73 袁中郎全集 袁宏道 世界書局 民国二十五年 一冊 一冊

74 英漢標準漢訳外国人名地名表 何崧齢 商務印書館 民国十三年 一冊 一冊

75 英和新撰兵語辞典 圖南社編輯 大正九年 一冊 一冊

76 英和海語辞典 内藤信夫 有明堂 大正七年 一冊 一冊

No.13

77 英和雙譯論語（全）
レッグ博士英訳、清水起正編
二三子堂書店　昭和七年
一冊　一冊

78 恵比須と大黒（稿本研究）
長沼賢海
丙午出版社　大正十一年
一冊　一冊

79 英和和製秘辞典
芸文堂　昭和六年
一冊　一冊

80 江戸年中行事
三田村鳶魚
芸文堂　昭和二年
春陽堂
関彰
一冊　一冊

81 建築式流圖説
一冊一帙　帙欠

資料 12（目録・List of 364 missing or imperfect books）

No. 14

| | 書名 | 冊数 | 欠及未還 |
|---|---|---|---|
| 82 | 白山獄凝煙 昭和九年 田中慶太郎 編・発行 | 一冊 | 一冊 |
| 83 | 八丈島 東京 晃文館 薄悲一 大正三年 | 一冊 | 一冊 |
| 84 | 博物新編 明治八年 | 五冊 | 五冊 |
| 85 | 白絹衣絨製造販賣組合規約書 | 一冊 | 一冊 |
| 86 | 荻日記 明治四十年 | 一冊 | 一冊 |
| 87 | 繭に関する俗信一覧表（全） | 一冊一帙 | 一冊一帙 |
| 88 | はるのかたみ 荘原好一編 | 一冊 | 一冊 |
| 89 | 白牛略考 橘元周 寛政壬子（明治十六年一月十五日に農務局報告課にて修史館楓山文庫蔵本を臨写） | 一冊 | 一冊 |
| 90 | 版本通義（百科小叢書） 錢基博 商務印書館 民国二十二年 | 一冊 | 一冊 |

91 平賀源内集（全） 塚本哲三編 有朋堂 昭和九年 一冊 一冊

92 悲恋の為恭 藤森成吉 詩道社 昭和十三年 一冊 一冊

93 日向文献史料 若山甲蔵 日向文献史料刊行会 昭和九年 一冊一帙 一冊一帙

94 表具のしをり（新修版） 山本元 芸草堂 昭和十二年 一冊 一冊

95 平田篤胤全集 平田学会編・刊 明治四十四年～大正七年 十五冊 十五冊

96 廣島県樹木目一覧表 一冊 一冊

97 雁鶴雑考 武津長平 一冊 一冊

98 福翁自傳 福澤諭吉述 大正四年 時事新報社 昭和五年 一冊 一冊

99 福島県山叢誌・附録 明治四十三年 二冊 附録一冊欠

No.15

資料 12（目録・List of 364 missing or imperfect books）

No.12

| No. | 書名 | 著者 | 発行所 | 年 | 冊数 | 冊数 |
|---|---|---|---|---|---|---|
| 100 | 藤田博士記念展覧会陳列図書目録 | | 東洋文庫 | 昭和五年 | 一冊 | 一冊 |
| 101 | 福翁自伝 | | 時事新報社 | 昭和九年 | 一冊 | 一冊 |
| 102 | 扶桑略記 | | | 文政三年 | 十五冊二帙 | 十五冊二帙 |
| 103 | 風雅論 | 大西克礼 | 岩波書店 | 昭和十五年 | 一冊 | 一冊 |
| 104 | 普通術語辞彙 | 徳谷豊之助 | 敬文社 | 明治三十八年 | 一冊 | 一冊 |
| 105 | 古本屋 創刊号—第十号 目録 特刊号 | 荒木伊兵衛 著 | | | 十二冊 | 十二冊 |
| 106 | 平家物語略解 | 御橋悳言 | 宝文館 | 昭和四年 | 一冊 | 一冊 |

107 平家納経図録　京都　便利堂　奈良帝室博物館編　昭和十五年　一冊一帙　一冊一帙

108 硯箋（持眞人傳硯記、硯道人硯術述）　一冊　一冊

109 硯史（昭和八年春及秋号）　西川一草亭　二冊　二冊

110 繍子生抄　享保三年　一冊　一冊

111 凹（内外不出）　白　ロヲジマ　凸凹寺　久保盛丸　昭和六年三月　一冊　一冊

112 本草便覧　光緒丁亥　成化嘉　二冊一帙　二冊一帙

113 方言　一巻一号 ― 五巻十二号（全揃）　高橋武馬　春陽堂

114 方彙　甲賀通元　享保癸丑　一冊　一冊

№19

訂正。104「普通術語辞彙」は既還本故還要 リストより御消し下さい

115 方丈記評釈　内海弘蔵　明治書院　昭和十三年　一冊　一冊

116 本邦四書訓點並に註解の史的研究　大江文城　関書院　昭和十年　一冊　一冊

117 方言と土俗　橘正一　一言社　第一巻第一号——第二巻第九号　昭和五年——七年　二十一冊　二十一冊

118 筆園　林柾木　第一〇二・一〇四——一三〇　二十八冊　二十八冊

119 法制史論集　中田薫　岩波書店　第一——大正十五年　第二——昭和十三年　二冊　二冊

120 法隆寺建築論附図（東京帝国大学紀要工科第一冊第一号附図）　伊東忠太　明治三十一年　一冊　一冊

No.18

No.19

121 法隆寺論攷　地人書館　喜田貞吉選　昭和十五年　一冊　一冊

122 本草和名　寛政丙辰板（原版）　二冊一帙　二冊一帙

123 本草和名　江戸和泉屋庄治郎発行（原版もう一部）　二冊一帙　二冊一帙

124 細井平洲の生涯　巌松堂　高瀬代次郎　昭和十一年　一冊　一冊

125 法隆寺国宝保存工事報告書　法隆寺国宝保存事業部編・発行　昭和十年—十二年　四冊　一冊欠（四冊目）

126 北平歳時志　国立北平研究院史学研究会発行　張江裁　二冊一帙　二冊一帙

127 北蒙植物の概観　昭和十二年　村松七郎　一冊　一冊

No. 23

128 訪餘錄　大正十年　田中廣太郎編纂　一冊　一冊

129 本草序例　芋野居作十郎　一冊　一冊

130 本草衍義　寇宗奭　一冊　一冊

131 本草蒙筌　汪訒菴　四冊一帙　四冊一帙

132 法制史料古文書類纂　瀧川政次郎　有斐閣　昭和二年　一冊　一冊

133 大福寺本方丈記　古典保存会編・發行　大正十五年　一冊一帙　一冊一帙

134 本草通串證圖　二冊一帙　二冊一帙

135 增訂本草備要　二冊　二冊

136 法隆寺金堂壁画解説（法隆寺金堂壁画十大講演版複製附録） 一冊 一冊

137 本邦書誌学概要 植松安 図書館事業研究会 昭和四年 一冊 一冊

138 平安朝文法史（全） 山田孝雄 宝文館 大正二年 一冊 一冊

139 宝雲 第一冊—第五冊 宝雲社 昭和七年—八年 五冊 五冊

140 本草書目抄 昭和三年 一冊 一冊

141 本草百書若葉序（全） 一冊 一冊

142 輔仁学誌 第一巻第一号—第六巻第二 （合本及合本） 六巻 六巻

143 皕宋楼蔵書志目録 光緒八年 三十二冊四帙 八冊（第三帙目）

No. 21

No. 22

| | 書名 | | 冊数 | 缺佚未還 |
|---|---|---|---|---|
| 144 | 一切経音義　西東書房 | 山田孝雄編　昭和七年 | 七冊一帙 | 七冊一帙 |
| 145 | 一切経音義索引（全）　西東書房 | 山田孝雄編　大正十四年 | 一冊 | 一冊 |
| 146 | 伊勢物語　岩波書店 | 屋代弘賢校訂　昭和六年 | 一冊 | 一冊 |
| 147 | 井上頼圀翁小傳　大正十年 | 田辺勝哉編著 | 一冊 | 一冊 |
| 148 | 印文学　三圭社 | 方田俊　昭和四年 | 一冊 | 一冊 |
| 149 | 今鏡（畠山本）　大塚巧藝社 | 和田英松校訂　昭和十三年 | 二冊一帙函入 | 二冊一帙函入 |
| 150 | 異態習俗考　六文館 | 金城朝永　昭和八年 | 一冊 | 一冊 |

No.23

151 現代醫学大辞典　第十四巻
小児科学篇　・沖田豊穂
春秋社　昭和四年　一冊　一冊

152 石川啄木全集
改造社　昭和六年　一冊　一冊

153 岩波文庫　古今著聞集
黒板勝美　一冊　一冊

154 偉人野口英世　池田宣政
大日本雄辯會講談社　昭和十六年　一冊　一冊

155 異国草木会目録（全）賀島信近　一冊　一冊

156 いかもの趣味　礒部鎮雄編
いかもの会　昭和八年―十年　四冊二帙　四冊二帙

No. 24

157 韻鏡考　大正十三年　大矢透著　一冊　一冊

158 栄花物語　二十一冊　二十一冊

159 板碑概説　服部清五郎　鳳鳴書院　小冊子挿入　昭和八年　二冊　二冊

160 一癖隨筆　成光館　第一号、宮武外骨　昭和五年　一冊　一冊

161 色葉字類抄及解説　育德財團　大正十五年　三冊函入　三冊函入

162 佚存書目　服部宇之吉編　田中慶太郎發行　昭和八年　一冊　一冊

No.25

| | 書名 | 冊数 | 缺及び未還 |
|---|---|---|---|
| 163 | 学畫問答崋椿尺牘 上下 神木猶之助 明治卌四年 | 二冊 | 二冊 |
| 164 | 学畫問答崋椿尺牘 神木猶之助 明治四十四年 | 三冊一帙 | 三冊一帙 |
| 165 | 銜署名目 | 一冊 | 一冊 |
| 166 | 雁皮栽培録（三部） | 三冊三帙 | （三部の中一部帰還）二冊二帙缺 |
| 167 | 藝文（未製本） 一巻―二十二巻 全揃 | 全揃 | 全揃 |
| 168 | 字音便覧 佐藤重治 東京陸軍経理学校内陸軍主計團記事部發行 大正九年 | 一冊 | 一冊 |
| 169 | 重校神農本草 光緒丙午 | 二冊 | 二冊 |
| 170 | 畫灰書、畫水書 蓬翁用九 | 写本一無帙 | 写本一無帙 |
| 171 | 藝林間歩 岩波書店 木下杢太郎 昭和十一年 | 一冊 | 一冊 |

No. 28

172 現代挿花圖集 第三輯 日本花道之院 昭和三年 一冊 一冊

173 現代挿花圖集 第二輯 西阪華之栞社 昭和十一年 一冊 一冊

174 現代挿花圖集 西阪清華、大阪第一藝文社 昭和十一年 一冊 一冊

175 諺草 貝原好古 茶川善兵衛 元禄十四年 七冊 七冊

176 解題叢書（全） 図書刊行会、編・発行 大正五年 一冊 一冊

177 元朝駅傳雑考 東洋文庫叢刊第一附篇 羽田 亨 東洋文庫 昭和五年 一冊 一冊

178 壹岐島方言集　山口麻太郎　一冊　一冊
刀江書院（言語誌叢刊のうち）

179 滋賀県方言集　太田栄太郎　一冊　一冊
刀江書院（言語誌叢刊のうち）

180 飛騨の方言　荒垣秀雄　一冊　一冊
刀江書院（言語誌叢刊のうち）

181 疑問假名遣　前・後　二冊　二冊
国語調査委員会　編
前編　大正元年
後編　大正四年

182 御物看聞日記複製　領布趣旨書　一冊　一冊
貴重図書影本刊行会

183 儀礼図　（官版）　八冊一帙　八冊一帙
寛政十二年

No. 27

No. 28

184 群書類従（上製本 平革） 昭和四年ー十二年 内外書籍株式会社 二十四冊 二十四冊

185 續群書類従 續群書類従完成会 昭和六年ー八年 七十二冊 七十二冊

186 群経概論（百科小叢書） 周豫同 商務印書館 一冊 一冊

187 能楽資料全集 東京 能楽資料頒布会 写真版 五音曲条々書、上下一冊 以外ノ分ナク全部 （写真版、解説、注釈版）闕

188 漢書 （殿刻） 六冊 五八○ 五九 二冊欠

189 五山文学全集 上村観光編 五山文学全集刊行会 昭和十一年 五冊 五冊

No.29

| No. | 書名 | 著者・発行 | 年 | 冊数 | 冊数 |
|---|---|---|---|---|---|
| 190 | 五山の四大詩僧 | 今関天彭 | 昭和八年 | 一冊 | 一冊 |
| 191 | 若樹文庫入札略目録 | | 昭和十三年 | 一冊 | 一冊 |
| 192 | 重要樹苗説明 | 稲井群芳園 | 明治三十四年 | 一冊 | 一冊 |
| 193 | 五雑組 | | 寛文元年 | 八冊 | 八冊 |
| 194 | 十二月図帖 | 聚楽社 | 昭和六年 | 一冊一帙 | 一冊一帙 |
| 195 | 實例今女習字帖 | 藤村耕一 宝文館 | 昭和三年 | 一帖 | 一帖 |
| 196 | 女子学習院五十年史 | 女子学習院 | 昭和十年 | 一冊 | 一冊 |

No.30

197 世界中何にても用文　関東竹二郎　松陽堂　明治三十二年　一冊　一冊

198 実験音声学上より見たるアクセントの研究　千葉勉　冨山房　昭和十年　一冊　一冊

199 爾雅註疏　五冊　五冊

200 順聖公年譜　伊地知季安　大正甲寅　一冊　一冊

201 尋常小学読本
巻一　大正七年　一冊
巻二―巻十二（東京の分なり）十二冊　昭和三年―六年
十三冊　十三冊

202 成吉思汗ハ源義経也　小谷部全一郎　冨山房　大正十三年　一冊　一冊

203 隋唐燕楽調研究　林謙三　商務印書館　民国二十五年　一冊　一冊

| No. | 書名 | 発行 | 著者 | 年 | 冊数 | 冊数 |
|---|---|---|---|---|---|---|
| 204 | 寺社宝物展覧目録 | | | | 二冊一帙 | 二冊一帙 |
| 205 | 実用文字のつゞり方 | 立川熊次郎 | 春花山人 | 大正十二年 | 一冊 | 一冊 |
| 206 | 女子手紙の文（完） | 大倉書店 | 小野鵞堂 | 明治四十四年 | 一冊 | 一冊 |
| 207 | 字音假字用 | 錢屋利兵衛 | 本居宣長 | 安永五年 | 一冊 | 一冊 |
| 208 | 女子消息文のゆきゝ | 落合長吾 | 多田合子 | 明治四十年 | 一冊 | 一冊 |
| 209 | 豆州熱海誌 | 直試社 | 大内青巒 | 明治十一年 | 一冊 | 一冊 |
| 210 | 女子風俗化粧秘傳 | 好古堂 | 佐山半七丸 | 文化十年 | 三冊一帙 | 三冊一帙 |
| 211 | 圖訓異義 和漢辞典 | 厚生閣 | 堀江與一 | 昭和十二年 | 一冊 | 一冊 |

212 五經 後藤先生訓點 目黒氏藏版 十一冊 十一冊

213 現行法律語の史的考察 海部万藏 万里閣書房 昭和五年 一冊 一冊

No.33

| 書名 | 冊数 | 献及未還 |
| --- | --- | --- |
| 214 假名源流考及證本寫眞 国語調査委員会 編 明治四十四年 | 合本一冊 | 合本一冊 |
| 215 漢文の訓讀によりて傳へられたる語法 山田孝雄 寶文館 昭和十年 | 一冊 | 一冊 |
| 216 漢篆千字文 芙蓉深先生稿本 菡萏居藏版 | 四冊一帙 | 四冊一帙 |
| 217 寛政版記録附信夫顯祖予跋 江島伊兵衛 わんや書店 | 一冊 | 一冊 |
| 218 花傳書改訂版 野上豊一郎編 岩波書店 昭和十四年 | 一冊 | 一冊 |
| 219 花傳書 (全) (三部) 江島伊兵衛 明治三十一年 | 二冊二帙 | 二冊二帙 |

No.34

220 懐風藻註釈　沢田總清　大岡山書店　昭和八年　一冊　一冊

221 花伝書（室町古写本の近世写）　一冊一帙　一冊一帙

222 鎌倉室町時代の儒教　足利知夫　日本古典全集刊行会　昭和七年　一冊　一冊

223 華山印譜（[illegible]華山実印使用のもの）　一冊一帙　一冊一帙

224 新釈観音経講話　古家東洋　東京観音布教会　昭和十年　一冊　一冊

225 かわさき物語　岡靖　横浜土地新報社　昭和十三年　一冊　一冊

226 観古雑帖　一帖一帙　一帖一帙

227 かながきろんご　安田文庫編発行　一冊一帙函入　一冊一帙函入
昭和十年

228 関八州印象記
神奈川県郷土研究聯盟編発行　一冊　一冊
昭和十六年

229 金沢文庫所蔵浄土宗に関する未傳
稀観の鎌倉鈔本
塚本善隆

230 化学工業全書（第十五冊）
高松豊吉編　一冊　一冊
丸善京都支店　大正五年

231 官衙名目　一冊　一冊

232 華山研究　土月孔
弘文書院　明治四十二年　一冊　一冊

No.35

No.36

233 漢方と漢字 第一～第五 日本漢方医学会 昭和九年～十四年 三省堂 林一 六十二冊 六十二冊

234 漢籍解題 明治書院 桂湖邨 明治三十九年 一冊 一冊

235 鹿児海魚譜 明治四十四年 日野夏実 一冊 一冊

236 かまの跡 精版印刷社 三好富之助 昭和二年 一冊一帙 一冊一帙

237 会話教本（巻一） 日語文化学校 一冊 一冊

238 管窺愚考（全） 伊地知氏宅蔵 天保癸下 脱稿 一冊 一冊

No.37

239 管窺愚考附録（全）　瀋陽　于孝安　一冊　一冊

240 甘露堂文庫稀覯本攷覧（全）　尾崎久彌　名古屋書史会　昭和八年　一冊　一冊

241 化学工芸 第九号　化学工芸社　大正十四年　一冊一帙　一冊一帙

242 かなのしらべ 上・下　桑田明　一和書院　昭和六年　二帙　二帙

243 漢文進階　卜郎特　北平法文圖書館　民国二十五年　一冊　一冊

244 漢字詳解　高田忠周　西東書房　大正十四年　三冊一帙　三冊一帙

資料 12（目録・List of 364 missing or imperfect books）

No.38

| No. | 書名 | 著者・編者 | 発行所 | 発行年 | 冊数 | 冊数 |
|---|---|---|---|---|---|---|
| 245 | 国宝重要美術品、絵画展覧會圖録（全） 及目録 | 朝日新聞社編 | 大塚巧藝社 | 昭和九年 | 六冊 目録一冊 函入 計七冊 | 七冊一帙 |
| 246 | からし言葉の索引 | 宮本光玄 | 誠文堂 | 昭和四年 | 一冊 | 一冊 |
| 247 | かまくら | 大森金五郎 | 吉川弘文館 | 明治四十四年 | 一冊 | 一冊 |
| 248 | 五段排列漢字典 | オ・ロビンベルグ | 興文社 | 大正五年 | 一冊 | 一冊 |
| 249 | 金澤と六浦荘時代 | 手田恒吾 |  | 大正三年 | 一冊 | 一冊 |
| 250 | 和英海語辞典 | 尾崎主税 | 水交社 | 昭和三年 | 一冊 | 一冊 |

No.39

251 下学集　上・下　元和三年　二冊　無帙　一冊　無帙

252 官刻沿革略史總目録　東京帝国大学　明治三十三年　一冊　一冊

253 韓語研究法　薬師寺知朧　明治四十二年　一冊　一冊

254 郷土研究（第一巻―第四巻）岡村千秋　郷土研究社　大正三年―六年　チヨコレート色　洋本
土俗と傳説　牛島軍平　文武堂書店　大正七年　五冊　五冊

255 切支丹宗門の迫害と潜伏　姉崎正治　同文館　大正十五年　一冊　一冊

256 近代文藝筆禍史　斎藤昌三　崇文堂　大正十三年　一冊　一冊

257 稀本零本　諸書会刊　一冊一帙　一冊一帙

258 欽定盛京通志　圖書集成局　武英殿聚珍版本　光緒二十七年　六冊　第一冊目　第六十冊目　缺

259 麒麟　松本行太郎編著　昭和七年　一冊　一冊

260 郷土趣味　田中緑紅　京都郷土趣味社　大正七年—十四年　揃　揃

261 舊刊影譜　日本書誌学会編著　昭和七年　一冊　一冊

262 貴重圖書影本刊行会目録　貴重圖書影本刊行会編纂　便利堂　一冊　一冊

263 貴重圖書影本刊行会趣意書規定　昭和四回配本目録　貴重圖書影本刊行会　便利堂　一冊　一冊

no. 40

264 全生樹譜（全） 長生舎主人 柳蔭藏版 二部 六冊 六冊

265 近代東洋音楽研究（第一巻之書） 岸辺成雄 一冊 一冊

266 近世畸人傳中遺物会目録 一冊 一冊

267 [illegible]荒圖録（完） 中田印春江編 明治十八年 一冊 一冊

268 欽定續通典 圖書集成局 武英殿聚珍版 光緒二十七年 十二冊 十一〇十二 缺

269 郷土志料目録 昭和四年 一冊 一冊

270 吉利支丹文字抄 村岡典嗣 弘道社 大正十五年 一冊 一冊

271 京華春報（第一－五号迄） 京春社 明治二十二年十月・十一月 一冊 一冊

No.41

272 京都圖書館和漢圖書分類目録
京都圖書館
大正十一年―昭和七年
六冊
二冊缺
註 現在あるもの
○叢書予彙之部
（大正十一年）
○社会産業之部
（大正十一年）
○歴史地誌之部
（大正十一年）
○法政経済之部
（昭和四年）

273 郷土志料分類目録
鹿児島県立圖書館 昭和四年
一冊
一冊

274 救荒野菜圖説（全）
嘉永四年
一冊
一冊

275 氣象の研究と其の應用
藤原咲平講演
東京啓明会 昭和十年
一冊
一冊

276 朴陽
昭和四年
宮里 本校訂
三冊
帙
三冊一帙

No.42

no.43

277 桐生織物史　昭和十五年　桐生織物史編纂会編　一冊　一冊

278 吉利支丹教義の研究　東洋文庫論叢 第九　東洋文庫　昭和三年　二冊一函（一冊は英文）　二冊一函

279 近代日本文学大系（17）　式亭三馬集（全）　昭和二年　一冊　一冊

280 頭書増補訓蒙圖彙大成　（日本語版）　一冊　一冊

281 君台観左右帳記研究　中央美術社　昭和六年　松本宗衛　一冊　一冊

282 懐徳堂印存　二冊一帙　二冊一帙

283 熊毛郡沿革誌　鹿児島県熊毛支庁編　昭和七年　一冊　一冊

資料 12（目録・List of 364 missing or imperfect books）

284 國語新辭典（國定教科書） 昭和十五年 一冊 一冊

285 國語と日本精神 保科孝一 實業之日本社 昭和十一年 一冊 一冊

286 國語國字國文改良諸說梗概 教育調查會 大正三年 一冊 一冊

287 校讎學（百科小叢書）胡樸安 商務印書館 民國二十四年 一冊 一冊

288 古代漢文を基礎とする言語文化の一研究 濱名寬祐 日本ツーラン協會 昭和八年 一冊 一冊

289 五部心觀（園城寺藏版） 便利堂東京出張所 一冊 一冊

240 國語の中に於ける漢語の研究 山田孝雄 寶文館 昭和十五年 一冊 一冊

20.44

291 光海君時代の満鮮関係　稲葉君山　大阪屋号書店　昭和八年　一冊　一冊

292 古硯美の鑑賞　井上清太　坂上書院　昭和十一年　一冊　一冊

293 古文孝経　足利学校遺蹟図書館　昭和六年　一冊一帙　一冊一帙

294 古活字版之研究　川瀬一馬　安田文庫　昭和十二年　二冊　二冊

295 皇室史の研究　黒板勝美　東伏見宮蔵版　昭和七年　一冊　一冊

296 古方薬品考（増補）　内藤尚賢　天保十三年　五冊一帙　五冊一帙

297 光悦遺芳　京都博物館　便利堂　昭和十年　一冊一帙　一冊一帙

298 古風土記逸文考證　栗田勤　大日本図書株式会社　明治三十六年　二冊　二冊

No.95

No.46

| 番号 | 書名 | 著者・編者 | 出版者 | 年 | 冊数 | 冊数 |
| --- | --- | --- | --- | --- | --- | --- |
| 299 | 好色本目録 | | | | 一冊一帙 | 一冊一帙 |
| 300 | 胡蝶後水尾院御製 | | 金尾文淵堂 | 大正十一年 | 一冊 | 一冊 |
| 301 | 皇室制度講話 | 酒巻芳男 | 岩波書店 | 昭和九年 | 一冊 | 一冊 |
| 302 | 古代研究 | 折口信夫 | 大岡山書店 | 昭和四年 | 三冊 | 国文学篇 一冊缺 |
| 303 | 皇室関係大阪府郷土資料陳列目録 | | 大阪府立図書館 | 大正五年 | 一冊 | 一冊 |
| 304 | 米澤藩学問所興譲館年志 | 石田勘四郎編 | | 昭和二年 | 一冊 | 一冊 |
| 305 | 皇室と基督教 | 曽我部四郎 | 丁未出版社 | 昭和二年 | 一冊 | 一冊 |
| 306 | 高麗史節要補刊附録 | | 朝鮮史編修会 | | 一冊 | 一冊 |

| 番号 | 書名 | 著者・発行 | 年 | 冊数 | 冊数 |
|---|---|---|---|---|---|
| 307 | 皇室事典 | 井原頼明　冨山房 | 昭和十三年 | 一冊 | 一冊 |
| 308 | 古代日本精神文化の研究 | 大西貞治　至文堂 | 昭和六年 | 一冊 | 一冊 |
| 309 | 口語法（全） | 国語調査委員会編　大日本図書株式会社 | 昭和十一年 | 一冊 | 一冊 |
| 310 | 国史大系（甘四版） | 経済雑誌社 | 明治三十年―三十四年 | 十七冊 | 七―九、十二―十四　六冊缺 |
| 311 | 首訓玉字格（全） | | 文政八年 | 一冊 | 一冊 |
| 312 | 康熙幾暇格物編 | | | 二冊 | 二冊 |
| 313 | 黒龍江墾殖説略 | | | 一冊 | 一冊 |
| 314 | 古典保存会趣旨類[illegible] | 古典保存会 | 昭和十二年 | 一冊 | 一冊 |
| 315 | 言余の塵　巻一―巻四 | 居行遠里 | 安永八年 | 四冊 | 四冊 |

No.411

| | 書名 | 冊数 | 缺本未還 |
|---|---|---|---|
| 316 | 古文 | 十六冊二帙 | 十六冊二帙 |
| 317 | こもこも草　嘉永六年十一月 | 二冊一帙 | 二冊一帙 |
| 318 | 国語学書目解題　吉田澄夫 | 一冊 | 一冊 |
| 319 | 高野版展覧目録　大阪府立図書館　昭和四年 | 一冊 | 一冊 |
| 320 | 国学院雑誌　一巻〜四十三巻　国学院大学　明治二十七年〜昭和十四年 | 五百三十三冊 | 五百三十三冊 |
| 321 | コトバ　二月号　小林竹雄　東京文学社　昭和十二年 | 一冊 | 一冊 |
| 322 | 国語の「日本」と音声学　大西雅雄　昭和十年 | 一冊 | 一冊 |
| 323 | 国語 明治以後の一考察　松岡静雄　[illegible]社　昭和十一年 | 一冊 | 一冊 |

No.47

324 古鈔本 伊勢物語　古典保存会　昭和六年　一冊一帙　一冊一帙

325 国語国文雑誌研究論文索引　京都国語国文学会　東京文献書院　昭和六年　一冊　一冊

326 蘇野山植物　明治三十九年　川瀬三治郎　一冊　一冊

327 古代木綿手染織絵彌展　昭和十一年　一冊　一冊

328 古文孝経私記 上・下　文化八年　南部泉沢充　二冊　二冊

329 こはらしまん　今村秀太郎　古染織はり込帖　昭和十五年　二冊（二部）　二冊（二部）

330 古事記裏書　古典保存会　大正十四年　一冊一帙　一冊一帙

No. 50

| No. | 書名 | 著者・発行 | | |
|---|---|---|---|---|
| 331 | 叩解機ノ研究 | 高知県内務部 | 一冊 | 一冊 |
| 332 | 公文式語 | | 一冊 | 一冊 |
| 333 | 廣西猺歌記音 | 趙元任 上海国立中央研究院 民国十九年 | 一冊 | 一冊 |
| 334 | 古典研究 第一 第二巻 | 昭和十一年 | 四冊 | 四冊 |
| 335 | 古典研究別冊附録 | 雄山閣 昭和十二年 | 五冊 | 五冊 |
| 336 | 弘道館記述義 | 藤田彪 明治十六年 | 一冊一帙 | 一冊一帙 |
| 337 | 交通文化 一〜八。十。十二。 | 東京 国際交通文化協会 昭和十二年〜十五年 | 十冊 | 十冊 |
| 338 | 国語法調査報告書 上・下 | 文部省内国語調査委員会 明治三十九年 | 二冊 | 下冊 欠 |

339 此花　宮武外骨
明治四十三年—四十五年
全揃　全揃

340 穀菜辨　印編　竹中卓郎
明治二十三年
一冊　一冊

341 皇道より見たる書経　加藤虎之亮
国民精神文化研究所
昭和十三年
一冊　一冊

342 国際茶会
わが祖国におもむ
国際を知る大徳寺茶会
国際茶会年代
一袋　四点一袋

343 国語の組織　大島正健
長風社　大正元年
一冊　一冊

344 古書句讀釈例　楊樹達
商務印書館　民国二十四年
一冊　一冊

No.51

no.52

345 廣惠濟急方　寛政元年　三冊一帙　三冊一帙

346 国史経籍志　野田庄右衛門梓行　五冊一帙　五冊一帙

347 国史経籍志　明曼山館刊　五冊一帙　五冊一帙

348 古文舊書考　明治甲辰刊　四冊一帙　四冊一帙

349 国史の研究（總説 各説上・下）　黒板勝美　岩波書店　昭和十四年　三冊　三冊

350 古語拾遺　加藤玄智校訂　岩波書店　昭和十四年　一冊　一冊

351 古史辨　顧頡剛　景山書社　民国一五－二十四年　五冊　一、二、四、五、缺

352 弘道館記　明治聖德記念学会編著　昭和十二年　一冊　一冊

353 古代劇文学（日本文学大系二十一）
能勢朝次
河出書房
昭和十四年
一冊
一冊

354 故実叢書（増訂）
故実叢書編輯部編
四十一冊
四冊欠
(1)標注令義解校本
乾の部 一冊
(2)装束集成 一冊
(3)武器考證 第一冊目
(4)女官装束着用次第
一冊

355 敬語法の研究
山田孝雄
宝文館
昭和六年
一冊
一冊

356 蒹葭堂百会譜（全） 浪速 木孔恭編
一冊
一冊

357 経験良方
明治

358 啓明会第九回講演集
大正十二年
一冊
一冊

No.53

加54

359 啓明会第二十八回講演集　昭和三年　一冊　一冊

360 建康集　十一（八）　宣統三年　二冊　二冊

deleted (360) in item, 22 Frank Hawley

361 諸字様　上下　明治四十四年　二冊一帙　二冊一帙

362 慶長以来書賈集覧　井上和雄　彙文堂　大正五年　一冊一帙　一冊一帙

363 東京帝国大学工科大学第四、及第六号（清国北京紫禁城殿門ノ建築及韓国建物調査報告）　明治三十六年及三十七年　二冊　二冊

364 磬　田辺孝次　工芸美術会　大正十年　一冊一函　一冊一函

| | 書名 | 冊数 | 缺ハ未還 |
|---|---|---|---|
| 365 | 万葉集古義 北村宇之松 昭和七年 | 十二冊 | 一・五・六・八・ 四冊缺 |
| 366 | 万葉集 文会堂書店 大正五年—六年 折口信夫 | 三冊 | 三冊 |
| 367 | 万葉集辞典 文会堂書店 大正八年 折口信夫 | 一冊 | 一冊 |
| 368 | 万葉集講義 巻一 漢字索引 山田孝雄 宝文館 | 一冊 | 一冊 |
| 369 | 万葉植物要覧 愛知県第一師範学校編 名古屋国文学会 昭和十年 | 一冊 | 一冊 |
| 370 | 満文書籍聯合目録 北平図書館 故宮博物院 | 一冊 | 一冊 |
| 371 | 満洲史 大原利武 京城近沢書店 昭和八年 | 一冊 | 一冊 |

No.55

372 蒲清記中（全） 一冊一帙 一冊一帙

373 前田下まくらの草子 東京育徳財團 昭和二年 一冊 一冊

374 贈従三位松平斉典公御手蹟 大康彬 大正二年 一冊 一冊

375 増鏡詳解 和田英松 《東京》球会 一冊 一冊

明治書院 昭和十四年

376 馬氏文献通考 圖書集成局 武英殿聚珍版 光緒二十七年 四十四冊 四九 四十二。 二冊缺

377 新刊萬病回春 寛永板 八冊 八冊

378 萬葉集解説 京都貴重圖書影本刊行会編 昭和十四年 二冊一帙 二冊一帙

379 松平春嶽公芸苑漫筆（五種） 福井久藏編 昭和十二年 一冊 一冊

No.57

380 まんじ 谷崎潤一郎 改造社 昭和六年 一冊 一冊

381 曼荼羅の研究 栂尾祥雲 高野山大学出版部 昭和七年 一冊 一冊

382 南の昔話(全) 喜捌緑村 京南書院 昭和十一年 一冊 一冊

383 鳴沙餘韻 附解説 矢吹慶輝編 岩波書店 昭和八年 一帙函入 附解説一冊 一帙函入一帙

384 明治以後日蓮主義著述目録 守屋貫教編 立正大学出版部 昭和八年 一冊 一冊

385 明治文学書目 村上浜吉 村上文庫 昭和十二年 一冊 一冊

386 明治の文章 明治の文学 厚生閣 昭和十三年 一冊 一冊

No.58

387 媽祖（雑誌） 台北媽祖書房 昭和九年 全揃 全揃

388 媽祖（單行詩集） 台北媽祖書房 昭和十年

389 明治天皇御傳 金尾文淵堂 [illegible]光輝 大正元年 一冊 一冊

390 物語支那史大系 早稲田大学出版部 昭和四年一五年 十二冊 十二冊

391 桃太郎の誕生 三省堂 柳田国男 昭和八年 一冊 一冊

392 満漢合璧五方元音 一冊一帙 一冊一帙

393 蒙古寇紀（全） 賀茂百樹 昭和六年 二冊（二部） 二冊（二部）

394 民族芸術（第五巻・第六巻） 民族芸術の会 昭和七年 十二冊 十二冊

395 民族と歴史（第一巻―第八巻）
日本学術普及会　大正八年―十二年
合綴　　合綴

396 昔話研究　第二巻第一号―第十二号
（未刊成本）
壬生書院　昭和十一年―十二年
合綴　　合綴

397 民俗芸術　第一巻―第三巻
小寺融吉　地平社
昭和三年――六年
六冊　　六冊

398 室町初期に於ける国語史の一考察
岸田定雄
一冊　　一冊

399 無盡方
一冊　　一冊

400 明治天皇御集謹解
佐々木信綱
一冊　　一冊

401 民族　第一巻―第四巻
民族発行会
大正十四年―昭和四年
四冊　　四冊

資料 12（目録・List of 364 missing or imperfect books）

| | 書名 | 冊數 | 缺及未還 |
|---|---|---|---|
| 402 | 奈良朝文法史（全）　山田孝雄　大正二年 | 一冊 | 一冊 |
| 403 | 續南方隨筆　南方熊楠　昭和十一年 | 一冊 | 一冊 |
| 404 | 南島方言資料　東條操　昭和五年 | 一冊 | 一冊 |
| 405 | 南島沿革史論（完）　幣原坦　明治三十二年 | 一冊 | 一冊 |
| 406 | 南蠻寺興廃記　宗水子　慶應四年 | 一冊一帙 | 一冊一帙 |
| 407 | 南蠻広記　新村出　大正十四年 | 一冊 | 一冊 |
| 408 | 内外教育小史（全）　金港堂書籍株式会社発行　明治二十九年 | 一冊 | 一冊 |
| 409 | 南總里見八犬傳　塚本哲三　大正十五年 | 六冊 | 第一冊目缺 |

No.61

410 南島同韻録　昭和九年　楊東仲二他　一冊　一冊

411 長崎方言に於ける外来語の研究　本山桂川　昭和六年　一冊　一冊

412 南洲号　八十九号　雑誌日本及日本人　大正十五年一月一日号　政教社　一冊　一冊

413 日本刀（岩波新書）　本間順治　昭和十四年　一冊　一冊

414 日本猥談集　昭和三年　坂田俊夫　一冊　一冊

415 日本讀史年表　昭和九年　大森金五郎　一冊　一冊

416 日光東照宮の写真　東照宮社務所　昭和十四年　一冊　一冊

417 日本的性格　昭和十四年　長谷川如是閑　一冊　一冊

No.62

418 日本畫論大觀 坂崎坦 昭和二年～四年 二冊 二冊

419 日本古代語音組織考 北里闌 大正十五年 写真二百枚一帙 目次一枚 解説一冊 目次一枚 写真二十四枚一帙 解説一冊 既還 缺

420 日蘭交通 第一輯 日蘭協会 昭和四年 一冊 一冊

421 日韓両国語同系論 金沢庄三郎 明治四十三年 一冊 一冊

422 日光廟建築論附図 (東京帝国大学紀要工科第一冊第二号 附図上下) 塚本靖 大沢三之助 明治三十六年五月 上下二冊 合一冊 合一冊

423 日本帝国郵便規則 附罰則 駅逓局 明治十一年 一冊 一冊

No.63

424 日本民族（第二巻 第一、二、十二号） 北野博美 昭和十一年 三冊 三冊

425 日鮮史話 第一編ー六編 松田甲 昭和五年 九冊 三冊欠（七ー九）

426 日本その日その日 上・下 モース、石川欣一訳 昭和四年 二冊 二冊

427 日本産貝殻和名索引（横山氏日本産貝殻標本目録附録） 一冊 一冊

428 新撰忠元勲功記（全） 薩藩史学会編 大正八年 一冊 一冊

424 日本臺灣雑誌（第四二号四三号の一部） 高橋利威 昭和五年ー六年 三冊 三冊

430 日本の國体と日蓮上人 清水梁山 明治四十四年 一冊 一冊

No. 64

| No. | 書名 | 年 | 著者・発行者 | 冊数 | 冊数 |
|---|---|---|---|---|---|
| 431 | 日本法制史 | 明治四十三年 | 三浦菊太郎 | 一冊 | 一冊 |
| 432 | 日本語読本 巻一－巻六 | 昭和六年 | 布哇教育会 | 六冊 | 六冊 |
| 433 | 日本古代法釈義 | 明治四十一年 | 有賀長雄 | 一冊 | 一冊 |
| 434 | 日伊文化協定 | 昭和十四年 | 国際文化振興会 | 一冊 | 一冊 |
| 435 | 日本銅版畫志 | 昭和十六年 | 西村貞 | 一冊 | 一冊 |
| 436 | 日仏文化 | 昭和二年－四年 | 日仏会館文芸部 | 三冊 | 第三輯目 一冊 欠 |
| 437 | 日本古[illegible]面 | 昭和十年 | 秋艸堂 | 一冊 | 一冊 |
| 438 | 日本女礼式 | 明治二十五年 | 坪谷善四郎 | 一冊 | 一冊 |

No65

| 番号 | 書名 | 著者 | 発行所 | 年 | 冊数 | 冊数 |
|---|---|---|---|---|---|---|
| 439 | 日本圖書目録 及解説 | レオン・パジェス | | 昭和二年 | 二冊 函入 | 二冊 函入 |
| 440 | 日本職業協会規約 | | | | 一冊 | 一冊 |
| 441 | 日本儒学史 | 安井小太郎 | 冨山房 | 昭和十四年 | 一冊 | 一冊 |
| 442 | 日本法制史 | 三浦菊太郎 | 博文館 | 明治三十三年 | 一冊 | 一冊 |
| 443 | 日本盲人史 正・續 | 中山太郎 | 成光館 | 昭和十二年 | 二冊 | 續一冊缺 |
| 444 | 日本法制史 | 池辺義象 | 博文館 | 明治四十五年 | 一冊 | 一冊 |
| 445 | 日韓古代史資料 | 太田亮 | | 昭和十五年 | 一冊 | 一冊 |
| 446 | 日本語文典 | コイャード・大塚高信訳 | 坂口書店 | 昭和九年 | 一冊 | 一冊 |
| 447 | 日本のポリ長崎 | 京郎月 | 長崎文化振興会 | 昭和十三年 | 一冊 | 一冊 |

No.66

448 日本及汎太平洋民族の研究　堀岡文吉　冨山房　昭和二年　一冊　一冊

449 日本古語大辞典　正・續　松岡静雄　刀江書院　（正　昭和十二年）（續　〃　四年）　二冊　二冊

450 日本耶蘇会刊行書志及その解説　明治文化研究会編　大正十五年　二冊　二冊

451 日本文学大辞典　藤村作　新潮社　昭和十一年、十二年　七冊　七冊

452 新渡辺博士追憶集　前田多門他　一冊　一冊

453 新渡辺博士文集　前田多門他　昭和十一年　一冊　一冊

454 日本郵便切手史論　樋畑雪湖　日本郵券倶楽部　昭和五年　一冊　一冊

455 日本書紀私見聞　貴重図書複製会　昭和十二年　一冊一帙　一冊一帙

456 日本郵便切手詳解　大柴峰吉編　日本郵券倶楽部発行　昭和七年　一冊　一冊

457 日本文法講義　山田孝雄　宝文館　昭和五年　一冊　一冊

458 日本文学の世界的位置　勝本清一郎　協和書院　昭和十一年　一冊　一冊

459 日本神代史　中村徳五郎　成光館　昭和九年　一冊　一冊

460 古写本日本書紀（秘籍大観日本書紀）　大阪毎日新聞社　大正十五年　七巻附一帙　八巻附一帙　解題一冊一帙　七巻附一帙　八巻附一帙　解題一冊一帙

461 日本思想　中世武民の精神生活　清原貞雄　昭和十四年　一冊　一冊

462 日本ローマ字史　川副佳一郎　岡村書店　大正十一年　一冊　一冊

463 日本戯曲全集　第四十一巻　現代篇九輯　長田秀雄他　春陽堂　昭和三年　一冊　一冊

464 ニッポン　ブルーノ・タウト　明治書房　昭和十六年　一冊　一冊

465 日本風俗沿革圖説（全） 江馬務編 大正十一年 五冊三帙 五冊三帙

466 日本考古学 歴史講座刊行会 後藤守一 昭和八年 一冊 一冊

467 日本性的崇拝資料一覧 正・續 昭和二年、七年 二冊 二冊

468 日本のもとり 久保田金僊 審美書院 昭和十三年 一冊 一冊

469 日本法制史 瀧川政次郎 有斐閣 昭和七年 一冊 一冊

470 日本生殖器崇拝概論 沢田四郎作著 大正十一年 一冊 一冊

471 日本法制史研究 瀧川政次郎 有斐閣 昭和十六年 一冊 一冊

472 日本法制史 瀧川政次郎 昭和十一年 一冊 一冊

no. 68

No.69

| No. | 書名 | 発行所・著者等 | 年 | 冊数 | 冊数 |
|---|---|---|---|---|---|
| 473 | 日本生殖器崇拝略説 | 山口米吉 | 大正九年 | 一冊 | 一冊 |
| 474 | 日本詩歌と外国語 | 国際文化振興会　ジヨルジユ、ボイ | 昭和十年 | 一冊 | 一冊 |
| 475 | 日本文法論 | 宝文館　山田孝雄 | 昭和四年 | 一冊 | 一冊 |
| 476 | 日本文法史 | 刀江書院　小林好日 | 昭和十一年 | 一冊 | 一冊 |
| 477 | 日本口語法講義 | 宝文館　山田孝雄 | 昭和六年 | 一冊 | 一冊 |
| 478 | 日本諸学研究 | 刀江書院　日本文化中央聯盟編 | 昭和十四年 | 四冊函入 | 四冊函入 |
| 479 | 日本漢字学史 | 明治書院　岡井慎吾 | 昭和九年 | 一冊 | 一冊 |
| 480 | 日本教育史資料 | 文部省 | 明治三十六年―三十七年 | 九冊　グリン色布装 | 九冊 |
| 481 | 日本性語大辞典 | 文芸資料研究会編輯部　東京良 | 昭和三年 | 一冊 | 一冊 |

No.90

482 日韓両国語同系論　三省堂　明治四十三年　金沢庄三郎　一冊　一冊

483 日光の今昔　文献社　昭和十一年　城田興法　一冊　一冊

484 日独文化（創刊号）　日独文化協会　昭和十五年　一冊　一冊

485 日用方物略　嘉永三年　小野蕙畝

486 熱河省産両棲類爬蟲類　第一次満蒙学術調査研究団　昭和十年　一冊　一冊

487 鼠はまだ生きてゐる　岩波書店　チエムバレン著　昭和十四年　一冊　一冊

488 年中行事　年中行事刊行会　北野博美　昭和八年―十年　十二冊　十二冊

489 年中行事秘抄　昭和六年　育徳財団　一巻 [illegible]　解説一冊　解説一冊欠

490 能楽古今記　春陽堂　野々村戒三　昭和六年　一冊　一冊

491 日本農具図説図譜　大正二年　帝国農会　一冊　一冊

492 能の栞　明治三十六年　一～六　一～三十七年　大和田建樹　三冊　三冊

493 能楽全史（改訂版）　わんや書店　横井春野　昭和十二年　三冊　三冊

494 能楽画譜　能楽新報社　勝野嘉一郎　明治四十四年

495 能楽盛衰記　能楽会　上・下　池田信嘉　大正十四年　二冊　二冊

496 農諭（全）　天保二年　一冊　一冊

497 農業全書　岩波書店　土屋喬雄校訂　昭和十一年　一冊　一冊

No.71　498 農桑輯要　元司農撰　二冊　二冊

No.72.

499 農村問題文献資料 日本評論社 大正十四年 一冊 一冊

500 野口英世 小泉丹 岩波書店 昭和十四年 一冊 一冊

501 能楽古面集 京都博物館 昭和七年 一冊一帙 一冊一帙

502 南都十大寺大鏡
南都七大寺大鏡 } 三十八冊
南都十大寺大鏡分類索引
南都七大寺大鏡所在別索引 } 一冊
東京 美術工藝 編
昭和十三年
二十八冊 二十九冊

No.93

| | 書名 | 冊数 | 献本書選 |
|---|---|---|---|
| 503 | 沖縄志略字引 明治十一年 河原田盛美 | 一冊一帙 | 一冊一帙 |
| 504 | 沖縄女性史 大正八年 伊波普猷 | 一冊 | 一冊 |
| 505 | 沖縄県女子師範学校郷土教育研究 全校郷土室編 昭和九年 | 一冊 | 一冊 |
| 506 | 近江奈良朝の漢文学 東洋文庫 岡田幹之助 昭和四年 | 一冊 | 一冊 |
| 507 | 往来物展覧会出陳目録 日比谷図書館 所蔵 | 一冊 | 一冊 |
| 508 | 欧米人の極東研究（全） 大日本文明協会編 大正元年 | 一冊 | 一冊 |
| 509 | 織田信長 鷲尾雨工 | 一冊 | 一冊 |
| 510 | 大沼枕山先生略傳 村松七郎 | 一冊 | 一冊 |
| 511 | 日本憲法（全） 明治二十九年 大宮兵馬 | 一冊 | 一冊 |

512. 大鏡詳解（全） 佐藤球 明治書院 昭和十四年 一冊 一冊

513 欧米の隅々 市河三喜・晴子 研究社 昭和八年 一冊 一冊

514 千葉氏藏東大鏡 古典保存会 大正十四年 一冊一帙 一冊一帙

515 言語学雑誌 第一巻第一号―第十期 北京[illegible]東路道社 民国十七年―二十年 十冊 十冊

516 萬葉物語 富田俊 昭和十一年 一冊 一冊

517 櫻誌 梅村甚太郎 昭和十二年 一冊 一冊

518 大奥の女中 池田晃淵 富山房 明治三十四年 三冊 三冊

519 小原流盛花瓶華傑作選集 中央華社 昭和十二年 一冊 一冊

520 小原流盛花瓶華傑作第二輯 小原豊雲 昭和十三年 一冊 一冊

No.74

No.75

521 音韻調査報告書 明治三十八年 文部省 一冊 一冊

522 ちりかみぶくろ 昭和十三年 中島健二 一冊 一冊

523 おれ博士の観た東海道 大正五年 スター 一冊 一冊

524 大橋図書館第三拾壹回年報 昭和十五年 一冊 一冊

525 音楽辞典 商務印書館 劉誠甫 民国二十五年 一冊 一冊

526 ポルトガルを訪ねる 昭和五年 岡本良知 一冊 一冊

527 蘭学鏡原 尾張 東壁堂 吉田先生訳 三冊一帙 三冊一帙

528 琉球人御暇之節覚 一帖一帙 一帖一帙

329 六書合訣 十二冊二帙 十二冊二帙

530 六書通 明治二十七年 上・中・下 秦貽自鞭甫 三冊 三冊

No.46

| 番号 | 書名 | 著者・編者 | 年 | 冊数 | 冊数 |
|---|---|---|---|---|---|
| 531 | 六書音均表　一編―十五編 | 段玉裁 | | 十五冊二帙 | 十五冊二帙 |
| 532 | 琉球 | 沖縄県教育会 | 大正十四年 | 二冊（二部） | 二冊（二部） |
| 533 | 琉球の宗教 | | | 一冊一帙 | 一冊一帙 |
| 534 | 琉球の織物 | 柳宗悦 | 昭和十四年 | 一冊 | 一冊 |
| 535 | 琉球の研究（啓明会第八回、第十五回講演集） | | 大正十四年 | 一冊 | 一冊 |
| 536 | 琉球と鹿児島 | | 大正十三年 | 一冊 | 一冊 |
| 537 | 琉球大観 | 石野瑛 | 大正四年 | 一冊 | 一冊 |
| 538 | 琉球浄瑠璃 | 杉山淳千郎 | 明治三十二年 | 一冊 | 一冊 |
| 539 | 律令の研究 | 瀧川政次郎 | 昭和六年 | 一冊 | 一冊 |
| 540 | 龍笛要録假名譜 | | | 四冊一帙 | 四冊一帙 |
| 541 | リットン報告書 | 牧野武夫 | 昭和七年 | 一冊 | 一冊 |
| 542 | 両周金文辞大系 | 郭沫若　文求堂 | 昭和七年 | 二冊 | 二冊 |

No.77

543 連理秘抄　古典保存会　昭和三年　一冊一帙　一冊一帙

544 令集解　広谷雄太郎　大正十三年　一冊　一冊

545 令義解講義（全）　明治三十六年　小中村清矩　一冊　一冊

546 厂木園草木記（完）　一冊　一冊

547 論語抄　文友社　大正六年　六冊一帙　六冊一帙

548 論語（東方古典叢刊　第六巻）五十沢二郎　昭和八年　一冊　一冊

549 老子（東方古典叢刊　第十巻）五十沢二郎　昭和九年　一冊　一冊

550 ローマ字論語　宮崎静二　学而篇　為政篇　昭和八年・十年　二冊　二冊

551 ローマ字の研究　田丸卓郎　大正十一年　一冊　一冊

552 琅玕記　新村出　昭和五年　一冊　一冊

No. 78

| | 書名 | | 冊数 | 欠本未還 |
|---|---|---|---|---|
| 553 | 西郷隆盛、青春と自覚篇 | 山中峯太郎 昭和十六年 | 一冊 | 一冊 |
| 554 | 西郷隆盛傳 | 佐々弘雄 昭和十二年 | 一冊 | 一冊 |
| 555 | 西郷隆盛 | 富田常雄 昭和十六年 | 一冊 | 一冊 |
| 556 | 西郷南洲先生傳 | 勝田孫彌 昭和二年 | 一冊 | 一冊 |
| 557 | 清荒外備 | 光緒己卯 | 一冊 | 一冊 |
| 558 | 清斎記聞 | 旦暮庵野 天保丙申 | 二冊（二部）（一部ハ一冊） | 二冊（二部） |
| 559 | 嵯峨本考 | 和田維四郎 大正五年 | 一冊 函入 | 一冊 函入 |
| 560 | 雅文大鑑（巻物）及解題 | 貴重図書影本刊行会 昭和九年 | 十冊 巻物 | 十冊 巻物 |
| 561 | 酒の文言 | 武井水戎 | 一冊 | 一冊 |
| 562 | 申楽談義 | 世阿弥、野上豊一郎校訂 昭和十年 | 一冊 | 一冊 |

deleted from inventory one item (560)

563 左傳の思想的研究　津田左右吉　一冊　一冊
昭和十年

564 薩道先生景仰録（吉利支丹研究史回顧）　一冊　一冊
新村出
昭和四年

565 山東玉篇　一〜六　山東直砥　六冊　六冊
明治九年

566 山陽頼先生百年祭紀念号　佐久節　一冊　一冊
昭和六年

569 山東書房図書目録　一冊　一冊

568 傘業随筆大観　小林久良治編　一冊　一冊

569 山水並野形図
古傳園方書
尺素往来抜粋
前栽秘抄（一名作庭記）
山本浩然館　一冊　一冊
昭和三年

570 薩藩経緯記（全）　佐藤信淵　一冊　一冊

571 薩州土風傳（全）　久保紀之英　一冊　一冊

No.79

572 四書（表紙、帙共にドンス） 六冊一帙 六冊一帙

573 シーボルト資料展覧会出品目録 一冊 一冊

574 シーボルト先生渡来百年記念展覧会出品目録 大正十三年 一冊 一冊

575 残叢雑誌 第二十七巻 第二号 昭和七年

576 史学年報 第二巻第一期—第四期 第十周年記念特刊号 燕京大学歴史学会 民国二十二年—二十七年 五冊 五冊

577 尺八史考 栗原広太 大正七年 一冊 一冊

578 植字略史 宇田川榕庵 天保四年 一冊 一冊

579 書物趣味（雑誌）一巻二号—二巻四号 昭和七年九月—八年十月 八冊 八冊

580 書譜 上中下 吉岡貞雄 昭和十二年 三冊 三冊

581 書物礼讃 一—七 大正十四年 七冊 七冊

582 古文書書目録 国学院大学 昭和五年 一冊 一冊

No. 80

583 ~~内庫本書珍本和装本標本~~ 冊 冊 deleted F.H.

583 第三次改定版四部叢刊目録 一冊 一冊

584 四季酒の肴 画君帯吉 昭和十年 一冊 一冊

585 新来古書販賣目録 昭和三年 一冊 一冊

586 昌平学寮学規簿 一冊一帙 一冊一帙

587 小学国語読本 文部省 昭和九年－十一年 尋常科用 巻三、五、六、七(三部) 十二冊 十二冊

588 袖珍字説(上・中・下) 明治三年 柳河春蔭 三冊 三冊

589 新撰字總案内 ブリンクリー 明治四十二年 一冊 一冊

590 静岡県郷土研究 第十二輯 栢植清 昭和十四年 一冊 一冊

591 字便ふう見め(全) 江戸仮字風研究 一冊桐箱入 一冊桐箱入

592 習字楷様(上) 山本竟山 大正六年 一冊 一冊

加81 593 信濃郷土研究 昭和七年－十三年 町田修三 全揃 全揃

594 七福神物語　尾崎静葉　大正六年　一冊　一冊

595 食道楽　第一巻―第五巻　村井寛　昭和三年　五冊　五冊

596 塩原の奥　新田寸彦　一冊一帙　一冊一帙

~~597 習字兼用常用書翰文　森田富次郎　昭和七年　一冊　一冊~~

597 捷引　十四篇目録　一冊　一冊

598 春鶯曲　芳也無題　三冊　三冊

599 紹述編年　薩藩史料纂編所　大正八年　二冊　二冊

600 支那香艶叢書　第一―第六　池田信雄　上海支那香艶叢書刊行会　大正十一年　六冊　六冊

601 支那社会の科学的研究　ウィットフォーゲル　平野義太郎訳　昭和十四年　一冊　一冊

602 支那長生秘術　杉[illegible]朝太郎　昭和四年　一冊　一冊

No. 82

九・八三

603 支那歴代年表　山根倬三　昭和五年　正・續　二冊　續ノ冊欠

604 支那法制史研究（全）　東川徳治　大正十三年　一冊　一冊

605 支那法制史　浅井虎夫　明治三十七年　一冊　一冊

606 支那の豫言　中野江漢　大正十四年

607 支那小説史　魯迅・増田渉訳　昭和十三年

608 支那文学概論講話　塩谷温　大正十五年

609 支那法制史論叢　桑原隲蔵　昭和十二年　一冊　一冊

610 支那詩論史　鈴木虎雄　昭和十四年

611 支那の孝道　桑原隲蔵　昭和十年　一冊　一冊

612 最新支那語大辞典　石山福治　昭和十年

613 支那銭鈔考　高木英彦　昭和十一年　一冊　一冊

~~615~~ 614 支那思想と日本　昭和十四年　津田左右吉　一冊　一冊

~~616~~ 615 支那語研究　第一号　昭和十三年　平岩彦次郎　一冊　一冊

~~617~~ 616 支那法制史研究　昭和十五年　瀧川政次郎　一冊　一冊

~~618~~ 617 支那の馬　中野江漢　大正十三年　一冊　一冊

~~619~~ 618 支那文字概論　青木正児　昭和十三年　一冊　一冊

~~620~~ 619 支那小説戯曲史概説　大正十四年　宮原民平　一冊　一冊

~~621~~ 620 支那絵画史　内藤湖南　昭和十三年　一冊　一冊

~~622~~ 621 支那風俗　井上紅梅　大正九年－十一年　三冊　三冊

~~623~~ 622 植物名彙　吉田義秀　昭和四年　一冊　一冊

~~624~~ 623 嶋の南洲先生　安藤佳翠　昭和十年　一冊　一冊

~~625~~ 624 書論　木村一郎　第一巻－第三巻合本　昭和八年－九年　三巻三冊　三冊

No.84

No. 35

~~626~~ 625 四角号碼検字法　王雲五　一九二八年　一冊　一冊

~~627~~ 626 支那に於ける佛教と儒教道教　常盤大定　昭和五年　一冊　一冊

~~628~~ 627 紫藤園攷證　弘化二年　二冊　二冊
（昭和九年京都小川睦治氏蔵書を写す）

~~629~~ 628 習字専用商業書翰文初歩（定）　森[?]富[?]次郎　昭和四年　十冊　十冊

~~629~~ 628 職人[?]畫　久保田米[?]　大正[?]年　一冊一帙　一冊一帙

~~630~~ 630 上海自然科学研究所彙報（一ー七）　一九二九ー一九三七年　七冊　七冊

~~631~~ 634 釈尊山遺形傳来史　小室重弘　明治三十六年　一冊　一冊

~~632~~ 632 ~~東亜[?]雑誌　中[illegible]編　[illegible]　栃[?][illegible]嘉[?][illegible]編　[illegible]年　十冊　十冊~~

~~633~~ 633 續日本紀　大正十四年　二十冊　二十冊

~~634~~ 634 書道之友[?]　木村一郎　四巻一号ー十四巻　全揃　十冊　全揃　十冊

635 和蘭日独交通小史　丸山国雄　昭和六年　一冊　一冊

636 書苑　創刊号—二号、第二巻六号　第三巻一　昭和十二年—十三年　三冊　三冊

637 四庫未收書目提要（三十七年本叢書）　阮元　民国二十四年　一冊　一冊

638 類瑜东日本書紀和見聞解説　一冊一帙　一冊一帙

639 春香傳　張赫宙　昭和十三年　一冊　一冊

640 岐阜県製紙工業試験場　昭和十年　十二年業務報告　二冊　二冊

641 書話　小見山寿海　昭和六年　一冊　一冊

642 書翰文講話及文範　芳賀矢一　昭和九年　一冊　一冊

643 書物の趣味　昭和二年—七年　七冊　七冊

644 書物之見　井上和雄　昭和十四年　一冊　一冊

645 書窓刊行会之輯（合）　恩地孝四郎　昭和十六年　一冊　一冊

645 書目集覧 昭和三年―六年 青木稲禅 二冊 中一冊欠

649 嶋 昭和八年―九年 二冊 二冊

648 社会教育 昭和十四年 社会教育会 一冊 一冊

659 聖徳太子御代御絵伝巻 一巻函入 一巻函入

650 静岡県市史編纂資料（廿六巻） 昭和四年 一冊 一冊

~~652 周秦漢三代の古典研究報告 東畑彦治郎 京都東方文化学院 十冊 十冊~~

656 真福寺本古事記 大正十三年―十四年 古典保存会 三冊一帙 三冊一帙

652 新文典 橋本進吉 昭和十三年 一冊 一冊

653 新文典別記 上級用 昭和十一年 橋本進吉 一冊 一冊

654 神品百碑（書道宝鑑） 昭和三年 渋川玄耳 一冊 一冊

No.89

657 神道叢説 大正十二年 山本信哉 纂刊 一冊 一冊

658 神祇史綱要 宮地直一 昭和十三年 一冊 一冊

659 新撰字鏡及索引 昭和八年 七冊一帙 七冊一帙

660 神札考 矢部善三 昭和九年 一冊 一冊

661 神霊と霊火 大矢康蔵 昭和七年 一冊 一冊

662 清文満漢蒙古指南 四冊一帙 四冊一帙

663 清文擡字 一冊 一冊

664 新作都々逸小唄 一冊 一冊

665 真福寺古事記上巻 昭和五年 古典保存会 一冊一帙 一冊一帙

666 四書集註 上帙 論語 七冊 下帙 大学・中庸・論語 六冊 十三冊二帙 七冊一帙 ~~十三冊二帙~~

667 スカーレットレター 大正十三年 ホーソン 神芳郎訳 一冊 一冊

668 水鏡及解説 昭和十三年 貴重図書影本刊行会 四冊一帙 四冊一帙

No.88

No.89

669 椎園　安田文庫　昭和十二年―十三年　四冊　四冊

670 酔夢　第二巻　島添達夫 他　昭和十年　一冊　一冊

671 ✓水平運動　高橋貞樹　大正十三年　一冊　一冊

672 生殖崇拝論　久澤参丸　大正十年　一冊　一冊

673 生殖器崇拝語彙集成　久澤参丸　大正十一年　一冊　一冊

674 世説新語補考　白鹿桃　宝暦十三年　二冊一帙　二冊一帙

675 西夏研究　王静如　民国二十一年―二十二年　三冊　三冊

676 西洋学家訳述目録　穂亭主人輯　大正十五年　一冊　一冊

677 聖教日課　ベルナルド　明治四年　一冊一帙　一冊一帙

678 千家文及傑人遺墨集　昭和六年　一冊　一冊

679 千頃堂書目　十六冊二帙　下帙の「帙」及上帙所収の七・八巻一冊欠

680 千種の花　幸埜楳嶺画　明治二十四年　四冊一帙　四冊一帙

no 90

| 番号 | 書名 | 年 | 著者 | 冊数 | 冊数 |
|---|---|---|---|---|---|
| 681 | 製紙の学理及実際 | 大正六年 | 今関歓 | 一冊 | 一冊 |
| 682 | 箋注倭名類聚抄 | 明治十六年 | 狩野棭斎 | 十冊二帙 | 十冊二帙 |
| ✓ 683 | 先秦時代文法研究 | 昭和七年 | 新東金橋 | | |
| 684 | 戦争と二人の婦人 | 昭和十三年 | 山本有三 | 一冊 | 一冊 |
| 685 | 成簣堂古文書影百種 | 昭和十二年 | | 一函 | 一函 |
| 686 | 征吏木路記（中空家島に於ける討究書） | | | 五冊一帙 | 五冊一帙 |
| 687 | 川柳語彙 | 昭和四年 | 宮武外骨 | 一冊 | 一冊 |
| 688 | 草字彙 | 大正五年 | 物集高見 | 一冊 | 一冊 |
| 689 | 叢書目録拾遺 | 民国二十三年 | | 四冊一帙 | 四冊一帙 |
| 690 | 蘇峰随筆叢書 五十二年 | 昭和八年 | | 一冊 | 一冊 |
| 691 | 蘇峰先生著作五十選 | 昭和十一年 | | 一冊 | 一冊 |

No.91

692 草叢　博文館　明治二十九年　十二冊一帙　十二冊一帙

693 草字彙　堅菴石梁書　乾隆五十二年　六冊一帙　六冊一帙

694 孫子の新研究　阿多俊介　昭和五年　一冊　一冊

695 宗達畫集　昭和五年　日本美術協会編　一冊　一冊

696 太平広記　北京　文友堂　五百巻六十冊六帙　五百巻六十冊六帙

697 太平記物語　鷲尾雨工　昭和十六年　一冊　一冊

698 大唐西域記に記せる東南印度諸国の研究　高桑駒吉　大正十五年　一冊及附録地図　附録地図欠

699 大寛実録　一名島津世禄記　上・中・下　薩藩史編纂所　大正八年　三冊　三冊

700 大宝令新解　窪美昌保　大正十二年　一冊　一冊

701 竹取物語　久松潜一訳　至文堂　昭和十二年　一冊　一冊

702 竹取物語 島津久基 校訂 岩波文庫 昭和十五年 一冊 一冊

703 竹取物語俚言解（上・下全） 佐々木信綱 明治廿七年 一冊 一冊

704 篆刻新解 柳瀬日章 昭和七年 一冊 一冊

705 高砂 大隈言道 一冊 一冊

706 泰西辞書の攝取と其の展開 啓明会 昭和十五年

707 篆字彙 五冊一帙 五冊一帙

708 高木利太遺書古活字版展観目録 川瀬一馬 編 昭和八年 一冊 一冊

~~[illegible][illegible]聊齋志異~~ 二十四冊六帙 二十四冊六帙

709 田中宣三 書簡 一通（桐箱第七三号） 一通（桐箱第七三号）

No.9 710 朝鮮の習俗 昭和九年 朝鮮總督府 一冊 一冊

711 朝鮮の俚諺集附物語 高橋亨 大正三年 一冊 一冊

712 中国雕板源流考（文学小叢書） 孫毓修 民国二十三年 一冊 一冊

713 中世丁番傳播考 —「史学」第十六巻一號所載— 岡本良知 昭和十二年 一冊 一冊

714 中部カロリン島俗家屋 田中鎮彦 大正十年 一冊 一冊

715 中央大学国学圖書館 同圖書館編 民国十七年—二十六年 十冊 十冊

716 中西交通史料 第一—第六冊 張星烺撰 六冊 六冊

717 中世に於ける精神生活 平泉澄 大正十五年 一冊 一冊

718 中小工業製品高級化施設實施状況報告書 昭和十二年 一冊 一冊

No. 93

資料 12（目録・List of 364 missing or imperfect books）

No.94

719 竹田翁尺牘 桐箱入唐物

720 椿山翁印譜 一冊一帙 一冊一帙

721 椿山印譜 一冊 一冊一帙

722 椿説弓張月（上下） 曲亭馬琴 十冊二帙 下帙五冊缺

723 直斎書録解題書名索引 東洋史研究会 一冊 一冊

724 西蔵語文典綱要 明石恵達 昭和十二年 一冊 一冊

725 張州府志（上下） 花見朔巳 大正六年／大正五年 七冊二帙 七冊二帙

726 知友新稿 蘇峰先生古稀祝賀記念刊行会 昭和六年 一冊 一冊

727 諦拭名印集 一冊 一冊

728 千代田城大奥（朝野叢書） 明治二十五年 二冊 二冊

no.95

| | | | | | |
|---|---|---|---|---|---|
| 729 | 珍籍展覧会目録附録 | 丸善 昭和七年 | | 一冊 | 一冊 |
| 730 | 潮音 第八巻第一号―第十二号 | 大正十一年 | | 十二冊 | 十二冊 |
| 731 | 通俗成業発達史 | 大正十五年 | 西嶋東洲 | 一冊 | 一冊 |
| 732 | 豆州熱海改正全図 | 明治二十七年 | 長谷川久美之助 | 一枚 | 一枚 |
| 733 | 徒然草解釋(全) | 大正十四年 | 塚本哲三 | 一冊 | 一冊 |
| 734 | 徒然草解釋(全) | 昭和五年 | 塚本哲三 | 一冊 | 一冊 |
| 735 | 都農郡自治史要 | | 大正十二年 | 一冊 | 一冊 |
| 736 | 帝室制度史 | 昭和十二年 | 帝国学士院 | 四冊 | 四冊 |
| 737 | 粘葉考 | 昭和七年 | 田中敬 | 二冊 | 二冊 |

No.96

738 天爾乎波の論理的研究　新井無二郎　昭和九年　一冊　一冊

739 天一閣蔵書考　陳登元　民国二十一年　一冊一帙　一冊一帙

740 天狗名義考序　宝暦四年　一冊　一冊

741 天正年間遣欧使節関係文書　新村出　浜田耕作　解説　昭和四年　書簡図四枚　解説　一冊　書簡図四枚　解説　一冊

742 典籍叢談　新村出　昭和九年　一冊　一冊

743 天徳地福傳

744 塔影　第十七巻第一号　渡辺華山特輯
〃　第二号　正倉院御物特輯　二冊　二冊

745 東瀛珠光　宮内省蔵版　昭和十六年　六冊六帙　六冊六帙

No.97

746 陶庵素描 うの陳徳器 昭和十一年 一冊 一冊

747 東京文理科大学文科紀要 第三巻 中山久四郎 昭和六年 一冊 一冊

748 東山水墨畫集 秋葉啓 昭和十五年 七十九枚 解説七輯 一帙 七十九枚 解説七輯 一帙

749 當流間仕舞付 五冊一帙 五冊一帙

750 當世書生氣質 坪内逍遙 大正十五年 一冊 一冊

751 東洋音楽研究（第一巻第一号—第二号） 昭和十二年 一冊 一冊

752 土佐製紙工業組合定款 一冊 一冊

753 土州商會大意併約件 一冊一帙 一冊一帙

754 土州淵岳志産物編 一冊 一冊

資料 12（目録・List of 364 missing or imperfect books）

755 圖書館辭典（昭和増訂） 間宮不二雄編 大正十四年 一冊 一冊

756 圖書館雜誌 第一号－第百九十四号 日本文庫協会 明治四十年－四十一年

757 圖書刊行会古版目録附日本古刻書史（合） 圖書刊行会編 明治四十二年 一冊 一冊

758 讀史論略 二冊一帙 二冊一帙

759 富山市史 昭和十一年 二冊 二冊

760 富岡文庫旧蔵書入札目録 昭和十三年－十四年 二冊 二冊

761 敦煌雜鈔 釣和亭輯 民国二十六年 一冊 一冊

762 東洋文化 東洋文化学会編 昭和三年 三冊 三冊

763 東洋歴史参考図譜 第一輯－第十五輯 石田幹之助 昭和五年 三函帙 三函帙

No 98

764 東洋史参考圖譜解説 第一輯—第十二輯 石田幹之助 大正十四年—昭和六年 十二冊 十二冊

765 東洋法制史本論 広池千九郎 大正四年 一冊 一冊

766 東洋法制史序論 広池千九郎 明治三十八年 一冊 一冊

767 東洋思想の研究 小柳司気太 昭和十三年 二冊 二冊

768 東洋美術史の研究 澤村専太郎 昭和七年 一冊 一冊

769 東方染色文化の研究 上村六郎 昭和八年 一冊一帙 一冊一帙

770 東西交渉史の研究 藤田豊八 昭和七年—八年 二冊 南海篇欠

771 東洋文化史研究 内藤虎次郎 昭和十二年 一冊 一冊

No.99

No.100

772 東亜語源志 昭和五年 新村出 一冊 一冊

773 唐宋法律文書の研究 昭和十二年 仁井田陞 一冊 一冊

774 堤中納言物語 昭和十年 藤村作著 一冊 一冊

775 謡の本
（内之部）
羽衣。高砂、杜若、三輪、八島、
阿漕、百万、鞍馬天狗、蝉丸
熊野、紅葉狩、桜川、鉢木。
葵上 三井寺 加茂、松風
船弁慶 山姥、隅田川 田村 忠則
（外之部）
草紙洗、求塚、絃上、松虫
西王母 [illegible]栖、小督 [illegible]師
熊坂、鐵輪、巴、花月

内之部 二十二
外之部 十二
内・外共 三十四 ~~冊~~ 欠

776 遊仙窟（全） 慶安五年 一冊一帙 一冊一帙

777 謠の調子 斎藤吉之助 昭和七年 一冊 一冊

778 有用植物図説 明治廿四年 田中芳男 七冊一帙 七冊一帙

779 浮世絵師略傳 大正八年 河浦謙一 一冊一帙 一冊一帙

780 有不為斎文庫善本入札目録 昭和十四年 一冊 一冊

781 袖海樓雑箸 民国二十年 燕京大学図書館蔵版 二冊一帙 二冊一帙

782 羽陵餘蟫 田中慶太郎 昭和十二年 一冊 一冊

宇治大納言源隆国御撰 今昔物語 明治十九年 二冊 二冊

783 浮世絵師傳（全） 昭和六年 井上和雄 一冊一帙 一冊一帙

【著者紹介】

**横山　學**（よこやま・まなぶ）

1948年、岡山市生まれ。1983年、筑波大学大学院歴史・人類学研究科史学日本史専攻博士課程修了。現在、ノートルダム清心女子大学名誉教授、早稲田大学招聘研究員。文学博士。

（主要著書）

『琉球国使節渡来の研究』（吉川弘文館、1987年）『書物に魅せられた英国人　フランク・ホーレーと日本文化』（吉川弘文館、2003年）『江戸期琉球物資料集覧』（本邦書籍、1981年）『琉球所属問題関係資料』〈編著〉（本邦書籍、1980年）『神戸貿易新聞』〈編著〉（本邦書籍、1980年）『文化のダイナミズム』〈共著〉「フランク·ホーレー探検　人物研究の面白さ」（大学教育出版、1999年）『描かれた行列—武士・異国・祭礼』〈共著〉「琉球国使節登城行列絵巻を読む」（東京大学出版会、2015年）『生活文化研究所年報』〈編著〉（ノートルダム清心女子大学生活文化研究所、１輯1987年～30輯2016年）"Journalist and Scholar Frank Hawley", British & Japan Vol.5, Edited by Hugh Cortazzi, 2004. "Frank Hawley and his Ryukyuan Studies", British Library Occasional Papers 11, Japan Studies, 1990.

書誌書目シリーズ⑪⓪
フランク・ホーレー旧蔵「宝玲文庫」資料集成
第2巻

二〇一七年三月十日　印刷
二〇一七年三月二十四日　発行

編　著　横山（よこやま）　學（まなぶ）
解　題　横山　學
発行者　荒井秀夫
発行所　株式会社ゆまに書房
〒一〇一—〇〇四七
東京都千代田区内神田二—七—六
電話〇三（五二九六）〇四九一（代表）
印　刷　株式会社平河工業社
製　本　東和製本株式会社
組　版　有限会社ぷりんていあ第二



定価：本体21,000円＋税

ISBN 978-4-8433-5132-1 C3300